THE FALLOUT OF WAR

THE FALLOUT OF
WAR

THE REGIONAL CONSEQUENCES OF THE CONFLICT IN SYRIA

WORLD BANK GROUP

1818 H Street NW, Washington, DC 20433
Telephone: 202-473-1000; Internet: www.worldbank.org

1 2 3 4 23 22 21 20

ISBN (paper): 978-1-4648-1614-7
ISBN (electronic): 978-1-4648-1615-4
DOI: 10.1596/978-1-4648-1614-7

Cover and interior design: Design and Development Minds

Library of Congress Control Number: 2020914232

CONTENTS

BOXES, FIGURES, MAPS, AND TABLES

Boxes

Figures

Maps

Tables

ACKNOWLEDGMENTS

This study was prepared by a multidisciplinary team led by Harun Onder (lead author and Senior Economist) and Haneen Sayed (Lead Social Protection and Jobs Specialist) under the guidance of Eric Le Borgne (Practice Manager). Contributing authors (alphabetically, by field) are as follows (their affiliation is World Bank unless otherwise noted):

- *Agriculture*: Bekzod Shamsiev (Senior Agriculture Economist), Garry Christensen (Consultant), Mekbib Haile (Economist), and Yulia Mitusova (Consultant)
- *Demography*: Emi Suzuki (Demographer) and Georgia Christina Kosmidou (Consultant)
- *Education*: Almedina Music (Economist) and Dina Abu-Ghaida (Lead Economist)
- *Energy*: Javier Gustavo Inon (Consultant), Mohammed Qaradaghi (Senior Energy Specialist), Victor B. Loksha (Consultant), and Waleed Saleh I. Alsuraih (Lead Energy Specialist)
- *Environment*: Andres Fernando Chamorro Elizondo (Consultant), Bjorn Klavdy Larsen (Consultant), and Craig Melsner (Senior Environmental Economist)
- *Finance, competitiveness, and innovation:* Alan Andrew Moody (Consultant), Haocong Ren (Senior Financial Sector Economist), John Speakman (Consultant), Kinley Salmon (Economist), Ethan Kapstein (Princeton University), Daniel Lowery (Consultant), Ola Hisou (Consultant), Patricia Haydamous (Consultant), and Tulu Balkir (Consultant)
- *Fiscal*: Juan Pradelli (Consultant) and Ariel Melamud (Consultant)
- *Fragility, conflict, and violence:* Elizabeth Dodds (Consultant), Stephan Massing (Senior Strategy and Operations Officer) and Bledi Celiku (Economist)
- *Governance and political economy*: Ali Halawi (Senior Public Sector Specialist), Izzah Akram Malik (Public Sector Specialist), Klaus Decker (Senior Public Sector Specialist), Michael Christopher Jelenic (Public Sector Specialist), Roland Lomme (Senior Governance Specialist), Shilpa Pradhan (Senior Country Officer), Jon Alterman (Center for Strategic and International Studies), and Will Todman (Center for Strategic and International Studies)
- *Health*: Nadwa Rafeh (Senior Health Specialist), Nour Aoun (Consultant), Rim Atoui (Consultant), and Toni Joe Lebbos (Consultant)
- *History*: Eyup Ozveren (Middle-East Technical University) and Omer Karasapan (Senior Operations Officer)
- *Information and communications technology*: Marolla Haddad (Senior Digital Development Specialist) and Suhail Shersad (Consultant)
- *Labor*: Angela Elzir Assy (Labor Specialist), Belal Fallah (Consultant), Carole Chartouni (Labor Economist), and Samer Hamati (Consultant)
- *Macroeconomy*: Christos Kostopoulos (Lead Country Economist), Harun Onder, Cevdet Denizer (Consultant), Ibrahim Saif (Jordan Strategy Forum), Swati Ghosh (Consultant), Majid Kazemi (Consultant), and Gulbin Yildirim (Consultant)

- *Models (computable general equilibrium and synthetic control method)*: Csilla Lakatos (Senior Economist), Harun Onder, and Claudio Rojas (Consultant)
- *Poverty*: Lokendra Phadera (Economist) and Matthew Wai-Poi (Senior Economist)
- *Regional analysis*: Cem Karayalcin (Florida International University) and Harun Onder
- *Trade*: Erhan Artuc (Senior Economist), Nicolas Gomez Parra (Consultant), Yulia Vnukova (Consultant), and Amevi Rocard Kouwoaye (Consultant)
- *Transport*: Abdulhakim Ali Ahmed Al-Aghbari (Senior Highway Engineer), Atsushi Iimi (Senior Economist), Ibrahim Dajani (Program Leader), Igor Jokanovic (Consultant), Louccas Bou Jaoude (Consultant), Mira Morad (Transport Specialist), Samy Rene Louis Mdihi (Consultant), and Soran Hama Tahir Ali (Senior Infrastructure Specialist)
- *Water and sanitation*: Amal Talbi (Lead Water Resources Management Specialist), Anders Jagerskog (Senior Water Resources Management Specialist), Dominick Revell de Waal (Senior Economist), and Sally Zgheib (Water Supply and Sanitation Specialist)

We would like to express our sincere gratitude to H. E. Mohamad Al-Ississ (Minister of Finance, Jordan), H. E. Mansour Bteish (Minister of Economy and Trade, Lebanon), Bayan Sami Abdul Rahman (Kurdistan Regional Government Representative to the United States), Joel Rayburn (Special Envoy for Syria Deputy and Assistant Secretary for Levant Affairs, US Department of State), Richard Albright (Deputy Assistant Secretary, Bureau of Population, Refugees and Migration, US Department of State), Michael Koehler (Deputy Director-General, DG ECHO, European Commission), Amin Awad (Director of the MENA Bureau, UNHCR), and other colleagues who participated in several consultation meetings throughout the report's preparation.

The team is grateful for guidance and support from Ferid Belhaj (MENA Vice President), Ceyla Pazarbasioglu (EFI Vice President), Anna M. Bjerde (MENA Director of Strategy and Operations), Saroj Kumar Jha (Mashreq Country Director), Najy Benhassine (EFI Regional Director), and Marcello Estevao (MTI Global Practice Director). This report benefited from valuable comments and inputs provided by peer reviewers Kevin Carey, Tito Cordella, Ishac Diwan, Ewen Macleod, Xavier Devictor, and William G. Battaile, and the following colleagues: Naila Ahmed, Amatalalim Ali Mohamed Al-Soswa, Benu Bidani, Sergio de Cosmo, Mireille Girard, Katrin Hager, Ellen Hamilton, Wissam Harake, Mirjam Kalle, Daniel Lederman, Wael Mansour, Piers E. Merrick, Tania Meyer, Lili Mottaghi, Francesca Recanatini, and Sajjad Shah. Throughout the project cycle, excellent support was provided by Ekaterina G. Stefanova, Jihane Rached, Mirvat Haddad, Muna Salim, and Syviengxay Creger. Editorial review was conducted by Nora Mara, and design and typesetting were performed by Design and Development Minds.

This study was financed by generous financial contributions from the governments of Canada, Germany, the Netherlands, the United Kingdom, and the United States and was supported technically by UNHCR.

ABBREVIATIONS

BOP	balance of payments
BTI	Bertelsmann Transformation Index
CAGR	compound annual growth rate
CDS	credit default swap
CGE	computable general equilibrium
CIP	Capital Investment Plan
CPI	Corruption Perceptions Index
CSO	civil society organization
DTM	Displacement Tracking Matrix (International Organization for Migration)
EAA	Euromed Association Agreement
EDL	Electricité du Liban
EITI	Extractive Industries Transparency Initiative
EMDEs	emerging markets and developing economies
EMIS	Educational Management Information System (Jordan)
EU	European Union
EYE	expected years of education
FCV	fragility, conflict, and violence (countries affected by)
FDI	foreign direct investment
GBI	Gulf Bridge International
GBPTP	Greater Beirut Public Transport Project
GCC	Gulf Cooperation Council
GCFF	Global Concessional Financing Facility
GDP	gross domestic product
GTAP	Global Trade Analysis Project
GWh	gigawatt hours
HBS	Household Budget Survey (Lebanon)
HCI	Human Capital Index
HEIS	Household Expenditure and Income Survey (Jordan)

HSES	Household Socio-Economic Survey (Iraq)
IDP	internally displaced person
IMF	International Monetary Fund
IOM	International Organization for Migration
IRU	International Road Transport Union
ISIC	International Standard Industrial Classification
IT	information technology
JADI	Jeddah, Amman, Damascus, and Istanbul
JLMPS	Jordan Labor Market Panel Survey
km	kilometer
KRG	Kurdistan Regional Government
KRI	Kurdistan Region of Iraq
kWh	kilowatt-hour
LFPR	labor force participation rate
MENA	Middle East and North Africa
MIC	middle-income country
MICS	Multiple Indicator Cluster Surveys
MODS	Mobility of Displaced Persons
MoPH	Ministry of Public Health
MPWT	Ministry of Public Works and Transport
MSW	municipal solid waste
MTEF	Medium-Term Expenditure Framework
MW	megawatt
NDP	National Development Plan
NGO	nongovernmental organization
NPTP	National Poverty Targeting Program
OBI	Open Budget Index
ODA	official development assistance
OECD	Organisation for Economic Co-operation and Development
OLS	ordinary least squares

PAFTA	Pan-Arab Free Trade Area
PDS	Public Distribution System (Iraq)
PEFA	Public Expenditure and Financial Accountability
PHCC	primary health care center
PIM	public investment management
$PM_{2.5}$	fine particulate matter
RCN	Regional Cable Network
RMSPE	root mean squared prediction error
SCM	synthetic control method
SWIFT	Rapid Welfare Monitoring Survey (Iraq)
TADAT	Tax Administration Diagnostic Assessment Tool
TFP	total factor productivity
TIR	Transports Internationaux Routiers
UCDP	Uppsala Conflict Data Program
UN	United Nations
UNHCR	United Nations High Commissioner for Refugees
UNICEF	United Nations Children's Fund
UNRWA	United Nations Relief and Work Agency for Palestinians in the Near East
VASyR	Vulnerability Assessment of Syrian Refugees in Lebanon
WEO	World Economic Outlook
WGI	Worldwide Governance Indicators
WHO	World Health Organization

All dollar amounts are US dollars unless otherwise noted.

KEY MESSAGES

As a region, the Mashreq has seen more than its share of deaths, economic losses, and instability over the past decade. The region has braved massive economic and social shocks that would challenge even the most advanced economies in the world. The conflict in the Syrian Arab Republic has contributed to the region's challenges, but the region's problems have other causes, too. As countries in the Mashreq look toward recovery, an approach that both takes account of the region's interconnectedness and seeks to build on it provides better prospects for the people of the region. Adopting such an approach will require a scaled-up international effort.

THE NATURE OF THE IMPACT

- The conflict in the Syrian Arab Republic has imposed a heavy economic and social toll on the country's neighbors in the Mashreq region. From 2011 onward, average annual gross domestic product (GDP) growth rates were reduced by 1.2 percentage points in Iraq, 1.6 percentage points in Jordan, and 1.7 percentage points in Lebanon in real terms solely because of the conflict in Syria. Cumulatively, these reductions correspond to 11.3 percent of the combined preconflict (2010) GDPs across the three countries.
- The fallout was transmitted through multiple channels. With decreasing transit trade through Syria and stalling service exports like tourism, the marginal effect of the trade shock on GDP reached –3.1 percentage points in Jordan and –2.9 percentage points in Lebanon. In comparison, the demographic shock (refugee arrivals) boosted GDP by 0.9 percentage points in both countries by increasing aggregate demand and labor supply.
- GDP effects are only a relatively small share of the overall impact. Despite some unquantifiable effects, the conflict had far-reaching consequences in the Mashreq:
  - The GDP impact of the conflict pushed up poverty rates by 4.0 percentage points in Jordan, 7.1 percentage points in Lebanon and, with internal displacement, 6.0 percentage points in Iraq.
  - Labor market conditions for locals, especially women, deteriorated in all three countries after 2011. These dynamics are correlated with overall economic slowdown but not necessarily with subnational refugee intensity.
  - The arrival of refugees boosted demand for public services, resulting in a mix of congestion and fiscal effects. In education and water, adaptations in service provision largely prevented congestion. In transport, health, and energy, congestion was observed (with fiscal costs through built-in energy subsidies).
  - The demographic shock has unambiguously increased municipal solid waste, but refugee-driven increases of pollution in water and air bodies have been detected only in some local settings.
  - Many other dimensions of the impact, including those in political, cultural, and security areas, are equally, if not more, important; but these dimensions could not be analyzed in the absence of relevant metrics or data.

THE PRECONDITIONS

- The overall economic impact of the Syrian conflict on Iraq, Jordan, and Lebanon has been disproportionately high compared to similar situations elsewhere in the world in the last few decades. This difference is driven by three factors: (i) the sheer scale of the Syrian conflict and ensuing forced displacement, (ii) the high exposure of neighboring countries to a possible fallout, and (iii) the low institutional resilience in neighboring countries, which propagated the shock further.
- The high exposure stemmed from unconventional channels. Although bilateral merchandise trade with Syria was low in all countries, the conflict still affected their external balances. Lebanon and Jordan relied heavily on foreign direct investments and service exports (tourism), which reacted strongly to instability. Iraq's exposure also materialized through a bolstered Islamic State insurgency.
- Institutional resilience was low in the three countries for different reasons. Before 2011, Iraq had one of the lowest state capacities in the world. Jordan had one of the best in the Middle East and North Africa region, but its fiscal space was narrowing as revenues decreased. Lebanon had both problems: driven by a complex political economy, its state capacity suffered from years of underinvestment; and an excessive public debt burden, along with an ineffective tax system, suffocated its fiscal space.

WHAT IS TO BE DONE GOING FORWARD?

- In the medium term, a strong economic recovery in Syria and an associated positive fallout are unlikely. In the three security and service restoration scenarios analyzed in this report, economic recovery in Syria remains modest with limited effects on neighboring countries, not exceeding a percentage point even in the best-case scenario. In the top-five materials that would be required for reconstruction, all three neighboring countries are net importers themselves.
- Regardless of what happens in Syria, neighbors can unilaterally improve upon the current outcomes. The complex political economy dynamics in the region have so far restrained building better institutional resilience and mitigating the Syrian crisis shock more effectively. A persistent short-termism in both cases has led to costly and ineffective service provision, lost economic opportunities, and underfunded programs. A medium-term strategy is needed to both address Syria's own structural problems and mitigate the adverse effects of the conflict. These two objectives can be pursued in a joint manner because the synergies between them are high, especially in the following areas:
    - *Enhancing social safety nets.* Potential complementarities are strong between refugee assistance systems and national assistance mechanisms.
    - *Improving service access for all.* Significant overlaps exist between building delivery capacity for own constituents and replacing ad hoc solutions for refugees.
    - *Investing in state capacity.* While exploiting the above two synergies, and building capacity, authorities can benefit from civil society and international organization participation.

- A regional approach can generate a better equilibrium. In the Mashreq region, both problems and opportunities are transboundary. As the conflict in Syria has shown, instability expands beyond borders, but so do public goods (connectivity for transit trade). Thus, a regional approach can help better internalize these spillovers to minimize public bads and maximize public goods.
  - *Gains from a regional perspective.* Intraregional complementarity of merchandise trade is limited; however, potential gains from service market integration and infrastructure cooperation are large. Scale economies in energy, transport, and information and communications technology are particularly promising.
  - *Barriers against regionalism.* Major asymmetries within countries (elite capture and exclusion) and across countries (imbalances in economic power) can trigger protectionist reflexes. Breaking these constraints often requires major changes.
  - *Lessons from the region's long history.* A review of successful regional cooperation episodes in the Mashreq (from the 7th to the 19th century) shows that demographic shocks can provide an opportunity to overcome unilateralism by facilitating economic interlinkages. Similarly, factors like major openings of external markets (bottom-up) or third-party promotion of stability and infrastructure cooperation (top-down) can also help. In all cases, a balance between intraregional competition and cooperation is essential for a dynamic regional economy.
- Adopting a regional focus for stability and prosperity necessitates a concerted international effort. A supranational commitment to stability at the regional level can potentially make elites feel safe enough to perform deep social and economic reforms, relaxing economic exclusion and alleviating the inherently interdependent fragility. Can such consensus be mustered? This report is optimistic, because the alternative is in no one's interest.

OVERVIEW

Since the 2011 onset of the conflict in the Syrian Arab Republic, Syrians have suffered an unimaginable tragedy. A previous World Bank (2017a) report, *The Toll of War: The Economic and Social Consequences of the Conflict in Syria*, documented the magnitude of devastation and losses suffered by Syrians. More than 400,000 deaths have been directly attributed to the conflict so far with millions more nonlethal casualties. More than half of the country's preconflict population (20.7 million) has been displaced—the largest displacement crisis since World War II—and, by 2017, the economic activity in the country had collapsed by more than 60 percent compared to that in 2010. A subsequent World Bank (2019b) report, *The Mobility of Displaced Syrians: An Economic and Social Analysis*, analyzed the conditions faced by Syrians inside and outside Syria, with a special focus on how those conditions could shape the spontaneous returns of Syrian refugees. That report emphasized the challenges faced by Syrians everywhere and showed that return has not been a real option for many Syrians. Refugees opt for safety regardless of the conditions they face in countries of asylum.

The repercussions of the brutal war have spread beyond the borders of Syria. The conflict in Syria has shaped conditions in neighboring countries in many ways. At its peak, the number of Syrian refugees registered by the United Nations High Commissioner for Refugees (UNHCR) represented more than a fifth of local populations in Jordan, Lebanon, and the Kurdistan Region of Iraq (KRI), leading to a massive policy challenge even by advanced economy standards. The broader insecurity in Syria and Iraq (including the Islamic State insurgency) disrupted economic connectivity and reduced confidence in economic prospects in these countries. Together, these factors have contributed to a toll that has been paid so far not only by Syrians but also by their neighbors.

This report aims to analyze the regional consequences of the conflict at a critical juncture. With persistent delays in the resolution of the conflict, and absent a swift economic recovery in Syria, the conflict-driven challenges in Mashreq are increasingly becoming protracted. The ideal response to this setback is a gradual transition from short-term mitigation policies pursued by regional authorities and the international community toward a medium-term strategy. Such a transition will help address the adverse impact of the conflict in a more effective and efficient manner going forward. This report aims to inform this transition by taking stock of the conflict-driven economic and social outcomes in Iraq, Jordan, and Lebanon and by explicitly analyzing the mechanisms through which such impact is manifested.[1]

ANALYTICAL STRATEGY

Analyzing the spillovers from the Syrian conflict is complicated by a plethora of factors that affected the region simultaneously. The onset of the Syrian conflict overlapped with the tail end of the global financial crisis and the subsequent global recession. At the regional level, the Syrian conflict was part of a broader Arab Spring movement, which led to widespread protests in the region, the collapse of governments (for example, of the Arab Republic of Egypt and of Tunisia), and violent conflicts (for example, in Libya, Syria, and the Republic of Yemen). Moreover, as the conflict progressed, other shocks like the major oil price collapse starting in mid-2014 materialized. Historically, Iraq, Jordan, and Lebanon have always been susceptible to external shocks. In Iraq, where hydrocarbon sales generated more than 90 percent of fiscal revenues, oil price dynamics were the primary source of vulnerability. In Jordan and Syria, foreign direct investment (FDI), remittances, and exports, especially tourism and financial services, played this role. Thus, even without a conflict in Syria, these factors alone would have affected the region in different ways. The challenge is to isolate the impact of the Syrian crisis from that of other shocks. In this study, we pursue a pragmatic approach to analyzing how the conflict in Syria has affected the economic and social outcomes in Iraq, Jordan, and Lebanon. Overall, the analyses pursue the following sequence:

1. *Analyze the conditions before the onset of the Syrian conflict.* Other things being equal, a greater exposure to the developments in Syria (such as through deep economic ties) could lead to a bigger impact in the region when Syrian economic activity takes a hit. Similarly, a lack of resilience could lead to an ineffective response to the shock, which would then further propagate the initial shock inside the country. Thus, to analyze exposure, we focus on cross-border flows including refugee arrivals, international trade, and capital flows (figure O.1). For institutional resilience, we assess state capacity (revenue and expenditure management, strategic planning, and capacity for service delivery and public accountability) and fiscal space (as measured by key fiscal indicators including debt burden and revenue/expenditure structures).

2. *Take stock of economic and social outcomes.* This step involves analyzing the outcomes of the exposure-resilience system described in the previous step, without a systematic effort to estimate the marginal effects of different underlying mechanisms. The analysis covers the following areas: macro-fiscal trends (economic growth and public debt dynamics), labor market trends (where we also exploit the heterogeneity of refugee populations across subnational areas to infer the relationship between refugee arrivals and labor market outcomes), poverty trends (brief assessment of distributional consequences), trends in access to publicly provided services (supply and demand dynamics in transportation, education, health care, water and sanitation, and energy services, as well as the likely fiscal implications of supply adaptation in selective cases), and environmental trends (water, land, and air pollution).

3. *Isolate the impact of the Syrian conflict on the Iraqi, Jordanian, and Lebanese economies.* We next turn to a more technical analysis of different channels through which the Syrian conflict has manifested its impact on the gross domestic products (GDPs) of Syria's neighbors. For this analysis, we use several models in an integrated manner (figure O.2). First, we use a synthetic control method (SCM) to estimate counterfactual GDPs, which helps to control for other global and regional factors that may have driven some of the economic outcomes. Next, we plug those GDPs into a structural gravity model to generate counterfactual trade patterns. Then, we use a computable general equilibrium (CGE) model, together with the counterfactual GDP and trade series, to analyze the marginal effects of different shocks (trade, demography, and total factor productivity [TFP]). Finally, we analyze counterfactual poverty rates and debt burden by using a macro-micro simulation model and debt dynamics framework.

4. *Last, analyze future prospects and policy options.* Using the framework constructed in the previous steps, we discuss how possible future recovery scenarios in Syria could affect the region. Policy options are discussed in two stages: a unilateral approach (the policy choices that can be pursued within each country, while holding other things constant) and a regional approach, which includes the effects of policy coordination among the countries to internalize cross-border spillovers. Insights from historical episodes are also sought.

FIGURE 0.1. **Analytical strategy**

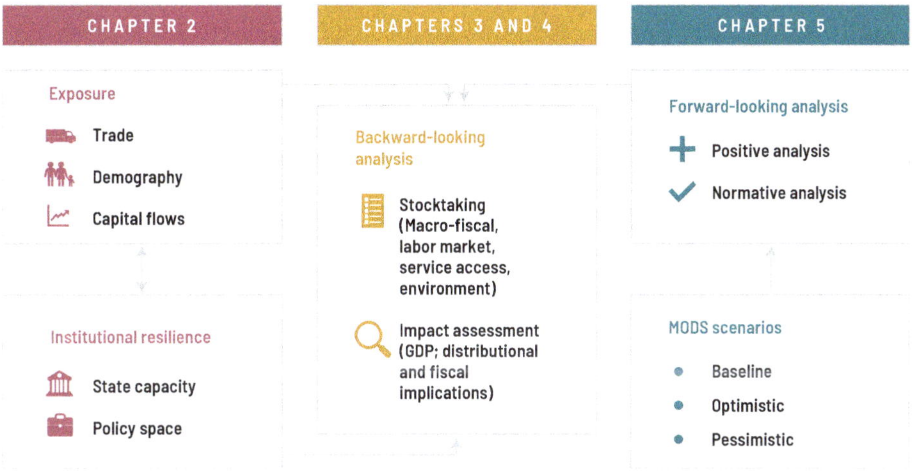

Source: Original figure for this report.

Note: MODS = Mobility of Displaced Persons.

FIGURE 0.2. **Technical strategy for analyzing the impact**

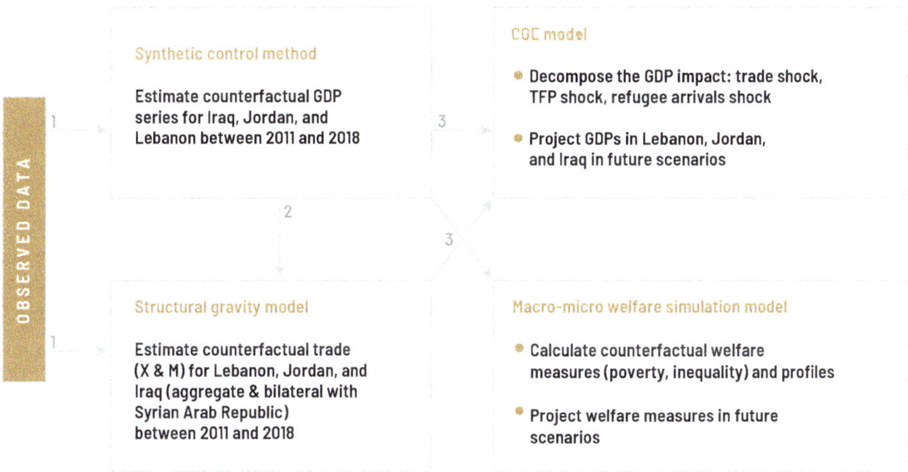

Source: Original figure for this report.

Note: CGE = computable general equilibrium; TFP = total factor productivity; M = imports; X = exports.

Next, we present a summary of key results. In the remainder of this overview, we first discuss the results concerning the nature of the impact, which includes the impact on GDP, poverty, fiscal balances, access to publicly provided services, and the environment. Next, we discuss the underlying conditions that led to the proliferation of the impact. Finally, we consider the possible future trajectories of the impact and two alternative approaches to addressing such underlying conditions and mitigating the adverse consequences of the conflict.

THE NATURE OF THE IMPACT

We analyze several dimensions of the impact, but with varying degrees of causal inference. For the GDP impact, we can infer some counterfactual series by using the SCM. For a limited number of issues, like poverty and fiscal, we use these counterfactual GDP estimations to analyze the likely effects of the Syrian conflict. In cases where a subnational heterogeneity can be exploited—such as for labor market analysis in Iraq and Jordan and environmental analysis in all three countries—we map outcome indicators onto refugee intensity to consider correlations. For others, where neither of these approaches is feasible, we discuss trends and parallelism with the conflict even if it is not possible to establish causality. This approach is based on a simple concern: to avoid reaching a conclusion that mistakes the absence of evidence for the evidence of absence (that is, data-poor issues are not relevant). With data limitations, some of the most important aspects (such as political outcomes) are not possible to quantify.

GDP GROWTH IMPACT

Compared to the decade before, the years with conflict in Syria were marked by an oil-driven recovery in Iraq and major economic slowdowns in Jordan and Lebanon. From an economic point of view, all three countries are critically susceptible to global and regional developments. In Iraq, this takes the form of vulnerability to oil price volatility, and in Jordan and Lebanon through the important roles played by FDI, remittances, and services exports like tourism. Therefore, not only the conflict in Syria but also global factors like the lingering effects of the 2008 global financial crisis and the 2014 oil price collapse, as well as regional dynamics like the Arab Spring, played important roles in shaping the economic dynamics in Mashreq after 2011.

- In Iraq, favorable oil production boosted growth despite a heightened Islamic State insurgency. Following a war-driven economic collapse in the 2000s, Iraq's growth accelerated as oil production increased from 2.4 million barrels per day to 3.4 million barrels per day between 2011 and 2014. This increase, and rising oil prices, boosted fiscal revenues and expenditures by half, which fueled growth in nonoil sectors. Industry (mainly oil) added to growth by about 4.8 percentage points annually during this period, and services contributed by 2.3 percentage points. In the following four years, oil production grew by another 40 percent despite the heightened Islamic State insurgency. With decreasing oil prices, however, oil revenues decreased by about 40 percent in 2015 and only caught up to the 2014 level by 2018. In this period, industry (oil) contributed to growth by 3.2 percentage points per year, whereas services remained stagnant.

- The Jordanian economy began to decelerate in 2008, and this trend has persisted since then. The slowdown in the Jordanian economy began with the global financial crisis, with GDP growth decreasing from 7.2 percent to 2.3 percent between 2008 and 2010 (largely a result of a sudden stop in external flows, including a 41 percent decrease in FDI inflows[2]). After 2010, average growth rate averaged 2.5 percent, with disruptions in gas imports from Egypt being a contributing factor. On the demand side, the largest drawback of the post-2010 episode in Jordan has been the decrease in exports' contribution to growth—from 4.7 percentage points during 2000–07 to only 0.1 percentage points. This decrease was driven by the fall of merchandise exports growth from 22.0 percent to only 2.7 percent and of services exports growth from 19.0 percent to 3.1 percent. Other contributions also decreased but in a more limited manner.

- Lebanon's growth record is marked with episodic spurts and long pauses in between. About three-quarters of the country's GDP comprises financial, trade, and tourism services; and these sectors are more susceptible to external shocks and risk than others. Between 2007 and 2010, Lebanon enjoyed a rapid growth episode, averaging above 9 percent per annum, primarily driven by the service sector (6.5 percentage points contribution). With Syrian crisis–led trade disruptions and instability in the region after 2010, growth decreased to an average 1.4 percent between 2011 and 2018. On the supply side, this decrease was largely driven by a service sector slowdown, with the sector contributing only 1.2 percent to growth after 2010.

Analyzing the drivers of shifting economic dynamics requires a nuanced approach. The macroeconomic trends exhibited by Jordan and Lebanon in the last two decades—that is, a rapid economic growth in the 2000s followed by a significant slowdown in the next decade—were common among developing countries. The magnitudes, however, are vastly different. Between the 2000s and the 2010s, annual GDP growth in Jordan and Lebanon slowed by 3.9 percentage points and 4.4 percentage points, respectively. In comparison, other middle-income countries experienced a slowdown of only 1.3 percentage points and other countries in the Middle East and North Africa (MENA) only 1.2 percentage points. Therefore, it is unlikely that global or regional factors alone shaped the economic performances in Jordan and Lebanon. Isolating the specific role played by the Syrian conflict, however, requires adopting a more technical approach.

The conflict in Syria had a significant dampening effect on neighbors' GDPs

To separate the impact of the Syrian conflict from that of global and regional factors, we first create counterfactual GDP series. In the absence of a direct measure of the impact of the conflict, the analysis in this report employs SCM, a statistical technique to generate counterfactual series for analyzing the impact of a treatment (for example, an exogenous shock). It involves assigning weights to a control group (other countries) not subjected to the treatment (conflict). This group becomes a synthetic benchmark. Once the weights are optimized to match the pretreatment series, the posttreatment (after-shock) performances are compared with the actual data to assess the impact of the treatment. For the purposes of this study, we estimated three different specifications, spanning various degrees of trade-offs between model fit and dimensionality of characteristics (for example, MENA-specific shocks) and used the average as the preferred specification.

Estimates show that the Syrian conflict had a sizeable negative impact on neighbors' GDPs (figure O.3). In Iraq, the average GDP growth rate in the counterfactual scenario (no Syrian conflict or associated events) is estimated at 6.7 percent annually, which is 1.2 percentage points higher than the actual growth rate between 2010 and 2018. In Jordan, it is estimated at 4.1 percent, which is 1.6 percentage points higher than the actual growth rate.[5] In Lebanon, the counterfactual growth rate is estimated at 3.1 percent, 1.7 percentage points greater than the actual rate. Thus, not all slowdown in Jordan and Lebanon between 2000–10 and 2010–18 can be attributed to the Syrian conflict. Even without a conflict, global and MENA-specific factors alone would lead to a decrease in average annual GDP growth by 2.0 percentage points in Jordan and 2.3 percentage points in Lebanon during 2010–18.

FIGURE 0.3. GDP growth rate comparison, 2000-10 versus actual 2010-18 versus counterfactual 2010-18

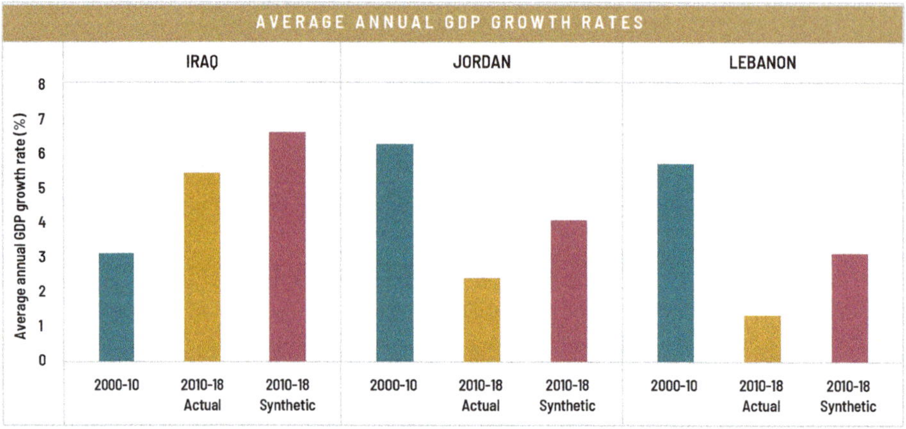

Source: World Bank staff calculations.

Trade and TFP shocks account for most of the GDP impact

To further analyze the GDP impact, we investigate the marginal impact of the demographic, trade, and TFP shocks. To assess the roles played by different factors, we use a CGE model based on the Global Trade Analysis Project model. The CGE model helps take general equilibrium links into consideration. First, the model is estimated using actual outcomes in 2011–18. Next, the actual outcomes are replaced with the counterfactual GDPs estimated via SCM. Then, one step at a time, counterfactual shocks for population (no refugee arrivals), trade (estimated by using a structural gravity model), and TFP growth (residual) are used to isolate the marginal impact of these factors on GDP growth in Iraq, Jordan, and Lebanon between 2011 and 2018. This process gives us the marginal effects of each shock, which cannot be interpreted additively—that is, the sum of marginal effects is not equal to the aggregate effect because of general equilibrium and feedback effects.

- The marginal effect of the demographic shock on GDP was positive in all countries but most pronounced in Jordan and Lebanon. The model-based analysis shows that, other things being equal, in the absence of refugees, the Jordanian and Lebanese GDPs would have grown on average 0.9 percentage points more slowly between 2011 and 2018. As expected, the impact of the refugees on growth in Iraq was positive but modest, about 0.1 percentage point. Note that GDP is an indicator of aggregate economic activity, yet it does not capture distributional consequences. Thus, although overall economic activity increases with a hike in population, per capita income of certain individuals or groups can still be reduced by the shock.
- Trade shocks associated with the Syrian conflict had a significant dampening effect on growth in Jordan and Lebanon. Other things being equal, with the higher counterfactual trade growth, the Lebanese GDP would have grown on average 2.9 percentage points faster between 2011 and 2018 (by 4.3 percent instead of the actual 1.4 percent). Similarly, in the absence of refugees, Jordan's GDP would have grown 3.1 percentage points faster (at 5.5 percent instead of 2.4 percent). The analysis couldn't be repeated for Iraq in a reliable manner given the extreme volatility of oil exports in the country. It is important to note that the higher export growth in the "no conflict"

counterfactual boosts the output not only of export-oriented industries but also of other domestic sectors indirectly, through higher input demand. Thus, effects are more than proportional to the share of trade in each economy.

- The marginal effects of negative TFP shock were substantial in all three countries. Other things being equal, the Lebanese GDP would grow 2.8 percentage points faster on average between 2011 and 2018, by 4.2 percent instead of the actual 1.4 percent, in the absence of the TFP shock imposed by the Syrian conflict. Similarly, results show that GDP in Jordan would grow 2.6 percentage points faster, at 5.0 percent instead of the observed 2.4 percent. Although Iraq did not experience a large trade and refugee arrival shock, lower TFP growth associated with the conflict had a dampening effect on growth of 1.9 percentage points for 2011–18.

The GDP impact is only a part of the effect, and probably not the most important one

GDP provides a convenient but imperfect metric for measuring the impact. The analysis so far has focused on the GDP impact of the Syrian conflict; however, it should be noted that GDP impact by itself is not a sufficient indicator. No single indicator on its own can capture the scope and depth of the conflict's economic impact. Because it is a metric for aggregate economic activity, GDP comes close, but even that suffers from multiple shortcomings. First, being a flow variable, it misses stock effects like changes in a country's physical (built), human, and environmental capital. Second, it does not capture the distributional dynamics of aggregate economic activity. Third, it does not measure directly many important consequences of the conflict, including those In political, cultural, and some social areas. Nevertheless, it provides a partially useful indicator because it is readily available and avoids major aggregation problems (for example, double-counting while using multiple indicators.

The marginal impact on GDP estimates should be interpreted with caution. GDP trends and individual welfare do not always overlap even in normal times. This is especially true in the case of this study because changes in aggregate economic activity are accompanied by a rise in population. The GDPs after the arrival of refugees include the production and consumption of refugees as well as those of the host country constituents. Given very high poverty ratios among refugees, the share of GDP that corresponds to refugee consumption is likely to be relatively small. Nevertheless, this situation shows that GDP trends before and after refugee arrivals cannot strictly be interpreted as indicators of well-being among host communities even in average terms. Moreover, considering the fact that all three shocks (demographic, trade, and TFP) are likely to affect different groups differently, the interpretation of the GDP effects should further be disassociated from welfare-based interpretations.

FISCAL CONSEQUENCES

After 2011, countries in Mashreq, especially Jordan and Lebanon, observed deteriorating fiscal trends. In all three countries, fiscal performances exhibited stark differences between the two consecutive decades (before and after 2011) but for different reasons, some unrelated to the conflict in Syria.

- In Iraq, fiscal dynamics driven by oil revenue have dwarfed other effects. As a share of GDP, average annual revenues decreased by 10.7 percentage points between the 2008–10 and 2011–19 periods; grants decreased by 5.0 percentage points and oil revenues by 6.0 percentage points. Expenditures declined by 14.0 percentage points in the same time frame, driven by contractions in spending for goods and services (6.0 percentage points) and capital expenditures (3.7 percentage points). The ratio of public debt to GDP remained stable after 2011 with contributions from higher real GDP growth (decreasing debt burden by 20.3 percentage points) and higher primary deficits (increasing debt burden by 19.3 percentage points) offsetting each other.

- In Jordan, fiscal imbalances were deepened by decreasing revenues and a delayed expenditure adjustment. Between the 2000–10 and 2011–19 periods, revenues decreased by 7.3 percentage points as a share of GDP: grants fell by 3.0 percentage points, indirect taxes by 1.8 percentage points (driven by the 2008 expansion of tax exemptions), and other revenues by 2.5 percentage points. Primary expenditures also fell by 3.0 percentage points, however, with a delay. Until 2015, expenditures remained well above revenues, leading to fiscal deficits at 10.4 percent of GDP, annually. This delay in adjustment was partly driven by the gas supply disruptions from Egypt. Beginning in 2016, a large consolidation program brought down the deficits to a range of 3–4 percent. Overall, with primary deficits adding 40.5 percentage points to the debt-to-GDP ratio, and with GDP growth subtracting only 17.3 percent (as opposed to the 37.4 percent in 2001–07), the ratio of public debt to GDP increased from 67 percent in 2010 to 94 percent in 2019.

- In Lebanon, the debt burden increased as the modest deficit reduction was overtaken by a larger GDP slowdown. Revenues decreased from 23.3 percent of GDP in 2008–10 to 21.0 percent in 2011–19. Indirect taxes decreased by 2.5 percentage points and grants by 0.9 percentage points, and direct taxes increased by 1.7 percentage points. Primary expenditures averaged 21.0 percent of GDP in 2008–10 and 20.4 percent of GDP in 2011–19. Interest payments dropped from an average of 10.8 percent in 2008–10 to 9.0 percent in 2011–19 with lower nominal interest rates. Overall, fiscal deficits remained persistent (8.5 percent in 2008–10 and 8.3 percent in 2011–19). With subdued growth after 2010, the debt-to-GDP ratio increased by 18.2 percentage points, reaching 155.0 percent in 2019.

To what extent can the increasing debt burden in the region be attributed to the GDP shock imposed by the Syrian conflict? On the revenue side, shocks in demography, trade, and capital flows, as well as the broader instability stemming from the conflict, can change the tax base. On the expenditure side, an increase in demand for publicly provided goods and services can affect the scale and composition of expenditures. These effects, however, are to a certain extent discretionary (relying on the government's willingness and ability to adjust service provision). In addition, conflict can also affect below-the-line factors. With the possibility of broader instability and cross-border spillovers, the country's risk outlook can change. This change may be reflected in its market access conditions and the terms of debt rollover, possibly worsening liquidity constraints and the sustainability of fiscal balances.

In the absence of counterfactuals for fiscal line items, we analyze the responsiveness of debt dynamics to changes in GDP, fiscal stance, and interest rates. Specifically, we consider three scenarios: first, we simulate the debt-to-GDP ratio by using the counterfactual (no Syrian conflict) GDP series, holding other things equal; second, we assume (in addition to the first scenario) that the revenue-to-GDP and primary expenditure–to-GDP ratios were maintained during the 2011–19 period at the historical levels and five-year average ratios observed prior to the conflict (no changes in fiscal stance); and, third, we assume (in addition to the second scenario) that the real interest rate facing the government during the conflict is 200 basis points lower than the actual rate.

- In Iraq, the counterfactual growth rates by themselves would not have driven the debt-to-GDP ratio down significantly. In contrast, had the country managed to maintain preconflict fiscal trends (in which, on average, the primary balance was near zero), the debt-to-GDP ratio in 2019 would have been nearly 20 percentage points lower than the actual ratio. Finally, a lower real interest rate may not have had a significant impact. With all factors (counterfactual GDP, preconflict primary balance, and an improved interest rate) taken into consideration, the debt-to-GDP ratio would have decreased from an actual of 49.3 percent to 25.9 percent.

- In Jordan, even all three factors together would have just maintained the debt-to-GDP ratio and not reduced it. Without an annual 1.6-percentage-point reduction in GDP growth imposed by the Syrian conflict, Jordan's debt-to-GDP ratio in 2019 would have been 10 percentage points lower than the actual one. Maintaining the preconflict primary balance would not have helped either (because the difference was only 0.7 percentage points), resulting in only a 3.9-percentage-point reduction. A lower real interest rate would have had a more uniform depressing effect on the debt-to-GDP-ratio, a 10-percentage-point reduction by 2019. Even with all three factors combined, however, the debt-to-GDP ratio (at 70.7 percent) would not have decreased below its preconflict level (67.1 percent in 2010).

- Lebanon's debt-to-GDP ratio could have decreased with either one of the three factors and much more so with all of them together. Without the conflict's GDP impact (a 1.7-percentage-point decrease in growth annually), Lebanon's debt-to-GDP ratio in 2019 would have been 23 percentage points lower than the actual one. With the preconflict primary surplus (2.3 percent of GDP) rather than the actual primary surplus (0.7 percent of GDP), the debt-to-GDP ratio in 2019 would have been reduced by another 15 percentage points. Finally, a 200-basis-point decrease in the real interest rate would reduce the debt-to-GDP ratio by an additional 20 percentage points. With all factors combined, the debt-to GDP ratio would have decreased from about 130 percent in 2010 to 97 percent in 2019, instead of climbing to 155 percent.

IMPLICATIONS FOR POVERTY

How did the GDP impact of the Syrian conflict affect the well-being of Iraqis, Jordanians, and Lebanese? To answer this question, we evaluate the welfare and distributional effects of the conflict in Syria on households in its neighboring countries of Iraq, Jordan, and Lebanon using a microsimulation-based analysis. This approach integrates the GDP impact analysis with a complete household distribution analysis based on national surveys that capture spatial and income distributions and, thus, incorporates multiple channels through which a shock affects households. Specifically, it accounts for changes in a country's employment shares and sectoral GDP, overall population growth, and changes in social assistance programs. Additionally, the microsimulation model is designed to explicitly account for large-scale displacement in Iraq due to the Islamic State crisis.

- The poverty rate in Iraq would be 6 percentage points lower without the Syrian crisis, the Islamic State insurgency, and internal displacement. Poverty analysis for Iraq used national poverty rates in 2012 and 2017. Replacing the actual growth with the counterfactual growth leads to a 6-percentage-point drop in the overall poverty headcount. Households in rural locations and households with male heads were most affected by the crisis; poverty in those households was 6.8 and 6.2 percentage points higher, respectively, than in the counterfactual scenario. Among households in urban areas and those with female heads, the impact of the crisis on poverty was an increase of 5.7 and 4.6 points, respectively. The crisis has also worsened the welfare of those who were already poor. The poverty gap—a measure of how far below the poverty line the average poor household's consumption is—has increased by almost 2 percentage points because of the crisis.

- The impact on poverty in Jordan was more modest but still significant. With lower GDP growth, overall poverty headcount in Jordan increased by 4.0 percentage points. As in Iraq, households in Jordan's rural areas suffered the most—poverty there increased by 6.3 percentage points. Poverty effects among both male- and female-headed households and in urban locations were similar to the overall impact, with increases of between 3.3 and 3.9 percentage points. The impacts on the gap and severity indexes were also lower compared to the impacts in Iraq. In contrast, vulnerability increased more significantly (6.0 percentage points) in Jordan: although few households fell below the poverty line, many came close to it.

- The poverty impact of the Syrian conflict was most pronounced in Lebanon. Poverty there is 7.1 percentage points higher in the counterfactual than the actual outcome—the highest difference estimated among the three countries. The crisis had similar impacts on male- and female-headed households (7.0 and 7.6 percentage points, respectively). Similarly, the gap and severity indexes were affected more significantly than in the other two countries. Impacts on vulnerability and inequality are near zero.

LABOR MARKET IMPACT

Unambiguously, the tragic forced displacement since 2011 has been the most dramatic consequence of the Syrian conflict for others in Mashreq. The arrival of refugees in all three countries and the internal displacement of Iraqis have created the world's highest displacement concentrations in proportion to the populations of host countries.[4] At peak values, Syrians who formally took refuge in the KRI, Jordan, and Lebanon (by registering with UNHCR) exceeded a fifth of the local population. By the end of 2019, UNHCR had registered about 5.6 million refugees, and 1.8 million of those refugees were hosted by Iraq, Jordan, and Lebanon. In Iraq, 1.5 million Iraqis were displaced internally as a result of the Islamic State insurgency. In general, these displaced populations faced different labor market conditions than their local peers:

- In Iraq, Syrian refugees have been more active in the labor market than their Iraqi peers, but they have also been more likely to be unemployed. In 2017, the formal and informal labor force participation rates (LFPRs) of Syrian males and females exceeded that of Iraqi peers by 12.4 percentage points and 9.0 percentage points, respectively. Their unemployment rates also exceeded the Iraqi averages by 5 percentage points for males and 20 percentage points for females. The unemployment rate difference was particularly high for those older than 40, reaching 40 percentage points for those between 50 and 54, and for those with higher education, reaching 20 percentage points for holders of postgraduate degrees.

- In Jordan, Syrian refugees, especially females, are less economically active than their Jordanian peers. In 2016, about half of Jordanians were economically active as opposed to a quarter of Syrians in Jordan. For males, the difference was large (78 percent among Jordanians and 51 percent among Syrians), but participation among Syrian women has been particularly low at 4 percent compared to 21 percent among Jordanian women. Both Jordanian and Syrian women faced about 30 percent unemployment.

- In Lebanon, the LFPRs of the Lebanese and of Syrian refugees were similar with the exception of women with tertiary education. Among Lebanese women, more educated females were more active economically. Among the non-Lebanese (also including other nationalities), this was not true: the highest LFPR was among illiterate women (52 percent). Overall, although the LFPRs of Syrian and Lebanese men were similar (about two-thirds), Syrian women had a significantly lower LFPR than did Lebanese women (11 percent versus 27 percent, respectively). Meanwhile, the unemployment rates of Syrian men and women were about 20 percentage points higher than those of their Lebanese peers.

In all three countries, labor markets for locals deteriorated significantly after 2011; however, attributing this trend to specific factors is not always possible. In the case of refugee arrivals, we compare different subnational areas to assess if exposure to refugee shocks can explain the observed subnational variation in labor market outcomes. This analysis, however, is not always feasible. Some factors, like policy changes and general concerns about security and stability, have countrywide effects. In such cases, we do not have enough variation to analyze the drivers of labor market outcomes.

- In Iraq, the areas with conflict or with arrivals of refugees and internally displaced persons (IDPs) faced significant labor market deterioration, with women suffering the most. The Iraqi LFPR and unemployment rate increased by 1.5 and 6.5 percentage points, respectively, between 2012 and 2017. Results differed significantly, however, by governorate, gender, and age group. In Baghdad, the LFPR increased (for both males and females) and the unemployment rate decreased. In contrast, the male LFPR decreased by 5.7 percentage points and the female LFPR collapsed from 26.0 percent to just 6.3 percent in Kirkuk, which was at the center of the conflict. Unemployment rates increased by 24.5 percentage points in Duhok (where local population increased by about 80 percent after the arrival of refugees and IDPs) and by 21.6 percentage points in Anbar (where violent battles with the Islamic State took place). Female unemployment was particularly affected: it increased by 52 percentage points in Anbar, 43 percentage points in Duhok, and 26 percentage points in Erbil. Overall, between 2012 and 2017, a 10.0-percentage-point increase in the share of displaced people in the population was correlated with about a 1.2-percentage-point increase in LFPR and a 3.7-percentage-point increase in unemployment across governorates. Although these results do not imply causality (refugee concentration and the conflict incidence were correlated), they are in line with other circumstantial evidence.
- In Jordan, the LFPR decreased (more severely for males) and unemployment increased (more severely for females). From 2010 to 2016, the LFPR of all Jordanians decreased from 54 percent to 49 percent, largely driven by the decrease in the male LFPR (from 86 percent to 78 percent), and the unemployment rate increased from 11 percent to 16 percent. Female unemployment increased faster (from 18 percent to 30 percent). Controlling for gender, LFPR and unemployment differences between educated and uneducated groups were not significant nationwide; however, they differed across governorates. For instance, the unemployment rate for low-educated males increased by 3 percentage points in Amman, remained stable in Irbid and Zarqa, and increased by 8 percentage points in Aqaba. Overall, there is no correlation between Syrian refugee shares and LFPR changes across governorates and a negative correlation between increasing unemployment and refugee intensity—that is, governorates with a lower refugee concentration experienced a higher increase in unemployment rate. This result also holds for wage trends. Many governorates that did not receive many refugees performed worse in wage growth than those that did.

- In Lebanon, the labor market preserved its characteristic inertia between 2011 and 2018, but severe data constraints prevent further analysis. Labor market conditions in Lebanon had responded to economic growth in a muted manner even before 2011. For instance, between 1997 and 2009, real GDP expanded at an average rate of 3.7 percent per year, yet employment grew only by 1.1 percent, indicating an employment growth elasticity of only 0.2, considerably lower than observed in other countries in the region. The labor market inertia continued after 2011 with the exception of the female LFPR, which grew from 18.0 percent to 27.1 percent between 2010 and 2018. Currently, unemployment rates among Lebanese are 30.0 percent for youth, 17.0 percent for women, and 9.9 percent for men. Severe data limitations made it impossible to assess the correlation between within-country heterogeneity in labor market outcomes and refugee intensity.

Overall, the conflict in Syria likely contributed to labor market deterioration in Mashreq. Although it is difficult to isolate the channels through which the conflict changed labor market outcomes, we are able to infer some patterns by exploiting within-country differences in refugee intensity and labor market dynamics. In Jordan, where data are in relatively better shape, there is no significant correlation between the two. In Iraq, we observe a strong correlation, but it is not possible to separate the effect of the refugees and IDPs from direct effects of the conflict. In Lebanon, data were not available. These observations do not refute a possibly large effect of the Syrian conflict on neighboring countries; as the rest of the report discusses, there is indeed such a large effect. It just does not seem to be through the labor market impact of the demographic shock. Similarly, these results do not suggest that refugees and IDPs did not pose any burden on host communities. As we discuss next, in certain areas, like access to public services, the demographic shock played a significant role in transmitting the negative fallout of the Syrian conflict.

ACCESS TO PUBLIC SERVICES

A sudden increase in demand for public services could overwhelm any country in the world; the people of Mashreq, and their governments, must be commended for their efforts in this regard. Public service provision systems are not often built to absorb a sudden 20 percent increase in demand. Thus, when such a demand shock hit the governments of KRI, Jordan, and Lebanon, they faced monumental challenges. On theoretical grounds, this demand can be met by either an equal adjustment of service provision (increase in supply) or sharing of existing provision levels (decrease in host community access to services). In the former case, the impact is primarily fiscal. In the latter, it is a direct welfare (consumption) impact. What happens in practice is often somewhere in between these boundary cases. Some adjustments in supply (possibly with the help of international aid) and some losses in the host community's access to services take place simultaneously. The exact magnitude of these adjustments, however, may differ by sector, country, and time. We analyze these aspects in the transportation, education, health care, water and sanitation, and energy sectors.

In transportation, the demographic shock increased depreciation and congestion. Before the Syrian conflict, the region's dominant transportation infrastructure, the road network, was well established but poorly maintained. Road densities were high because they supported a trucking-based domestic transportation system. The conflict in Syria has influenced the demand for transportation in Iraq, Jordan, and Lebanon, with consequences for depreciation and congestion. The transport sector provides ways for refugees to commute within a country or across borders, and it is directly affected by border closures and movement restrictions. To assess how these factors have influenced the quality of infrastructure and congestion, we analyze road density and demographic patterns between 2010 and 2019, using the results to produce indexes of host community accessibility to education and health care facilities.

- In Iraq, conflict-driven damage to transportation infrastructure compounded the displacement-driven depreciation. World Bank (2018) estimated $3.3 billion worth of physical damages in transportation infrastructure. Refugee and IDP arrivals, and associated humanitarian relief efforts, increased the rehabilitation and upgrade needs of the road network by an estimated $80 million to $100 million, annually. With large-scale displacement and infrastructure destruction, the share of population with access to a school within a 10-minute driving distance decreased from 41 percent in 2010 to 36 percent in 2019 (congestion adjusted) and the share with access to a hospital within a 30-minute driving distance fell from 69 percent to 63 percent.

- In Jordan, according to the Jordanian Ministry of Transport, the number of registered vehicles increased by half between 2010 and 2018. It is not possible, however, to attribute this change to a single factor. The resulting congestion (sometimes lasting all day) increased travel times and decreased accessibility, yet the proportion of people who live within a 30- or 10-minute distance from a health facility or school was estimated to increase slightly between 2010 and 2019. This increase is likely driven by the urban bias in population growth, which dominated the congestion effect.

- In Lebanon, high motorization density, insufficient maintenance of roads, and the influx of refugees have made a bad traffic problem worse. Road transport is by far the dominant form of transport in Lebanon, with reliable public transport being nearly absent. The influx of Syrian refugees put extra pressure on the road networks, which already suffered from the absence of rehabilitation and routine maintenance. The result was a worsening condition over the years, which led to Lebanon's ranking of 121st worldwide in terms of road quality in 2018, dropping 20 places from 2010. The share of people who live within a 30- or 10-minute distance from a health facility or school was estimated to increase marginally between 2010 and 2019 (by 0.2 and 0.5 percentage points, respectively). As in Jordan, this increase is likely driven by the urban bias in population growth dominating the congestion effect.

In education, the demographic shock posed a major challenge to service delivery systems. Of the 1.9 million registered refugees in Iraq, Jordan, and Lebanon, nearly half were under the age of 18. Since the onset of the crisis, the Mashreq governments have aimed boldly to provide these refugees with education services. The international community has contributed to the cost of service provision, but funding gaps remain. Expanding the coverage would require additional finances and may be costlier in the future.[5] Estimates show that the provision of education services to all refugee children (excluding tertiary education and demand-side problems) could cost at least $50 million in Iraq, $198 million in Jordan, and $392 million in Lebanon, annually.[6]

- In Iraq, conflict, displacement, and inefficiencies in the education system translated into growing student–teacher ratios. With about 70,000 Syrian refugee children registered in Iraq, 30,000 of whom were enrolled in schools in 2018, combined with natural population growth and conflict-driven service disruptions, student–teacher ratios have deteriorated since 2010. The number of teachers grew by only 1.2 percent per year between 2007 and 2017 in preprimary and primary levels, and by 3 percent in the secondary level. Overall, student–teacher ratios increased from an average of 16 to 23.

- In Jordan, a three-tier system helped provide Syrian refugees with education services without sacrificing the quantity or quality of Jordanian education. Jordan has allowed Syrian children to access tuition-free public schools since the start of the conflict. More than half (56 percent) of school-age Syrian refugees were enrolled in formal education, making up 9 percent of all public school attendees in 2017–18. One in four Syrian students attended the first shift with Jordanian children, and others attended either camp schools or the second shift. A recent body of research suggests that the arrival of Syrian refugees did not have a significant effect on the attainment and learning outcomes of Jordanian students.[7]
- Lebanon has almost doubled the size of its national public education system since 2010. Of the 370,000 school-age Syrian refugee children (numbers vary by source) in the country, about 20 percent attended the first (morning) shift together with Lebanese students, and 60 percent attended the second (afternoon) shift dedicated for Syrian refugee education. Combining those two groups, Syrian refugee children made up half of the enrolled students in public schools. Between 2011 and 2018, enrollment rates for Lebanese children increased from 67 percent to 78 percent in the lower-secondary level and from 55 percent to 65 percent in the secondary level.

In health care, refugee arrivals aggravated structural problems in service provision systems. In Iraq, the demand shock was compounded by a major fiscal crisis faced by the Kurdistan Regional Government (KRG). In Lebanon, a flawed system of procurement from private providers had already left many Lebanese with insufficient care. In Jordan, the private sector spearheaded a rapid adaptation in response to the demand shock; however, the magnitude of the shock was large enough to overwhelm the provision system.

- Iraq suffered from both demand and supply shocks. In camps, Syrian refugees benefited from primary health care centers (PHCCs) free of charge; they could access other PHCCs with a 500 dinar consultation fee (like locals). Services were provided by the KRG with financial support from UNHCR, the United Nations Population Fund, and the World Health Organization. With KRG's own fiscal constraints (driven by the dispute with Baghdad), the total number of PHCCs decreased from 984 to 812 (from 1.80 per 1,000 persons to 0.12) between 2013 and 2017. Nationwide, Iraq lost 3,938 physicians and 6,787 nurses and midwives (through casualties and outmigration), decreasing the number of physicians per 1,000 persons by 0.17 points, between 2013 and 2015. The fiscal share of health spending decreased from 4.8 percent to 1.7 percent between 2010 and 2016, which increased private expenditure for health—all out of pocket—from 26.1 percent in 2010 to 78.5 in 2016.
- In Jordan, a private sector–driven adaptation helped cope with the surge in demand. From 2012 to 2014, registered Syrian refugees paid the same rate as insured Jordanians at public facilities (almost free of charge). Facing an increasing fiscal burden, however, authorities introduced a copayment (the same that locals would pay) in November 2014. The number of PHCCs increased from a total of 1,453 to 1,594 between 2010 and 2018, and the number of physicians increased drastically from 4,620 to 6,591. The increase in PHCCs was driven mostly by private sector responses in governorates with the highest numbers of refugees (Amman, Irbid, and Mafraq). With slower response on the public side (the fiscal share of health care expenditures

decreased from 18.4 percent to 12.0 percent), PHCCs per 1,000 persons decreased from 0.20 to 0.16, whereas the density of physicians remained comparable between 2010 and 2018.

- In Lebanon, policy-driven obstacles prevented a more dynamic private sector response and led to sluggish adaptation. Lebanon's health care system struggled to ensure financial coverage to vulnerable Lebanese even before the crisis. The Ministry of Public Health contracted hospitals and allocated a budget ceiling for their services, which often fell short of the health care demand of uninsured Lebanese. This shortfall led to $1.4 billion in arrears for private hospitals in 2012–17 and a hospital waitlist of 94,000 Lebanese citizens, annually. Although the total number of PHCCs increased from 870 to 965 between 2010 and 2018, PHCCs per 1,000 persons decreased from 0.18 to 0.14, and the number of physicians per 1,000 persons dropped from 2.46 to 2.01 between 2010 and 2017.

In the energy sector, the demographic shock reduced energy access and increased fiscal burden through embedded subsidies. A recent World Bank assessment pointed to considerable stress to the energy systems of the host countries, particularly Lebanon and Jordan, caused by the Syrian refugee crisis (World Bank 2019b). According to this analysis, fuel and electric power use have risen sharply since 2011, as have subsidy bills for the host country governments.

- In Iraq, the effects on the energy sector were relatively small. Although all Syrian refugees were connected to the electricity grid, they received only about 9 hours of electricity per day on average. In comparison, residents of KRI received 18 hours of electricity per day. In Iraq, the cost of electricity supply was about $0.12 per kilowatt-hour (kWh) on average in 2017. With half of this cost recovered through tariffs, the cost of the additional demand covered by the treasury in 2018 was estimated at about $15 million, annually.

- In Jordan, higher demand and the associated subsidy bill aggravated energy insecurity. Jordan was already an energy-insecure country, importing 96 percent of its fuel demand before the Syrian crisis. Between 2009 and 2014, the total annual electricity consumption rose markedly from 4,296 Gigawatt-hours (GWh) to 6,560 GWh, and liquefied petroleum gas consumption increased from 300,000 tonnes per year to 366,000 tonnes. The cost of generation was estimated at $0.20/kWh on average, and the tariff charged to households was about $0.05–$0.10/kWh, depending on the level of consumption per month (World Bank 2017b). Thus, the fiscal cost of the subsidy in refugee-induced demand was estimated at about $60 million to $100 million.

- In Lebanon, a persistent excess demand prevailed despite improvements in capacity. Lebanon was subject to significant load-shedding even before the arrival of Syrian refugees, resulting in supply cuts of roughly 3 hours (12.5 percent) daily in Beirut, and up to 12 hours (50 percent) outside the capital, forcing locals to rely on diesel generators on a regular basis. Despite the addition of 715 megawatts (MW) of total capacity since 2010, the arrival of Syrian refugees necessitated the addition of 486 MW of additional power supply (inclusive of 15 percent technical losses during generation) to cover increased net demand. On average, between 2012 and 2016, residents had about 14 hours a day of grid power. At $0.20/kWh average cost of production, and $0.095/kWh tariff charged by EDL (Electricité du Liban, the state-owned utility), the subsidy cost of the additional power catered to refugees would be about $132 million, annually.

ENVIRONMENTAL OUTCOMES

The conflict in Syria could have direct and indirect effects on environmental trends in neighboring countries. With data limitations, we describe these environmental trends in three categories and try to correlate them with refugee intensity subnationally: (i) water pollution, which uses a water clarity index to investigate changes in water bodies' pollution levels; (ii) land pollution, which focuses on solid waste management records and remote-sensing imagery to infer changes in land pollution between 2010 and 2019; and (iii) air pollution, which examines whether high or increasing levels of fine particulate matter ($PM_{2.5}$) exist in areas of high refugee presence by using the Emerging Hot Spot Analysis.

- Refugees increased solid waste generation in all three countries. At the aggregate country level, the districts with the highest numbers of Syrian refugees registered the highest increases in solid waste. In Jordan, districts with relatively high refugee intensity, including Al-Jizah and Al-Quwasimah Districts of the Amman Governorate and Al-Kurah District of the Irbid Governorate, registered the greatest change in municipal solid waste (MSW) generation (at least 256.7 percent, 172.1 percent, and 240.9 percent, respectively). Similarly, in Lebanon, districts with high intensity of refugees exhibited much higher MSW generation. On the basis of assessment of United Nations Development Programme district-level data for MSW sites that were operational in both 2011 and 2016, the districts in Lebanon with the greatest increase in MSW were El Hermel District (12-fold increase), Aley (6-fold), and El Batroun (3-fold). In Iraq, many official landfills analyzed using LANDSAT and Google Earth imagery did not exhibit significant area (m^2) expansion, but any vertical expansion can be missed in satellite images.

- The water pollution effects of the refugee footprint were mixed. Jordan exhibited the most significant degradation in water clarity over time. Iraq was relatively stable, even though minor water clarity degradation over time was apparent. Lebanon registered the most year-to-year variation, trending toward minor water clarity improvements during the period under examination, although periods of significant water clarity degradation were apparent. At the country level, there is no significant correlation between high refugee density and increasing water pollution in any of the countries. Nevertheless, the locations with higher refugee concentration were more likely to have an increase in water pollution, especially in Lebanon and Iraq.

- Some correlations between air pollution and refugee settlements are observed in Jordan and Lebanon. In Jordan, urban air pollution is primarily driven by the country's heavy reliance on fuel oil and diesel, which emit high levels of sulfur dioxide, carbon monoxide, and nitrogen oxides. Some sporadic hot spots found in the urban core, and near refugee clusters (Irbid and Mafraq), were in this group. In Lebanon, relatively high levels of fine particulate matter were observed along the western urban centers (Beirut and Tripoli). These levels have been persistent since 2005, reflecting the role played by increasing population. Intermittent hot spots were also identified in the northeast (Baalbek), where refugees have settled in large numbers, and the southwestern districts. Overall, these findings show that air pollution trends have largely been driven by demographic dynamics rather than climatic conditions in Lebanon. Iraq shows the highest levels of fine particulate matter, with some decrease since 2010; but there is no correlation observed between these trends and the refugee intensity across the country.

THE PRECONDITIONS OF THE FALLOUT

Overall, how significant has the impact of the Syrian conflict been on the neighboring countries? The analysis in this report shows that the Syrian conflict is accountable for about 1.2 percent, 1.6 percent, and 1.7 percent reduction in average annual growth rates in Iraq, Jordan, and Lebanon, respectively. To put these numbers into perspective, we compared them with global experiences by estimating the average GDP effects of conflicts on neighboring countries by using simple cross-country growth regressions. This estimation covers both all civil conflicts (intrastate) and high-intensity civil conflicts only. Results shows that, on average, conflicts did not have a statistically significant effect on the neighbors' GDPs. Even when we ignore the significance problem, the estimated magnitude of effects, especially on Jordan and Lebanon (1.7 percent and 1.6 percent, respectively), is larger than the global estimates in any given year after the onset of the conflict.

What makes the Mashreq different for such large effects to take place? It is difficult to find precise answers to this question without comparing all conflict cases in detail. A number of contributing factors, however, are potential culprits: (i) the sheer scale, composition, and duration of the Syrian conflict, which have made it an outlier among all global civil conflict cases, with the scale of the economic collapse in the original conflict country being much larger than average; (ii) the high exposure of Mashreq economies to the Syrian crisis, including dependence for transit trade, sensitivity of major economic sectors (such as tourism) to regional instability, and a large demographic shock, which increased the bandwidth of impact; and (III) the low institutional resilience of the Mashreq economies (with low state capacity and policy space), which has propagated the shocks and magnified the impact of the conflict. The first factor (the scale of the shock) has been analyzed in great detail elsewhere. In what follows, we focus on the second (exposure) and third (institutional resilience) issues.

Exposure to fallout from the conflict was high, especially in Jordan and Lebanon

To assess the initial exposure to the fallout from the Syrian conflict, we focus on three cross-border movements: refugees (people), trade (goods), and capital flows (money). The conflict is expected to affect the economic and social outcomes in neighboring countries in a manner that is proportional to the bandwidth of bilateral economic connectivity. The greater the economic interaction between two countries, the larger the economic shock. To assess the magnitude of these interactions, we analyze the cross-border transmissions of goods and money (forced displacement was analyzed in the labor market discussion) starting from before the onset of the conflict, but also assessing how they changed in its aftermath.

Although Syria was not a major merchandise export destination for Jordan and Lebanon, the conflict dampened their overall trade. Conflicts can affect neighboring countries' trade in many ways: (i) with reduced production capacity and income in the conflict-struck country, bilateral trade with neighbors can be affected; (ii) trade flows between the neighboring country and third countries could be disrupted; and (iii) increased regional insecurity and uncertainty could deter importers elsewhere from committing to future purchases and could reduce exports of services like tourism. For Mashreq, the first channel was modest. Syrian imports decreased from $18.7 billion in 2010 to $5.7 billion in 2018; however, the direct impact of this decrease on neighboring countries remained small. Jordan's exports to Syria decreased from about $240 million to about $50 million (from 3.9 percent to 0.6 percent of all merchandise exports). In Lebanon, the decrease was less pronounced, from $220 million to $210 million (from 7.0 percent to 5.8 percent of total merchandise exports). Notwithstanding these modest bilateral effects, however, total merchandise exports of Jordan slowed from 17.0 percent average annual growth in the decade before to 0.1 percent after 2010, and Lebanon's fell from 15.0 percent to 1.5 percent in the same period.[8]

The closure of transit trade routes expanded the trade impact beyond bilateral flows. For Jordan, the closure of the main border-crossing point Jaber-Nasib in 2015 led to a halt in southbound trucks from Lebanon, Syria, and Turkey, and in northbound trucks with cargo from Egypt, Jordan, and the Gulf states. The number of Syrian vehicles entering Jordan dropped from 331,636 in 2010 to only 8,172 in 2018. Jordan's borders with Iraq also closed as a result of the Islamic State insurgency; however, that closure affected only the bilateral trade between the two countries. For Lebanon, Syria provided the only viable land connection to the rest of the world and was a major supplier of inputs to Lebanese producers. Although bilateral trade between Jordan and Lebanon continued at a smaller scale, transit trade through Syria became costly, and often impossible.

The slowdown in services exports, especially in tourism, dwarfed that of merchandise trade. Jordan's services exports (three-quarters of which are travel services) are as large as merchandise exports and grew by 3.1 percent annually over 2011–18 as opposed to the 18.9 percent growth in the decade before. Lebanon's exports in services shrank by half a percentage point after 2011 as opposed to the 8.1 percent growth in the decade before. This drop was particularly problematic because services exports in Lebanon, half of which are travel services, exceeded merchandise exports by a factor of four ($15.4 billion versus $3.6 billion), and made up nearly half of the GDP.

The Syrian crisis reinforced other factors in decreasing capital inflows in the Mashreq. Conflicts can affect capital flows to neighboring countries because (i) investments by foreigners may be diverted from the conflict-struck country to its neighbors, (ii) foreign investors' purchases may be diverted from the region altogether, (iii) residents in neighboring countries may acquire or sell off foreign assets abroad, and (iv) with the influx of refugees, recorded or unrecorded cash may be brought into neighboring countries. In Mashreq, we observe a strong effect along the second channel (foreigner's investments have been diverted away from the region) and a weaker effect in the third channel (residents have sold off some foreign assets). There is also some indication of the fourth channel (unrecorded capital flows), especially for Lebanon. Comparing the 2011–17 averages with those of 2006–10, we observe the following:

- In Iraq, net capital inflows declined from 0.6 percent of GDP to –2.8 percent, driven by a decrease in foreigners' purchases of Iraqi assets from 1.4 percent of GDP to –2.0 percent. About 84 percent of this decline came from a decline in FDI inflows, and another 20 percent from a decline in other inflows. At the same time, Iraqi residents' purchases of assets abroad also fell from an average of 2.1 percent of GDP to 0.7 percent.

- In Jordan, net capital inflows decreased from 16.0 percent of GDP to 9.3 percent. Whereas FDI inflows fell from 13.7 percent of GDP to 5.0 percent in this period, other flows and portfolio flows rose by 0.7 percentage points and 4.3 percentage points, respectively. As in Iraq, the decrease in net capital flows in Jordan was driven by shrinking foreigners' purchases of Iraqi assets, which decreased from 17.6 percent of GDP to 9.6 percent (almost all FDI). Jordanian residents reduced their acquisition of foreign assets from 1.7 percent of GDP to 0.3 percent.

- In Lebanon, net capital flows declined from 28.0 percent of GDP to 21.6 percent, largely driven by a decline in net FDI from 10.0 percent of GDP to 3.4 percent, and despite an increase in portfolio flows from −1.8 percent of GDP to 4.4 percent. As a share of GDP, both foreigners' purchases of Lebanese assets and Lebanese residents' acquisition of foreign assets declined (from 26.5 percent of GDP to 15.7 percent and from −1.8 percent of GDP to −5.9 percent, respectively), but the former effect dominated.

Some evidence supports the view that the conflict in Syria has driven at least a portion of these trends. To control for other global and regional factors that may have driven the downward trend in capital inflows, we considered a panel data analysis with year and distance fixed effects. The results suggest that the greater the distance between the capital-receiving country and Syria, the greater the FDI inflows to the country. FDI inflows for Syria's immediate neighbors (as measured by the Syria neighbor dummy) also experienced a statistically significant (negative) trend during 2011–15 after controlling for other factors. This impact appears to be limited in the case of portfolio flows.

Unrecorded capital flows out of Syria may have occurred, especially into Lebanon. Measuring unrecorded capital flows is, by definition, very difficult. The capital flight literature suggests two approaches in estimating them: an errors and omissions–based approach and an indirect approach.[9] The two approaches yield positive but different results in Lebanon: 1.5 percent of GDP versus 6.5 percent annually in 2011–17. In Jordan and Iraq, results are inconclusive because the two measures provide opposite results for Jordan (1 percent versus −3 percent, respectively) and because only one approach could be tried in Iraq (which suggests an insignificant effect).

Institutional resilience was weak, and it has weakened further since

Besides exposure, the ability to mitigate shocks can determine the size of the impact. In this study, we follow Cordella and Onder (2020) and Besley and Persson (2011) to characterize institutions as factors that restrain different interest groups from appropriating the country's wealth. Accordingly, noncohesive institutions can lead to insufficient productive activities and excessive rent-seeking, including underinvestment in state capacity and fiscal space. Moreover, any political settlement between contesting parties about the allocation of resources may also be more fragile under weak institutions. In such cases, as external shocks (like a conflict) reduce the returns to productive spending, rent-seeking can deepen and state capacity and fiscal space can weaken further. These results translate into a relatively lower planned provision of public services and, thus, a greater propagation of the initial shock in the economy. Although institutions cover a wide array of factors, not all of those are quantifiable or comparable across countries and years. Thus, in this report, we analyze the relatively more observable manifestations of such institutional background: state capacity and fiscal space.

State capacity is characterized by the following five categories: (i) capacity to collect fiscal resources for the delivery of public services; (ii) ability to conduct budgeting and public investment management within a medium-term vision; (iii) ability of the state to effectively perform budget execution, procurement, and auditory functions; (iv) service delivery capacity with a sustainable, efficient, and meritocracy-based management of civil service; and (v) public accountability.

- Iraq's state capacity was one of the weakest in the world in the early 2010s. In 2010, Iraq ranked 180th out of 183 countries in terms of ease of trading across borders. Its fiscal budget suffered from insufficient strategic planning, poor execution, and weak oversight (less than 64 percent of capital expenditures were executed). The country's Open Budget Index score in 2010 was zero out of 100—that is, the country did not inform the public about the central government's budget or financial activities. Iraq also struggled with pervasive corruption and ranked 175th out of 183 countries on the 2010 Corruption Perceptions Index (CPI). Since 2011, some improvement in strategic planning capacity and accountability has been achieved, including medium-term budgeting and monthly budget execution reports. Public jobs, however, continued to be an avenue for rent-seeking while merit-based selection regressed further.

- Jordan performed above the MENA average in all dimensions of governance, but discretionary constraints abounded. The 2010 Worldwide Governance Indicators (WGI) reported better scores for Jordan than for any other MENA country; however, policy- and politics-driven constraints were binding at times. For instance, whereas tax and customs administrations were relatively efficient, various tax exemptions depressed revenues. Human resource and public administration capacities were good, but political economy–driven exclusion and favoritism prevailed. Two-thirds of Jordanians believed that corruption existed in both the public and private sectors (Bertelsmann Stiftung 2009). Since 2011, budget credibility has prevailed and internal audit practices have improved despite emerging challenges; however, revenue and public administration practices have deteriorated. According to *Doing Business 2019*, Jordan ranked 95th in terms of the ease of paying taxes, which is a sharp decline from 26th in 2010 (World Bank 2019a).

- Lebanon was below MENA averages in government effectiveness. According to the WGI, Lebanon suffered from insufficient tax and customs administration capacities, absent strategic planning, and a politically driven bottleneck in budgeting. Parliament had not approved a budget since 2005, which paralyzed fiscal policy and increased quasi-fiscal activities, contingent liabilities, and arrears. Budget execution was often less than half, and oversight capacities were dismal. Human resource and public administration capacities were also weak and reflected political and sectarian divisions. Public accountability was mixed: civil society has been traditionally vocal in Lebanon and one of the major catalysts of political change; however, access to financial information about public enterprises remained limited. Since 2011, several indicators, including revenue and public administration capacities and budget execution and oversight, have deteriorated. Lebanon's ranking declined from 34th to 113th for the ease of paying taxes, while the wage bill and overstaffing continued to grow and state capacity decreased further.

Fiscal space, in combination with state capacity, is an essential element of governments' ability to mitigate the unanticipated fallout from a conflict. The term "fiscal space" defines the budgetary room that allows a government to deliver the necessary public goods and services without undermining fiscal sustainability. This space includes the ability to increase spending or cut taxes without triggering public debt distress and limiting market access. In the case of the Syrian conflict's impact on neighboring countries, this space could determine the governments' ability to shield their constituents from a sudden increase in demand for publicly provided services like education, health care, and water and sanitation.

- With rising oil prices and large debt relief operations, Iraq was beginning to build fiscal space before the Syrian crisis. In 2010, fiscal revenues constituted about 45 percent of the Iraqi GDP, 92 percent of which were oil revenues. Government expenditures were very volatile, averaging around 50 percent of GDP. The country managed to bring down an excessive debt to manageable levels with historically high oil prices, rebounding production, and major international support. From 2005 to 2010, public debt decreased from 227 percent of GDP to 54 percent (more than half of the external debt was forgiven). Thus, although the debt burden was reduced, a deep reliance on oil revenues and the absence of fiscal buffers limited fiscal space in the country. This situation proved to be costly in the following years when oil revenues plummeted.

- In the years leading up to the Syrian crisis, Jordan was losing the fiscal space it had built in the decade before. With favorable external conditions, public debt was reduced in the previous decade (from 100 percent of GDP in 2000 to 60 percent in 2008); however, deteriorating external conditions and tax exemptions were gradually turning the tide against further build-up of fiscal space after 2008. Fiscal revenues decreased from 32 percent of GDP in 2006–07 to 25 percent in 2010 and continued to fall with regressive changes to the Income Tax Law in 2010. Grants also decreased as a share of GDP (from 5.0 percent to 2.1 percent) between 2005 and 2010. Fiscal spending adjusted by decreasing from 38.9 percent of GDP to 32.9 percent in the same period, especially capital expenditures—which did not rebound afterward. In contrast, energy subsidies and pension transfers continued to increase after 2010. Thus, when the fallout of the Syrian conflict hit the country, it found an already weakening fiscal space.
- Lebanon suffered from structural fiscal weaknesses. A high burden of debt, inefficient public spending, loss-making utilities, and corruption complicated fiscal management. With narrow income tax bases, and as nominally fixed consumption excises were reduced by inflation, total revenues declined from 25.0 percent of GDP in 2006–07 to 21.7 percent of GDP in 2010. On the expenditure side, interest payments represented the largest expenditure item (10.2 percent of GDP in 2010), exceeding the public sector wage bill and public investments. Utilities were lavishly subsidized, particularly the electricity sector (for example, subsidies to EDL were about 4 percent of GDP, annually). Despite these expenses, a small primary surplus (1–3 percent) and the rapid economic growth helped reduce the ratio of public debt to GDP by nearly 50 percentage points (to 137 percent) between 2006 and 2010. Trends after 2010, however, showed that Lebanon's fiscal space was indeed narrower than it looked in 2010, as stalling growth and emerging primary deficits reescalated the public debt burden in later years.

Overall, before the Syrian crisis, all three countries exhibited relatively high exposure to potential fallouts and weak institutional resilience, but in different ways. Iraq's exposure through three channels (demography, trade, and capital flows) was limited in aggregate terms, but was concentrated in KRI. The country suffered from one of the worst state capacities in the world, and its fiscal space carried intrinsic weaknesses (excessive oil dependence with no buffers). Jordan's exposure was high in all three channels. Its state capacity was one of the best in the region before the conflict, but that capacity deteriorated over time. The country's relatively favorable fiscal position was already worsening with deteriorating external conditions and controversial fiscal policy choices like extensive tax exemptions. Finally, Lebanon shared the disadvantages of Iraq and Jordan. Like Jordan, its exposure was high with a large demographic shock, a significant trade shock mostly in services trade, and a sizeable capital flow shock. Like Iraq, its institutional resilience was low: state capacity suffered from years of underinvestment as a result of a complex political economy, and an excessive public debt (and debt service) burden suffocated its fiscal space along with an ineffective tax system.

LOOKING AHEAD: A TALE OF TWO FUTURES

Going forward, the economic and political trajectories of the Mashreq countries will remain intertwined. Future developments in Syria will continue to affect other Mashreq economies. To capture these prospects, we rely on the three security and service restoration scenarios from *The Mobility of Displaced Syrians* report (World Bank 2019b). In the first scenario (which we adopt as our baseline), the insecurity index decreases from 1.70 to 0.54 and only 5 percent of the damaged infrastructure is rebuilt by 2025. In the second scenario, the insecurity index decreases further to 0.15 and the reconstruction ratio reaches 16 percent. Finally, the third scenario considers a decrease in the insecurity index of 0.07 points and a reconstruction ratio of 30 percent. We analyze the implications of these scenarios for economic recovery in Syria and the future fallout of the war in neighboring countries. Next, we provide a discussion on desired policies. For the purposes of this study, we consider two policy frameworks:

1. *A unilateral approach.* Each country implements its desired policies by taking the conditions and policies of other Mashreq countries as given at their current specifications. International support in a given country is not linked with other cases either.

2. *A regional approach.* Mashreq countries coordinate their efforts in addressing cross-boundary issues including migration, trade, and infrastructure. Likewise, support from the international community is determined within a regional strategical framework as well.

The main idea here is to internalize cross-border externalities for promoting stability and prosperity in the region. Whereas the unilateral approach presents an adaptive policy path where countries implement their best responses to the changes in regional factors with the support of the international community (which shares the same country-specific focus), the regional approach pursues jointly beneficial policies to be implemented with the support of the international community (which shares the same regional perspective). This process is not necessarily about economic–political integration but about cooperation for internalizing cross-border externalities, including negative and positive spillovers.

The fallout of the Syrian conflict is not likely to be reversed in the medium term

Economic recovery in Syria will be slow. In the first scenario (baseline), Syrian GDP growth increases by 0.8 percentage points annually in the next five-year period. The second and third scenarios yield 1.7 and 2.5 percentage points additional GDP growth, respectively. These are incremental growth rates brought about by security improvements and service restoration only (not overall GDP growth projections). They capture the productivity-enhancing aspects of better security and greater infrastructure stock, and endogenous return of refugees.

Any positive fallout from Syrian recovery will be through regional stability rather than immediate economic opportunities. The muted economic recovery in Syria will translate into a slow reversal of the adverse effects on Iraq, Jordan, and Lebanon so far (figure O.4). In the baseline case (Scenario 1), the additional GDP growth in Iraq, Jordan, and Lebanon is estimated to be limited to 0.2–0.3 percentage points. In the other two scenarios, where security improvements and service restoration are both more significant, the growth increments are 0.3–0.6 percentage points and 0.6–0.9 percentage points, respectively. A large share of these additional growth rates (more than 90 percent) is driven by the

FIGURE O.4. GDP growth gains in selected Mashreq countries from security and service restoration in the Syrian Arab Republic

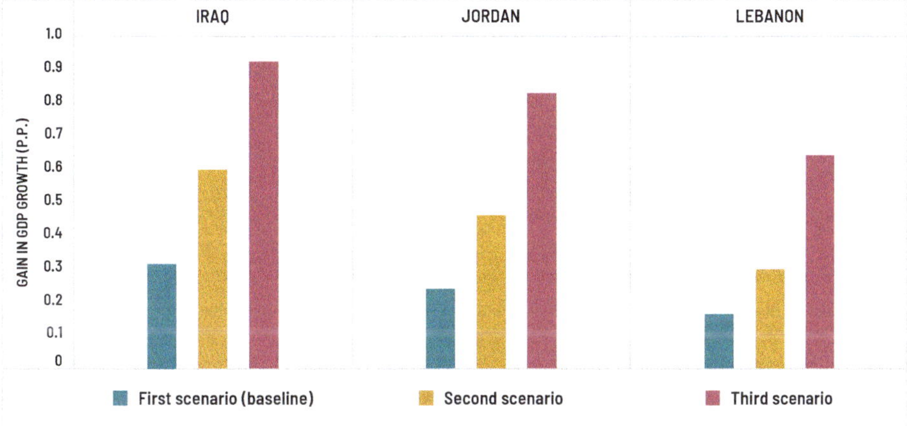

Source: World Bank staff calculations, using scenarios from World Bank 2019b.

Note: Figure shows gains in annualized GDP growth five years ahead depending on security and service access scenarios in Syria. In the first scenario (baseline), the insecurity index decreases from 1.70 to 0.54 and only 5 percent of the damaged infrastructure is rebuilt by 2025. In the second scenario, the insecurity index decreases further to 0.15 and the reconstruction ratio reaches 16 percent. The third scenario considers a decrease in the insecurity index of 0.07 points and a reconstruction ratio of 30 percent. p.p. = percentage point.

security- and confidence-driven TFP improvements. To see why export opportunities are likely to be low, we calculated the material demand for reconstruction. For the top-five (by value) items across all three scenarios (concrete structure, rebar steel, wood, concrete block, and waterproofing) all countries exported very little and ran significant trade deficits in recent years.

Opportunities prevail for unilateral policies, but they need longer-term perspectives

A persistent short-termism suffocates economic prospects in the region. In dealing with the adverse impact of the Syrian conflict, a chronic lack of medium-term planning is a common problem among the governments of the region and the international community and donors alike. On the government side, this short-termism takes the form of formulating mitigation policies as a series of ad hoc measures in sequence, which is costly and open to political exploitation. On the donors' side, an annual funding cycle remains the norm, and it reduces incentives for multiyear, cross-agency, and cross-sector planning. Inefficiencies emanating from the lack of a medium-term perspective include the following:

- *Costly and ineffective service provision.* Ad hoc solutions to protracted issues are less effective and more costly. For instance, in Lebanon and Jordan, water supply to refugees, especially to those living in temporary shelters or in camps, is often provided by tanking or trucking. Such water is more prone to quality (E. coli) problems than piped water and, in 2018, cost Jordan and Lebanon 0.55 percent and 0.74 percent of GDP in health care, respectively.
- *Lost economic opportunities.* Despite all efforts, school attendance of Syrian refugees is lower than that of their host country peers. Currently, Syrian refugee children are expected to complete about 3.7 fewer years of education than Jordanian children

and 5.4 fewer years than Lebanese children. Our estimates show that offsetting these losses in human capital would increase the GDP growth rate by 0.4 percentage points in Jordan and 1.1 percentage points in Lebanon.

- *Underfunded programs.* The inability of host country governments to commit to a medium-term path could reduce their access to aid. With costly and inefficient service provision, and thus lower marginal impact of an additional dollar, donors may transfer money elsewhere to increase returns to their investment, for example, to have greater impact on the ground.

Adopting a medium-term mitigation strategy can also help build countries' own institutional resilience. A comprehensive approach that carefully exploits the synergies between the deployment of a medium-term strategy for addressing the protracted challenges of the Syrian crisis and reinforcing public service delivery to own constituents can achieve great results. Some of these results are as follows:

- *Bring "Robin" into the "hood."* Refugee arrivals can create both winners and losers. An important role that governments can play is to smooth out the gains and losses by means of proper public policies. Progressive social insurance and assistance mechanisms are examples in this regard. All the countries we cover in this study have weak automatic stabilizers like unemployment insurance, especially in nonpublic employment. In comparison, social assistance programs were more prevalent but not sufficiently targeted or progressive, especially in Iraq and Lebanon. Overall, better protection of the vulnerable and redistribution of gains from the winners to the losers are needed. Achieving such improvements requires exploring the synergies between refugee assistance mechanisms and national social assistance systems.

- *Improve service access for all.* The provision of public goods and services for host communities can be improved in several areas. For instance, insufficient attention is paid to periodic maintenance in transport (all countries), and costly options like diesel generators are used too often in the energy sector (mainly Lebanon). Refugees also face similar problems: costly and unhealthy provision of water by tanking and trucking and the economic losses due to low school attainment among Syrian children are some examples. In addition, the presence of refugees makes the prevailing inefficiencies more costly and visible (for example, the higher subsidy bill in energy provision). Thus, while trying to improve the efficiency and effectiveness of service provision to own constituents and refugees, countries can exploit synergies between the two provision systems.

- *Invest in state capacity and build policy space.* The successful implementation of such activities requires building further public sector capacity and policy space. Currently, major discrepancies exist between public sector shares of employment (too much) and the service delivery capacities (too little) in the region. Developing a medium-term strategy for better service delivery for locals and refugees alike can provide an opportunity in this regard. The presence of international organizations and civil society organizations could provide an opportunity to align the two systems in a transparent manner.

While aspiring to deliver on these fronts, reformers should not ignore the complex political economy dynamics that surround the policy decisions. The short-termism and the low institutional resilience of countries should not be regarded as poor policy choices only. Low investments in state capacity, low fiscal responsibility, and ad hoc mitigation strategies for coping with the fallout of the Syrian conflict are all outcomes of a complex political economy surrounding policy decisions. In the case of low institutional resilience, the inability of different political or interest groups to commit to inclusiveness, and the lack of broader institutional checks and balances that force those in power to do so, may be driving low investments in state capacity and fiscal resilience. Thus, public offices and employment may be seen as prizes in such cases. These factors also feed the short-termism in dealing with the Syrian crisis' fallout, but there is more to it. The inability of the international community to commit to long-term support and a moral hazard problem in host countries (that is, the lack of incentives to produce long-term solutions when the country is protected from costly consequences through the international community's commitment to long-term support) feed into each other in creating the dual short-termism. What can change the dynamics of such political economy constraints?

A REGIONAL APPROACH TO THE REGION'S PROBLEMS

In the Mashreq region, both problems and opportunities are transboundary. From broader regional insecurity to sudden demographic changes, the conflict in Syria has imposed numerous changes on neighboring countries. But this conflict has not been the only one. The region's history teems with conflicts whose effects go beyond borders; however, it is not only "public bads" but also "public goods" that have cross-border effects. For instance, better roads in Syria made transportation costs lower not only for Syrians but also for Iraqis, Jordanians, and Lebanese through transit trade. This effect became evident during the conflict when road closures inside Syria affected the trade patterns of neighboring countries. Similarly, economies of scale in many areas like energy and information and communications technologies can help countries like Lebanon and Jordan overcome market size problems.

A regional approach can exploit these spillovers. In a unilateral framework, governments do not take these spillovers into consideration when deciding the level of public services (thus, they do not provide enough when spillovers are not internalized). In a regional framework, cooperation among countries can address this problem. With greater perceived benefits, the optimal levels of public goods and services could increase. Consequently, higher investments in state capacity would become incentive compatible and the conflictual and rent-seeking activities within a country would decrease at the margin (Karayalcin and Onder 2020). But this argument will need to be substantiated further. What are the mechanisms though which regional cooperation can contribute to peace, stability, and prosperity in each country? Are there clear gains for everyone from a regional approach? If yes, why have these gains so far failed to mobilize policy makers for such an approach?

Important gains are possible in service market integration and infrastructure cooperation. Although the intraregional complementarity of merchandise trade has been relatively low,[10] the potential gains from removing the barriers to service market integration and infrastructure cooperation are large. Opportunities to exploit cross-border synergies in energy, transport, and information and communications technologies are particularly promising.

- *Energy*. There is much room for deeper mutual integration of countries' electricity infrastructure and markets at the regional level. Coordinated expansion of generation and transmission capacity, joint building of transmission interconnections, and joint efforts to build and strengthen the institutions for a common electricity market can all contribute to cost savings and better security of supply. Cross-border interconnectors of Jordan with West Bank and Gaza, Saudi Arabia with Iraq, Jordan with Iraq, and

Saudi Arabia with Jordan can generate an estimated $9.2 billion in benefits—derived mainly from avoided capital expenditures as well as reliability benefits and fuel cost savings. Such integration can also encompass other major regional markets.

- *Transportation.* The lack of integrated transport systems and infrastructure constitutes a bottleneck, preventing regional value chains and participation in the global system of production and distribution. Main action areas are the following. First, accelerate railway systems: all countries in Mashreq suffer from weak railway interconnectivity, with Lebanon entirely lacking railway lines. According to the Agreement on International Railways in the Arab Mashreq,[11] 60 percent of the total railway network remains to be built. Second, improve cross-border facilities and procedures: underdeveloped transit systems cause delays and increase freight rates. Finally, expand the TIR (Transports Internationaux Routiers) system to streamline the transit system and improve the transportation sector locally.

- *Digital market.* The digital transformation of the Mashreq with regional integration of infrastructure and data markets can generate additional GDP growth between 1.6 percent and 2.4 percent in all countries. Main action areas are as follows. First, increase connectivity through infrastructure, reduce the costs of access to regional networks, and position the region as a hub in Europe–Asia traffic. Second, lower regional transit costs, and standardize an open-access regime for backbone interconnection, including the possibility of purchasing wholesale transit capacity. Finally, improve affordability and quality of connectivity services; survey telecom policies to take stock of interconnection fees, number portability, infrastructure sharing challenges, and price regulation of dominant market players.

Potential gains alone do not suffice for a regional perspective. Although the region has maintained economic interconnectivity throughout its history, it has not always sustained a true cooperative framework at the regional scale. Domestic political economy (for example, majority-minority dynamics) and significant economic or political asymmetries between the region's economies can hinder regional efforts. For the purposes of this report, we studied three episodes of regional integration in the region's long history, each driven by different dynamics, in order to gain insights for a contemporary problem with a medium- to long-term perspective. From these episodes—the Umayyad and Abbasid caliphates (661–1258), the Pax Ottomanica during the early modern period, and the Euro-Ottoman modus vivendi of the long 19th century (1800–1945)—we have distilled the following lessons:

- Demographic shocks may provide an opportunity to increase cross-border connectivity by supporting trade. With a slow economic recovery in Syria, trade benefits for neighboring countries are likely to remain modest. With a common regional vision, however, and with infrastructure cooperation (including physical and institutional dimensions), gains can be transformative. Demographic networks can play a facilitating role in this case as in the Umayyad and Abbasid caliphates period.

- External factors can play a major role in facilitating economic integration. In the 19th century, expansion of trade with Europe promoted a bottom-up economic integration, in which the market dynamics shaped labor mobility and infrastructure provision across the Mashreq. The role of external factors becomes more important when none of the regional actors can be the locomotive of growth, as is currently the case.

- The right balance between competition and cooperation is essential. The Pax Ottomanica period suffered from stagnant economic dynamics as urban guilds, empowered by imperial institutions, reduced incentives for innovation and competition. In comparison, the 19th century witnessed a chaotic race to establish natural monopolies through infrastructure investments, which led to incompatibility across regions. Overall, a regional framework should encourage market principles and contestability, yet it should nurture markets with strategic and supportive infrastructure and institutional systems.

With the right approach, today's challenges can beget tomorrow's opportunities. Currently, there are several impediments to a regional perspective: major asymmetries within and across the countries of the region have so far prevented a regional perspective. Nevertheless, history shows us that a better outcome is possible. Although the conflicts in Syria and Iraq have fundamentally changed the conditions faced by other countries in Mashreq, they have also created the conditions to build a better equilibrium. Under the right circumstances, service restoration and economic recovery in Syria can provide an opportunity to foster a regional perspective.

A DEUS EX MACHINA FOR THE MASHREQ THEATER?

Shifting to a regional focus for stability and prosperity necessitates a concerted international effort. A supra-national commitment to stability at the regional level is a prerequisite of a successful regional approach. Only such a commitment can make elites feel safe enough to perform deep social and economic reforms, relaxing economic exclusion and alleviating the inherently interdependent fragility. The right combination of local, regional, and international inputs can thus help surpass the inherent limitations observed in the past. This is not an easy task, yet there seems to be no alternative that is equally desirable or feasible, at least not for the foreseeable future. The global spillovers from an unstable Mashreq region, including emigration and security threats, should provide incentives for all parties to wish for better stability and prosperity for all in the region.

In sum, although the conditions are less than ideal for a regional drive, such a motive can provide a feasible exit from a fragile regional equilibrium. Studies on regional cooperation often highlight the importance of stability before attempting cooperation. Mashreq, however, does not have this option. Drivers of instability in the Mashreq are numerous and powerful, and overcoming them is a formidable task. Past experience shows that the region requires all the help we can muster to begin stabilizing and tackling its structural problems. Thus, this report took a different approach and asked a fundamental question: Can a regional perspective that is owned locally but supported internationally help stabilize the region? Our answer is affirmative, albeit cautiously so. If and when a consensus is established, the international community has the means to facilitate such a vision. Will there ever be such a consensus? We are optimistic because the alternative is in no one's interest.

NOTES

1. Other countries that have also been affected by the conflict, including those that host large numbers of Syrian refugees (Greece, Turkey, and other countries in Europe) and those that were directly or indirectly a party to the conflict, have been excluded from the analysis because of data limitations and the regional focus of the study.
2. An important share of the high FDI inflows in the 2000s was linked to the arrival of Iraqi refugees fleeing the 2003 war.
3. Note that country-specific shocks that overlapped with the Syrian conflict are only imperfectly separated in this analysis. For instance, the gas pipeline problem faced by Jordan is partially controlled for by our MENA effects in the growth regression that feeds into the SCM estimates, but this is unlikely to capture the entire effect.
4. The economic effects of refugee arrivals are highly context-specific. Alix-Garcia, Artuc, and Onder (2017) provide an overview of different channels through which refugee arrivals could influence labor markets (and welfare). As refugees' consumption is typically financed by wages and transfers (international aid, remittances, or both), they increase in demand for goods and services. In nontradable (cannot be imported) sectors, prices would increase in the short term, with a possible supply adjustment in the medium term. This increases demand and wages for skills that are used more intensively in these sectors. As workers, refugees may compete with host country members for jobs; with a greater labor supply, equilibrium wages may decrease, unemployment may increase, or both may happen. The magnitude of these effects, however, will depend on skill composition and regulations. For instance, if refugees are proportionately less skilled than local workers, then the unskilled host community workers would face a greater impact through the labor supply channel. The net effects of refugee arrivals on labor markets are determined by both the demand- and the supply-side effects.
5. If refugees decide on enrollment by comparing the direct and indirect (opportunity) costs of enrollment with potential benefits of doing so, then, by a revealed preferences argument, the nonenrolled must be facing greater costs, lower perceived benefits, or both. Thus, financing service provision cost may not be sufficient to achieve universal enrollment.
6. Based on the forthcoming joint World Bank and UNHCR report "The Global Cost of Inclusive Refugee Education," which relies on a modified unit cost approach (using the unit cost of host country students and a percentage adjustment to account for refugee-specific constraints).
7. See Assaad, Ginn, and Saleh (2019) and Rozo and Sviatschi (2018) for examples. Using household surveys with school-level records and using a differences-in-differences design across refugee density and birth cohort, the former paper found no evidence that a greater exposure to Syrian refugees affects the attainment quantity or quality of Jordanian students.
8. In Iraq, merchandise exports (almost all oil) increased from $51 billion in 2010 to $103 billion in 2018.
9. The first approach relies on sudden changes in errors and omissions entry in the balance of payments data to estimate the unrecorded flows. The indirect approach involves treating unrecorded capital movements as a residual of those balance of payments components that are assumed to be more accurately measured.
10. For detailed analyses of trade and trade policy issues in MENA, see Rouis and Tabor (2012) and World Bank (2014).
11. Adopted on March 14, 2003, and entered into force on May 23, 2005. The Agreement has been ratified by 16 countries in the region.

REFERENCES

Alix-Garcia, J., E. Artuc, and H. Onder. 2017. "The Economics of Hosting Refugees: A Host Community Perspective from Turkana." Report No. 113183, World Bank, Washington, DC.

Assaad, Ragui A., Thomas Ginn, and Mohamed Saleh. 2019. "Impact of Syrian Refugees on Education Outcomes in Jordan." CEPR Discussion Paper No. DP14056, Center for Economic and Policy Research, Washington, DC.

Bertelsmann Stiftung. 2009. *Bertelsmann Transformation Index (BTI) 2010*. Berlin: Bertelsmann Stiftung and the Center for Applied Policy Research at Munich University.

Besley, Timothy, and Torsten Persson. 2011. "Fragile States and Development Policy." *Journal of the European Economic Association* 9 (3): 371–98.

Cordella, Tito, and Harun Onder. 2020. "Sharing Oil Rents and Political Violence." *European Journal of Political Economy* 63 (June).

Karayalcin, Cem, and Harun Onder. 2020. "Domestic Conflict, Public Services, and Regional Integration." Background paper, *The Fallout of War*, World Bank, Washington, DC.

Rouis, M., and S. R. Tabor. 2012. *Regional Economic Integration in the Middle East and North Africa: Beyond Trade Reform*. Directions in Development. Washington, DC: World Bank Group.

Rozo, S., and M. M. Sviatschi. 2018. "Are Refugees a Burden? Impacts of Refugee Inflows on Host's Consumption Expenditures." Working Paper. http://www.micaelasviatschi.com/wp-content/uploads/2018/11/RozoSviastchi_Nov1_2018.pdf.

World Bank. 2014. "Over the Horizon: A New Levant." Report No. 86946-IQ, World Bank, Washington, DC.

World Bank. 2017a. *The Toll of War: The Economic and Social Consequences of the Conflict in Syria*. Washington, DC: World Bank.

World Bank. 2017b. "Quasi-Fiscal Deficits in the Electricity Sector of the Middle East and North Africa: Sources and Size." Policy Research Working Paper 8280. December 2017. World Bank, Washington, DC.

World Bank. 2018. "Iraq Reconstruction and Investment: Part 2: Damage and Needs Assessment of Affected Governorates." World Bank, Washington, DC. http://documents.worldbank.org/curated/en/600181520000498420/pdf/123631-REVISED-Iraq-Reconstruction-and-Investment-Part-2-Damage-and-Needs-Assessment-of-Affected-Governorates.pdf.

World Bank. 2019a. *Doing Business 2019: Training for Reform*. Washington, DC: World Bank.

World Bank. 2019b. *The Mobility of Displaced Syrians: An Economic and Social Analysis*. Washington, DC: World Bank.

World Bank and UNHCR (United Nations High Commissioner for Refugees). Forthcoming. "The Global Cost of Inclusive Refugee Education." Washington, DC, and New York: World Bank and UNHCR.

1. PRELUDE

Undoubtedly, the largest burden of the conflict in the Syrian Arab Republic has fallen onto Syrian shoulders. Since the onset of the conflict in 2011, the country has gone through an unimaginable tragedy. A previous World Bank (2017) report, *The Toll of War*, documented the magnitude of devastation and losses suffered by Syrians. More than 400,000 deaths have been directly attributed to the conflict with millions more nonlethal casualties. More than half of the country's preconflict population (20.7 million) has been displaced, and the economic activity in the country collapsed by more than 60 percent by 2016. A subsequent World Bank (2019) report, *The Mobility of Displaced Syrians*, analyzed the conditions faced by Syrians inside and outside Syria, with a special focus on how those conditions could shape the spontaneous returns. That report highlighted the challenges faced by Syrians everywhere and showed that return has not been a real option for many of them. Refugees choose safety and endure the conditions they face in countries of asylum.

Syria's neighbors have also been troubled by the brutal conflict. Perhaps one of the most vexing consequences of the conditions created by the conflict in Syria was the surge of an Iraq-born armed group, the Islamic State of Iraq and Levant (later the Islamic State, also known as ISIS, ISIL, or Da'esh). From its stronghold in the Syrian town of Raqqa, the Islamic State was able to overrun a third of Iraq's territory in 2014, sowing death and destruction in its path and leading to the internal displacement of over 3 million Iraqis (EPRS 2017). The setbacks created by the Syrian conflict, however, go well beyond the battlefields. The Syrian crisis produced not only the largest displacement crisis since the Second World War but also the largest hosting of refugees in host countries relative to their own populations. At their peak value, Syrian refugees exceeded a fifth of local populations in Jordan, the Kurdistan Region of Iraq (KRI), and Lebanon. Moreover, insecurity in Syria and Iraq has disrupted economic connectivity and reduced confidence in economic prospects for the neighboring economies. All these factors have contributed to a toll paid not only by Syrians but also by their neighbors.

This report primarily focuses on the impact of the Syrian conflict on economic and social outcomes in Iraq, Jordan, and Lebanon.[1] It is important to consider this impact for several reasons. First, and most important, developing effective policies to mitigate the adverse effects of the conflict requires an explicit recognition of the mechanisms through which such effects are manifested. Second, when such mechanisms are well defined, more public support can be amassed for nuanced and well-targeted mitigation programs. Third, and finally, potential reversals in specific channels can be used to project future outcomes more accurately. Considering these benefits and building on the preceding methodologies developed in *The Toll of War* (World Bank 2017) and *The Mobility of Displaced Syrians* (World Bank 2019) reports, this study pursues a systematic analysis of these mechanisms. Doing so is, however, a complex task. Over the nine years of active conflict in Syria, many global and regional factors have affected the economic and social trajectories in Iraq, Jordan, and Lebanon. Thus, effects from different channels need to be disentangled to the extent permitted by data limitations. The remainder of this introductory chapter first provides an overview of the global and regional events that may have contributed to the economic and social trends in the Mashreq. The chapter then discusses the analytical approach to disentangling the impact of the Syrian conflict from that of other factors.

MASHREQ: A TIMELINE RETROSPECTIVE

Although the Syria crisis has been detrimental for the whole Mashreq, it has not by any means been the first or the only destabilizing factor in the region. The Mashreq experienced numerous crises in the second half of the 20th century, and their effects continue to be felt in the region. The burden of such rocky history comes in the form of rounds of instability. Successive waves of mass forced displacement have crashed through the Mashreq in the last century, including hundreds of thousands of Armenians who fled to the Mashreq after 1915 and more than 700,000 Palestinians who took refuge in neighboring countries decades ago (McDowall 1987). More than a quarter of Lebanon's population fled during the Lebanese civil war, and Iraq's invasion of Kuwait in 1990 led to a mass exodus of Arab and foreign workers. After the US-led coalition's invasion of Iraq in 2003, 6 million Iraqis took refuge in Iraq's immediate neighbors and an additional 6 million Iraqis were displaced internally (Lynch and Brand 2017).

When conflict broke out in Syria, the Mashreq Region was in the midst of important transformations. Figure 1.1 shows a timeline of important global, regional, and local events that potentially affected the economic and social outcomes in Iraq, Jordan, and Lebanon since 2007. The onset of each event is marked at the beginning of the bars (from left to right), and the length of each bar denotes the period over which the event has remained in effect. The following paragraphs briefly describe these events and how they influenced the conditions in the countries of interest in this report.

The conflict in Syria arrived at the tail end of the global financial crisis, which led to the largest global recession since the Great Depression. Although the crisis originated in advanced economies, it had substantial short-term consequences for emerging economies (figure 1.2). Global merchandise exports decreased by 22.5 percent, from $16.2 trillion in 2008 to $12.6 trillion in 2009 (WTO 2019). On average, the gross domestic product (GDP) growth rate in middle-income countries (MICs) decreased from 8.5 percent in 2007 to 5.6 percent in 2008 and 2.3 percent in 2009. This drop resulted partially from a 16 percent decrease in the export-to-GDP ratio and a 22 percent decrease in foreign direct investment (FDI) inflows in 2009. Despite strong economic recovery in 2010 (7.4 percent), GDP growth hovered around 4–5 percent from then on.

In Jordan, the onset of the global financial crisis marked the beginning of a significant economic slowdown. Although the crisis affected emerging economies that had closer financial ties (banking, portfolio, and FDI) with the developed economies, Mashreq countries, especially Jordan and Lebanon, were not immune to negative spillovers. In Jordan, GDP growth slowed from 8.2 percent in 2007 to a meager 2.3 percent in 2010. This drop was accompanied by decreases in receipts in several items, the most interesting of which include the following:

- Exports, whose dynamics mimicked that of the MICs and fell by about 16 percent in proportion to GDP in 2009. Whereas the MIC exports shares stabilized somewhat after a modest recovery in the subsequent years, Jordan's exports continued their downward pattern.
- FDI, which had already started to decrease after its prior peak (23 percent of GDP in 2006). This trend continued and stabilized at about 5 percent of GDP from 2010 onward. The MICs also experienced a decrease in FDI in 2009 and a modest recovery in the following years, but these magnitudes were small (within a band of 1 percent of GDP).

FIGURE 1.1. **Timeline of key events**

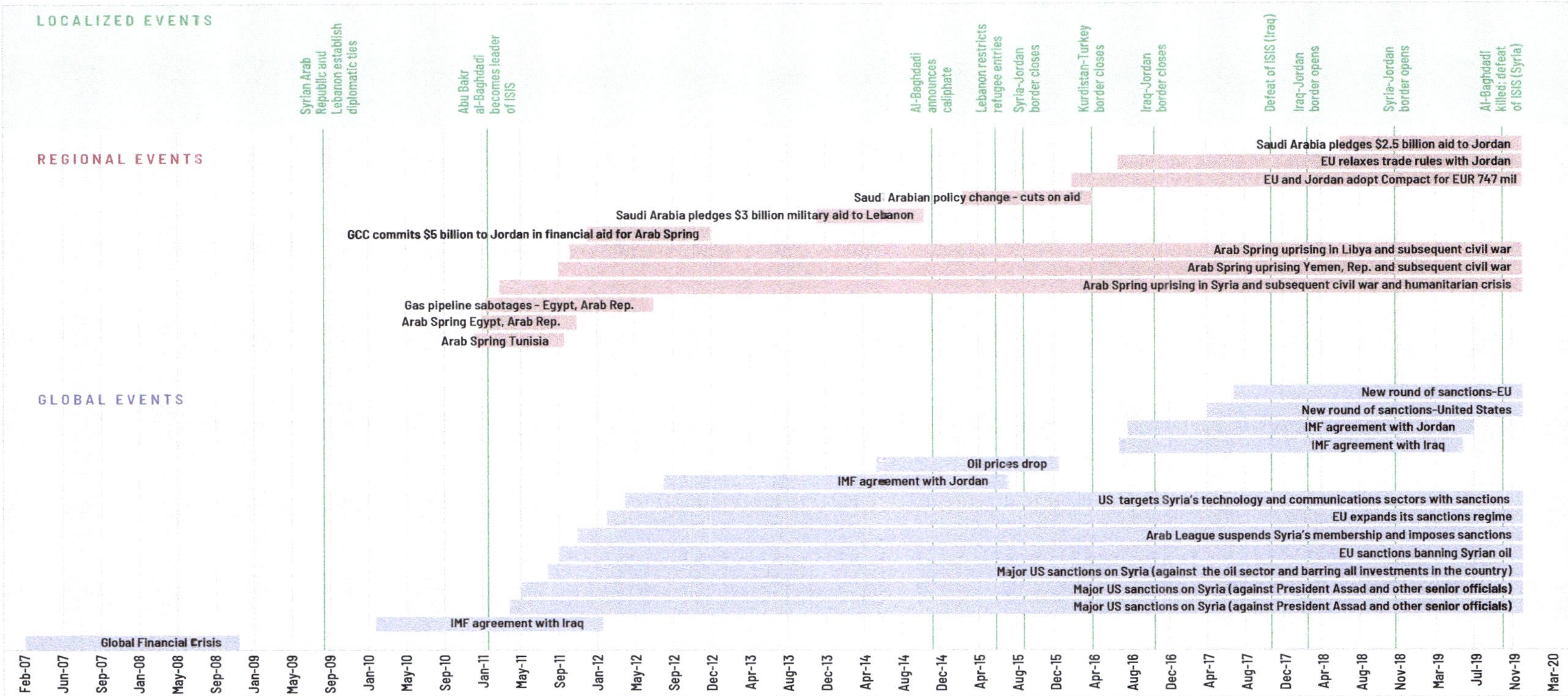

Source: Original figure for this report.

Note: EU = European Union; GCC = Gulf Cooperation Council; IMF = International Monetary Fund.

FIGURE 1.2. Growth and external receipts in Iraq, Jordan, Lebanon, middle-income countries, and MENA countries

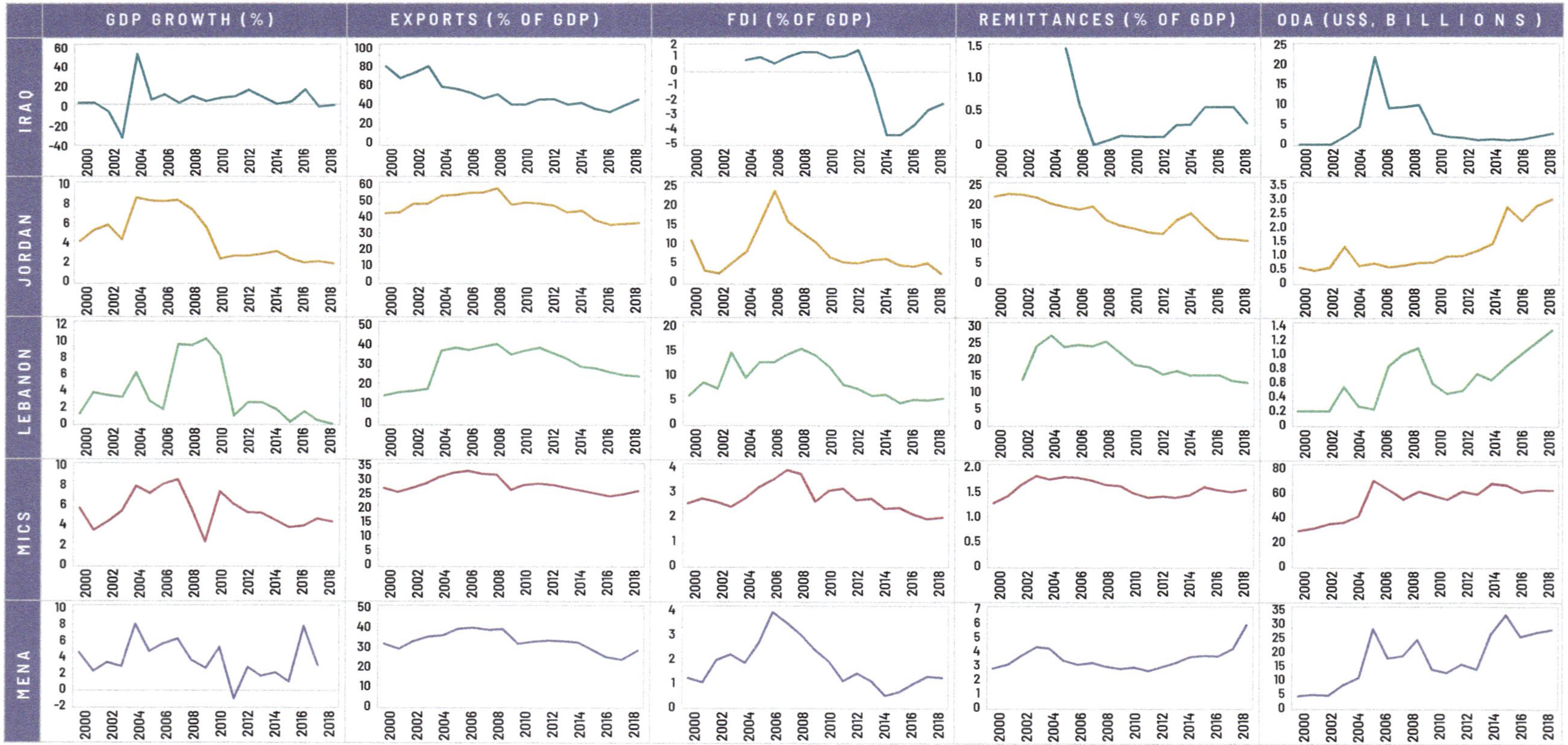

Source: Original figure for this report.

Note: FDI = foreign direct investment; MENA = Middle East and North Africa; MICs = middle-income countries; ODA = official development assistance. MENA countries exclude high-income countries.

- Remittances, which as a share of GDP dropped from about 19 percent in 2007 to 13 percent in 2010 despite a 9 percent increase in nominal terms. The latter is roughly comparable to the 13 percent increase in the total remittance outflows in Jordan's top-five remittance source economies (Germany, Oman, Saudi Arabia, the United States, and West Bank and Gaza) in the same period.

The Lebanese economy was in the middle of a boom when the global financial crisis unfolded, and the crisis did not immediately interrupt that boom. On average, the Lebanese GDP grew at a record high of 9.2 percent annually during 2007–09. This growth did not occur in other countries in the Middle East and North Africa (MENA) or in MICs, and happened despite some impact on its receipts:

- Export dynamics mimicked those of Jordan, with about a 5-percentage-point decrease in 2009 as a share of GDP, a 3-percentage-point recovery in 2010, and then a secular decrease since 2011.

- FDI inflows remained strong in 2008 and 2009, near 15 percent of GDP, but gradually decreased afterward to stabilize at about 5 percent of GDP in the medium term.

- Remittances reached a high of nearly 25 percent of GDP in 2008 and exhibited a trend of secular decline after that, which continues. In nominal dollar terms, the changes between 2008 and 2010 constitute a 4 percent decrease, which is different than the 2 percent increase in the remittance outflows of Lebanon's top-five remittance source countries (Australia, Canada, Germany, Saudi Arabia, and the United States) in the same period.

- Official development assistance (ODA) fell sharply from $1.1 billion in 2008 (3.7 percent of GDP) to $445 million in 2010 (1.2 percent of GDP).

While the systemic effects of the global financial crisis were unfolding, in December 2010, Mohamed Bouazizi, a Tunisian citizen, marked the beginning of a new era. In protest of authorities' confiscation of his only livelihood, a fruit cart he used to support his family, Mr. Bouazizi from Sidi Bouzid in Tunisia set himself on fire on December 17, 2010 (Reuters 2010). Having borrowed about $200 the night before to buy produce to sell that day, he did not have the funds to bribe local officers, which led to the confiscation of his produce. His death triggered mass protests against the Tunisian government and eventually led to the resignation of President Ben Ali on January 14, 2011, after 23 years in office (Abouzeid 2011). With the success of political transition in Tunisia and broadly shared growing dissatisfaction with the quality of life in many countries in the region, political turmoil spread rapidly (Ianchovichina, Mottaghi, and Devarajan, 2015). Within months, protests spread in Algeria, Bahrain, the Arab Republic of Egypt, Jordan, Libya, Saudi Arabia, Syria, and the Republic of Yemen.

The gravity of the events that followed the Arab Spring and their economic impact surpassed expectations. Despite the difficulty of disentangling the economic effects for each singular Arab Spring event in the region, in combination, those events led to major political, social, and economic outcomes. The protests in Iraq, Libya, Syria, and the Republic of Yemen turned into protracted and intense conflicts. Extremist networks increasingly challenged governments' monopoly over violence. The consequences of these events for development in the MENA region were grave, erasing decades of progress: millions of people were thrust back into poverty, and dependence on humanitarian assistance increased. Child and maternal mortality skyrocketed, and life expectancy slumped as hundreds of thousands of people died either directly from violence or indirectly from hunger, neglect, and lack of access to health services (Devarajan et. al. 2016). The wars forced millions of children out of school, hurting their future earning potential and dooming the countries' human capital to low skills (Ianchovichina 2018). In many countries, inflation soared, tourism collapsed, investment plummeted, and the state's ability to finance public services was eroded as governments increased spending on national security at the expense of productive investments in public services and infrastructure.

The conflict in Syria constituted the most brutal outcome of the process triggered by the Arab Spring movement. Although the protests in Syria started in March 2011, by the summer they had already escalated to an armed conflict. The conflict, which came to be known as one of the most brutal of our times, displaced more than half of the country's preconflict population. More than 5.5 million people became refugees in neighboring countries, and about 6.2 million were displaced internally (UNHCR 2020). According to *The Mobility of Displaced Syrians*, by June 2018 about 20.3 percent of all housing units were estimated to be either partially damaged or fully destroyed in 15 major conflict-affected cities (World Bank 2019). Damage ratios for education and health facilities have been higher: about 6.8 percent of schools were destroyed and 35.2 percent partially damaged, and about 11.2 percent of health facilities were destroyed and 37.2 percent partially damaged. About 44.0 percent of schools and 40.4 percent of health care facilities were not functioning as of June 2018.

The Syrian conflict quickly became a problem that spread well beyond Syria's borders. The conflict in Syria created security problems not only for the region but also globally. From its controlled territory, the Islamic State and other extremist organizations orchestrated numerous attacks in dozens of economies on all continents. The Islamic State ran over a large swath of Iraqi territory and conquered large cities like Mosul. Missiles from Syria landed several times in Jordanian and Lebanese cities and towns, intensifying the burden on their security forces. The repeated attacks on the Arab Gas Pipeline, which supplied Jordan with approximately 80 percent of its gas needs from Egypt prior to February 2011, caused major losses (Hochberg 2015).[2] Similarly, the refugee crisis emanating from the conflict in Syria created severe political problems in both immediate neighbors of Syria and other destinations like Europe.

Another major event that significantly affected the region was the oil price collapse between mid-2014 and early 2016. The collapse was one of the largest declines, about 70 percent, since World War II, and the longest lasting since the supply-driven collapse of 1986 (World Bank 2018). The sharp fall in oil prices negatively affected oil-exporting countries in the region: as receipts for oil exports shrank, so did fiscal spending, which constrained the demand for nonoil goods and services. Theoretically, the oil-importing economies in the region should have benefited from the price collapse through terms of trade effects. In practice, however, this effect was stymied by the economic slowdown in oil-exporting countries like the Gulf Cooperation Council (GCC) countries, because many oil-importing countries also relied on remittances from them. In Jordan and Lebanon, the impact of the oil price collapse on remittance inflows was not significant; however, fiscal grants took a large hit.

Because other events besides the Syrian conflict would have also affected Iraq, Jordan, and Lebanon, isolating their marginal effects is difficult. The economic trends observed in Iraq, Jordan, and Lebanon after 2010 reflect the composite effect of everything that happened at global, regional, and national levels. Take the Arab Spring events, for example: each political turmoil or conflict in a given country could produce a political, social, and economic impact on other countries in the region (and beyond). Theoretically, the magnitude of such impact should be a function of the economic and physical distance between the countries. For instance, if a country is a direct neighbor to the country that suffers from the conflict, or has deep economic ties, then the impact could be expected to be greater. For each Arab Spring event, therefore, we would expect a gradient of effects. The problem is that almost all Arab Spring events began around the same time, therefore making it difficult to systematically isolate their effects on a given country. Thus, we should not rush to attribute all changes after 2010 to the Syrian conflict per se. The next section describes this problem and other methodological issues in more detail, and then describes attempts to address these issues to the extent allowed by the available data and assessment techniques.

MEASURING THE IMPACT: METHODOLOGICAL ISSUES

The analysis of the post-2010 changes in economic and social outcomes in Iraq, Jordan, and Lebanon is impeded by complexity. As described in the previous section, many other global, regional, and local factors possibly influenced the outcomes in these countries regardless of the conflict in Syria. This section provides an overview of the challenges faced in analyzing the impact of the Syrian conflict. The challenges fall into three categories: correctly identifying the source of the impact (isolating the impact of the conflict from the impact of other factors); defining and measuring what has been affected; and accounting for the fact that the impact is driven not only by the shock but also by the prevailing conditions in the areas affected.

First problem: The impact of what? The first challenge in evaluating the impact of the Syrian conflict is to separate this shock from other confounding factors. Typically, the impact of a shock (often called an intervention or a treatment in the impact evaluation literature) is assessed by comparing outcomes between the cases where the shock takes place and where it does not take place in a manner that is not driven by conditions in these cases (that is, the shock is truly exogenous). In a strict interpretation, this assessment would entail comparing the economies of Iraq, Jordan, and Lebanon with other identical economies that have not been subjected to the Syrian conflict in any way. Unfortunately, the lack of any such "counterfactuals" makes this type of comparison impossible. Also, as described in the previous section, other global and regional factors possibly affected the economic and social outcomes in these countries simultaneously with the Syrian conflict. Thus, a simple comparison of indicators before and after the Syrian conflict does not constitute an impact analysis.

Second problem: The impact on what? Identifying the shock brings us to the problem of assessing the impact of the shock properly. Here, we face two issues: imperfect measurement and indicator selection. These issues are interrelated but, nevertheless, distinct problems:

- *Imperfect measurement.* A conflict can influence many outcomes in neighboring countries, including those in economic, social, political, and cultural dimensions. Some of these changes are quantifiable and measurable, but some are not. For instance, economic indicators like prices, fiscal revenues, and labor market statistics are directly measurable unless capacity constraints render them otherwise. In comparison, social and political processes are less measurement-friendly although some indicators in this group can be generated by means of indexes. For instance, changes in social trust can be assessed by means of survey questions relying on the Likert Scale (a ranked numerical scale, where the lowest number is associated with the lowest amount of trust, and the highest number is associated with the highest amount of trust). Some other very important issues, like cultural effects, may not be conducive to such assessments.

- *Indicator selection*. The measurability of an indicator is a necessary condition—but not a sufficient one—for a quantitative impact assessment. Although many indicators can be useful by themselves, it is unlikely that a single indicator can capture the whole impact of a conflict. To do so often requires an array of indicators. When using such an array, however, proper aggregation is crucial as double-counting or not capturing all relevant components of the impact can distort the assessment. For instance, when refugee arrivals lead to an increase in housing prices (rent), it reduces the well-being of local consumers because they pay more for housing; but increased housing prices cannot be used alone as the impact indicator because the accompanying increase in the incomes of landlords must also be taken into consideration.

Third problem: The "Pisa fallacy." How a shock affects outcomes on the ground also depends on the resilience of the area hit by the shock. To use an analogy, assume that the leaning tower of Pisa has an unusually low wind resistance threshold, and a modest wind exceeds this threshold. In this case, although the wind is the final blow that drives the catastrophe, attributing the whole impact to wind, with no reference to prevailing structural issues, could provide an incomplete picture.[3] Thus, any assessment of the impact of a shock should also consider existing conditions in the area hit by the shock.

In the end, the solutions to these problems are determined by data quality. Assessments in active conflict situations or in countries where institutional capacity is low can severely constrain methodological options: ideal counterfactual assessments may be impossible to pursue, and data constraints may hamper systematic assessments that could help provide a comprehensive view. Nevertheless, in the absence of alternatives, second-best approaches are often used to answer questions that are pertinent to developing effective policies. The next section defines the approach used to analyze the impact of the Syrian conflict on the economic and social outcomes in Iraq, Jordan, and Lebanon in the presence of numerous data constraints.

THE ANALYTICAL STRATEGY OF THIS STUDY

In light of the discussion above, we pursue a pragmatic strategy in analyzing pertinent issues in a systematic manner. Limitations in data restrict the technical analysis—that is, it is not always possible to identify causal effects in all areas. Regardless, we take stock of issues that are commonly thought to be pertinent for understanding the impact. These issues are distilled from experience in other conflict and forced displacement situations; anecdotal references in the case of Iraq, Jordan, and Lebanon; and pure economic reasoning. The report is structured in two main blocks: a backward-looking assessment and a forward-looking section that builds on the backward-looking assessment (figure 1.3). In the following three chapters, we

- Analyze the initial conditions in Mashreq before the onset of the Syrian conflict,
- Take stock of changes in economic and social outcomes in the course of the conflict without a systematic effort to attribute outcomes to causes, and
- Infer the marginal role played by the conflict in explaining a limited number of indicators.

The initial conditions are assessed in two dimensions: exposure and resilience. The analysis in the second chapter focuses on conditions in Iraq, Jordan, and Lebanon by dividing them across two categories, exposure and resilience. The idea behind that division is that,

FIGURE 1.3. **Analytical strategy**

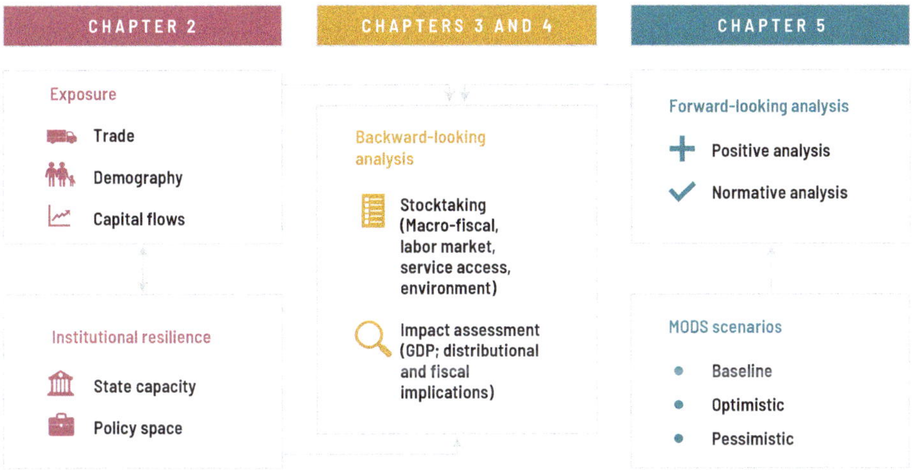

Source: Original figure for this report.

Note: MODS = Mobility of Displaced Persons.

other things being equal, a greater exposure to the developments in Syria (because of deep economic ties) could lead to a greater impact when the Syrian economic activity takes a hit. Similarly, other things being equal, a weaker resilience at the outset could lead to an ineffective response to the shock, which would then further propagate the initial shock inside the neighboring country. More specifically,

- For exposure, we focus on cross-border flows including refugee arrivals, international trade, and capital flows. The analysis of refugee arrivals relies on registration data from the United Nations High Commissioner for Refugees (UNHCR) (as recorded in the pro-Gres system) for the scale and spatial distribution of registered refugees and administrative and survey data from national sources (for example, Jordan's Labor Market Panel Survey), as well as WorldPop data for spatial aspects of demographic changes (which are also used to consider unregistered refugees).[4] The trade analysis relies on UN Comtrade trade statistics, often in the mirror format.[5] To analyze capital flows, we primarily use Balance of Payments (BOP) data from the International Monetary Fund.[6]

- For resilience, we assess state capacity, policy space, and broader stability in 2010. The indicators of state capacity include revenue and expenditure management, strategic planning, capacity for service delivery, and public accountability, and are assessed by using cross-country indexes including Worldwide Governance Indicators (WGI), Public Expenditure and Financial Accountability (PEFA) scores, Open Budget Index (OBI), and previous World Bank assessments. Policy space indicators include fiscal space and rigidity and social protection system characteristics (insurance and assistance). Fiscal indicators are drawn from the International Monetary Fund's World Economic Outlook database for comparability across countries, and social protection system information is based on national descriptions.[7]

Taking stock of the economic and social outcomes during the conflict involves a plethora of areas to consider. Chapter 3 provides an overview of key outcomes in Iraq, Jordan, and Lebanon during the conflict, which intrinsically reflect the outcomes of the exposure-resilience system described in the chapter before. Trends in the following areas are studied:

FIGURE 1.4. Technical strategy for analyzing the impact

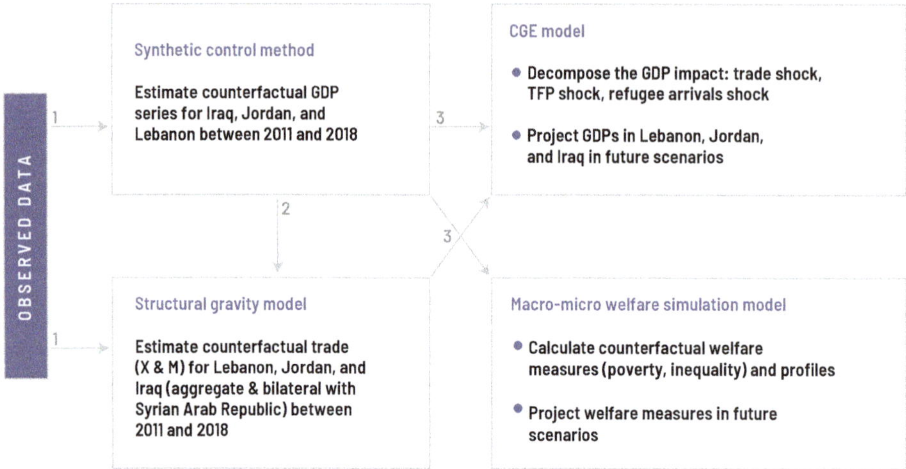

Source: Original figure for this report.

Note: CGE = computable general equilibrium; TFP = total factor productivity; M = imports; X = exports.

- *Macro-fiscal.* The analysis begins with a description of macroeconomic and fiscal trends between 2011 and 2019. We decompose (in an accounting framework) changes in key indicators like economic growth and debt-to-GDP ratios; however, we refrain from attributing causality at this stage.

- *Labor markets.* We analyze labor market trends in the three countries of interest. Here, we exploit the heterogeneity of refugee populations across subnational areas to infer the relationship between refugee arrivals and labor market outcomes. Again, these relationships give us correlations rather than water-tight causal mechanisms, but we found them indicative nevertheless.

- *Poverty.* Data on poverty are scarce and not always comparable across years; thus, we provide only a brief assessment of distributional trends.

- *Access to publicly provided services.* We focus on how the service access of host community members has changed over years. We analyze the supply and demand dynamics in transportation, education, health care, water and sanitation, and energy services. Specifically, we aim to assess to what extent service provision has adapted to the sudden increase in demand and what have been the fiscal implications of such adaptation. Data come mainly from national sources and are not always conducive to decomposing supply and demand effects.

- *Environment.* We consider water (above-surface lakes and ponds), land (solid waste), and air pollution trends by combining a novel remote-sensing based dataset with existing sources (such as government data and United Nations surveys). Correlations between refugee settlement intensity and pollution indicators provide some inference about the relationship between the demographic shock and environmental outcomes.

To isolate the impact of the Syrian conflict on Iraqi, Jordanian, and Lebanese economies, we then analyze the GDP dynamics in more detail. Chapter 4 provides a more technical perspective that focuses on analyzing different channels through which the Syrian conflict has manifested its impact on Iraqi, Jordanian, and Lebanese GDPs. To do this, we proceed with the following technical strategy (figure 1.4):

- *First, estimate counterfactual GDP series.* In an attempt to eliminate global and regional factors that may have driven some of the economic results since 2011, we estimate "counterfactual" GDP series by using a synthetic control method (SCM). This method searches for a weighted combination of other countries (termed "donors") that resemble as closely as possible the characteristics of the target country or countries (Iraq, Jordan, and Lebanon) in the preconflict period in terms of an outcome—in this case GDP—and a set of other specific covariates. We use different specifications for this estimation: a purely statistical model with no additional covariates, a model with common covariates for growth SCM analyses, and an extension of this latter model with a regional adjustment estimated from cross-country growth regression with a MENA fixed effect.
- *Second, estimate counterfactual trade patterns.* Using the counterfactual GDP and the preconflict trade shares across countries, we generate counterfactual export and import patterns using a structural gravity model.
- *Third, analyze the marginal roles played by different factors.* We analyze the conflict's impact on GDP through three different channels—trade, demographics, and total factor productivity—using a computable general equilibrium (CGE) model based on a Global Trade Analysis Project model together with the counterfactual trade and GDP series estimated in the previous two steps. We are interested in the marginal effects of each of the three shocks. For instance, say the question we answer for the trade shock is the following: What would have happened to GDP growth if the country had had the counterfactual (no Syrian conflict) trade pattern? This treatment holds the other two shocks in place but removes only the trade shock. The gap between GDPs in these two cases shows the marginal (flow) impact of the trade shock over the period of our analysis.

As the last step of the backward-looking analysis, we consider the poverty and fiscal implications of the GDP impact. We employ a macro-micro simulation model, where the GDP impact estimates are used together with household survey–based poverty–growth relationship analysis. This method helps produce estimates of counterfactual poverty trends in the absence of the Syrian conflict. Similarly, we take our counterfactual GDP estimates to a debt dynamics framework. Doing so allows us to analyze the extent to which such GDP impacts could explain the deteriorating debt burdens in Lebanon and Jordan over the last decade. We also run a few additional thought experiments by incrementally changing assumptions regarding fiscal position (that is, the revenue-expenditure balance) from the preconflict period and an arbitrary variation in real interest rate that is effectively used on interest payments on outstanding public debt.

Finally, building on the backward-looking analysis, we analyze prospects ahead in the region and associated policy options. The uncertainties about the future loom large in the Mashreq. The framework we construct to analyze the impact of the Syrian conflict on three neighboring countries, however, enables us to consider a scenario-based analysis going forward. Chapter 5 discusses how possible recovery scenarios in Syria could affect economic and social outcomes in its neighbors going forward.[8] The chapter then offers a discussion of desirable policies in two stages: a unilateral approach and a regional approach. The former considers, other things being equal, the policy choices that can be pursued and supported by the international community, within each country. The latter adds to the former the effects of policy coordination among the countries to internalize cross-border issues.

NOTES

1. Other countries that have possibly been affected by the conflict, including those that host large numbers of Syrian refugees (Turkey, Greece, and other countries in Europe), and those that were directly or indirectly a party to the conflict have been excluded from the analysis because of data limitations. The three countries covered in this report (Iraq, Jordan, and Lebanon) are listed and analyzed alphabetically unless entailed otherwise by expositional constraints. For the purpose of this study, we will refer to these three countries, along with Syria, as "the Mashreq" simply to avoid frequently repeating the country list.
2. The recovery in Egyptian gas production has enabled gas to flow to Jordan from 2018. In 2020, the pipeline also began distributing gas from Israel inside Jordan.
3. Technically, this example describes a case with binary outcomes, where the marginal effect of a treatment could vary drastically (perhaps because of a discontinuity) when it is not interpreted at mean values of other covariates.
4. For more information on WorldPop and its data, see https://www.worldpop.org.
5. The UN Comtrade database (the United Nations International Trade Statistics Database) is available at https://comtrade.un.org.
6. For more information on Balance of Payments data, see https://data.imf.org/?sk=7A51304B-6426-40C0-83DD-CA473CA1FD52.
7. For more information on the World Economic Outlook database, see https://www.imf.org/external/pubs/ft/weo/2018/02/weodata/index.aspx.
8. These recovery scenarios are based on World Bank (2019).

REFERENCES

Abouzeid, Rania. 2011. "Bouazizi: The Man Who Set Himself and Tunisia on Fire." *Time*, January 21. http://content.time.com/time/magazine/article/0,9171,2044723,00.html.

Devarajan, Shantayanan, Lili Mottaghi, Quy-Toan Do, Anne Brockmeyer, Clément Joubert, Kartika Bhatia, Mohamed Abdel Jelil. 2016. "Economic and Social Inclusion to Prevent Violent Extremism." *Middle East and North Africa Economic Monitor* (October), World Bank, Washington, DC. doi: 10.1596/978-1-4648-0990-3.

EPRS (European Parliamentary Research Service). 2017. "Syrian Crisis: Impact on Iraq." Briefing, European Parliamentary Research Service, April.

Hochberg, Michael. 2015. "Jordan's Energy Future: A Path Forward." Middle East Institute, Washington, DC, August 19. https://www.mei.edu/publications/jordans-energy-future-path-forward.

Ianchovichina, Elena. 2018. *Eruptions of Popular Anger: The Economics of the Arab Spring and Its Aftermath.* MENA Development Report. Washington, DC: World Bank. https://openknowledge.worldbank.org/handle/10986/28961.

Ianchovichina, Elena, Lili Mottaghi, and Shantayanan Devarajan. 2015. "Inequality, Uprisings, and Conflict in the Arab World." *MENA Economic Monitor* (October). Washington, DC: World Bank.

Lynch, Marc, and Laurie Brand. 2017. "Refugees and Displacement in the Middle East." Carnegie Endowment for International Peace, March 29. https://carnegieendowment.org/2017/03/29/refugees-and-displacement-in-middle-east-pub-68479.

McDowall, David. 1987. *The Palestinians.* New ed. Report / the Minority Rights Group, No. 24. London: Minority Rights Group.

Reuters. 2010. "Witnesses Report Rioting in Tunisian Town." Reuters, December 19. https://af.reuters.com/article/topNews/idAFJOE6BI06U20101219.

UNHCR (United Nations High Commissioner for Refugees). "Syria Regional Refugee Response." https://data2.unhcr.org/en/situations/syria, accessed on March 30, 2020.

World Bank. 2017. *The Toll of War: The Economic and Social Consequences of the Conflict in Syria.* Washington, DC: World Bank.

World Bank. 2018. *Global Economic Prospects, January 2018: Broad-Based Upturn, but for How Long?* Washington, DC: World Bank.

World Bank. 2019. *The Mobility of Displaced Syrians: An Economic and Social Analysis.* Washington, DC: World Bank.

WTO (World Trade Organization). 2019. *World Trade Statistics Review 2017.* Geneva: WTO.

2. THE MECHANISMS OF THE FALLOUT

Geographic Syria as an economic sphere existed for 2,000 years before the Syrian Arab Republic emerged in the eastern Mediterranean in the 20th century. Greater Syria, or Bilad Al-Sham encompassed the major cities of Aleppo, Beirut, Damascus, Homs, and Jerusalem; a series of smaller cities such as Bethlehem and Salt; surrounding rural areas; and nomadic tracts with small populations. Although conquerors, caliphs, and emperors have come and gone, trade networks (partly connected to the Muslim Pilgrimage and anchored by cosmopolitan urban elites) have prevailed. These networks helped maintain a relatively well-connected business environment and ensure that Greater Syria was a relatively integrated region for most of this time.

Postcolonial independence led to efforts to consolidate power domestically, which came at the expense of interstate connectivity. The postcolonial states of the Mashreq developed unevenly, resulting in political and economic disparities. Initially, leaders of the smaller countries, such as Jordan and Lebanon, had a stake in fostering nationalism to guard against external political domination.[1] Mashreq leaders sought to protect their economies from external competition by raising new barriers to trade. They also developed separate financial and commercial links with industrialized countries (Owen and Pamuk 1998). During the Cold War, the changing world order added an extra layer of obstacles to integration in the Mashreq. Mashreq states became members of alliances with opposing superpowers that blocked their political and economic interactions. Such alliances severed many of the historical webs that connected Mashreq cities. A recent wave of bilateral agreements aimed to liberalize trade, investment, and labor mobility across borders; however, their effects remained partial and fragile. We will discuss this issue in more detail in the subsequent analysis in this report.

Despite the obstacles, people-to-people ties within the region remain strong. The deep connectivity of the region, driven by historical and cultural interactions, has so far prevailed. Dialects of Arabic in Lebanon, Jordan, and Syria are mutually intelligible; and most people in these countries can also understand Iraqi Arabic. Tribal networks cut across today's borders and are more salient in areas where state control is at its weakest, such as eastern Syria, southern Iraq, and northern Jordan. Waves of migration and displacement inside the region have also strengthened people-to-people ties. Millions of civilians fleeing violence and instability in Iraq, Lebanon, and most recently Syria, have tended to settle elsewhere in the Mashreq. This displacement has enhanced the intermingling of different Mashreq states and increased intermarriage. Although national, ethnic, and sectarian identities often champion regional identity despite these common ties, in the long term these identities have proven to be somewhat fluid as well (Kausch 2018).

These dynamics shaped two key factors that are essential in understanding the Syrian conflict's impact: (i) exposure to shocks and (ii) institutional resilience. In principle, the greater the economic interaction between two countries the larger the transmission of an economic shock from the conflict-struck country to the other. For instance, if the conflict-struck country acted as a major export destination for its neighbor, then the market loss would be substantial. Conversely, this trade shock may be negligible if the conflict country did not import much from the neighbor to begin with. Even though exposure to a shock is an important driver of the impact, it is not the only one. The ability of the shock-receiving country to respond to the shock effectively is another major driver. For our purposes in this study, we consider state capacity, fiscal space, and public perceptions as part of this institutional resilience concept. We now turn to analyzing those issues.

EXPOSURE TO SHOCKS

To assess exposure to the conflict, we focus on key cross-border channels of transmission: refugees (people), trade (goods), and capital flows (money). The conflict in Syria likely had multifaceted effects on people's well-being inside Syria and in its neighbors. Some of these effects, like cultural and political influences, are not easy to measure and quantify despite having the utmost importance. In this report, we restrict attention to measurable dimensions for assessing the exposure of local economies in Iraq, Jordan, and Lebanon to the conflict in Syria. While doing so, we focus on what might cross the border (physically or digitally), that is refugees (people), trade (goods), and capital flows (money). In what follows, we investigate the characteristics of these flows in detail.

DEMOGRAPHY

Unambiguously, the tragic forced displacement since 2011 has been the most important channel through which the Syrian conflict has affected others in the Mashreq. Over the nine years of the Syrian conflict, the demographic map of Syria changed drastically. More than half of the country's preconflict population (20.8 million in 2011) was displaced, internally or has taken refuge outside the country. By the end of 2019, the United Nations High Commissioner for Refugees (UNHCR) had registered about 5.6 million refugees, 1.8 million of whom were hosted by Iraq, Jordan, and Lebanon. About 6.2 million internally displaced persons (IDPs) remained in Syria, including 2.5 million children, and in Iraq another 1.5 million were displaced by the conflict with the Islamic State (UNHCR 2020).

Although population dynamics have far-reaching socioeconomic consequences in the region, demographic statistics are often plagued with ambiguity. Data quality and availability are major problems in the region, especially in Iraq and Lebanon. Significant discrepancies often exist between demographic estimates from different agencies, for refugee and host community populations alike, and underlying data sources are not always available. These constraints place significant limitations on the analyses we can conduct.

In the absence of better options, we use available sources pragmatically. Information on registered refugees was obtained from UNHCR. For consistency across countries, the number of unregistered refugees, a statistic which differs drastically across different sources, was calculated using information from the Regional Refugee and Resilience Plan (3RP). For labor market statistics in Jordan, we used the Jordan Labor Market Panel Survey (JLMPS), which provides information on socioeconomic and demographic characteristics, among other indicators, of residents in Jordan.[2] The JLMPS was first fielded in 2010, before the breakout of the Syrian conflict, and then repeated in 2016. In Iraq, we used the Household Socio-Economic Survey (HSES) from 2012 and the Rapid Welfare Monitoring Survey (SWIFT) from 2017.[3] In Lebanon, because microdata access has proven daunting, we relied on aggregate tabulations from Central Administration of Statistics data, including the Labour Force and Household Living Conditions Survey 2018–19. More details about these sources are provided at the end of this chapter. Finally, for nationwide population dynamics, we used the estimates of United Nations (UN) Population Division for comparability. When analyzing subnational dynamics of overall population, we used WorldPoP estimates, not for the scale of the population but for changes in its spatial composition.[4]

Population dynamics: A bird's-eye view

At the outset of the Syrian conflict, population growth in Iraq had begun slowing, and the arrival of Syrian refugees did not change this long-term trend. Between 2010 and 2019, total population in Iraq grew by 31.5 percent, from about 30 million to about 40 million. On average, this total growth corresponds to a 3.3 percent change annually. The actual growth rate of population, however, was not uniform over those years. It was at 3 percent in 2010 and climbed to 3.9 percent in 2012–13 with the arrival of refugees. Since 2014 the growth rate decreased steadily, reaching a low of 2.3 in 2019.

A nationwide decrease in fertility rate explained the slowdown. In Iraq total fertility data for women between the ages of 15 and 49 are available for the years 2011 and 2018. Those come from the Multiple Indicator Cluster Surveys (MICS) without disaggregation by population group (local community, refugees, migrants, and so on). Overall, the average fertility rate during the seven years between the two surveys dropped from 4.4 children per woman to 3.6 children per woman across the country. In Salah ad Din and Anbar, the decrease was more than 2.8 and 2.3 children per woman, respectively. Even the governorates that host the largest numbers of refugees recorded decreases in fertility (Duhok had 1.4 fewer children per woman and Erbil 1.1 fewer children per woman).

Forced displacement changed the spatial composition of demography significantly, especially in the Kurdistan Region. The flow of Syrian refugees to Iraq increased gradually after 2012, mirroring the expansion of the Islamic State in Syria. By March 2015, the total number of registered Syrian refugees in Iraq reached 246,000. After that, the number mainly remained stable, with some reductions facilitated by returns during the period of relative stability in Northeast Syria, which reduced the number to 224,000 by mid-2017 (however, the more recent wave of displacement during the Turkish offensive has brought the number back to its peak). Partially because of geographical proximity, Duhok had the highest share of Syrian refugees (figure 2.1) compared to the other two governorates by March 2014 (48 percent); however, because of low economic opportunities, many refugees later moved to Erbil, so Duhok's share decreased to 35 percent by September 2019. Thus, although refugees represented about 0.7 percent of the country's total population, a considerably smaller portion than in Lebanon and Jordan, they represented a significant share of local population because of their concentration.

Another significant component of the demographic shift in Iraq was the large number of IDPs. The expansion of the Islamic State in Iraq, and the ensuing conflict, displaced many Iraqis internally. According to International Organization for Migration (IOM), about 3.4 million Iraqis were displaced in 2016–17, at the peak (IOM 2016). Even though many IDPs returned after the liberation of Islamic State–controlled territories, 1.4 million Iraqis remained displaced in December 2019, highlighting the long-term nature of displacement. Regarding their governorate of origin, the largest share of IDPs came from Ninewa, followed by Anbar and Salah ad Din. About one-third were displaced within their own governorate. Duhok, Erbil, and Sulaymaniyah received almost all the IDPs who moved elsewhere.

Overall, conflicts significantly altered the demographic distribution in Northern Iraq. Map 2.1 (panel a) shows the estimated demographic change in Iraq between 2010 and 2019, evaluated at a grid cell level (about 3 arcs, which corresponds to about 100 meters on the equator). In figure 2.2 (panel a), this information is converted to a histogram of grid cell numbers (vertical axis) for each population level (in natural logarithms on the horizontal axis). The figure shows, for 2010 to 2019, a shift from the middle of the distribution (the blue bars over the red bars) to the right (the red bars over the blue bars), denoting an

FIGURE 2.1. Shares of Syrian refugees, by governorate in Iraq, 2012–19

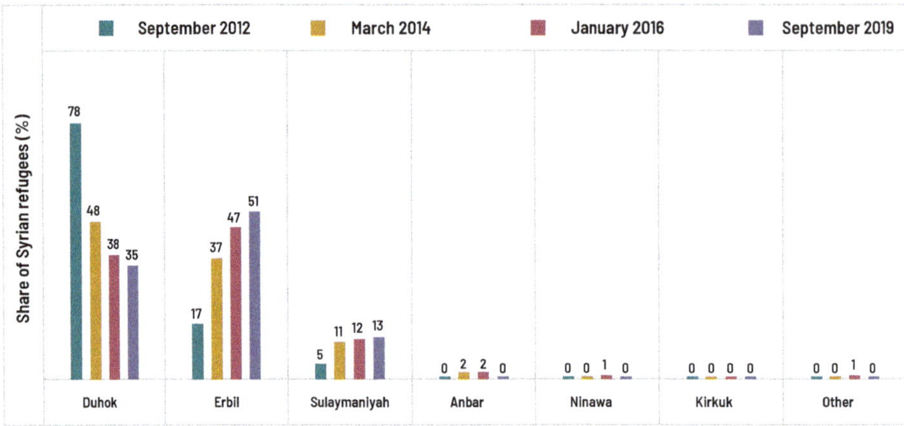

Source: UNHCR 2020.

increase in grid cells with higher population in that range. To a limited extent, these increases may have been driven by an overall population growth for smooth transitions, but some shifts are large after exponential corrections to the logarithmic scales. This finding implies that displacement likely played an important role. Overall, most Iraqi governorates grew about 30 percent between 2010 and 2019 demographically, with the striking exception of Duhok, whose population increased by almost 80 percent. The next fastest growing governorates for this period were At-Ta'mim and Karbala (38 and 37 percent, respectively), and the slowest growth rates were observed in Diyala (15 percent) and Baghdad (17 percent).

The Syrian displacement caught Jordan at the turning point of a population growth episode. According to UN Population Division estimates, the total population in Jordan grew by about 5.3 percent in 2010. This remarkable rate was the peak of a gradual increase in population growth rate since the early 2000s and was mostly explained by net migration patterns.[5] Between 2010 and 2019, the total population of Jordan increased by 36 percent, from slightly less than 7.5 million to more than 10.1 million, about 4 percent annually on average. Currently, the annual rate of population growth for Jordan hovers slightly lower than 1 percent.

With the onset of the Syrian conflict, many refugees found a safe haven in Jordan. Beginning in 2012, refugee arrivals increased gradually, with the peak inflow reached in 2013. By mid-2014, the number of registered refugees reached above 600,000 and stabilized around that number since then. As of December 2019, 655,000 Syrian refugees had registered in Jordan (123,000 in refugee camps, mainly in Za'atari, Azraq, and the Emirati Jordanian Camp), with official estimates suggesting the presence of a large group of unregistered refugees (a group as large as or larger than registered ones) in the country. Most refugees reside in the governorates of Amman, Irbid, Mafraq, and Zarqa. Because Amman was already the most populous governorate of Jordan, the ratio of refugees to local population there remained low (5 percent in 2015 and 6 percent in 2018). Mafraq, however, featured a much higher ratio, because it started with a local population of about 229,000 and received more than 350,000 registered and unregistered refugees. By comparison, Irbid had the second-highest refugee concentration: it hosted almost 300,000 refugees (both registered and unregistered) and had a local population of more than 1.5 million people.

MAP 2.1. **Population change in Iraq, Jordan, and Lebanon between 2010 and 2019**

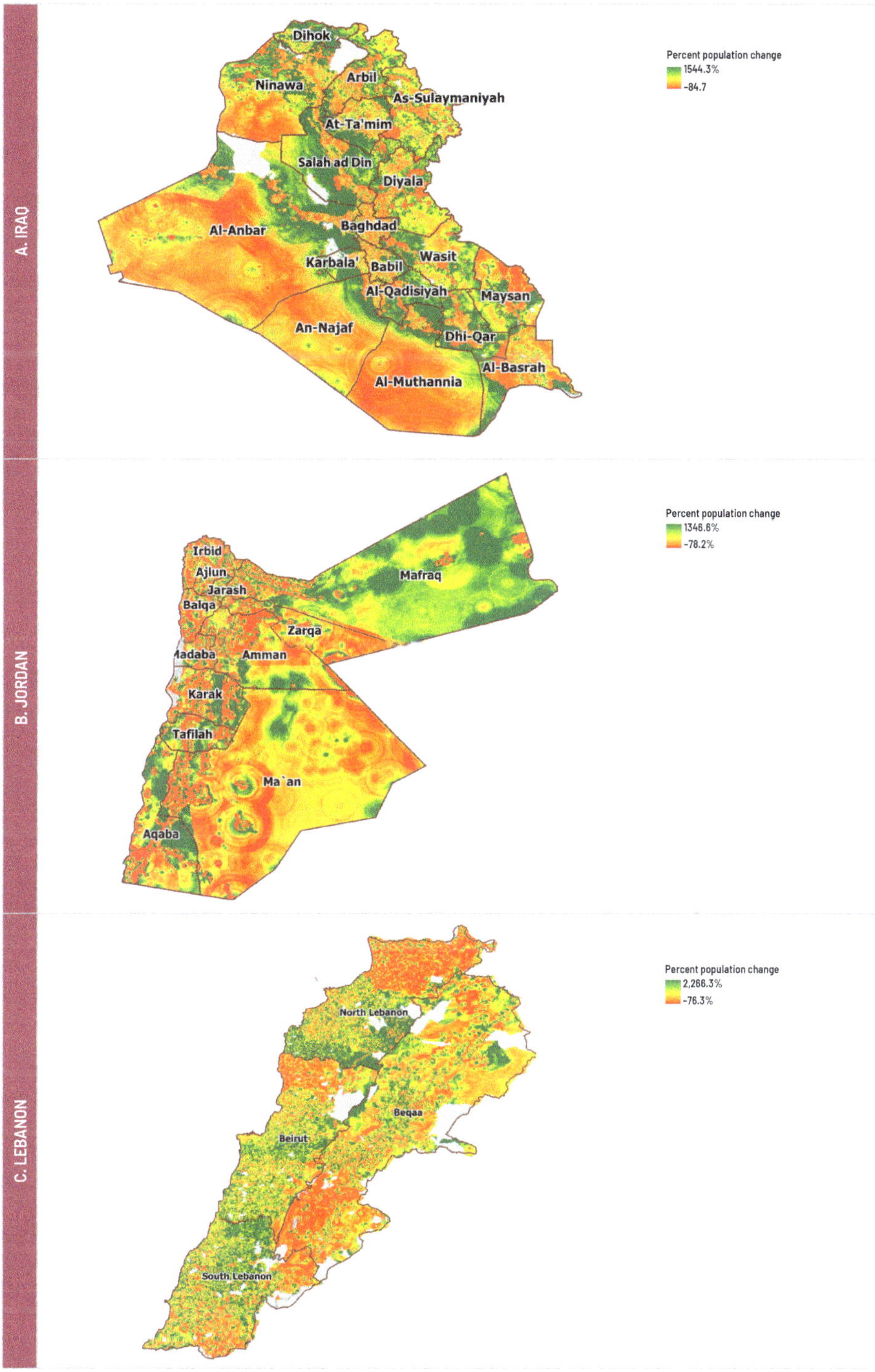

Sources: WorldPop data and World Bank staff calculations.

Note: Figure shows percent population change by pixel (about 100 meters). Artifacts in the form of borderline effects and radials are original. Mismatches at national borders stem from differences in specifications across different sources, which do not indicate World Bank endorsement.

FIGURE 2.2. **Population distribution in Iraq, Jordan, and Lebanon, 2010 versus 2019**

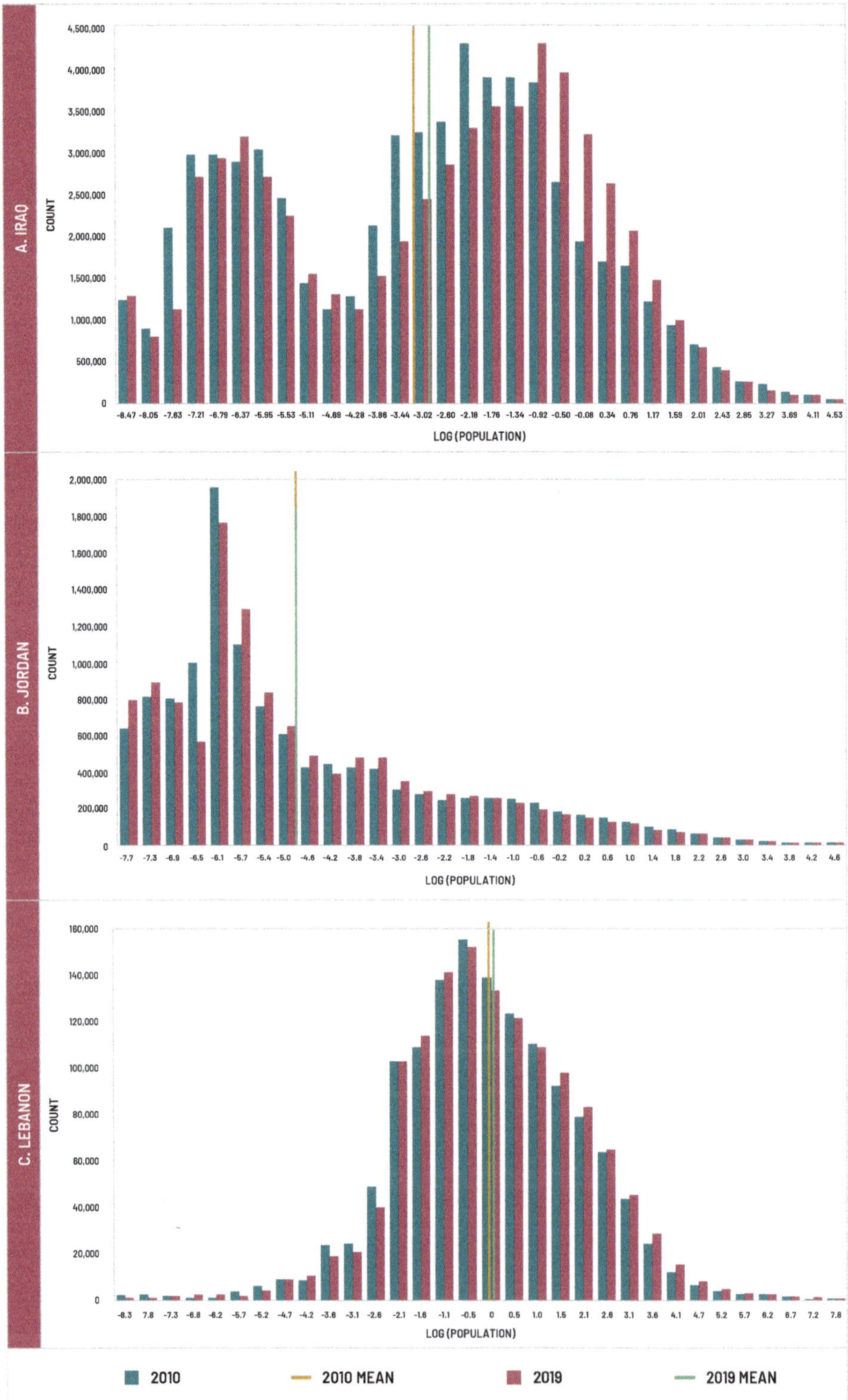

Sources: WorldPop data and World Bank staff calculations.

Note: Populations (horizontal axis) in log scale by pixel (about 100 meters); pixels with zero population excluded.

The arrival of refugees was mean-preserving for Jordan's spatial composition of population. Map 2.1 (panel b) shows the grid cell level estimates for demographic change in Jordan between 2010 and 2019, with the associated histograms in figure 2.2 (panel b). Overall, changes are distributed in a balanced manner around the mean, leading to no change. Despite some clear population increases in cells with low 2010 levels, these increases are counterbalanced by two sizeable reductions to the mean and a rather smooth increase in above-mean cells. At the governorate level, this balance is reflected in a relatively similar population growth pattern. The average population growth rate was 40 percent between 2010 and 2019, and the highest population growth took place in Mafraq (52 percent), followed by Amman (45 percent). In 2019, the governorate of Amman represented 42 percent of the total population of Jordan. It is also the governorate that shows the largest increase in total population, having grown by 45 percent during 2010–19. Irbid is the second most populous governorate, with almost 19 percent of the country's total population, followed by Zarqa (with 14 percent of the population). Meanwhile, Tafilah, with its small population (about 100,000 in 2019), recorded the lowest growth rate (18 percent).

In Jordan, not all Syrians were refugees, and not all refugees were Syrians. According to the JLMPS in 2016 Syrian refugees made up about 92 of all Syrians in Jordan, who in turn represented about 9 percent of Jordan's total population. Table 2.1 compares the population share of Syrian refugees and other groups relative to the total governorate population. In several governorates, Syrians, refugees and nonrefugees together, did not constitute the largest non-Jordanian group. According to United Nations Relief and Work Agency for Palestinians in the Near East (UNRWA), Jordan had about 2.2 million registered Palestinian refugees; according to UNHCR, Jordan hosted about 68,000 Iraqi persons of concern (UNHCR 2019; UNRWA 2018).

Lebanon was coming out of a period of slow population growth when the Syrian conflict broke out. From 2006 to 2010, total population in Lebanon grew by only 1 percent annually, which was significantly lower than earlier years when rates of over 4 percent were not uncommon. This reduction was driven by net outmigration and a decrease in birth rates. These trends were already being reversed in 2010, when the population grew by 3.9 percent, with the outmigration coming to an end.

The arrival of Syrian refugees in Lebanon created one of the world's highest concentration of refugees in any country. The total population of Lebanon increased by more than 38 percent between 2010 and 2019, rising from 4.9 million to 6.9 million.[6] Much of this increase resulted from the arrival of Syrian refugees, whose numbers peaked in 2013 with more than 700,000 arrivals that year. With almost no attrition (that is, no returns or third country repatriation) in refugee numbers in the following years, the total registered refugee numbers reached a total of 1.2 million in 2015, nearly a fifth of the country's total population. Since then, Lebanon has experienced a slow attrition with some returns and repatriations, bringing the number down to 915,000 in December 2019. Official estimates put the total (registered and unregistered) refugee count close to 1.5 million.

The concentration of refugees varied across regions. About 38 percent of all refugees resided in the Beqaa region of Lebanon. This region is the most sparsely populated area of Lebanon and was home to about 12 percent of the total population in 2010. Similarly, North Lebanon, accounting for only 17 percent of the total population in 2017, received almost 27 percent of the total stock of refugees. The Beirut region, in contrast, hosted 25 percent of the refugee population while serving as home to 51 percent of the Lebanese population in 2010. South Lebanon hosted only 11 percent of Syrian refugees. These changes are captured by the increases in grid cell counts with populations on either side of the averages in figure 2.2 (panel c), where the mean population per pixel exhibited a small increase between 2010 and 2019.

TABLE 2.1. Distribution of refugees and composition of nationalities, by governorate in Jordan, 2016

GOVERNORATE	DISTRIBUTION OF SYRIAN REFUGEES ACROSS GOVERNORATES	WITHIN GOVERNORATE DISTRIBUTION OF GROUPS				
		JORDANIANS	SYRIANS	EGYPTIANS	OTHER	TOTAL
AMMAN	33	71	10	7	13	100
BALQA	3	78	3	9	9	100
ZARQA	12	73	8	5	13	100
MADABA	2	81	10	4	5	100
IRBID	29	80	15	2	3	100
MAFRAQ	19	66	29	3	2	100
JARASH	0	76	0	3	21	100
AJLOUN	0	99	0	0	0	100
KARAK	2	92	6	1	1	100
TAFILEH	0	100	0	0	0	100
MA'AN	0	98	0	1	0	100
AQABA	0	68	2	18	12	100
TOTAL	100					

Source: Jordan Labor Market Panel Survey 2016.

The growth of the Lebanese population appears to have stalled in recent years. UN Population Division estimates show that Lebanon's population growth rate has slowed to near zero and even became negative in 2019. One reason for the slowdown is that arrivals of Syrian refugees have almost completely stopped in recent years. With fewer arrivals, and with some returns and repatriations, the Syrian refugee population in Lebanon was nearly 250,000 less in 2019 than its peak value in 2017. A secondary source of this slowdown in the population growth has been the country's plateauing births, which are estimated to have remained stable after 2017.

Socioeconomic dimensions of the demographic shock

How refugees affect economic outcomes in host countries is shaped by the characteristics of both, among other factors. The economic impact of refugee arrivals on host country residents depends on numerous factors including the labor market policies in the host countries, effectiveness of markets, and other institutional characteristics in the host country. The impact also depends on refugees' own characteristics like skills, education, age, and gender, which determine their willingness to participate in labor markets. In this section, we compare refugee and the host country constituents with respect to these factors to the extent permitted by our data.

TABLE 2.2. Labor force participation rates across groups in Iraq, 2017

	IRAQIS		IDPs		SYRIAN REFUGEES		WITHIN GROUP SHARES (PERCENTAGE)	
	MALE	FEMALE	MALE	FEMALE	MALE	FEMALE	SYRIAN REFUGEES	IDPs
DUHOK	69.6	12.1	74.1	9.5	86.5	21.9	34.9	14.4
SULAYMANIYAH	75.8	20.7	73.9	8.8	75.9	32	12.7	5.6
ERBIL	75.4	19.0	71.7	18.6	89.3	19.6	51.6	12.7
TOTAL	74.8	12.4	75.8	10.3	87.2	21.5	99.1	32.7

Source: World Bank staff calculations.

Note: IDPs = internally displaced persons.

In Iraq, Syrian refugees, both males and females, had a higher labor force participation rate (LFPR) than that of Iraqis. In 2017, the Iraqi LFPR was 74.8 percent for males and 12.4 percent for females (table 2.2). The rates were similar across Iraqi IDPs. In comparison, Syrian refugee men and women had significantly higher LFPRs (87.2 percent and 21.5 percent, respectively). For men, the differences were most stark in Erbil, where the LFPR of Syrian refugees was 14 percentage points greater than the LFPR of Iraqi men. For women, the difference was highest in Sulaymaniyah, where the Syrian refugee women's LFPR exceeded that of Iraqi women by more than half (32 percent versus 20.7 percent, respectively). In contrast, female Iraqi IDPs had a remarkably lower LFPR (8.8 percent) than other women in Sulaymaniyah.

Syrian refugees, especially older ones, faced a greater unemployment threat than Iraqis. For Syrian refugees in Iraq, higher LFPR did not always translate into higher employment. In 2017, the average unemployment rate in Iraq was about 13 percent for males and 38 percent for females in refugee hosting governorates. In comparison, the unemployment rates of Syrian refugees were about 17.8 percent for males and 58.0 percent for females. Strikingly, almost no gap exists between unemployment rates of younger refugees and younger Iraqis. Panel a in figure 2.3 shows the unemployment rates across Syrian refugees (red line), Iraqi IDPs (green line), and Iraqis in general (yellow line) by age. Although no significant differences exist between the unemployment rates of Syrian refugees and those of Iraqis before age 30, the unemployment gap between the two groups increased dramatically after age 30. At its peak, the Syrian refugees' unemployment rate was greater than that of Iraqis by almost 40 percentage points for the 50–54 age group. The age bias in the unemployment rate differential also appears between IDPs and Iraqis in general, but with smaller gaps.

Reflecting an education bias in employment, Syrian refugees were more likely to be unemployed than Iraqis, especially in higher education categories. Syrian refugees were more likely to be unemployed than Iraqis at all education levels, but greater unemployment was especially the case for refugees with more education (figure 2.3, panel c). The unemployment rate of Syrian refugees with only elementary or basic education was nearly 20 percent, about 50 percent (or 7 percentage points) higher than that of Iraqis in the same category. In comparison, the difference between the two groups increased to 70 percent (or 16 percentage points) in the case of having a university degree, and about two and

FIGURE 2.3. Unemployment rates in Iraq, by age, education, and gender, 2017

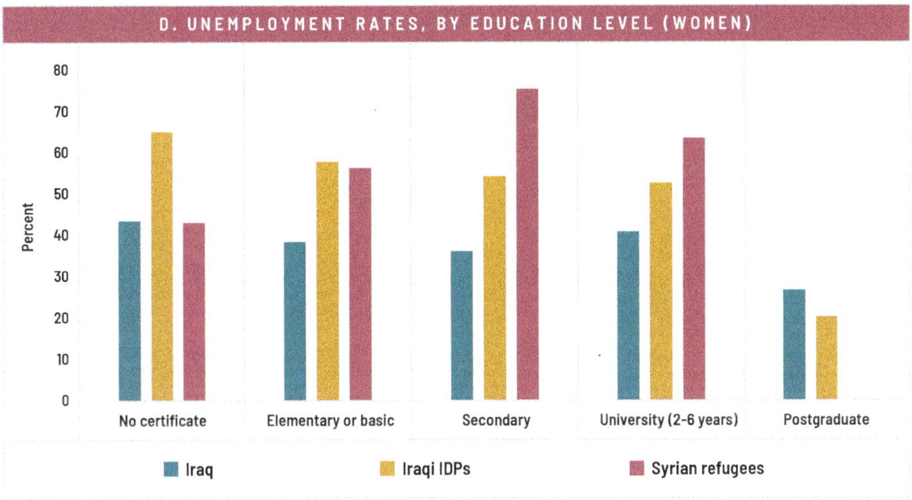

Source: World Bank staff calculations.
Note: IDPs = internally displaced persons.

a half times (about 20 percentage points each) for secondary and postgraduate degrees. The results for women were similar: they experienced a 45 percent gap for elementary or basic education and about 108 percent and 56 percent gaps for secondary and tertiary education, respectively (figure 2.3, panel d). These gaps may suggest that higher-skilled individuals are more status-conscious; for example, refugees may be reluctant to work in jobs that are less skill intensive than their original profession. Without better data, however, we cannot confirm if this mechanism drives the education bias.

In Jordan, most Syrian refugees had lower education than Jordanians. More than 75 percent of Syrian refugees had not completed basic education, and 89 percent had not finished secondary education. Among Syrians, 28 percent are illiterate and only 11 percent completed secondary or higher education (table 2.3). In comparison, about 30 percent of Jordanians and Egyptians in Jordan had completed secondary or higher education. These observations do not significantly vary by gender decomposition.

Syrian refugees were economically less active in the labor market than their Jordanian peers. Overall, almost half of the Jordanian working-age population was economically active, compared to one out of four Syrian refugees and three out of four Egyptians. The LFPR was highest among Egyptians, distantly followed by the Jordanians and other nationalities. The lowest LFPR (25 percent) belonged to Syrian refugees, who made up only about 5 percent of the overall labor force. The meager LFPRs of Syrian refugees were driven by both relatively low male participation (51 percent as opposed to the Jordanian average of 78 percent) and very low female participation (4 percent as opposed to the Jordanian average of 21 percent). Except in the case of Syrian refugees, the male LFPR for all groups scored above 60 percent. Notably, the Egyptian labor force in Jordan comprised primarily males admitted to Jordan on work contracts.

Unemployment rates among Syrian refugees and Jordanians were roughly comparable. The LFPR dynamics broadly mirrored the unemployment rates: very low unemployment among economic migrants from the Arab Republic of Egypt, relatively higher unemployment rates among Jordanians, and the highest unemployment rates among Syrian refugees (table 2.4). In this case, however, the differences were more muted. For instance,

TABLE 2.3. Education attainment in Jordan, by nationality, 2016 (percent)

	ALL			
	JORDANIAN	SYRIAN	EGYPTIAN	OTHER
ILLITERATE	20	28	30	18
READ AND WRITE	25	51	24	30
BASIC EDUCATION	24	9	15	14
SECONDARY EDUCATION	14	5	16	15
POSTSECONDARY EDUCATION	6	1	9	3
UNIVERSITY EDUCATION	10	5	5	17
POSTGRADUATE EDUCATION	1	0	0	3
TOTAL	100	100	100	100
	MALES			
	JORDANIAN	SYRIAN	EGYPTIAN	OTHER
ILLITERATE	18	25	30	17
READ AND WRITE	25	53	22	26
BASIC EDUCATION	27	10	17	16
SECONDARY EDUCATION	14	6	17	17
POSTSECONDARY EDUCATION	5	1	9	3
UNIVERSITY EDUCATION	10	4	5	17
POSTGRADUATE EDUCATION	2	0	0	4
TOTAL	100	100	100	100
	FEMALES			
	JORDANIAN	SYRIAN	EGYPTIAN	OTHER
ILLITERATE	21	31	31	19
READ AND WRITE	24	49	31	35
BASIC EDUCATION	22	8	1	12
SECONDARY EDUCATION	14	5	14	13
POSTSECONDARY EDUCATION	7	0	10	4

UNIVERSITY EDUCATION	10	6	3	16
POSTGRADUATE EDUCATION	1	0	0	2
TOTAL	100	100	100	100

Source: World Bank staff calculations.

Note: Numbers in the table are rounded.

TABLE 2.4. Labor force participation and unemployment rates in Jordan, by nationality, 2016 (percent)

LABOR FORCE PARTICIPATION RATE				
	JORDANIAN	SYRIAN	EGYPTIAN	OTHERS
ALL	49	25	75	38
MALE	78	51	91	63
FEMALE	21	4	0	7
UNEMPLOYMENT RATE				
	JORDANIAN	SYRIAN	EGYPTIAN	OTHERS
ALL	16	18	3	11
MALE	12	20	3	11
FEMALE	30	31	–	9

Source: World Bank staff calculations.

Note: – = not available.

the unemployment rate of Syrian males was only 8 percentage points higher than that of Jordanians. As for females, unemployment rates were equally high among Jordanians and Syrian refugees, at 30 and 31 percent, respectively. Nonetheless, this high unemployment rate for females was especially disheartening given their already low participation rates. The coexistence of both extremely low participation rates and high unemployment rates points to major structural problems on the demand side (market related, not worker related).

Lebanon had a much larger education gap between the local population and Syrian refugees than that in other countries. According to UNHCR statistics, among Syrian refugees in Lebanon, about 72 percent had at most a primary education and only 6 percent hold a degree higher than high school. Compared to pre–Syrian crisis Lebanese statistics, these rates were significantly concentrated on the low end of the education spectrum. Before the crisis, 32 percent of Lebanese held a tertiary degree, 26 percent a secondary degree, and 36 percent at most a primary education (Robalino and Sayed 2012).

The Lebanese LFPR was lower than that of non-Lebanese populations, except for Lebanese women with tertiary education. In 2018, the LFPRs were significantly higher for foreigners than for the Lebanese, reaching 85.2 percent for men and 39.6 percent for women compared to 67.4 percent for Lebanese men and 27.1 percent for Lebanese women (table 2.5). Foreigners included all nationalities other than Lebanese and, therefore, were not limited to the Syrian refugees. Data from the Vulnerability Assessment of Syrian Refugees in Lebanon (VASyR), which sampled only a small portion of Syrian refugees, show that the LFPR of Syrian refugee women (11 percent) was much lower than that of their Lebanese peers (27.1 percent), whereas the LFPR of Syrian refugee men (66 percent) was comparable to that of Lebanese men (67.4 percent) (UNHCR, UNICEF, and WFP 2019). In comparisons of LFPRs across different education levels, both Lebanese men and women lag behind the non-Lebanese in all categories (table 2.6). Lebanese women with tertiary education provided the only exception to this finding. At that level of education, the LFPR of Lebanese women increased drastically to 52 percent, bringing their average above that of non-Lebanese residents with tertiary education. Among all women, only illiterate non-Lebanese women had such high LFPRs.

The Lebanese labor market preserved its inertia after the onset of the Syrian conflict. The labor market conditions in Lebanon responded to economic growth in a muted manner even before 2011. For instance, between 1997 and 2009, real gross domestic product (GDP) expanded at an average rate of 3.7 percent per year, yet employment grew by only 1.1 percent (World Bank 2012a). These rates indicate an employment growth elasticity of only 0.2, considerably lower than observed in other countries in the region. The labor market inertia continued after 2011 with the exception of female LFPR, which grew from 18 percent to 27.1 percent between 2010 and 2018. More recent data show that unemployment rates among the Lebanese have been 30 percent for youth, 17 percent for women, and 9.9 percent for men. In contrast, despite their high LFPRs, foreign youth and women have much lower unemployment rates (11.6 percent and 5.5 percent, respectively) than do their Lebanese peers. According to the 2019 VASyR, unemployment rates for Syrian refugees were higher, at 30 percent among men and 37 percent among women (table 2.7).

Unemployment rates among Syrian refugees and other non-Lebanese populations were higher in refugee-concentrated areas and for the highly skilled. According to the 2019 VASyR, the regions with high refugee concentration also accounted for the high refugee unemployment rates. The unemployment rate among Syrian refugees in Beqaa was twice the group average at 61.9 percent, followed distantly by Baalbek El Hermel at 49.3 percent and Mount Lebanon at 31.4 percent. Unemployment rates for illiterate foreign youth and women were low (3.9 percent and 1.0 percent, respectively) compared to those with a tertiary education (27.2 percent and 24.2 percent, respectively).

Overall, both the scale and the socioeconomic aspects of the demographic shock experienced by Iraq, Jordan, and Lebanon are hard to overstate. In this section, we characterized the nature of the demographic shock experienced by Syria's neighbors in the Mashreq; however, many aspects of the demographic shock have been left out either because of missing data or because the nature of the issue does not lend itself to measurement. Those other aspects include, but are not limited to, crime by or against refugees along with the demand for a greater provision of security services, political consequences of refugee arrivals, and cultural aspects. Even without accounting for such complex aspects, the sheer numbers make it clear that the exposure to the demographic shock was very large in the Kurdistan Region of Iraq (KRI), in Jordan, and in Lebanon. Before we look at the next exposure channel, however, we should note that the exposure to the demographic shock in these countries was not driven by their legal obligations. On the contrary, it reflected the willingness of the Mashreq people to adhere to the fundamental moral principle of helping other human beings in need.

TABLE 2.5. Labor force participation rates in Lebanon (percent)

LEBANESE (2010)		LEBANESE (2018)		NON-LEBANESE (2018)		SYRIAN REFUGEES (2019)	
MALE	FEMALE	MALE	FEMALE	MALE	FEMALE	MALE	FEMALE
71	18	67.4	27.1	85.2	39.6	66	11

Sources: Labour Force and Household Living Conditions Survey 2018–19; Employee-Employer Survey 2010 for Lebanon; UNHCR, UNICEF, and WFP 2019.

TABLE 2.6. Labor force participation rates in Lebanon, by education level (percent)

	LEBANESE (2018)			NON-LEBANESE (2018)		
	TOTAL	MALE	FEMALE	TOTAL	MALE	FEMALE
TOTAL	46.3	67.4	27.1	60.8	85.2	39.6
ILLITERATE	17.3	40.5	6.7	60.7	80.9	52
PRIMARY	45.1	73.0	14.9	59.5	88.5	27.8
SECONDARY	40.1	61.6	20.5	52.8	81.0	25.9
TERTIARY	60.9	70.9	52.5	58.2	76.5	32.6

Source: Labour Force and Household Living Conditions Survey 2018–19 for Lebanon.

TABLE 2.7. Unemployment rates in Lebanon (percent)

LEBANESE (2010)			LEBANESE (2018)			NON-LEBANESE (2018)			SYRIAN REFUGEES (2019)	
MALE	FEMALE	YOUTH	MALE	FEMALE	YOUTH	MALE	FEMALE	YOUTH	MALE	FEMALE
9	18	33	9.9	17.1	30	10.4	5.5	11.6	30	37

Sources: Labour Force and Household Living Conditions Survey 2018–19; Employee-Employer Survey 2010 for Lebanon; UNHCR, UNICEF, and WFP 2019.

Note: Youth are defined as 15–24 years of age.

TRADE

Conflicts can affect trade flows in neighbors in multiple ways, often, but not necessarily, negatively. First and foremost, reduced production capacity and income in the conflict-struck country can affect bilateral trade with the neighbor. Previously traded items can become untraded and vice versa. In the short term, these changes could bring about costs or opportunities for the neighboring countries. Costs could be large if the original trade entails a large relationship-specific investment that cannot be diverted easily to other markets. Similarly, benefits can also be large if the country in conflict has few options in terms of import sources. Second, conflicts could disrupt trade flows between neighboring countries and third countries. This disruption can occur when the country in conflict serves as a transit route for the neighboring country and that route closes because of physical and procedural obstacles. Finally, Qureshi (2013) suggests that increased regional insecurity and uncertainty could deter importers elsewhere from committing to future purchases, which can discourage investors from making investments in the tradable sector in the country in conflict and its neighbors—thereby reducing trade. Overall, the volume of trade could decrease in some channels and increase in others. The net effect is determined case by case. In the following paragraphs, we provide a brief summary of bilateral trade between Syria and its neighbors before the onset of the conflict, along with an assessment of the conflict-driven factors in trade.

In Iraq, the collapse of connectivity constituted the major impediment against trade. The rise of the Islamic State and its control of vast territories in Iraq halted trade in three directions. First, the Syria–Iraq border closed, preventing trade between them. Second, the Iraq-Jordan border also closed later, halting bilateral and transit trade between those two countries. Third, with the capture of Mosul, the Islamic State effectively controlled Iraq's main North–South trade routes as well as the western portion of the Iraqi main transport and trade route—Expressway No. 1 leading from Baghdad to Jordan—because of terrorist attacks and military operations. Trade therefore diverted to alternate routes, mainly via the Islamic Republic of Iran, disrupting business activity in the KRI-based logistics, transport, and trading sectors. The diversion of trade from Turkey to Baghdad and southern Iraq via the border crossing at Gurbulak added more than 1,000 kilometers to the journey and costs an estimated extra $2,000 per truck, according to Turkey's International Transporters' Union (World Bank 2015). The crisis forced the Kurdistan Regional Government (KRG) to source from refineries much further south, leading to an increase in the price of fuel—ranging from 14 percent in Sulaymaniyah to 15 percent in Erbil and 23 percent in Dohuk—which fed into higher electricity and transport costs. Trucks carrying imports into KRI returned empty rather than with exports from the rest of Iraq, which prompted truckers to charge higher freightage for the incoming traffic. These factors led to the decrease in transported goods via trucks from 519,000 tonnes in 2010 to 334,000 tonnes in 2017.[7] The eradication of the Islamic State from border regions and the reopening of Jordanian borders partially boosted trading.[8] In 2018, 750 million tonnes of goods were transported via trucks.

For Jordan, Syria provided a major transit trade route, which was shut down completely during the conflict. Jordan and Syria share a long border (362 kilometers), and the main border crossing point Jaber-Nassib accounted for billions of dollars' worth of trade between the two countries, and countries across the region. Before its closure in 2015, the Jaber-Nassib border-crossing accommodated southbound trucks from Lebanon, Syria, and Turkey, often carrying European imports, and northbound trucks with cargo from Egypt, Jordan, and the Gulf states. Jaber-Nassib also included a free trade zone in which transit businesses could set up shops under favorable terms. With the conflict in Syria and the closure of the border, the number of buses entering Jordan from Syria dropped from 6,866 in 2010 to only 225 in 2018 (Ministry of Transport 2010, 2014, 2018). Similarly, the number of private and public Syrian vehicles entering Jordan dropped from 331,636 vehicles in 2010 to only 8,172 vehicles in 2018. Despite the reopening in October 2018 of the Jaber-Nassib border crossing, its trade volume has not picked up because of obstacles and procedures imposed by the Syrian authorities on Jordanian exports. Although Jordan's borders with Iraq also closed as a result of the Islamic State insurgency, the impact of that closure fell largely on bilateral trade between Jordan and Iraq only.

Syria is Lebanon's only viable land connection to the rest of the world and a major supplier of inputs to Lebanese producers. With 394 kilometers of shared borders (83 percent of the Lebanese land border) and seven official border crossings, precrisis Syria was a vital trading partner for Lebanon. Before the war, many industries imported raw materials and intermediate goods at low prices from Syria to manufacture their products. In addition, Lebanon exported many goods, mainly agriculture, to the neighboring country. Because of the crisis, most of Syria became unsafe and trading with Syrian businesses stopped. This trade interruption had negative repercussions on the Lebanese market: rising import costs reduced the profit margins in industry, and lost export markets reduced revenues in agriculture.

Exports originating from Mashreq countries also faced a wavering trade policy environment after 2011. In the context of the Syrian refugee crisis, some countries have changed their trade policies regarding Syria and its neighboring countries. For instance, the European Union (EU) granted Jordan preferential access to its market in 2016 to support Jordan during the refugee crisis. This preference comprised relaxing or simplifying the rules of origin that Jordanian exporters use in their trade with the EU (European Commission 2016). The idea behind the change was to boost investment and create employment in Jordan, with the objective of creating about 200,000 jobs for Syrian refugees there. Jordan's exports also faced lower effective tariff rates in the United States and Egypt over the same time period. Unlike Jordan, Lebanon witnessed an increase in effective tariffs on its exports, with tariffs in Turkey, for example, rising from 3.8 percent in 2010 to 7.0 percent in 2018 and tariffs in Switzerland rising from 2.7 percent to 12.3 percent at the same time.

Overall, the conflict decimated Syrian trade; however, direct implications for bilateral trade represented only a small portion of the impact because of relatively low intraregional trade. As Syria's GDP collapsed by more than 60 percent between 2010 and 2016, both the scale and the composition of Syrian trade changed drastically (World Bank 2017). In merchandise goods trade, exports decreased from $11.1 billion to $0.7 billion. About half of exports in 2010 comprised crude and refined oils ($5.6 billion), but exports of oil ceased completely by 2013. In comparison, agricultural exports proved relatively more resilient. During the same time period, Syrian imports decreased from $18.7 billion to $5.7 billion, but the direct impact of this decrease on its neighboring countries has remained modest. Jordan's exports to Syria decreased from about $240 million in 2010 to about $50 million in 2018 but were, in relative terms, a small fraction of total merchandise exports: 3.9 percent (2010) and 0.6 percent (2018) of all merchandise exports. In Lebanon, the decrease was much weaker, from $220 million to $210 million (7.0 percent and 5.8 percent of total merchandise exports, respectively).[9]

The total dampening effect of the Syrian conflict on merchandise trade was large in Jordan and Lebanon but not in Iraq. Despite the ongoing Syrian conflict and Islamic State crisis, Iraq's merchandise exports increased twofold from $51 billion in 2010 to $103 billion in 2018, almost all driven by oil (table 2.8). Jordan's merchandise exports and imports remained stagnant during the conflict period with exports growing at 0.1 percent and imports declining at 0.2 percent compounded annually over the 2011–18 period. Precrisis growth rates for Jordan's exports and imports were significantly higher at 17 percent and 14 percent, respectively, during 2000–10. In Lebanon, merchandise exports and imports increased at 1.5 percent and 1.4 percent between 2011 and 2018, respectively, much weaker than the precrisis growth rates of 15 percent and 13 percent during the 2000–10 period.

Changes in destinations accompanied the changes in the scale of merchandise exports (table 2.9). The period after 2011 witnessed a shift in major export markets, especially for Iraq. Iraq's exports to the United States remained stagnant while its exports to other countries, especially India and China, boomed; however, the share of Iraq's exports going to the United States decreased from 24.5 percent to 11.8 percent between 2010 and 2018. In comparison, the US share of Jordan's exports increased from 16.4 percent to 24.4 percent, and the US share of Lebanon's exports increased from 2.8 percent to 3.1 percent in the same time frame. The share of exports to the EU remained stagnant or increased slightly for all three countries (from 17.4 percent to 18.3 percent for Iraq, from 5.2 percent to 5.1 percent for Jordan, and from 13.6 percent to 17.5 percent for Lebanon). Meanwhile, Gulf Cooperation Council countries remained an important export destination for both Jordan and Lebanon, with 2.3 percentage points reduction in total export share in Jordan and 5.3 percentage points increase in Lebanon.

The conflict in Syria has reduced the trade openness of the Mashreq economies. In the few years before the onset of the Syrian crisis, Iraq and Jordan were more open in terms of the share of trade in economy (measured as the ratio of total merchandise trade to total GDP) as compared to other countries at the same per capita income level (figure 2.4). In comparison, Syria and Lebanon were below the predicted levels. As the conflict slowed trade growth, all four countries observed a regression in their trade openness. During 2016–18, only Jordan remained above the predicted trade level but with a narrower margin than that during 2008–10. Iraq's trade openness also slid below the expected levels. The downward shift of Mashreq countries during 2016–18 compared to 2008–10 signifies the overall worsening of trade openness across all four countries, especially Syria.

During the Syrian conflict, trade in services among the Mashreq countries slowed even more radically than merchandise trade. Services trade in Iraq grew by only 8.8 percent annually during 2011–18 compared to a massive 51.5 percent during 2005–10, although starting from a low base. Jordan's growth of services trade slowed to an annual average rate of 3.1 percent over 2011–18, compared to an 18.9 percent growth rate during the preconflict period. It is important to note that, in Jordan, services exports are almost as large as merchandise exports ($7.3 billion and $7.6 billion, respectively). The sector comprises mainly travel services (72 percent of services exports in 2018), which grew at 6 percent annually over 2011–18 in comparison to 20 percent over the preconflict period of 2005–10. Lebanon's exports in services shrank by half a percentage point after 2011 as opposed to the 8.1 percent growth recorded in the previous decade. This drop was particularly problematic because services exports in Lebanon, about half of which comprise travel services, exceeded merchandise exports by a factor of four ($15.4 billion versus $3.6 billion), at 52 percent of GDP in 2018.

In sum, despite relatively limited bilateral trade with Syria, Mashreq economies suffered from a halt in merchandise and services exports during the Syrian crisis. Following the onset of the Syrian war in 2011, the trade in goods and services as a share of GDP declined drastically, especially in Jordan and Lebanon. From 2010 to 2018, the share of total goods and services exports in GDP decreased from 118 percent to 88 percent in Jordan, and from 126 percent to 90 percent in Lebanon (table 2.8). These effects were transmitted not only through a collapse in bilateral trade with Syria, which represented only a relatively small share of trade for these countries, but also through problems in input provision for exports to third parties. Perhaps most important, the broader instability in the region, stemming from the spillovers of the Syrian conflict, drove a sharp slowdown in services exports (mainly travel services).

TABLE 2.8. Exports and imports of goods and services, selected countries, 2000–18

GOODS		US$, BILLIONS			PERCENT CHANGE (CAGR)				PERCENT OF GDP		
	TRADE FLOW	2000	2010	2018	2000–18	2000–07	2008–10	2011–18	2000	2010	2018
IRAQ	EXPORTS	16.2	51.4	102.8	10.8	12.7	11.3	9.0	95.7	43.9	47.4
	IMPORTS	2.7	29.5	35.1	15.3	21.4	41.2	2.2	16.0	25.1	16.2
JORDAN	EXPORTS	1.3	6.2	7.6	10.4	21.7	6.6	2.7	15.0	23.2	18.0
	IMPORTS	4.0	15.0	17.6	8.6	15.4	11.4	2.0	46.6	56.4	41.6
LEBANON	EXPORTS	0.8	3.2	3.6	8.8	19.8	4.5	1.5	4.7	8.2	6.3
	IMPORTS	4.8	16.0	17.9	7.6	9.7	20.6	1.4	28.7	41.6	31.5
SYRIAN ARAB REP.	EXPORTS	4.9	11.1	0.7	-10.1	6.5	13.4	-29.0	25.0	18.4	3.7
	IMPORTS	3.6	18.7	5.7	2.6	21.5	10.0	-13.8	18.2	30.8	29.3

SERVICES		US$, BILLIONS			PERCENT CHANGE (CAGR)			PERCENT OF GDP		
	TRADE FLOW	2005	2010	2018	2005–18	2005–10	2011–18	2005	2010	2018
IRAQ	EXPORTS	0.4	2.8	5.6	23.6	51.5	8.8	1.0	2.4	2.6
	IMPORTS	6.1	9.9	18.0	8.7	10.1	7.8	16.8	8.4	8.3
JORDAN	EXPORTS	2.4	5.7	7.3	8.9	18.9	3.1	19.0	21.6	17.2
	IMPORTS	2.5	4.4	4.8	5.0	11.7	1.0	20.0	16.7	11.3
LEBANON	EXPORTS	10.9	16.0	15.4	2.7	8.1	-0.5	50.6	41.7	27.0
	IMPORTS	7.9	13.2	14.4	4.7	10.8	1.1	36.7	34.3	25.3
SYRIAN ARAB REP.	EXPORTS	2.9	7.3	–	-2.3	20.3	–	10.2	12.1	3.8
	IMPORTS	2.4	3.5	–	3.5	8.4	–	8.3	5.8	4.3

Sources: Calculations based on data from United Nations Comtrade database, World Development Indicators, and World Trade Organization.

Note: CAGR = compound annual growth rate; – = not available.

TABLE 2.9. Merchandise export markets, by Mashreq country, 2000–18

		US$, BILLIONS			PERCENT OF GOODS EXPORTS			PERCENT CHANGE (CAGR)			
EXPORTER	EXPORT MARKET	2000	2010	2018	2000	2010	2018	2000–18	2000–07	2008–10	2011–18
IRAQ	EU	5.7	9.0	18.8	35.4	17.4	18.3	7	7	0	10
	GCC	0	1.3	0.6	0	2.4	0.6	63	145	198	-9
	ROW	4.4	28.4	69.9	27.1	55.1	68.0	17	20	23	12
	SYRIA	–	0.1	–	–	0.2	–	–	–	–	–
	TURKEY	–	0.2	1.4	–	0.3	1.4	18	55	-38	32
	USA	6.1	12.6	12.1	37.5	24.5	11.8	4	10	2	-1
JORDAN	EU	0.1	0.3	0.4	9.6	5.2	5.1	7	13	3	2
	GCC	0.4	2.0	2.3	27.4	32.0	30.0	11	20	15	2
	ROW	0.7	2.6	2.9	53.4	41.9	38.6	8	16	11	2
	SYRIA	0	0.2	0.1	1.8	3.9	0.6	4	37	4	-18
	TURKEY	0	0	0.1	2.1	0.7	1.3	7	-11	54	11
	USA	0.1	1.0	1.9	5.7	16.4	24.4	20	52	-10	8
LEBANON	EU	0.2	0.4	0.6	29.2	13.6	17.5	6	10	-1	5
	GCC	0.18	1.12	1.45	22.3	35.4	40.7	12	26	9	3
	ROW	0.25	1.08	1.01	32.5	34.0	28.2	8	22	2	-1
	SYRIA	0.03	0.22	0.21	3.3	7.0	5.8	12	35	2	-1
	TURKEY	0.02	0.23	0.17	2.8	7.2	4.8	12	27	25	-4
	USA	0.08	0.09	0.11	9.8	2.8	3.1	2	5	-7	3
SYRIAN ARAB REP.	EU	3.36	4.78	0.13	68.4	43.0	17.9	-17	5	1	-36
	GCC	0.29	3.14	0.19	5.9	28.2	27.0	-2	25	31	-29
	ROW	0.56	2.30	0.32	11.4	20.7	44.6	-3	10	28	-22
	TURKEY	0.55	0.45	0.07	11.1	4.1	9.6	-11	-5	6	-21
	USA	0.16	0.45	0.01	3.2	4.0	0.9	-16	-4	55	-41

Sources: Data from United Nations Comtrade database; World Bank staff calculations

Note: For Iraq, with missing data, time periods are defined either as stated or by using latest available data. CAGR = compound annual growth rate; EU = European Union; GCC = Gulf Cooperation Council; ROW = rest of world; – = not available.

FIGURE 2.4 **Merchandise trade openness and the level of income per capita, 2008–10 versus 2016–18**

Source: World Bank calculations based on data from United Nations Comtrade database and World Development Indicators.

Note: The predicted relationship (as the fractional-polynomial prediction) between the merchandise trade as a share of GDP and income per capita has the concave shape indicating that countries' merchandise trade openness tends to slow down at the higher levels of income. The flatter curve of the fitted line in 2016–18 indicates a slower rate of increase than in 2008–10. MENA = Middle East and North Africa.

CAPITAL FLOWS

In principle, conflict can affect capital flows to neighboring countries through several channels. First, foreign investors may decide to redirect their investments or purchases of the conflict country's assets to other countries in the region (entailing higher capital inflows or an increase in the liabilities of Iraqi, Jordanian, and Lebanese residents). Second, foreign investors may decide to redirect their investments away from the region altogether, entailing lower capital inflows (or a decrease in the liabilities of Iraqi, Jordanian, and Lebanese residents). Third, (Iraqi, Jordanian, and Lebanese) residents may acquire greater foreign assets abroad given uncertainties in their region (higher capital outflows) or, conversely, may sell foreign assets and repatriate their earnings (lower capital outflows). Fourth, with the influx of refugees, unrecorded cash may be brought into neighboring countries. In the following paragraphs, we analyze the evolution of recorded capital flows—inflows (increase in net liabilities of residents), outflows (increase in net assets of residents), and net flows (change in net assets minus change in net liabilities)—into these countries.[10]

All three of Syria's neighboring countries witnessed a decline in net capital inflows during 2012–2017 relative to the period preceding the crisis. Foreign direct investment (FDI) flows have been the most affected, and all three countries' average share in the FDI inflows to emerging markets and developing economies (EMDEs) decreased. Lebanon and Iraq's share of net other inflows also declined. Jordan's share remained roughly constant. Portfolio flows recovered after being initially adversely affected, and all three countries' share of portfolio flows to emerging markets rose. Because portfolio investment is negotiable, it allows investors to diversify their portfolios and to withdraw their investment readily. It is not surprising, therefore, that these flows reacted more quickly to events.

In Iraq, net capital flows fell sharply in 2011 and 2012 as a result of the overall decrease in all categories and have been volatile thereafter. In absolute terms, net capital flows fell from a positive $0.3 billion (on average during 2006–10) to a negative $5.5 billion (on average during 2010–17), as shown in figure 2.5. Relative to GDP, net capital flows declined from an average of 0.6 percent of GDP in 2006–10 to –0.8 percent in 2011–17. All categories of net flows (FDI, portfolio, and other) declined between the same periods.

The decrease in net capital flows was driven by a decrease in foreigners' purchases of Iraqi assets. Foreigners' purchases of Iraqi assets declined from 1.4 percent of GDP during 2006–10 to –2.0 percent of GDP during 2011–17, on average. About 84 percent of this decline came from a decline in FDI inflows, and another 20 percent from a decline in other inflows. Portfolio inflows, negligible throughout the period, reached only 1 percent of GDP in 2017. Iraqi residents' purchases of assets abroad also fell from an average of 2.1 percent of GDP during 2006–11 to an average 0.7 percent of GDP during 2011–17. The decline in Iraqi residents' purchases of assets abroad was not enough to offset the decline in foreigners' purchases of Iraqi assets—and net capital flows declined on average as mentioned earlier.

In Jordan, while net capital flows remained stable in absolute terms, they declined relative to GDP. As a percentage of GDP, net capital flows to Jordan fell from an average of 16.0 percent of GDP during 2006–10 to an average of 9.3 percent of GDP during 2011–17 (in absolute terms, it remained stagnant, at $3.1 billion and $3.2 billion, respectively). Net FDI flows fell sharply from 13.7 percent of GDP to 5 percent of GDP, in average terms, during the corresponding periods. Both net flows in the "other" category and portfolio flows increased: net "other" flows rose from an average of 0.8 percent of GDP during 2006–10 to 1.5 percent of GDP during 2011–17 (and were as high as 11 percent of GDP in 2013) and net portfolio flows rose from –1.5 percent of GDP to 2.8 percent of GDP on average.

As in Iraq, the decrease in net capital flows in Jordan was driven by a reduction in foreigners' purchases of Iraqi assets. The acquisition of Jordanian assets by foreigners decreased from an average of 17.6 percent of GDP during 2006–10 to an average of 9.6 percent of GDP during 2011–17. Once again, the fall in FDI inflows accounted for almost all the decline, whereas portfolio flows increased in the latter period. Jordanian residents reduced their acquisition of foreign assets from an average of 1.7 percent of GDP during 2006–10 to 0.3 percent of GDP during 2011–17. Despite this reduction, the decline in the purchases of Jordanian assets by nonresidents dominated, leading to the decline in net capital flows during 2011–17 relative to 2006–10.

Lebanon, like Jordan, witnessed a significant reversal in FDI inflows between the two periods, which led to a large decline in net capital flows. As figure 2.5 shows, in Lebanon, net FDI flows declined from an average of $3 billion during 2006–10 to $1.6 billion during 2011–17. As a share of GDP, this decline corresponds to a decrease from an average of 10.0 percent of GDP to 3.4 percent of GDP during the mentioned time periods. Although net portfolio flows increased from -1.8 percent of GDP to 4.4 percent of GDP in the same time frame, that increase was not enough to offset the losses. Overall, net capital flows have declined from an average of 28.0 percent of GDP during 2006–10 to 21.6 percent of GDP during 2011–17.

Both foreigners' purchases of Lebanese assets and Lebanese residents' acquisition of foreign assets declined, but the former effect dominated. The foreigners' purchases of Lebanese assets declined as a percentage of GDP from an average of 26.5 percent during 2006–10 to 15.7 percent during 2011–17, two-thirds of which was driven by the FDI inflow reversals. Lebanese residents' acquisition of foreign assets declined from an average of -1.8 percent of GDP to -5.9 percent of GDP between the same time periods. This was mostly driven by a decrease in Lebanese portfolio flows abroad (from an average of 3.4 percent to an average of -1.2 percent of GDP).

Several key global events affected net capital flows to emerging markets, but Syria's neighbors experienced greater effects after 2011. The global events included the buildup of global liquidity and vulnerability that culminated in the global financial crisis of 2008; the subsequent quantitative easing of 2009, 2010, and 2011 in Europe and the United States; and several smaller events. Some of these events could be expected to have acted as a dampening force, whereas others could be expected to act as an impetus for capital flows to EMDEs as a whole. As table 2.10 shows, average net capital flows to EMDEs as a percentage of GDP declined during 2011–17 relative to 2006–10, as did all its components. As mentioned previously, the share of total capital inflows to EMDEs declined for all three countries following the onset of the Syrian crisis (with the exception of portfolio flows). This decline suggests that the spillover from the Syrian crisis, other regional developments, or country-specific events after 2011 may have further dampened capital flows to these countries. However, all three of Syria's neighboring countries witnessed a decline in their shares of total inflows to EMDEs. FDI flows were the most affected, and all three countries' average share in the FDI inflows to EMDEs decreased. Lebanon's and Iraq's share of "net other inflows" also declined. Jordan's share remained roughly constant. Portfolio flows, though, recovered after being initially adversely affected and all three countries' share of portfolio flows to EMDEs rose. This may not be surprising since these countries' shares of EMDE portfolio flows were relatively low to begin with: investors may have wished to hold these assets for portfolio diversification reasons, and since portfolio investment is negotiable, it allows investors to withdraw their investment readily if needed. The fact that all three countries' share of total capital inflows to EMDEs declined following

FIGURE 2.5. Net capital flows to Iraq, Jordan, and Lebanon, 2006–10 versus 2011–17

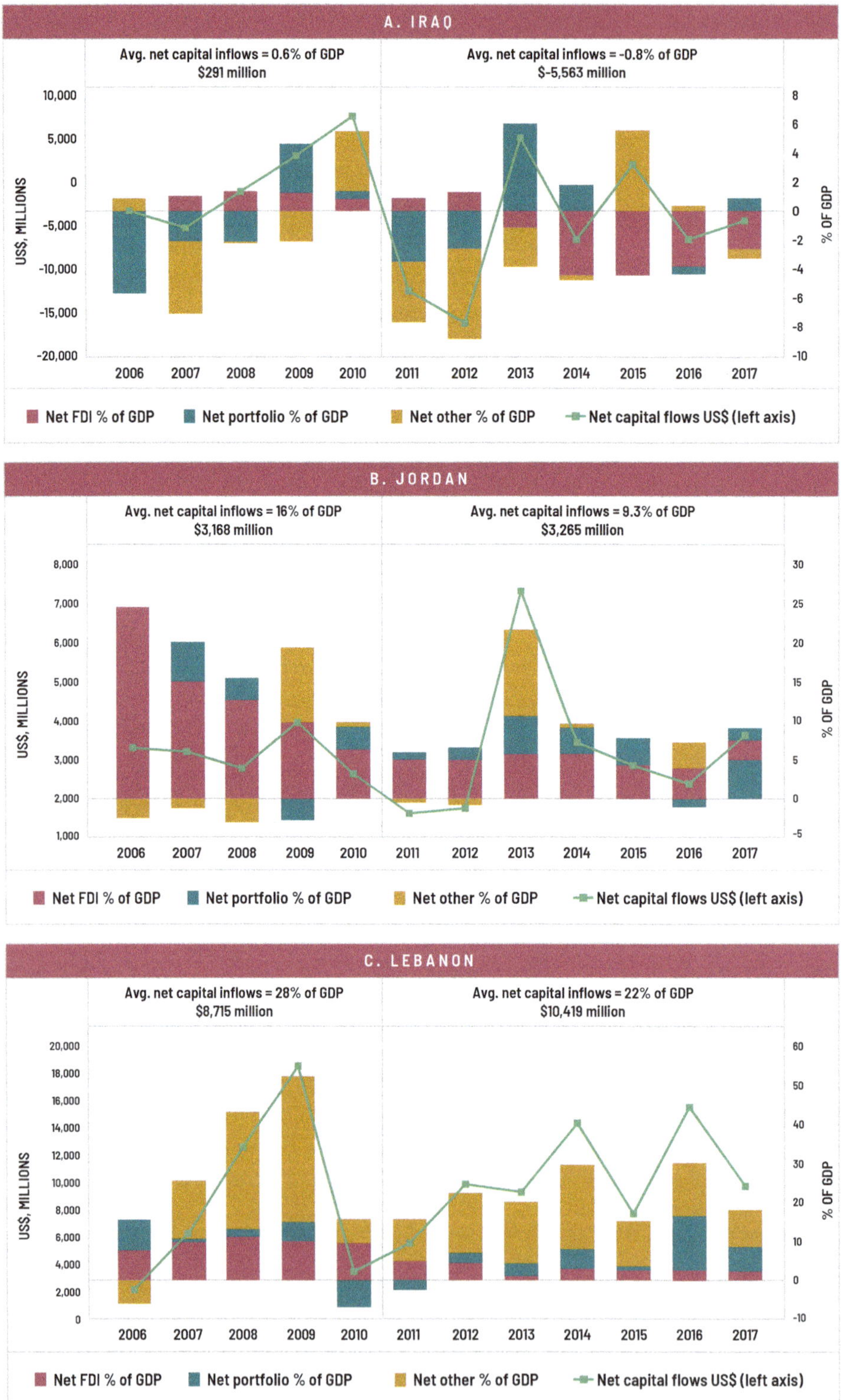

Sources: International Monetary Fund Balance of Payments data and World Bank staff calculations.

Note: FDI = foreign direct investment.

the onset of the Syrian crisis suggests that the spillover from the Syrian crisis, other regional developments, or country specific events post-2011 may have further dampened capital flows to these countries.

There is evidence to suggest that some of the decline in capital inflows to Syria's neighbors was driven by the conflict in Syria. As noted above, foreigners' purchases of Iraqi, Jordanian, and Lebanese assets—or capital inflows—declined during 2011–17. The impact of the conflict on capital inflows was analyzed based on panel data within a "push-pull" framework frequently used in the capital flows literature (appendix B). This framework divides the determinants of capital flows into global "push" factors (industrial country growth, global risk aversion, global interest rates) and domestic or country-specific "pull" factors that influence risks and returns to investors (macroeconomic fundamentals and the overall investment climate, including fiscal health). The underlying concept is a portfolio approach in which expected returns, risk, and risk preferences determine capital flows across countries.

In part, the conflict affected capital inflows through the deterioration in macroeconomic fundamentals. In addition to the global factors, domestic GDP growth is found to be a statistically significant determinant of total capital inflows. As noted in chapter 4, average annual GDP growth rates were reduced in Mashreq solely because of the conflict in Syria. Our results suggest that—holding other factors constant—this Syria-related lower GDP growth increased capital outflows from Iraq by 8 percent (purchases of Iraqi assets by foreigners were negative on average during 2011–17), and reduced capital inflows to Jordan by 13 percent and to Lebanon by 6 percent. The GDP growth impact also had adverse fiscal implications. In turn, this deterioration in the fiscal position increased investors' perceptions of risk and dampened investor sentiment. Indeed, the average five-year sovereign credit default swap (CDS) spreads during 2011–18 rose in all three countries relative to their averages during 2006–11.

There is a negative Syria effect on capital flows even controlling for these macroeconomic fundamentals. The statistical significance of the 2011 dummy interacted with the distance to Syria dummy suggests that other factors, such as perhaps heightened generalized uncertainty, may have further contributed to reducing actual capital inflows.

FDI flows were especially affected. As in the case of total inflows, the results show that the shorter the distance between the capital-receiving country and Syria, the lower the FDI flows into that country. FDI inflows for Syria's immediate neighbors (the Syria neighbor dummy) also experienced a statistically significant (negative) trend during 2011–15 after controlling for other factors. This impact appears to have been more limited in the case of portfolio flows. While portfolio inflows declined initially, they recovered in 2015 and 2016. As noted above, since portfolio investment is negotiable, it allows investors to react to developments more readily and may be less impacted by generalized uncertainty for prolonged periods.

Finally, some unrecorded capital flows out of Syria may have occurred, but estimates vary widely across different techniques. It is very plausible that Syrian refugees brought at least a share of their assets into neighboring countries through informal channels (mainly to avoid capital controls), as they have sought to reallocate into safer assets (IMF 2016). To the extent that they did so, these flows would have been in the form of unrecorded capital inflows into Iraq, Jordan, and Lebanon. Capturing unrecorded capital flow movements is, by definition, very difficult. Studies on capital flight have used several approaches to estimate such flows, but there is no consensus on the best method.[11] Moreover, the results of the various approaches vary widely and are, at best, indicative.

TABLE 2.10. Net capital flow movements, selected Mashreq countries, between 2006-10 and 2011-17

	NET CAPITAL FLOWS				NET FDI		NET PORTFOLIO		NET OTHER	
	$ BILLIONS		% OF GDP		% OF GDP		% OF GDP		% OF GDP	
	2006-10	2011-17	2006-10	2011-17	2006-10	2011-17	2006-10	2011-17	2006-10	2011-17
LEBANON	8.7	10.4	28.3	21.6	10.0	3.4	-1.8	4.4	16.5	13.8
JORDAN	3.2	3.3	16.0	9.3	13.7	5.0	-1.5	2.8	0.8	1.5
IRAQ	0.3	-5.6	-0.6	-2.8	1.0	-2.0	1.2	0.3	-0.4	-1.1
EMDES	–	–	2.8	0.7	2.0	1.5	0.4	0.4	0.56	-0.9

Source: IMF 2020.

Note: Data on net capital flows to emerging markets and developing economies (EMDEs) are from 2007-17. Data on the components of capital inflows to EMDEs are from 2006-15. FDI = foreign direct investment; – = not available.

FIGURE 2.6. Estimates of average unrecorded capital movements, selected Mashreq countries, 2011-17

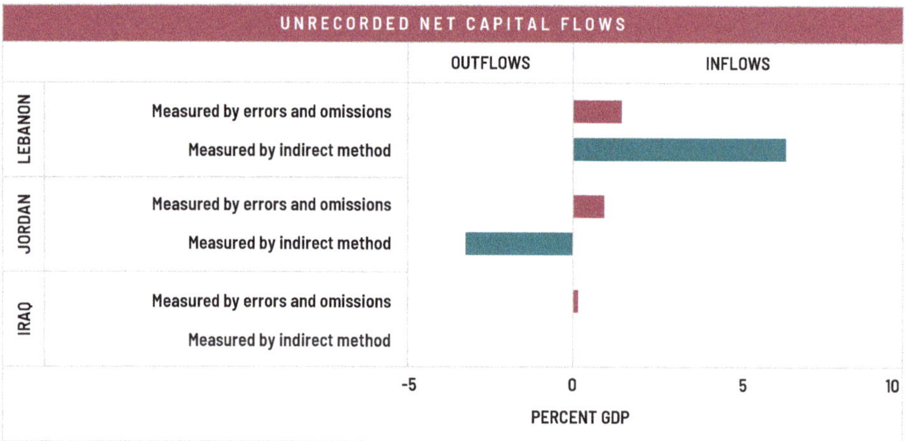

Source: World Bank staff calculations.

Estimates support a positive unrecorded capital inflow to Lebanon between 2011 and 2017, but results are not conclusive for Iraq and Jordan. Figure 2.6 shows the estimates of unrecorded net capital inflows using the two common methods (by errors and omissions and by the indirect method). According to both these approaches, no unrecorded capital inflows into Lebanon appear to have taken place during 2011–17. Measured by errors and omissions, capital inflows amounted to 1.5 percent of GDP; when measured by the indirect approach, they amounted to an average of over 6.5 percent of GDP during the period. In Jordan, the two measures provide opposite results: the errors and omissions method shows a small inflow averaging slightly over 1.0 percent of GDP, but the indirect method shows an outflow of about 3 percent of GDP during 2011–17. In Iraq, we can use the errors and omissions only from the balance of payments, because external debt data do not exist. As seen in figure 2.6, Iraq appears to have a slight positive inflow averaging less than 0.2 percent of GDP.

INSTITUTIONAL RESILIENCE

When analyzing political economy transitions, separating causes from effects is a daunting task. An important problem in analyzing how the Syrian conflict has influenced the political economy of neighboring countries is separating shocks from various outcomes. Exogenous variations constitute an external shock to the prevailing political economy equilibrium, upon which political actors change their actions. Their changes could take the form of a smooth adaptation (for example, small reallocation of funds or effort across alternative uses) or major shifts in the political economy equilibrium (for example, changes in governments or political systems). The mechanisms that generate such outcomes from exogenous shocks differ across cases, however, and are not always well identified even in a qualitative manner. In this section, we will employ a classification structure loosely based on Cordella and Onder (forthcoming) and Besley and Persson (2011) to examine the nature of such mechanisms in the case of the Syrian conflict's impact on Iraq, Jordan, and Lebanon.

As the conflict in the neighbor increases the risk associated with future economic benefits, investments in state capacity could decrease along with an increase in rent-seeking. In this political economy framework, opposing interest groups allocate their efforts or resources between productive (conducive to production of public or private goods) and rent-seeking (unproductive, predatory) activities to maximize their expected economic payoffs. As external shocks reduce the return to productive spending, these groups would allocate a greater share of their resources to rent-seeking activities. In the case of groups controlling the state apparatus, this reallocation would also translate into a lower planned provision of public services and, thus, a lower investment in state capacity to deliver such services. As a result, one could expect a growing popular dissatisfaction with institutions and an increasing likelihood of instability. With this analytical framework in mind, we next analyze the evolution of state capacity, trust in institutions, and overall stability conditions in Iraq, Jordan, and Lebanon since 2011 to the extent enabled by scarce data.

STATE CAPACITY

What functions, institutions, and capacities did governments in Iraq, Jordan, and Lebanon possess before the onset of the Syrian conflict? To answer this question, we evaluate several upstream and downstream governance dimensions, including the following (see also table 2.11):

- *Revenue mobilization and management* concerns the capacity to collect fiscal resources for the core functioning of government and the delivery of public services, including (i) tax administration capacity contributing to both direct and indirect fiscal outturns, and (ii) customs administration capacity.
- *Strategic planning and public expenditure management* focuses on the ability of the state to engage in (i) a timely, transparent, and effective annual budget process; (ii) multiyear budgeting to achieve strategic objectives over the medium term; and (iii)

public investment management, ensuring the quality and prioritization of capital projects.

- *Budget execution and oversight* focuses on the ability of the state to (i) reach desired budget execution rate and manage debt and arrears recording; (ii) implement financial management and reporting at appropriate frequency and consistency; (iii) realize best public procurement practices, including thresholds and transparency standards; and (iv) build oversight mechanisms, including internal audit and external oversight institutions.
- *Core capacities and resources for service delivery* includes the ability to (i) manage the wage bill in a fiscally sustainable manner; (ii) manage the civil service effectively, with meritocratic recruitment and capacity development; and (iii) ensure service delivery at both central and decentralized levels with appropriate fiscal and administrative actions.
- *Public accountability* is a demand-side aspect that includes current arrangements to ensure (i) capacity of nongovernmental institutions (for example, civil society organizations [CSOs]) in safeguarding public interests; (ii) the availability and transparency of public information regarding political processes; and (iii) the larger accountability environment—including negative externalities such as corruption, rent-seeking, state capture, and exclusion.

In 2010, Iraq was ranked in the lowest quintile of all six dimensions of governance. According to the Worldwide Governance Indicators (WGI), Iraq's governance capacity and quality scored significantly below the Middle East and North Africa (MENA) regional average performance in all six dimensions of the governance assessment—political stability, voice and accountability, rule of law, regulatory quality, government effectiveness, and control of corruption (figure 2.7).[12]

The revenue and customs administration had particularly weak capacities after a long history of dependence on oil revenues. Iraq's dependency on oil along with low tax collection resulted in a revenue structure dominated by oil receipts. Between 2005 and 2012, oil accounted for 80.4 percent of total revenues on average, whereas taxes accounted for only about 2 percent (World Bank 2014). This poor performance also reflected deficiencies in the tax administration system, including weak oversight (formal audits absent), inadequate fraud and corruption investigations, the lack of a tax appeals tribunal, and poor performance of the tax account reconciliation system (World Bank 2011a). Similarly, customs administration in the country had become a significant source of inefficiency and corruption. Despite modest efforts to rehabilitate the customs administration, significant deficiencies related to information technology (IT) and human resources undermined customs administration performance. According to the World Bank (2019b), Iraq ranked 180th out of 183 countries surveyed in terms of ease of trading across borders. It was among the slowest countries in trade, with an average delay of 101 days in either direction.

The fiscal budget suffered from insufficient strategic planning, poor execution, and weak oversight. In Iraq, a clear annual budget calendar existed and was largely adhered to before 2011. The annual budgeting process, however, remained a bottom-up exercise, so submissions from ministries were not affordable or aligned with strategic priorities (World Bank 2011a). Despite adoption of a multiyear budget framework, that framework lacked credibility, and the links between policy priorities and medium-term budgeting remained weak. Likewise, public investment management suffered from significant weaknesses, including a limited capacity to develop sector strategies, project feasibility studies, and realistic project appraisals. Bottlenecks abounded at every stage of the process, from procurement and contract management to commitment (World Bank 2008). Budget execution was unpredictable and actual expenditures deviated from budgeted expenditures by a significant amount (often more than 15 percent). According to the Public Expenditure and Financial Accountability (PEFA) assessment prepared at the beginning of the period, less than 64 percent of capital expenditures were executed for the years 2010–13, further undermining the credibility of budget (World Bank 2008; 2019a). Furthermore, the tracking of arrears was nonexistent over this period, because no consolidated system existed for monitoring payments due, which made doing business with the government through procurement "extremely difficult" (World Bank 2012b).

Meritocracy and performance orientation were not a concern, public accountability was low, and corruption was not controlled effectively. Iraq's Open Budget Index (OBI) score in 2010 was zero out of a possible 100, meaning that the central government did not provide the public with any information about its budget or financial activities. As a result, it was virtually impossible for citizens to hold the government accountable for its management of public sources (International Budget Partnership 2010). In 2011, Iraq released its first Extractive Industries Transparency Initiative (EITI) report, publicly disclosing data across several aspects of extractive sector operations (World Bank 2014). In this period, Iraq struggled with pervasive corruption, ranking last in the MENA region and 175th out of 183 countries and territories around the world with respect to Transparency International's 2010 Corruption Perceptions Index.[13] As noted by the Bertelsmann Transformation Index (BTI) 2010, corruption may have worsened in the period leading up to the Syrian conflict, as vast amounts of reconstruction funds from the international community were released and oil revenues flooded into the country (Bertelsmann Stiftung 2009).

After 2011, Iraq's public employment continued to be an avenue for rent-seeking in the aftermath of the Syrian conflict. The number of public sector employees more than tripled between 2004 and 2019, from 900,000 to almost 3 million, partly due to unchecked recruitment and poor payroll practices, including the proliferation of ghost workers and double dippers, the collection of salaries by chronically absent workers, and inflated allowance claims. As of 2018, employee compensation accounted for 41.9 percent of government expenditures, totaling $31.6 billion, and the 2019 approved budget provides for 57,000 additional public employees, increasing the aggregate wage bill to $36.7 billion (17 percent of GDP). In addition to these challenges, Iraq saw a steady fall in the percentage of employees recruited through standard meritocratic procedures, putting the country at the bottom of the scale regarding measures of merit-based public employment relative to comparators. Finally, the decentralized delivery of basic services remained weak all over Iraq, especially in territories liberated from the Islamic State.

More recently, Iraq has achieved some improvements in strategic planning capacity and accountability. The budget–policy link improved and now fits squarely within the articulation of the Cabinet Program for 2018–22, the country's Vision 2030, and the National Development Plan (NDP). Medium-term budgeting practices improved, with estimates now presented for up to three years using administrative and economic classifications, and a public investment management (PIM) Action Plan currently being implemented. Similarly, on public accountability, new laws were adopted over the period governing civil society through a largely consultative process; budget transparency increased, including the publication of regular in-year monthly budget execution reports as well as the establishment and publication of a Citizens' Budget. With respect to corruption, Iraq improved its standing, ranking 168th in the world according to Transparency International's 2018

Corruption Perception Index—a notable improvement from 175th in 2010 (Transparency International 2018).

In 2010, Jordan performed above the MENA regional average in virtually every dimension of governance at the outset of the conflict in Syria. WGI reported better scores for Jordan than other MENA countries, including for political stability, voice and accountability, rule of law, regulatory quality, government effectiveness, and control of corruption. Despite the better governance performance, constraints driven by policy and politics accompanied the good practices in public administration.

Tax and customs administrations were relatively efficient, but policy choices, like various tax exemptions, depressed revenues. Jordan performed well in 2010 on the ease of paying taxes, ranking 26th globally with a compliance time of just 101 hours. Automation and other measures like media campaigns helped improve access and compliance. Customs administration was also adequate; upgrades to IT systems made access to trade and customs data easy. *Doing Business* ranked Jordan 26th in terms of the ease of trading across borders (World Bank 2009), and Jordan was ranked 71st in the 2010 Logistics Performance Index. Despite the administrative reforms, however, distortions to the tax base, created by various exemptions, depressed tax revenues (IMF 2019a), which, as we will analyze later, created significant fiscal problems during the Syrian conflict.

Strategic planning measures were in place, but political factors led to occasional hiccups. Jordan had adopted an enhanced budget calendar to strengthen the initial strategic phase of budget preparation, during which budget performance, strategies, and priorities were reviewed and medium-term spending requirements were evaluated (World Bank 2011b). The 2010 budget was delayed by 15 months, however, as political factors blocked parliamentary approval, resulting in a 2011 PEFA score of a D. Nevertheless, adopting a Medium-Term Expenditure Framework (MTEF) as well as program budgeting with a results-oriented budget approach, establishing a capital expenditure database, and assessing performance of all capital projects, earned Jordan an A in the 2011 PEFA.

Jordan had adequate budget execution and oversight capacities. It received a budget credibility score of an A in the 2010 PEFA. The government produced in-year budget reports on a monthly basis, albeit with some inconsistencies, and submitted the end-of-year consolidated government statements for external audit. The legal framework for procurement was adequate, although no independent body could review the procurement complaint, resulting in a PEFA score of a C+ (World Bank 2011b). As of 2010, there was a general absence of internal audit functions in ministries, departments, and agencies, but a wide range of financial audits were performed in accordance with international standards and were submitted to the legislature.

Jordan's human resource and public administration capacities were good, but exclusion and favoritism driven by political economy prevailed systematically. In 2006, the Jordanian government introduced a code of conduct as a national priority, with human resource management practices at the center of the comprehensive public sector reforms (World Bank 2011b). The 2010 BTI noted the continued existence of problems resulting from favoritism (*wasta*, meaning nepotism or clout) exerted by the political elite. Positions in the state bureaucracy were generally awarded not meritocratically, but rather on the basis of kinship or personal relationships (Bertelsmann Stiftung 2009), with a major discrepancy between public employment and population distributions across these dimensions. Service delivery at a decentralized level was adequate, as demonstrated by the above-average human development indicators; however, the provision of government

FIGURE 2.7. Governance indicators, selected Mashreq countries, 2010 versus 2018

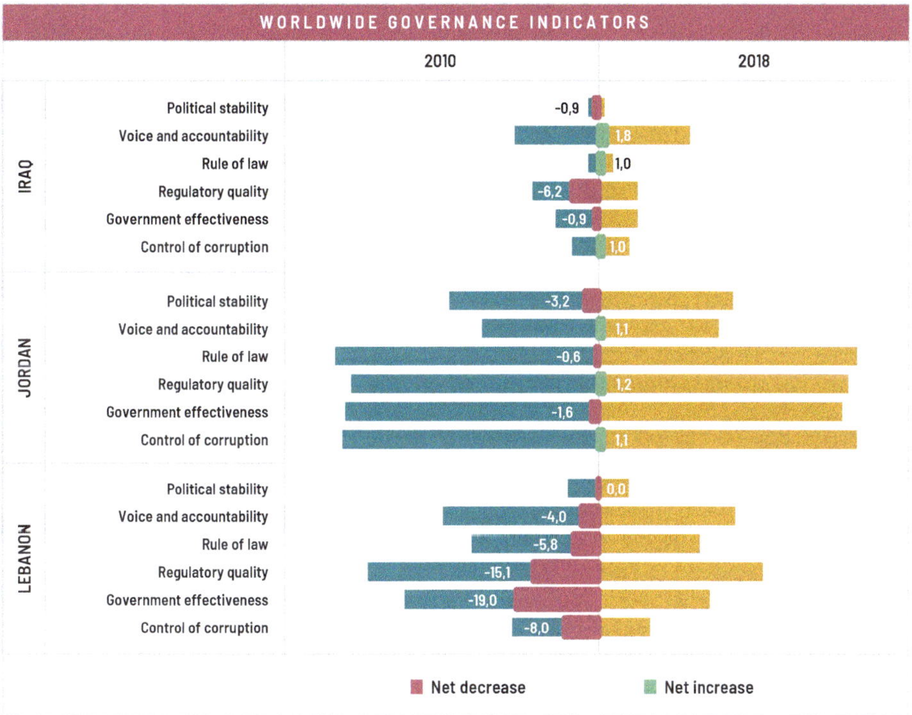

Source: Based on data from Worldwide Governance Indicators, 2010 and 2018.

services appeared to be uneven across the country, with Amman enjoying a favored position compared to rural areas.

Jordan's public accountability was among the highest in the MENA region. Jordan had the only freedom of information law in the region, although the law was criticized for falling below international standards (Bertelsmann Stiftung 2009). Likewise, Jordan's score of 50 on the 2010 OBI was the highest in the MENA region and above the world average (International Budget Partnership 2010). In terms of CSO and citizen engagement, legislative changes and government actions resulted in an enhancement of control over existing nongovernmental organizations (NGOs), including a law passed in 2008 that allowed for increased control by state officials over international and domestic NGOs (Bertelsmann Stiftung 2009). Authorities made some progress in combatting corruption, but still two-thirds of Jordanians believed that corruption existed in both the public and the private sectors. Jordan ranked 49th out of 180 countries surveyed in Transparency International's 2009 Corruption Perceptions Index.

Jordan's public financial management capacities registered important improvements after 2011. Despite the emerging challenges, Jordan's budget creditability remained intact over the 2011–18 period, with annual deviations contained to less than 5 percent of original projections. The Ministry of Finance kept a record of expenditure arrears, and procurement practices greatly improved, including enhanced completeness and accuracy of recordkeeping, adequate access to public procurement information, and competition used as the default method in almost all procurements (however, an independent mechanism to redress complaints still did not exist). Similarly, internal audit practices improved in a limited manner, with internal audit included in almost all government entities but external audit capacity remaining unchanged.

During the Syrian conflict, the most notable deterioration in Jordan's state capacity occurred in revenue and public administration areas. Tax administration continues to struggle with issues related to the reliability of the taxpayer register, high rates of tax arrears, and the low rate of e-service usage. According to *Doing Business 2019*, Jordan ranked 95th in terms of the ease of paying taxes, which is a notable decline in performance from a ranking of 26th in 2010 (World Bank 2019b). Conversely, customs administration performance of the country has improved, with its global ranking jumping from 71st in 2010 to 56th in 2019 and its customs administration score going from 2.31 to 2.49 in the 2018 Logistics Performance Index (World Bank 2019b). On the public administration side, payroll management capacities have increased with the integration of payroll and personnel records. Nevertheless, the wage bill grew at an average annual rate of 10 percent during 2010–14 and has remained around lower single digits since then.

Public accountability in Jordan continued to be the highest in the region, with notable improvements in improved transparency and control of corruption. Although civil society at large did not have an influential role in the political process, many local and international NGOs continued to operate freely in the country. In terms of transparency, Jordan had one of the few freedom of information laws in force in the region, and the country's score of 63 on the 2017 OBI was not only the highest in the MENA region but also higher than its performance in 2011, 2013, and 2015 (International Budget Partnership 2017). Finally, in terms of corruption, Jordan maintained its ranking of 49th out of 180 countries surveyed in Transparency International's 2019 Corruption Perceptions Index—the same score as 10 years earlier—but ratings for voice and accountability and control of corruption improved according to the 2010–18 WGI.

In 2010, Lebanon scored below MENA averages in terms of government effectiveness. According to the WGI, Lebanon suffered from insufficient tax and customs administration capacities, absent strategic planning, and a politically driven bottleneck in budget preparation and execution.

Lebanon had insufficient tax and customs administration capacities, with large scope for tax evasion —as well as tax exemptions—although reforms were ongoing. The 2011 PEFA rated Lebanon a D+ for its effectiveness in the collection of tax payments and customs duties and a C+ for its performance in the transparency of taxpayer obligations and liabilities (World Bank 2011c). The Tax Authority had made efforts to increase its tax collection through the introduction of an IT-based, multicriteria audit plan and electronic payments in 2009. As a result of these efforts, Lebanon ranked 34th globally according to *Doing Business 2010* on the ease of paying taxes, with a compliance time of 180 hours per year (World Bank 2009). Customs procedures in Lebanon were streamlined and simplified through computerization; however, agency coordination problems and corruption were prevalent (World Bank 2012a). Moreover, allegations of corruption in customs had been increasing, possibly revealing an increased intensity in corruption. In 2010, according to *Doing Business*, Lebanon ranked 95th globally in trading across borders, with 26 days needed to export and 35 days to import.

Lebanon's strategic planning measures were poor. In 2010, a key public financial management impediment was the absence of a Parliamentary-approved budget since 2005, which rendered fiscal policy virtually nonexistent (World Bank 2012a). According to the 2011 PEFA, multiyear programming of public expenditure in Lebanon was not a common practice. The Ministry of Finance started to prepare multiyear fiscal forecasts and quarterly updates; however, it did not prepare a rolling medium-term expenditure plan (World Bank 2011c). Instead, fiscal measures and responses to shocks were often decided on an ad hoc basis and outside of a consistent fiscal framework. This practice resulted in quasi-fiscal or off-budget activities, as well as the buildup of arrears and contingent liabilities. Public investment did not exceed 2.4 percent of GDP in the decade before, gradually diminishing infrastructure and public services, and constraining growth.

Budget execution and oversight capacities were dismal. The government did not manage to keep expenditures within the limits set forth in the proposed (but not formally approved) budget (World Bank 2011c). Budget execution fell to less than half at times. Annual financial statements had not been prepared since 2005, and were not submitted to the Court of Accounts, as reflected in Lebanon's 2011 PEFA score of a D+ (World Bank 2011c). With respect to procurement, there was no evidence at the time of the use of opened completion regarding national thresholds, nor was there a procurement complaints mechanism, resulting in a 2011 PEFA score of a D+. Internal controls were weak (with a PEFA score of a C+), with no clear indication of the extent of their application or compliance. External audits were inadequate because they did not cover substantial parts of government and public sector institutions, and were not in line with international standards, resulting in a PEFA score of a D+.

Human resource and public administration capacities were weak. Lebanon's public sector pay regime was highly compressed and fragmented among numerous special statutes, making progression and rotation difficult (World Bank 2012a). According to the 2011 PEFA, Lebanon scored a D+ for the effectiveness of its payroll controls, because the personnel database and payroll records were not linked, no internal audits took place, and external audits were ineffective (World Bank 2011c). Major personnel actions, such as recruitment and selection, promotions, and dismissals, reflected merit and performance; however, the appointment of management positions was generally based on political and sectarian grounds (World Bank 2012b). In terms of local service delivery capacity, the 2010 BTI notes that the bureaucracy remained slow, inefficient, and highly centralized, and plans for administrative decentralization had not been carried out (Bertelsmann Stiftung 2017).

Public accountability was mixed in Lebanon with opportunities for CSO and citizen engagement; however, transparency and control of corruption were limited. Civil society has been traditionally vocal in Lebanon and one the major catalysts of political change (World Bank 2012a). This influence was evident in the 2009 elections, during which the government cooperated intensively with civil society to raise public awareness (Bertelsmann Stiftung 2009). In 2010, Lebanon was ranked Partly Free by Freedom House, with a freedom rating of 4, a civil liberties rating of 3, and a political rights rating of 5. Despite those factors, access to financial information about public enterprises was limited, and the country had no freedom of information legislation or regulation. According to BTI, most integrity mechanisms and tools to curb corruption were nonexistent or ineffective in Lebanon—allowing political and petty corruption to abound. This poor performance was reflected in Transparency International's 2018 Corruption Perceptions Index, which ranked Lebanon 127th out of 178 countries.

After 2011, several indicators, including revenue and public administration capacities and budget execution and oversight, deteriorated in Lebanon. The 2018 Tax Administration Diagnostic Assessment Tool (TADAT) noted that, despite the existence of good international practice in several areas, the tax administration remained plagued by critical weaknesses, including (i) a tax identification number system that lacked integrity features;

TABLE 2.11. Key governance trends, selected Mashreq countries, 2010–19

	IRAQ	JORDAN	LEBANON
	REVENUE MOBILIZATION AND MANAGEMENT		
TAX ADMINISTRATION	DETERIORATION	DETERIORATION	DETERIORATION
CUSTOMS ADMINISTRATION	DETERIORATION	MODEST IMPROVEMENT	DETERIORATION
	STRATEGIC PLANNING AND PUBLIC EXPENDITURE MANAGEMENT		
ANNUAL BUDGETING	MODEST IMPROVEMENT	NO SIGNIFICANT CHANGE	NO SIGNIFICANT CHANGE
MULTIYEAR BUDGET PLANNING	MODEST IMPROVEMENT	NO SIGNIFICANT CHANGE	NO SIGNIFICANT CHANGE
PUBLIC INVESTMENT MANAGEMENT	MODEST IMPROVEMENT	NO SIGNIFICANT CHANGE	NO SIGNIFICANT CHANGE
	BUDGET EXECUTION AND OVERSIGHT		
EXECUTION MANAGEMENT	NO SIGNIFICANT CHANGE	MODEST IMPROVEMENT	UNKNOWN
FINANCIAL MANAGEMENT AND REPORTING	NO SIGNIFICANT CHANGE	NO SIGNIFICANT CHANGE	UNKNOWN
PROCUREMENT	NO SIGNIFICANT CHANGE	MODEST IMPROVEMENT	UNKNOWN
INTERNAL AND EXTERNAL AUDIT	NO SIGNIFICANT CHANGE	NO SIGNIFICANT CHANGE	UNKNOWN
	CORE HUMAN RESOURCE CAPACITIES AND RESOURCES FOR SERVICE DELIVERY		
PAYROLL CONTROLS/WAGE BILL	DETERIORATION	MODEST IMPROVEMENT	DETERIORATION
CIVIL SERVICE/PUBLIC ADMINISTRATION	DETERIORATION	DETERIORATION	DETERIORATION
MECHANISMS FOR DECENTRALIZED SERVICE DELIVERY	DETERIORATION	MODEST IMPROVEMENT	DETERIORATION
	PUBLIC ACCOUNTABILITY		
CSO/CITIZEN ENGAGEMENT	MODEST IMPROVEMENT	MODEST IMPROVEMENT	MODEST IMPROVEMENT
TRANSPARENCY	MODEST IMPROVEMENT	MODEST IMPROVEMENT	NO SIGNIFICANT CHANGE
CORRUPTION	MODEST IMPROVEMENT	MODEST IMPROVEMENT	DETERIORATION

Source: World Bank staff assessment.

Note: CSO = civil society organization.

(ii) the absence of multiyear compliance improvement plans to mitigate risks; (iii) high levels of old and uncollectible tax arrears; (iv) an internal audit that was not fully functional; and (v) a lack of transparency, external reporting, and oversight of tax administration performance. As a result of these challenges, Lebanon's rank in terms of the ease of paying taxes drastically declined from 34th to 113th globally (World Bank 2009) over the 2010–18 period. Similarly, in terms of customs administration performance, Lebanon's rank declined from 33rd globally in 2010 to 79th in 2018. Human resource and public administration capacities also declined further below the already poor performance in 2010. The wage bill continued to grow, with overall personnel costs, including retirement and end-of-service compensation, reaching 39 percent of total spending. At the same time, a lack of meritocracy led to overstaffing, limited competition, and declining capacity in public administration, deteriorating "government effectiveness" and "regulatory quality" as measured by WGI.

Public accountability remained limited in Lebanon. The constitutional right to association and assembly in Lebanon had historically supported a tradition of independent CSOs in the country. Over the period, Freedom House had noted improvements in Lebanon's 2019 Freedom in the World Index, with a freedom rating of 4.5 in 2018 (compared to 4 in 2010), a political rights rating of 5 in 2018 (the same as in 2010), and a civil liberties rating of 4 in 2018 (compared to 3 in 2010) (Freedom House 2019). With respect to transparency, the International Monetary Fund notes that the authorities passed public information transparency and anticorruption legislation, including the access-to-information law, the whistleblower protection law, the law establishing a national anticorruption commission, and the law on oil and gas sector transparency (IMF 2019b). Despite these gains, however, budget transparency decreased, with Open Budget Index scores declining below 2010 levels. Similarly, clientelism and corruption remained systemic, and engagement in petty corruption was ubiquitous, along with the use of contacts for gaining access to state resources (Bertelsmann Stiftung 2017). According to Transparency International's Corruption Perceptions Index, Lebanon ranked 138th out of 180 in 2019, a decline from a ranking of 127th in 2010. This poor performance was likewise reflected in the deterioration in the WGI for 2010–18 measuring control of corruption as well as voice and accountability.

Overall, the negative trends in state capacity were concentrated in the areas of revenue mobilization and service delivery capacities in all three countries. Tax administration capacity appeared to have significantly declined in Iraq, Jordan, and Lebanon over the period of 2010–18. This decline is reflected not only by decreasing tax revenue outturns but also by deteriorating direct and indirect tax administration practices and procedures. Likewise, customs administration capacity declined in Iraq and Lebanon, and remained largely the same in Jordan. Payroll practices deteriorated in Iraq and Lebanon over the period, and wage bills increased substantially. Paired with decreasing tax and customs revenues, these increasing recurrent expenditures represented a constraining factor, crowding out investment, hampering service delivery, and creating incentives for corruption through leakages in feeble payment systems. Human resource and public administration capacity have declined in all three countries since the conflict in Syria began nearly a decade ago. A poorly functioning civil service is a serious limitation against effective response to the fiscal, humanitarian, development, and security challenges posed by the conflict.

FISCAL SPACE

Fiscal space, in combination with state capacity, is an essential element of governments' ability to mitigate the adverse spillovers from the conflict. The previous section focused on state capacity, which refers to the organizational ability of governments to deliver public goods and services, including the soft power of the government—that is, the consent of its constituents. Fiscal space is an essential condition of such ability. The term "fiscal space" defines the budgetary room that allows a government to deliver the necessary public goods and services without undermining fiscal sustainability, including the ability to increase spending or cut taxes without triggering public debt distress and limiting market access. This space determines the government's ability to shield its constituents from a sudden increase in demand—such as following the Syrian conflict—for publicly provided services like education, health care, and water and sanitation. In this section, we will assess these conditions in Iraq, Jordan, and Lebanon.

Fiscal space is a multidimensional concept generally captured using several measures. Measures such as the fiscal balance/GDP, fiscal balance/total revenues, public debt/GDP, and public debt/total revenues can give an indication of budgetary scope, whereas a measure such as the five-year spread on CDS helps to capture market perceptions (and hence, eventually market access). In order to assess the extent to which the countries had built up fiscal space just before the Syrian conflict, we look at the average trends of these measures during 2005–10 as well as their levels in in 2005 and 2010 (table 2.12).

In 2010, Iraq was emerging from years of turmoil and, with rising oil prices, began to build fiscal space. The years preceding the onset of the Syrian conflict marked a significant economic rebound, mainly through the hydrocarbon sector. With historically high oil prices and major international support, Iraq managed to bring down an excessive debt to manageable levels; however, the country remained far from building sufficient fiscal buffers and generating a diversified and nonvolatile stream of revenues.

Iraq's fiscal revenues have depended solely on oil sales and exports, with little attempt to diversify revenue sources or smooth fiscal flows over the years. In 2010, fiscal revenues constituted about 45 percent of the Iraqi GDP (table 2.12). About 92 percent of all fiscal revenues depended on oil. In the years before, this ratio was smaller, mainly because of major postwar grants that decreased from 17.5 percent of GDP in 2005 to 2.9 percent in 2010. Around the time of the global financial crisis, simple rules were in place to build precautionary savings—for example, whenever actual revenues exceeded budgeted figures, the excess of funds had to be allocated to additional investment spending (50 percent) and to build up financial reserves (50 percent). Nonoil tax revenue did not exist around the time of the global financial crisis, although the sales tax had been already envisaged.

At the outset of the Syrian conflict, the Iraqi GDP and fiscal expenditures were recovering rapidly in a postwar environment, with the former growing faster. In Iraq, domestic, economic, and political instability prevailed all throughout the early 2000s; thus, it is not easy to identify the structural relationship between nonoil economy and fiscal spending. Government expenditure (and all its components) were very volatile because of domestic economic and political factors. In 2010, total fiscal expenditure was about 50 percent of GDP. Wages and salaries represented nearly 30 percent of total spending, capital expenditures 30 percent, and social transfers 8 percent.

Thanks to a rapidly increasing GDP and major debt relief programs, Iraq's public debt burden had become more manageable before the Syrian conflict. From 2005 to 2010, Iraq's gross public debt as a share of GDP decreased from 227 percent to 54 percent. Until 2008, the government ran primary surplus, GDP doubled (in current prices), and more than half of the country's external debt, about $66.5 billion out of $120.2 billion, had been forgiven. This debt-relief process was spearheaded by the Paris Club, which canceled a total debt of $42.3 billion.

Management of public finances was a challenging task for Jordan. Given its economic structure and openness, the country has depended on external assistance, grants from the Gulf Cooperation Council, and remittances from the Jordanian diaspora and FDI inflows when the global economy and source countries' economies were buoyant. In the years preceding the onset of the Syrian conflict, rapid economic growth helped reduce the public debt; however, deteriorating external conditions and some unanticipated consequences of tax policy reforms were gradually turning the tide against further build-up of fiscal space.

TABLE 2.12. Indicators of fiscal space, selected Mashreq countries, 2005-10 (percent unless otherwise noted)

	2005	2010	AVERAGE CHANGE 2005-10
IRAQ			
REVENUES/GDP	67.3	45.4	SIZEABLE DECREASE
TAX REVENUES/GDP	49.8	42.6	DECREASE
GRANTS/GDP	17.5	2.9	LARGE DECREASE
EXPENDITURES/GDP	63.2	49.6	DECREASE
INTEREST PAYMENTS/GDP	-0.1	0.5	INCREASE
FISCAL BALANCE/GDP	4.1	-4.2	LARGE DECREASE
FISCAL BALANCE/TOTAL REVENUES	-0.1	-9.3	LARGE DECREASE
PUBLIC DEBT/GDP	227.3	53.5	LARGE DECREASE
PUBLIC DEBT/TOTAL REVENUES	204	117.8	LARGE DECREASE
FIVE-YEAR CDS SPREAD (BASIS POINTS)	454	451.4	SLIGHT DECREASE
JORDAN			
REVENUES/GDP	33.3	24.9	LARGE DECREASE
TAX REVENUES/GDP	28.3	22.7	DECREASE
GRANTS/GDP	5.0	2.1	DECREASE
EXPENDITURES/GDP	38.9	32.9	DECREASE
INTEREST PAYMENTS/GDP	2.8	2.1	DECREASE
FISCAL BALANCE/GDP	-4.0	-8.0	SIZEABLE DECREASE
FISCAL BALANCE/TOTAL REVENUES	-21.4	-32.1	DECREASE
PUBLIC DEBT/GDP	84.3	67.1	DECREASE
PUBLIC DEBT/TOTAL REVENUES	238.5	269.5	INCREASE
FIVE-YEAR CDS SPREAD (BASIS POINTS)	286.0	326.7	INCREASE
LEBANON			
REVENUES/GDP	22.9	21.7	DECREASE
TAX REVENUES/GDP	22.9	21.7	DECREASE
GRANTS/GDP	0	0	n.a.

EXPENDITURES/GDP	31.4	29.2	DECREASE
INTEREST PAYMENTS/GDP	10.5	10.2	SLIGHT DECREASE
FISCAL BALANCE/GDP	-8.6	-7.5	SLIGHT INCREASE
FISCAL BALANCE/TOTAL REVENUES	-38.8	-34.6	INCREASE
PUBLIC DEBT/GDP	179	136.9	SIZEABLE DECREASE
PUBLIC DEBT/TOTAL REVENUES	681.9	630.9	SIZEABLE DECREASE
FIVE-YEAR CDS SPREAD (BASIS POINTS)	324	279.5	DECREASE

■ Improvement from perspective of fiscal space ■ Deterioration from perspective of fiscal space

Sources: International Monetary Fund World Economic Outlook database; Kose et al. 2017.

Note: CDS = credit default swap; n.a. = not applicable.

In the run-up to the Syrian crisis, Jordan had already been losing tax revenues and grants. Following the global financial crisis, Jordan introduced tax reforms as an incentive to boost the decelerating economy. These reforms, however, provided inefficient tax exemptions, narrowed tax bases, and did not avert the economic slowdown. For instance, Jordan reformed sales tax in 2008 and introduced exemptions on commodities, which largely undermined the resources collected. It had several different sales tax rates and a proliferation of zero-rated transactions. As a result, total revenues as a share of GDP declined from 32 percent of GDP in 2006–07 to 25 percent in 2010 and continued to decrease thereafter with regressive changes to the income tax law. The same time period also witnessed a decrease in grants as a share of GDP (from 5 percent of GDP in 2005 to 2.1 percent in 2010).

Fiscal expenditures were also downsized, but this adjustment did not match revenue losses or prevent the growth of the fiscal deficit. Between 2005 and 2010, fiscal spending decreased from 38.9 percent to 32.9 percent of GDP. The reduction took place in all spending categories, but the sharp decrease in capital expenditures in 2010 was particularly noticeable because it did not rebound afterward (in contrast to other expenditures like energy subsidies and pension transfers, which increased significantly after 2010). The fiscal deficit increased from 5 percent of GDP in 2008 to 8 percent in 2010.

With persistent fiscal deficits and sluggish growth, public debt burden began to increase. Despite the persistent deficits over the last decades, Jordan managed to bring down the ratio of public debt to GDP from 100 percent in 2000 to 60 percent by 2008, thanks to a rapid growth performance. After 2008, however, growth slowed and fiscal deficits increased to 9.1 and 8.0 percent in 2009 and 2010, respectively. As a result, the ratio of public debt to GDP started climbing again, reaching 67.1 percent by 2010. Thus, when the fallout of the Syrian conflict hit the country, it found an already weakening fiscal space.

In the years before the Syrian crisis, Lebanon had weak fiscal policy management. During most of the post-2000 period, as well as in the period after the civil war, the country could not put public finances on a sustainable path despite reform efforts on a number of occasions. This difficulty exposed Lebanon to large vulnerabilities. Frequent macroeconomic shocks, often triggered by conflicts and the absence of stability, complicated fiscal policy management in Lebanon. In addition, the relatively high cost of debt, inefficient public spending, loss-making power generation sector, and corruption and waste were the main drivers of a fiscal performance that left much to be desired.

Before 2011, the Lebanese fiscal system suffered from a structurally weak taxation system. Even prior to the global financial crisis, the tax system was already unable to provide sufficient resources to support government expenditures, which had traditionally been funded with both revenue and borrowings. Fiscal incentives and loopholes were used to encourage investment, although not always in an effective manner. Narrow income tax bases, together with low tax rates on corporate profits and individuals' capital gains, resulted in low revenue collection. Value added tax had numerous exemptions and low rates, and consumption excises were fixed in nominal terms and thus decreased in real value with inflation. Whereas total revenue was 25 percent of GDP in 2006–07, it fell to 21.7 percent of GDP in 2010.

In 2010, the interest payment on outstanding public debt was the largest expenditure item, exceeding the public sector wage bill and public investments. As capital expenditure decreased by more than 4 percentage points (as a share of GDP) between 2008 and 2010, interest payments on outstanding debt remained the largest expenditure item (10.2 percent of GDP in 2010). In the same period, utilities continued to be subsidized, particularly in the electricity sector (for example, Electricité du Liban [EDL] received subsidies amounting to 4 percent of GDP in 2009). Overall, the country managed to run a small primary surplus in the range of 1 to 3 percent in the years before the Syrian conflict. Together with the rapid economic growth between 2006 and 2010, these primary surpluses helped reduce the ratio of public debt to GDP by about 50 percentage points in the same period. Post-2010 trends in the country showed, however, that fiscal space in Lebanon was indeed narrower than how it looked in 2010, as stalling growth and emerging primary deficits escalated the public debt burden again in later years.

NOTES

1. The union between Syria and Egypt, the United Arab Republic, was the most serious project of pan-Arabism but failed after just a few years, lasting only from 1958 to 1961.
2. For more on the Jordan Labor Market Panel Survey, JLMPS 2016, see http://www.erfdataportal.com/index.php/catalog/139.
3. For more on the Iraq Household Socio-Economic Survey 2012, see https://microdata.worldbank.org/index.php/catalog/2334/study-description For more information on the World Bank's SWIFT 2017 dataset, see https://datacatalog.worldbank.org/dataset/iraq-rapid-welfare-monitoring-survey-2017.
4. For more on WorldPop, see https://www.worldpop.org.
5. In fact, over decades, the Jordanian population growth rate exhibited three major peaks, mid- to late 1960s, early 1990s, and the later 2000s, all driven by migration patterns. In contrast, fertility rates exhibited a secular decline over these decades.
6. Based on midyear total population, using UN Population Prospects 2019 data.
7. Public Transport Reports (2015, 2016, 2017, 2018) by Ministry of Transport.
8. Public Transport Reports (2015, 2016, 2017, 2018).
9. Bilateral trade data between Iraq and Syria are not available either in direct or mirror format.
10. For the purposes of this study, we categorize capital flows into three groups: foreign direct investment (FDI) flows, portfolio flows (comprising both debt and equity flows), and "other investment" flows. Other investment is a residual category that includes positions and transactions other than those included in direct investment, portfolio investment, financial derivatives and employee stock options, and reserve assets. To the extent that the following classes of financial assets and liabilities are not included under direct investment or reserve assets, other investments include (i) other equity; (ii) currency and deposits; (iii) loans (including use of credit and loans from the International Monetary Fund); (iv) nonlife insurance technical reserves, life insurance and annuities entitlements, pension entitlements, and provisions for calls under standardized guarantees; (v) trade credit and advances; (vi) other accounts receivable/payable; and (vii) Special Drawing Rights (SDR) allocations (SDR holdings are included in reserve assets).
11. One approach is to simply look at the net errors and omissions entry in the balance of payments data. These entries account for the difference between credit and debit entries of current and capital accounts. A large positive balance can be interpreted as unrecorded capital inflows in the literature. One should note, however, that errors and omissions are not identical to unrecorded capital flows. They include true measurement and recording errors and can also reflect unreported trade and lagged registration as suggested by Eggerstedt, Brideau Hall and Van Wijnbergen (1995). A second indirect approach involves treating unrecorded capital movements as a residual of those balance of payments components that are assumed to be more accurately measured: generally, these include the change in foreign debt, FDI, change in foreign reserves, and the current account balance. The underlying premise of this approach is that capital inflows in the form of increases in indebtedness and FDI finance change either the current account deficit or the official reserve accumulation; any shortfall (use of financing is less than available finance) is indicative of private foreign asset accumulation, associated, in this view with unrecorded capital flight/outflow. Conversely, any excess or use of financing greater than available finance, is indicative of unrecorded capital inflows.
12. For more on the Worldwide Governance Indicators, see www.govindicators.org.
13. For more on Transparency International's Corruption Perceptions Index 2010, see https://www.transparency.org/en/cpi/2010.

REFERENCES

Bertelsmann Stiftung. 2009. *Bertelsmann Transformation Index (BTI) 2010*. Berlin: Bertelsmann Stiftung and the Center for Applied Policy Research at Munich University.

Bertelsmann Stiftung. 2017. *Bertelsmann Transformation Index (BTI) 2018*. Berlin: Bertelsmann Stiftung and the Center for Applied Policy Research at Munich University.

Besley, Timothy, and Torsten Persson. 2011. "Fragile States and Development Policy." *Journal of the European Economic Association* 9 (3): 371–98.

Cordella, Tito, and Harun Onder. Forthcoming. "Sharing Oil Rents and Political Violence." *European Journal of Political Economy*.

Eggerstedt, Harald, Rebecca Brideau Hall, and Sweder Van Wijnbergen. 1995. "Measuring Capital Flight: A Case Study of Mexico." *World Development* 23 (2): 211–32.

European Commission. 2016. "EU-Jordan: Towards a Stronger Partnership." Press Release, Brussels, European Commission, July 20. https://ec.europa.eu/commission/presscorner/detail/en/IP_16_2570.

Freedom House. 2019. *Freedom in the World*. Washington, DC: Freedom House.

IMF (International Monetary Fund). *International Financial Statistics*. Washington, DC: IMF.

IMF (International Monetary Fund). 2016. "Syria's Conflict Economy." Working Paper WP/16/123. IMF, Washington, DC.

IMF (International Monetary Fund). 2019a. "Jordan: Technical Assistance Report–Monetary and Financial Statistics Mission." IMF Country Report 19/139, IMF, Washington, DC. http://elibrary.imf.org/view/IMF002/26071-9781498315753/26071-9781498315753/26071-9781498315753.xml.

IMF (International Monetary Fund). 2019b. "Lebanon 2019 Article IV Consultation." IMF Country Report 19/312, IMF, Washington, DC. http://elibrary.imf.org/view/IMF002/28437-9781513517049/28437-9781513517049/28437-9781513517049.xml.

International Budget Partnership. 2010. "Open Budget Survey 2010." International Budget Partnership, Washington, DC. https://www.internationalbudget.org/publications/open-budget-survey-2010/.

International Budget Partnership. 2017. "Open Budget Survey 2017." International Budget Partnership, Washington, DC. https://www.internationalbudget.org/open-budget-survey/downloads/#full-report.

IOM (International Organization for Migration). 2016. "Displacement in Iraq Exceeds 3.4 Million." IOM Iraq Mission, April. https://www.iom.int/news/displacement-iraq-exceeds-33-million-iom.

Kausch, Kristina. 2018. "Identity Politics and Regional Order in the Levant." *Uluslararası İlişkiler / International Relations* 15 (60): 21–29.

Kose, M. A., S. Kurlat, F. Ohnsorge, and N. Sugawara. 2017. "*A Cross-Country Database of Fiscal Space*." World Bank, Washington, DC.

Ministry of Transport (Jordan). 2010. "Annual Report." Transport Planning and Development Directorate, Amman.

Ministry of Transport (Jordan). 2014. "Annual Report." Transport Planning and Development Directorate, Amman.

Ministry of Transport (Jordan). 2018. "Annual Report." Transport Planning and Development Directorate, Amman.

Owen, Roger, and Şevket Pamuk. 1998. *A History of Middle East Economies in the Twentieth Century*. Cambridge, MA: Harvard University Press.

Qureshi, Mahvash Saeed. 2013. "Trade and Thy Neighbor's War." *Journal of Development Economics* 105 (C): 178–95.

Robalino, David, and Haneed Sayed. 2012. "Lebanon—Good Jobs Needed: The Role of Macro, Investment, Education, Labor and Social Protection Policies (MILES) - a Multi-Year Technical Cooperation Program." Report No. 76008-LB. World Bank, Washington, DC. http://documents.worldbank.org/curated/en/230521468089355499/Lebanon-Good-jobs-needed-the-role-of-macro-investment-education-labor-and-social-protection-policies-MILES-a-multi-year-technical-cooperation-program.

Transparency Internatonal. 2018. *Corruption Perceptions Index 2018*. Berlin: Transparency International. https://www.transparency.org/files/content/pages/CPI_2018_Executive_Summary_EN.pdf.

UNHCR (United Nations High Commissioner for Refugees). 2019. "Statistics for Registered Iraqi Refugees in Jordan." UNHCR, Geneva. https://data2.unhcr.org/en/documents/details/72386.

UNHCR (United Nations High Commissioner for Refugees). 2020. "Syria Emergency." UNHCR, Geneva. https://www.unhcr.org/syria-emergency.html.

UNHCR, UNICEF (United Nations Children's Fund), and WFP (United Nations World Food Programme). 2019. "2019 Vulnerability Assessment of Syrian Refugees in Lebanon." UNHCR, Geneva.

UNRWA (United Nations Relief and Works Agency for Palestine Refugees in the Near East). 2018. "Protection in Jordan." UNRWA, March. https://www.unrwa.org/activity/protection-jordan.

World Bank. 2008. "Iraq Public Expenditure and Financial Accountability (PEFA) Report." World Bank, Washington, DC.

World Bank. 2009. *Doing Business 2010: Reforming through Difficult Times*. Washington, DC: World Bank.

World Bank. 2011a. "Country Policy and Institutional Assessment (CPIA) Iraq." World Bank, Washington, DC.

World Bank. 2011b. "Country Policy and Institutional Assessment (CPIA) Jordan." World Bank, Washington, DC.

World Bank. 2011c. "Lebanon Public Expenditure and Financial Accountability (PEFA) Assessment." World Bank, Washington, DC.

World Bank. 2012a. "Country Policy and Institutional Assessment (CPIA) Lebanon." World Bank, Washington, DC.

World Bank. 2012b. "Oil Revenue Management for Economic Diversification." Report No. 69852-IQ, World Bank, Washington, DC.

World Bank. 2014. *Republic of Iraq Public Expenditure Review: Toward More Efficient Spending for Better Service Delivery*. Washington, DC: World Bank.

World Bank. 2015. "Kurdistan Region of Iraq: Economic and Social Impact Assessment of the Syrian Conflict and the ISIS Crisis." Draft Report, World Bank, Washington, DC.

World Bank. 2017. *The Toll of War: The Economic and Social Consequences of the Conflict in Syria*. Washington, DC: World Bank.

World Bank. 2019a. "Country Policy and Institutional Assessment (CPIA) Iraq." World Bank, Washington, DC.

World Bank. 2019b. *Doing Business 2019: Training for Reform*. Washington, DC: World Bank.

3. A SURVEY OF THE OUTCOMES

Conflicts have multidimensional economic and social consequences, even for the neighbors of conflict-struck countries. The previous chapter provided a detailed assessment of the channels through which the spillovers from the Syrian conflict could have been transmitted to neighboring countries. In it, we analyzed the institutional resilience of these countries, which can determine the extent to which such spillovers can affect the well-being of the constituencies. This chapter presents a survey of outcomes driven by these two factors. Specifically, it discusses how the conflict in the Syrian Arab Republic has affected actual economic and social outcomes in Iraq, Jordan, and Lebanon. As noted in the methodology section of the first chapter, however, such outcomes can take place in countless areas, and we need to restrict attention to issues where discussions rely on reliable evidence or data.

With data limitations, trade-offs arise between expanding analytical coverage and increasing confidence in the causality inference. We face a decision-making spectrum that spans a range between many issues with low degrees of causal inference and few issues with high degrees of causal inference. This chapter aims to get close to the first boundary, because acknowledging only the verifiable dimensions of the problem would not do justice to the issue at hand. Moreover, not including such relevant (but relatively data-poor) dimensions of the problem could inadvertently lead to a conclusion that mistakes the absence of evidence for the evidence of absence. To the extent possible, however, we also avoid discussions that are too general—that is, either generally true regardless of conditions (for example, advising to increase productivity) or unable to consider trade-offs between alternative policy actions, cardinally or ordinally (for example, providing a laundry list of policy recommendations). In the next chapter, we turn to the other boundary, restricting attention to the gross domestic product (GDP) impact of the conflict and tackling the causality problem to the extent allowed by our dataset and the nature of the problem.

In the remainder of this chapter, we discuss how certain economic and social outcomes in the Mashreq region changed since 2011 without asserting causality. In the following sections, we survey the developments in key areas between 2011 and 2018 (or the latest possible year). These developments include trends in macro-fiscal issues, labor markets, and access to key publicly provided services like education, health, and water and sanitation, as well as environmental trends.

MACROECONOMIC TRENDS

This section provides an analysis of economic growth performance in Iraq, Jordan, and Lebanon since 2011, compared with the decade before. The objective is to understand the key drivers of economic growth and compare the pre- and post-2011 periods, distinguished by the onset of the Syrian crisis. To this effect, we study the components of GDP growth from supply and demand sides, which helps to recognize changes in sectoral composition and expenditure patterns in each economy. The section includes, as needed, discussion of issues regarding sector-specific trends and macroeconomic policy problems.

For decades, Iraq suffered a series of wars, internal conflicts, and sanctions, which affected its economic growth, social development patterns, and institutional quality dramatically. The country has long suffered from instability, including an eight-year war with the Islamic Republic of Iran in the 1980s, oppression of marginalized populations, a long-lasting civil war leading to the use of chemical weapons[1] and mass displacement, two Gulf Wars, and the recent Islamic State insurgence. As a result of this long history of turmoil, the country could not translate its vast oil reserves into physical and human capital accumulation, and unemployment has been high. Growth since the early 1980s has been subject to boom-and-bust cycles reflecting large variations in oil prices and periods of armed conflict.

The 2000s witnessed the collapse of economic growth and a recovery driven by favorable oil production and oil prices. Figure 3.1 shows the evolution of real GDP since 2000. Overall, the average annual GDP growth between 2000 and 2007 was a modest 2 percent in real terms. With oil production rising from about 2 million barrels per day in 2004 (after the rebound from war) to 2.4 million barrels per day in 2010, and average oil prices increasing from $38 to $71 in the same time period, Iraq's growth performance also improved, averaging 6 percent between 2008 and 2010. In sectoral terms, industry (including hydrocarbons) contributed to this growth by 3.1 percent, annually, and services (which reflects the injection of oil money into the economy) by 2.2 percent (figure 3.2). On the demand side, the major difference between the two periods (2000–07 and 2008–10) was the revival of investments, which boosted growth by 3.1 percent in the latter period (figure 3.3). A strong rebound in imports was also noticeable in the same period.

Between 2010 and 2014, growth accelerated thanks to oil production increasing by more than one-third and fiscal expenditures increasing by more than half. According to the US Energy Information Administration, oil production in Iraq increased monotonically from 2.4 million barrels per day in 2010 to 3.4 million in 2014.[2] At the same time, average oil prices increased from about $75 to $108 just before June 2014. Together, these two factors alone boosted fiscal revenues by half in the same period. Fiscal expenditures adapted in a perfectly procyclical fashion and also increased by about half. Overall, in this short period, industry (mainly oil) boosted growth by about 4.8 percentage points annually, and services (driven by fiscal spending) contributed by 2.3 percentage points per year.

From 2014, oil price dynamics and Islamic State insurgency posed formidable challenges, but oil production continued to grow. Although the Islamic State in Iraq was established in 2006, it remained restrained until the opening of the Syrian front. Starting in 2011, a limited insurgency transformed into a territorial organization, which took control of Fallujah and parts of Ramadi in December 2013, Raqqa (in Syria) in January 2014, and Mosul in June 2014. In Iraq, however, this control did not significantly reduce oil production capacity. In 2014, oil production increased by 4.3 percent; between 2014 and 2018, it increased by more than 40 percent. With oil prices taking a sharp dive that brought the average crude oil price down to $30 per barrel by February 2016, fiscal revenues did not trail the production trend. In fact, oil revenues decreased on a nominal basis (close to 40 percent in 2015) and only caught up with the 2014 level by 2018. Fiscal expenditures decreased more gradually but remained suppressed by 30 percent by 2018 compared to 2014. In this subperiod, industry (oil) drove growth by contributions of 3.2 percentage points per year, whereas services remained stagnant and agriculture reduced growth by 0.9 percentage points annually.

Overall, before-and-after comparisons in Iraq do not reveal much insight about the macroeconomic effect of the Syrian conflict. From 2011 until 2018, Iraq's economy grew by 5.4 percent annually. On the supply side, this growth was driven mainly by industry (mostly oil), which contributed about 4.1 percentage points and presented a more oil-dependent growth than the previous decade. On the demand side, the growth contribution of investments decreased from 3.9 percentage points between 2008 and 2010 to 0.3 percentage points between 2010 and 2018, which follows from a near 70 percent decrease

FIGURE 3.1. **Real GDP levels and growth, Iraq, Jordan, and Lebanon**

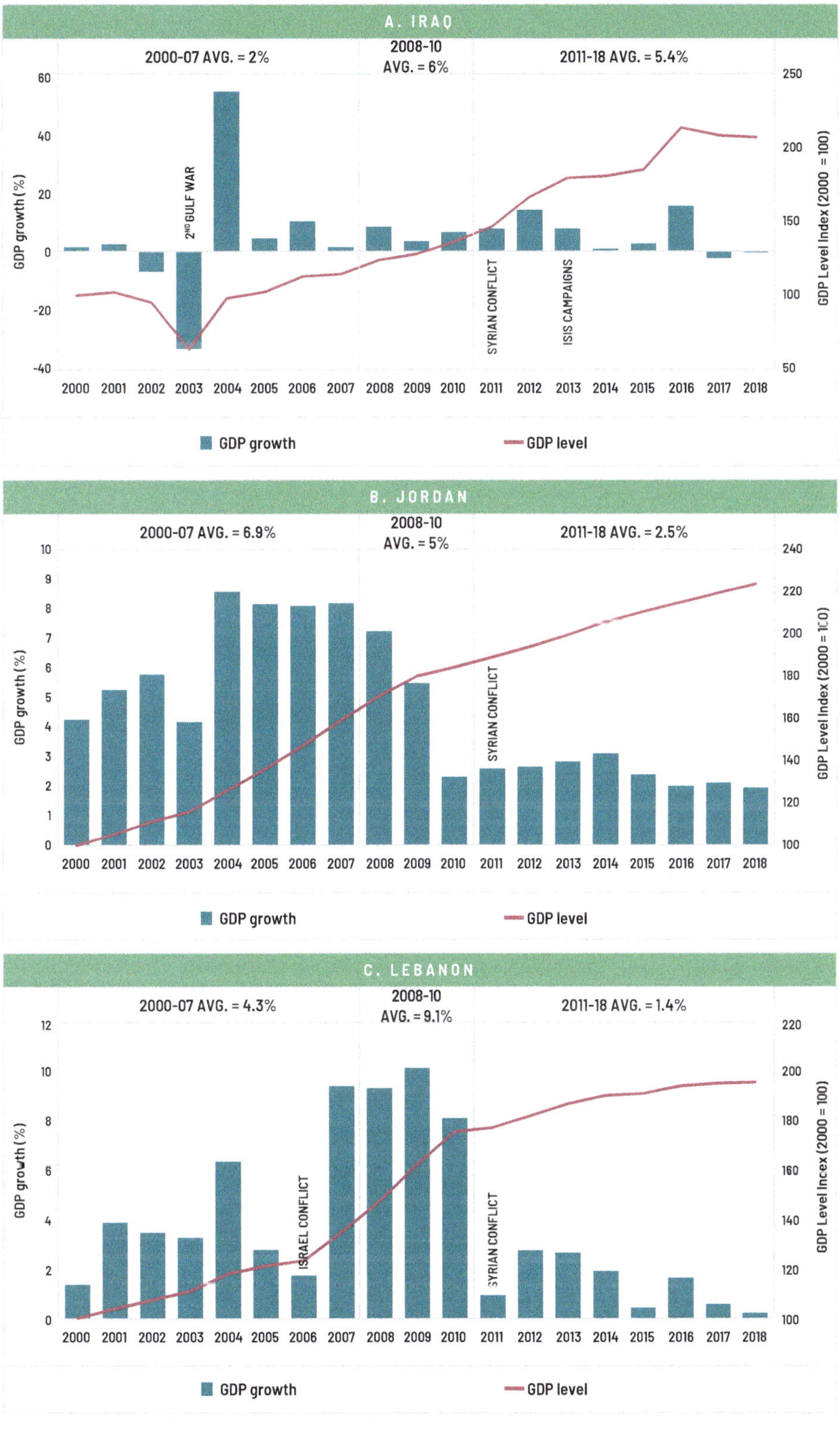

Source: World Bank staff calculations.

Note: Based on the 2010 US$ series.

in the country's capital expenditures in the latter period. These trends result from several interlinked factors, including the conflict in Syria, rebounding oil production, major oil price fluctuations, and Iraq's own insurgency problem. Thus, separating the marginal effects of each factor may be difficult. For instance, the ability of the Islamic State to impose control over territories in Iraq may not have been possible without the space provided by the conflict in Syria. Therefore, we cannot identify the roles of individual drivers without further controls, which we tackle in chapter 4.

Because Jordan has a small and remarkably open economy, its overall economic performance has been significantly dependent on external factors over the past few decades. Sitting at the crossroads of major tectonic plates in the Mashreq, Jordan has historically been affected by regional developments. The country hosted successive waves of Palestinian refugees (currently more than 2.2 million registered by the United Nations Relief and Work Agency for Palestinians in the Near East) since 1948 and up to a million Iraqi refugees in two waves (following the First Gulf War in 1991 and the Second Gulf War in 2003). Economically, it is more open than similar countries, as shown in the preceding chapter, and it imports more than 90 percent of its energy consumption (EIA 2014; Hochberg 2015). Together, these factors have shaped the ups and downs of the Jordanian economy to a significant extent.

In the mid-2000s, the Jordanian economy grew strongly with favorable external conditions. Between 2000 and 2007, GDP grew by 6.9 percent annually in real terms, and more than 8 percent in the last four years of that period (figure 3.1). This boom was fueled by rapid growth in real estate and manufacturing.[3] Increasing foreign direct investment (FDI)—some reported to be capital flight from Iraq after the Second Gulf War but which overall reached 23 percent of the GDP in 2006—facilitiated the earlier growth in the 2000–07 period. A special arrangement with the United States, which enabled significant investments in the garment sector in qualifying industrial zones, made possible the later growth. On the supply side, industry (including construction) boosted growth by 2.6 percentage points annually, and services contributed by 3.6 percentage points in this period (figure 3.2). On the demand side, private consumption and exports were the main drivers of growth at 5 percentage points and 4.7 percentage points, respectively (figure 3.3).

The period between 2008 and 2010 was characterized by sharply falling growth rates in Jordan. The advent of the global financial crisis had drastic and persistent impacts on Jordan's economy. Jordanian GDP growth decreased from 8.1 percent in 2007 to 2.3 percent in 2010. This decrease resulted mainly from a sudden stop in external flows, such as a 41 percent decrease in FDI inflows. Although the Jordanian financial sector weathered the crisis, other sectors including mining and quarrying, manufacturing, and tourism were hit the hardest in this period. On the supply side, the growth contribution of the industry fell to 0.8 percentage points (a 1.8-percentage-point decrease compared to the 2000–07 period), and that of services fell to 2.9 percentage points. On the demand side, all categories suffered losses in their contributions to growth as compared to the 2000–07 period, with the most notable losses occurring in exports, private consumption, and investments, which decreased by 3.7 percentage points, 3.1 percentage points, and 2.9 percentage points, respectively.

With counterbalancing factors, growth remained subdued after 2010. Between 2011 and 2018, Jordan's economy grew by 2.5 percent in real terms, annually (figure 3.1). This period, however, can be subdivided into two parts. First, until 2014, growth slowly crawled up from 2.6 percent in 2011 to 3.1 percent. During this period, in late 2012, Jordan sought assistance from the International Monetary Fund and signed a Stand-By Arrangement agreement. At the same time, it received a $5 billion grant from the Gulf Cooperation

FIGURE 3.2. **Growth decomposition for Iraq, Jordan, and Lebanon, supply side**

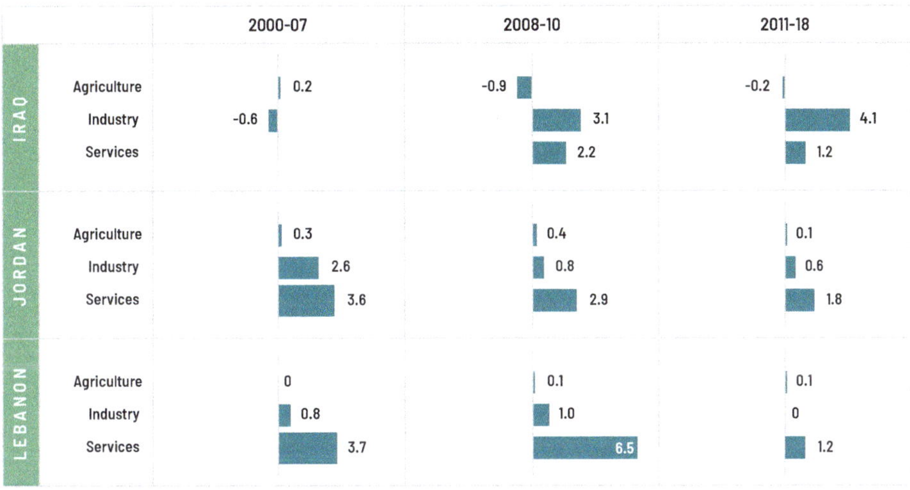

Sources: World Development Indicators 2020; World Bank staff calculations.

Notes: Calculations reflect contributions to compounded annual growth rate of constant GDPs (based on 2010 US$ values). Agriculture also includes forestry and fishing, and industry also includes construction and oil. Services data for Iraq were not available for the 2000-07 period, which was not evaluated. Similarly, Iraq's last figure covers 2010-17 as a result of a missing industry observation.

Council (GCC) countries to help the kingdom deal with the looming refugee crisis (IMF 2019). This grant was earmarked for infrastructure and productivity-enhancing projects. In this first subperiod, industry contributed to growth by 0.8 percentage points and services contributed by 2.1 percentage points. Agriculture remained stagnant. Second, the period after 2014 observed a renewed deterioration as Jordan's borders with both Iraq and Syria closed and, with the collapse in oil prices, the further decline of both remittances and FDI. As a result, growth fell from 3.1 in 2014 to 0.2 percent in 2017. On the supply side, most sectors suffered—with the exception of agriculture, whose contribution to growth increased slightly by 0.2 percentage points. The contribution from services fell to 1.5 percentage points and that of industry fell to 0.5 percentage points.

Overall, although the Jordanian economy had already begun to slow, the Syrian crisis seems to have aggravated and prolonged this trend. The slowdown in Jordanian growth began in the aftermath of the global financial crisis, decreasing from 7.2 percent to 2.3 percent between 2008 and 2010. Proportionally, this decrease corresponds to a 68 percent reduction in growth rate. Although large, this drop is comparable to that of other middle-income countries, where the growth rate fell by 60 percent (from 5.6 percent to 2.3 percent) after the global financial crisis. The real difference between Jordan and other middle-income countries in this regard lies in what happened next. Whereas the latter group recovered most of the losses and registered a 4.7 percent average annual growth after 2010, Jordan's average growth rate stalled at 2.5 percent in the same period. Although we need to leave estimating the GDP impact of the conflict to the next chapter in this book, the descriptive analysis so far offers a number of clues. Complementing the supply-side dynamics discussed above, the demand side also showed that the largest drawback of the post-2010 episode in Jordan was the decrease in exports' contribution to growth from 4.7 percentage points in the 2000–07 period to only 0.1 percentage point (figure 3.3). This drop is in line with the trade analysis in the previous chapter, which found that merchandise growth fell from 22 percent to only 2.7 percent and services growth fell

FIGURE 3.3. Growth decomposition for Iraq, Jordan, and Lebanon, expenditure side

Sources: World Development Indicators 2020; World Bank staff calculations.

Notes: Calculations reflect contributions to compound annual growth rate of constant GDPs (in 2010 US$ in Lebanon and Jordan, and in constant local currency units in Iraq). Bar lengths to scale, with the exception of Jordan 2000-07 and Lebanon 2000-07 and 2008-10 figures, in which the axis ranges (bar lengths) are truncated for visual clarity.

from 19 percent to 3.1 percent, in the same time frame. Border closures have played a key role in this process. Other factors at play include decreases in contributions from private consumption (by 3.0 percent), investments (by 2.4 percent), and government consumption (by 1.4 percent) between the two periods.

Lebanon's growth record was marked by episodic spurts and long pauses in between. Over the past few decades, Lebanon has experienced a civil war, spillovers from regional conflicts, and several waves of refugees. The country experienced two high-growth episodes since the early 1990s, both preceded by wars. The first episode came after 16 years of brutal civil war in Lebanon and boosted GDP by 2.5-fold (about 16.3 percent growth per year) between 1990 and 1996. From 1997 onward, growth stalled, leaving GDP only 30 percent larger a decade later, in 2006 (about 2.7 percent growth per year). Following the brief war with Israel, the economy took off once more and grew by about 9.1 percent per year until 2010 despite the global financial crisis.

The first and the second halves of the 2000s represent different episodes in Lebanon's growth performance history. The 15-year civil war between 1975 and 1990 had devastating impacts in terms of loss of human lives and infrastructure, and undermined social cohesion. Despite those losses, Lebanon enjoyed periods of rapid economic growth driven by its financial sector and made important strides in the achievement of a well-educated labor force after the conflict. In 1994 output growth was over 7 percent but gradually declined below zero percent in 1999. The early years of the new millennium in Lebanon fell on the tail end of this decline. From 2000 until 2005, growth remained less than 4 percent (figure 3.1). In 2006, with a conflict with Israel looming, growth fell to 1.7 percent. Starting from 2007, however, the country enjoyed a rapid growth episode that lasted until 2010, even at the height of the global financial crisis, and averaged above 9 percent, annually. On the supply side, growth in both episodes was primarily driven by the service sector. In 2000–07 and 2008–10, this sector contributed to growth by 3.7 percentage points and 6.5 percentage points, respectively (figure 3.2). On the demand side, the second episode differed from the first by a much higher contribution from private consumption (8.9 percentage points versus 3.0 percentage points), imports (–7.2 percentage points versus –3.0 percentage points), and investments (3.6 percentage points versus 1.1 percentage points), as shown in figure 3.3.

From 2011, the Lebanese economy struggled to grow. Economic growth in Lebanon took a deep dive in 2011, decreasing from 8.0 percent in the year before to 0.9 percent. Subsequently, growth remained subdued and averaged 1.4 percent per year. On the supply side, this trend was driven by a large reduction in service sector contribution to growth (from 6.5 percentage points in 2008–10 period to 1.2 percentage points after 2010), and to a limited extent by industry (from 1 percentage point to zero in the same time frame). On the demand side, contributions were suppressed at 2.8 percentage points, and both investments and exports decreased growth by 0.1 percentage point.

Overall, the Syrian crisis seems to have played an important role in suppressing growth in Lebanon after 2010. Lebanon historically had a service-oriented economy, with about three-quarters of its GDP made up of financial services, trade, and tourism services. Because these sectors are in general externally oriented and more risk-conscious than others, however, when the Syrian crisis disrupted trade and fueled instability in the region, the consequences for the Lebanese economy were significant. In this regard, the impact of the Syrian conflict on Lebanon could be considered an amalgamation of that on Jordan and Iraq. The similarity between Jordan and Lebanon lay in their exposure to external shocks, which was balanced between merchandise and service exports in Jordan but tilted heavily toward services in Lebanon. In comparison, the similarity between Iraq and Lebanon lay in the propagation of conflict in terms of uncertainty and risk, which, In Iraq, took the form of conflict spillover across borders in the form of Islamic State insurgency. In Lebanon it was less dramatic but nonetheless consequential for risk perceptions.

FISCAL TRENDS

Conflicts can affect fiscal outcomes in neighboring countries in multiple ways. All factors that affect economic and social outcomes in neighboring countries will also affect fiscal balances. Distilling the direct and indirect mechanisms through which such effects take place in a simultaneous manner is a daunting task. This difficulty arises because the shocks and their fiscal implications propagate throughout the economy and fiscal outcomes depend on prevailing revenue-spending structures as well as on discretionary responses.

- On the revenue side, all three channels identified before (demographic shock, trade shock, and capital flow shock) and broader instability stemming from the conflict can change the tax base. This change, however, does not need to be uniform in every channel and can change over time. For instance, with a negative trade shock, revenues from exporting firms may decrease, but if local prices are affected (for example, prices decreasing with an excess domestic supply) then those changes would propagate the real economy and fiscal effects to other sectors as well. These effects may be stronger in the short term and gradually phase out as exports are diverted to alternative destinations. In comparison, the arrival of refugees may boost some revenues as the higher demand for goods and services are matched with increasing supply. If a country receives international aid, that would be another channel through which fiscal balances are affected. In the end, the net effect comprises all such underlying factors.

- On the expenditure side, the main driver of change is the increase in demand for publicly provided goods and services. How such activities are reflected in fiscal balances depends, however, on the nature of the provision. If the services provided directly by donor-funded mechanisms or by private providers are paid through such funds, then fiscal balances may not capture them. In comparison, if the government finances the delivery, then these transactions will be reflected under fiscal expenditures (donor contributions could be captured separately in grants). In reality, it is likely to be a mix. Some donor funds reduce the effective demand for services faced by the government and others reimburse the government for such services. It is very possible that a significant share of such provisions is financed out of the country's own fiscal sources and not reimbursed.
- Other factors can also be affected. With the possibility of broader instability and cross-border spillovers of political economy problems, the neighbor's risk outlook can change. This outlook may be reflected in the neighbor's market access conditions and the terms of debt rollover, possibly worsening liquidity constraints and the sustainability of fiscal balances.

As in other cases, "change over time" and "impact" are not synonyms for analyzing fiscal balances. Fiscal balances reflect combined effects of conflict effects, other exogenous factors, and discretionary actions. Thus, the right benchmark for an impact analysis is not the base year in which the conflict had not yet taken place but counterfactual fiscal data for the current year, which reflect fiscal outcomes in the absence of the conflict, holding everything else constant. In the next chapter, we will explicitly consider the fiscal implications of the GDP shock with counterfactual GDP analysis. In this section, however, we summarize the fiscal trends in Iraq, Jordan, and Lebanon, without trying to assess strictly the impact of the Syrian conflict. Nevertheless, we highlight some conjectures in that regard based on the descriptive discussion below.

In Iraq, oil price–driven fiscal dynamics have historically dwarfed other effects. In the last two decades, more than 90 percent of Iraq's fiscal revenues stemmed from its hydrocarbon sector in every year—with the exception of a few years after 2004, when external grants were sizeable. Although the authorities tried to collect more direct and indirect taxes after the oil price collapse in 2014, the share of those taxes in the fiscal budget remained in the lower single digits in percentage terms. Average annual revenue decreased by 10.7 percentage points between 2008–10 and 2011–19, led by decreasing grants (by 5 percentage points) and commodity-related revenues (by 6 percentage points) following the oil price trajectory, all as shares of GDP (table 3.1). It appears that neither the onset of the Syrian conflict nor the escalation of the Islamic State insurgency led to a break in fiscal revenues, and oil sector dynamics were the dominant factor. Whereas oil production was stagnant between 2008 and 2010 (increasing by less than 1 percent annually), it increased by 7 percent per year between 2010 and 2014 and accelerated to 9.3 percent starting from 2014. Because prices decreased faster after 2014, however, the overall fiscal take from oil production decreased anyway.

TABLE 3.1. Main fiscal trends across key episodes, Iraq, Jordan, and Lebanon (percent of GDP unless otherwise noted)

	2000–07	2008–10	2011–19
IRAQ			
REVENUES	60.8	49.3	38.6
O/W TAXES ON INCOME, PROFITS, AND CAPITAL GAINS	0.4	0.7	0.8
TAXES ON GOODS AND SERVICES AND INT'L. TRANSACTIONS	0.3	0.4	0.7
GRANTS	10.1	5.0	0.1
COMMODITY-RELATED AND OTHER REVENUES	49.9	43.3	37.0
EXPENDITURES	53.2	55.3	41.4
O/W COMPENSATION OF EMPLOYEES	9.3	14.3	13.9
SOCIAL BENEFITS	3.0	3.2	3.7
INTEREST PAYMENTS	-0.2	0.2	0.7
CAPITAL EXPENDITURE	11.9	16.2	12.5
FISCAL BALANCE	7.5	-5.9	-2.9
PUBLIC DEBT	162.5	71.7	46.8
NOMINAL GDP GROWTH (PERCENT, CURRENT LCU SERIES)	23.1	13.3	5.6
JORDAN			
REVENUES	32.4	27.1	25.4
O/W TAXES ON INCOME, PROFITS, AND CAPITAL GAINS	3.1	3.9	3.2
TAXES ON GOODS AND SERVICES AND INT'L. TRANSACTIONS	14.3	13.0	12.6
GRANTS	5.9	2.9	3.2
COMMODITY-RELATED AND OTHER REVENUES	9.1	7.4	6.5
EXPENDITURES	36.2	34.6	32.9
O/W COMPENSATION OF EMPLOYEES	5.6	4.6	5.0
SOCIAL BENEFITS	5.7	5.4	6.8
INTEREST PAYMENTS	3.3	2.2	3.0
CAPITAL EXPENDITURE	6.8	6.3	4.0
FISCAL BALANCE	-3.8	-7.4	-7.5

PUBLIC DEBT	90.3	64.0	88.0
NOMINAL GDP GROWTH (PERCENT, CURRENT US$)	10.6	15.6	5.9
LEBANON			
REVENUES	22.0	23.3	21.0
O/W TAXES ON INCOME, PROFITS, AND CAPITAL GAINS	3.9	4.5	5.7
TAXES ON GOODS AND SERVICES AND INT'L. TRANSACTIONS	12.7	13.7	10.6
GRANTS	0.8	0.5	0.0
COMMODITY-RELATED AND OTHER REVENUES	4.6	4.7	4.8
EXPENDITURES	36.4	31.8	29.4
O/W COMPENSATION OF EMPLOYEES	10.4	9.0	10.0
SOCIAL BENEFITS	0.3	0.3	0.2
INTEREST PAYMENTS	14.3	10.8	9.0
CAPITAL EXPENDITURE	10.9	11.2	9.7
FISCAL BALANCE	-14.4	-8.5	-8.3
PUBLIC DEBT	168.3	147.3	142.2
NOMINAL GDP GROWTH (PERCENT, CURRENT US$)	5.6	15.6	4.8

Source: International Monetary Fund World Economic Outlook Database.

Note: In Iraq, the first column shows averages of 2005-07, because values before 2005 are missing or unreliable. LCU = local currency unit; INT'L. = international; o/w = of which.

The fall in oil and fiscal revenues was matched by an equally large decrease in fiscal expenditures. Average annual expenditures as a share of GDP declined by 14 percentage points between 2008–10 and 2011–19, driven mainly by contractions in spending for goods and services (6 percentage points) and capital expenditures (3.7 percentage points). Consequently, fiscal outturns, expressed as primary and fiscal deficit as a share of GDP, improved between 2008–10 and 2011–19, from 5.8 percent and 5.9 percent of GDP to 2.1 percent and 2.9 percent, respectively.

Iraq's public debt stock decreased dramatically before 2010 but remained stable afterward. From 2007 to 2010, Iraq's public debt stock decreased by 63.6 percentage points, from 117.1 percent of GDP to 53.5 percent. About 45 percentage points of this reduction was due to debt relief and forgiveness (figure 3.4). Real GDP growth reduced the debt-to-GDP ratio by another 14.4 percentage points, and primary deficits increased it by 17.3 percentage points. In comparison, the debt-to-GDP ratio did not change much after 2011 with contributions from higher real GDP growth (decreasing the debt-to-GDP ratio by 20.3 percentage points) and higher primary deficits (increasing the debt-to-GDP ratio by 19.3 percentage points) largely offsetting each other. Contributions from other factors remained small.

FIGURE 3.4. **Contributions to change in debt-to-GDP ratio, Iraq, Jordan, and Lebanon**

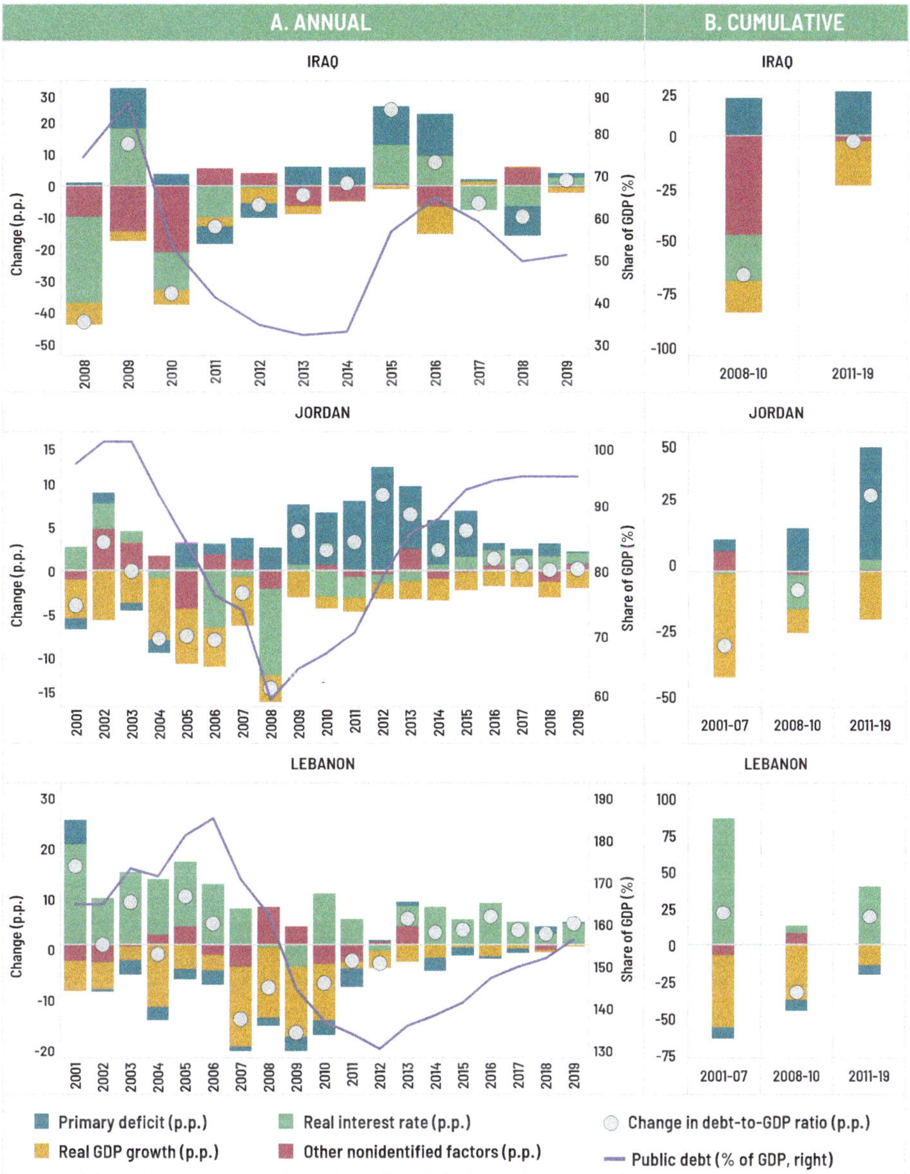

Source: World Bank staff calculations.

Note: Debt dynamics decomposition considers the following: (i) net borrowing to fund the budget deficit (including the primary balance and total interest payments on previously accumulated debt); (ii) net borrowing to fund other funding needs; and (iii) valuation effects resulting from exchange rate movements. The annual change in the debt-to-GDP ratio is given by:

$$d_t - d_{t-1} = pd_t + \frac{i_t - \pi_t + g_t\pi_t}{(1+g_t)(1+\pi_t)}d_{t-1} - \frac{g_t}{(1+g_t)(1+\pi_t)}d_{t-1} + of_t$$

where *pd* is primary deficit, the second term is the contribution of the real interest rate (i-π), the third term is the contribution of the real GDP growth (g), and the fourth term (of) captures other funding needs and the valuation effect (which is zero for countries with fixed parities). p.p. = percentage point.

In Jordan, management of public finances has been a challenge for policy makers over the past two decades, with fiscal balances in the red in every year. When the economy was growing rapidly thanks to favorable external flows, including grants, remittances, and FDI inflows in a buoyant global economy context in the mid-2000s, this deficit was not a problem. It became a problem, however, when the Jordanian economy slowed in the aftermath of the global financial crisis and subsequently entered an extended period of growth suppression in the wake of the Syrian crisis and associated regional turmoil.

Jordan's fiscal revenues decreased drastically between the 2000s and 2010s. In Jordan, tax collection, particularly indirect tax generated by international trade, is a main revenue component and fluctuates with external shocks. Similarly, the grant component of revenues has historically been high compared to other countries. Between the two episodes of interest, 2000–07 and 2011–19, average annual revenues as a share of GDP declined by 7 percentage points. This decline was led by falling grants (by 3 percentage points as a share of GDP), contraction of other revenues (by 2.5 percentage points), and decreasing indirect taxes (by 1.8 percentage points) driven by the expansion of tax exemptions and subsequently reduced tax base from 2008 onward (table 3.1).

Primary expenditures adjusted with a lag, generating large deficits between 2009 and 2015. Primary expenditures averaged from 32.9 percent of GDP in 2000–07 to 32.3 percent in 2008–10. The latter period, however, comprises two distinct episodes, with expenditures remaining well above revenues until 2015 and then, starting from 2016, a large consolidation program taking place, led by adjustments in other current expenditures like subsidies and capital expenditures. During this process, the public sector wage bill and social transfers did not decrease. Overall, the consolidation helped to stabilize the persistent fiscal deficit, which averaged 10.4 percent between 2011 and 2015 (more than 6 percentage points higher than the decade before) and brought it down to a range of 3–4 percent by the end of the decade.

Rapid growth had reduced the debt-to-GDP ratio in the 2000s; however, with sluggish growth and large deficits until 2015, the debt stock bounced it back in the 2010s. Public debt stock fell by 26.7 percentage points, from 100.5 percent of GDP in 2000 to 73.8 percent in 2007, and by another 6.7 percent between 2008 and 2010. The primary driver of these reductions was the real GDP growth, which led to a 37.4-percentage-point reduction in the former period and an 8.5-percentage-point reduction in the latter period, both in cumulative terms (figure 3.4). Primary deficits added to the debt-to-GDP ratio in these periods by 4.2 percentage points (2000–07) and 15.5 percentage points (2008–10). Between 2008 and 2010, decreases in real interest rates driven by the global financial crisis also reduced the debt-to-GDP ratio by 12.4 percentage points. After 2010, the debt-reducing effect of real GDP growth shrank to 17.3 percent. At the same time, increasing primary deficits increased the debt-to-GDP ratio by another 40.5 percentage points. As a result, public debt increased from 67 percent of GDP in 2010 to 94 percent by 2019 (World Bank 2017a).

Overall, the fiscal trends in Jordan would suggest that it was affected by the Syrian conflict. The analysis in this section shows that Jordan's fiscal deterioration began after the onset of the global financial crisis when growth slowed down significantly, and revenues shrank even faster as grants decreased and the tax base was cut after extended exemptions. Nevertheless, the Syrian conflict seems to have played an important role in two ways: (i) by suppressing economic growth for an extended of period and (ii) by making it more difficult for authorities to cut expenditures in light of increasing regional uncertainties after 2011. It is difficult to quantify the latter effect; however, we estimate the first effect in chapter 4.

Lebanon has long carried a burden of public debt. The country entered the new millennium with a debt burden that exceeded 160 percent of its GDP. Since 2000, the government has run primary surpluses in most years, yet these were not large enough to reduce the burden significantly. In the second half of the 2000s, the above-average growth rates brought down the debt burden to nearly 130 percent of GDP, but after that, with slower growth and heavy debt service obligations, the debt-to-GDP ratio picked up again. In fact, interest payments were so large that they often exceeded either the public sector wage bill or capital expenditures; in 8 of the past 20 years, interest payments exceeded both and become the largest spending item in public expenditures.

Fiscal revenues have been stable at a relatively low share of GDP. In Lebanon, tax collection, particularly indirect taxes including sales taxes and taxes on international trade, is the main source of revenue (representing nearly half of total revenue) and is sensitive to external shocks. Average annual revenues increased from 22 percent of GDP in 2000–07 to 23.3 percent in 2008–10. This decline was due to reductions in indirect taxes (falling by 2.5 percentage points) and grants (0.9 percentage points), which were partially offset by an increase in direct taxes of about 1.7 percentage points.

Whereas primary expenditure remained roughly the same across the last two decades, interest payments decreased significantly with lower nominal interest rates. In Lebanon, the public wage bill and capital expenditures jointly explain about two-thirds of total expenditures and have been relatively stable (table 3.1). Primary expenditures averaged 22.1 percent of GDP in 2000–07, 21 percent in 2008–10, and 20.4 percent in 2011–19. Interest payments dropped significantly from an average of 14.3 percent of GDP in 2000–07 to 10.8 percent in 2008–10 and 9 percent in 2011–19, owing to lower nominal interest rates; however, public debt stayed at high levels across the periods. Because the interest rate–driven decrease in expenditures more than offset the small decrease in fiscal revenues, the fiscal deficit decreased from 14.4 percent of GDP in 2000–07 to 8.5 percent in 2008–10 and to 8.3 percent in 2011–19, all in average terms.

After a short period of growth-driven reduction in the preceding years, the ratio of public debt to GDP took an upward trend in the last decade. Between 2000 and 2007, public debt stock increased by 20.8 percentage points, from 148.2 percent of GDP to 169 percent. This increase was driven mainly by the real interest rate (+83.6 percentage points), which was compounded by high outstanding public debt and low inflation rates (figure 3.4). During the high-growth years between 2008 and 2010, it took a downturn and decreased by 32.1 percent of GDP and reached 136.9 percent in 2010. In these three years alone, GDP growth reduced the debt burden as much as in the seven years of the 2000–07 period and the nine years of the 2010–19 period. With subdued growth after 2010, the debt-to-GDP ratio increased by 18.2 percentage points and the real interest rate added another 38.2 percentage points, bringing the debt burden to 155 percent in 2019.

As in the case of Jordan, the Syrian conflict seems to have aggravated and prolonged the prevailing structural problems in Lebanon's fiscal balances. Public debt in Lebanon has overwhelmed the country's fiscal balances for decades. A previous assessment attributed these conditions to the political gridlock and excessive rent-seeking that have left the Lebanese state apparatus hollowed and paralyzed and the country's markets underdeveloped. As the onset of the Syrian conflict increased regional instability and magnified short-termism among all key players, these dynamics could only worsen. Thus, such a political economy channel is likely to reinforce the more obvious growth-suppression channel of the conflict in explaining the impact of the Syrian conflict on fiscal balances.

LABOR MARKET TRENDS

The conflict in Syria could potentially have multifaceted and dramatic consequences for labor markets in the Mashreq. All three channels of transmission—namely trade, capital flows, and refugee arrivals—could significantly influence labor market outcomes in Iraq, Jordan, and Lebanon. Decreased demand for these countries' exports (or greater trade costs) could depress economic performance in export-oriented sectors (and other sectors through input-output links), which would then reduce demand for labor, potentially leading to unemployment, lower wages, or both. Similarly, concerns regarding security and stability in the region could depress economic activity and labor demand throughout the economy. In comparison, refugee arrivals could potentially have more nuanced effects. Alix-Garcia, Artuc, and Onder (2017) provide an overview of different channels through which refugee arrivals could influence labor markets (and welfare), specifically,

- *As consumers* whose consumption is typically financed by wages and transfers (international aid, remittances, or both), refugees could create increased demand for goods and services. To the extent that these goods and services are nontradable (that is, cannot be fully and immediately imported from abroad), their prices would increase in the short term, and supply would increase in the medium term as a result. These dynamics would increase labor demand in these sectors and lead to an increase in wages of skills used more intensively in these sectors.

- *As workers*, refugees may compete with host country members for jobs, and with a greater labor supply, equilibrium wages may decrease or unemployment may increase. The magnitude of these effects would depend, however, on skill composition and regulations. For instance, if refugees are proportionately more unskilled than host community workers, the unskilled host community workers would face a greater impact through the labor supply channel.

- *The net effect* of refugee arrivals on host community workers' employment and real wages would be determined by both the demand and supply sides of the labor market dynamics. It is certainly possible that some host community workers may lose jobs or purchasing power while others gain them.

Labor market changes in Iraq, Jordan, and Lebanon since 2011 reflect a synthesis of effects (in all channels) driven by the Syrian conflict as well as global, regional, and local factors. In the following paragraphs, we analyze the changes in labor market conditions in Iraq and Jordan (for Lebanon, we did not have access to microdata for conducting change analysis) since the onset of the Syrian conflict. Attributing these changes to a specific underlying cause, however, is not always possible. In the case of refugee arrivals, we compare different subnational areas to infer if exposure to refugee shocks can explain the observed variation in labor market outcomes across different areas. This comparison is not possible for other factors. Some factors like policy changes and overall concerns about security and stability have near countrywide effects. In those cases, we do not have enough variation to analyze the relationship between those factors and labor market outcomes.

Iraq's labor force participation rate (LFPR) remained low despite accelerating growth compared to the decade before. The LFPR in 2017 was about 43 percent (table 3.2), about 18 percentage points less than the world average and 5 percentage points less than the

TABLE 3.2. Labor market indicators in Iraq, 2012 versus 2017 (percent)

	MALE		FEMALE		TOTAL	
	2012	2017	2012	2017	2012	2017
LABOR FORCE PARTICIPATION RATE (% OF WORKING-AGE POPULATION)	73.1	74.6	12.0	12.4	42.0	43.4
EMPLOYMENT RATE (% OF WORKING-AGE POPULATION)	66.2	64.6	10.4	7.5	37.6	36.1
UNEMPLOYMENT RATE (% OF ACTIVE POPULATION)	9.4	13.4	15.9	38.4	10.4	16.9

Sources: Iraq's Household Socio-Economic Survey (HSES 2012) and Rapid Welfare Monitoring Survey (SWIFT 2017).

Middle East and North Africa (MENA) average. The 2017 average was only 1.4 percentage points higher than 2012, driven by an increase in the male LFPR (from 73.1 percent to 74.6 percent), whereas that for women remained very low at about 12 percent, even lower than the already meager MENA average.

Participation trends in the Kurdistan Region of Iraq, where most Syrian refugees and Iraqi internally displaced persons (IDPs) reside, were mixed but still somewhat better than the Iraqi trends. The overall LFPR increased by about 7 percentage points in Erbil and 1 percentage point in Sulaymaniyah and remained constant in Duhok despite the drastic increase in population. In Erbil, the increase was identical across genders (both 7 percentage points). In comparison, in Sulaymaniyah and Duhok, male and female trends went in opposite directions: a 4.2-percentage-point reduction in female LFPR and a 5.0-percentage-point increase in male LFPR in Sulaymaniyah, and a 2.5-percentage-point increase in female LFPR and a 3.3-percentage-point decrease in male LFPR in Duhok. In Baghdad, male and female LFPR both increased in a balanced way. In Kirkuk, which was at the center of a multiparty conflict in recent years, the male LFPR decreased by 5.7 percentage points, but the female LFPR nearly collapsed from 26 percent in 2012 to just 6.3 percent in 2017.

Unemployment rates increased drastically in governorates affected by the conflict and hosting refugees and IDPs. From 2012 to 2017, Iraq's unemployment rate increased by 6.5 percentage points to reach 17 percent nationwide. But this increase was largely driven by northern governorates. In Duhok, where the local population increased by about 80 percent after the arrival of refugees and IDPs, the locals' unemployment rate increased by 24.5 percentage points. Similarly, Erbil and Sulaymaniyah observed increases of 13.0 and 13.8 percentage points, respectively. In Anbar, where violent battles with the Islamic State took place, unemployment increased by 21.6 percentage points. At the same time, unemployment rates decreased in other governorates including Baghdad, Basrah, and Najaf, with improving outcomes for men.

Women and younger generations were particularly affected by decreasing job prospects. The overall Iraqi unemployment rate for women rose by 22.5 percentage points to reach 38.4 percent in 2017. In governorates where conflict and displacement has taken a heavy toll, these numbers were much higher (figure 3.5b). Women's unemployment rates reached 68 percent in Anbar (a 52-percentage-point increase), 58 percent in Duhok (a 43-percentage-point increase), and 54 percent in Erbil (a 26-percentage-point increase). Finally, unemployment rates in rural areas were lower because of the dominance of agricultural activities in these areas. Youth have also paid a disproportionate price for these dynamics. In 2012, an Iraqi aged 20–24 years was 8 percentage points more likely than an

FIGURE 3.5. **Unemployment rates in Iraq, by gender and governorate, 2012 versus 2017**

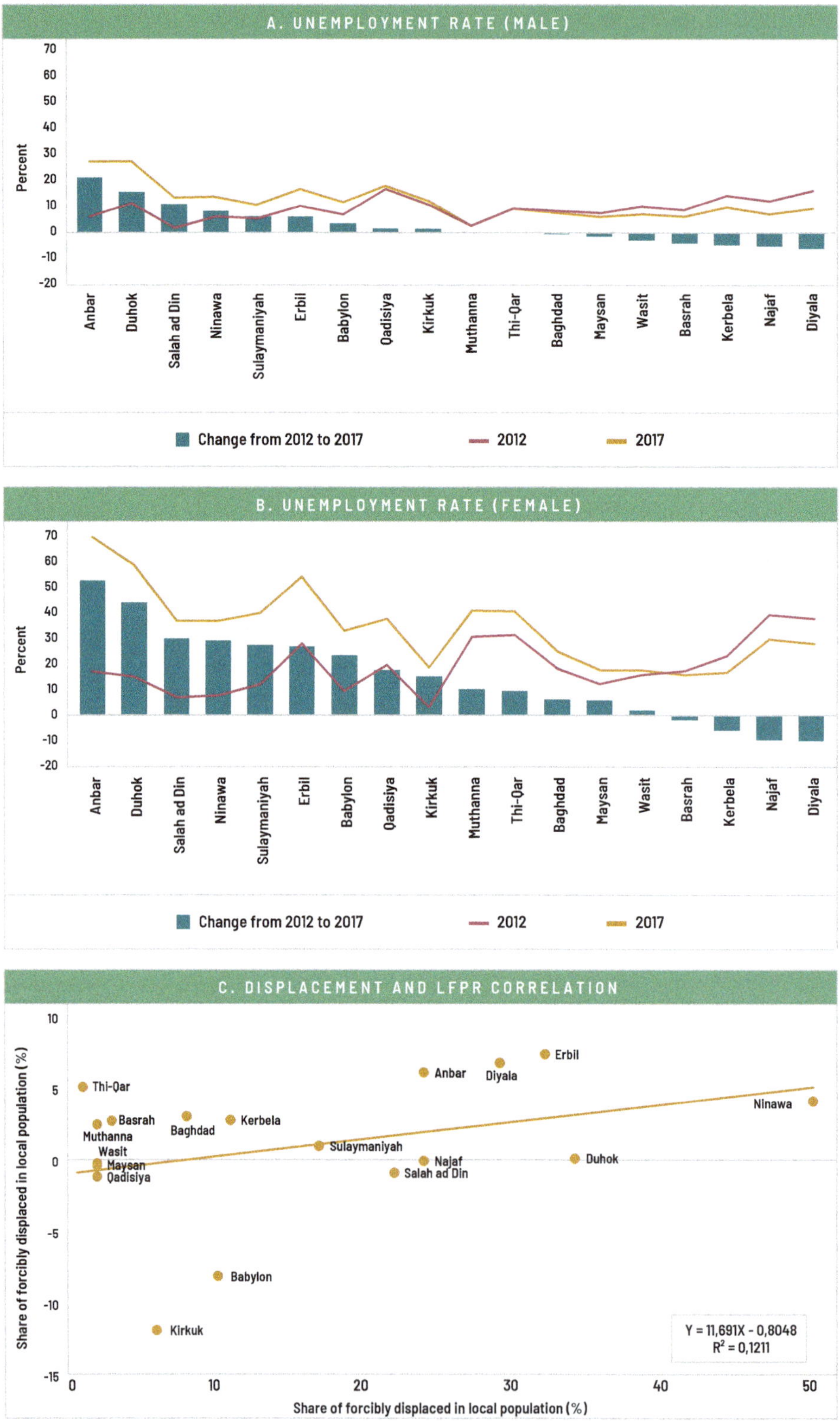

D. DISPLACEMENT AND UNEMPLOYMENT CORRELATION

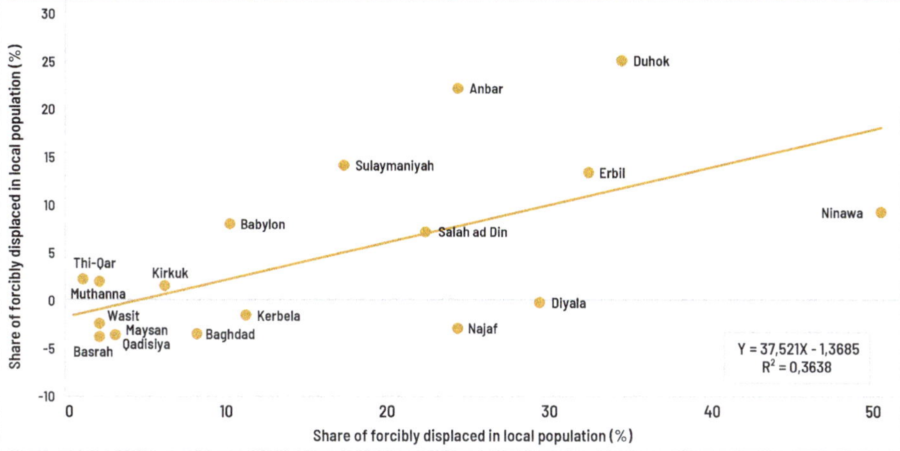

Source: World Bank staff calculations.

Notes: Share of forcibly displaced population includes internally displaced persons and Syrian refugees in 2017. Changes in labor force participation rate (LFPR) and unemployment rate are defined between 2012 and 2017.

average Iraqi to be unemployed. In 2017, this gap doubled to reach 16 percentage points. In comparison, the unemployment rate for an Iraqi aged 40–44 years increased by only 0.5 percentage points between 2012 and 2017.

The employment rate of locals decreased significantly in conflict- and displacement-affected areas but slightly improved elsewhere in Iraq. The employed share of the working-age population in all of Iraq decreased by 1 percentage point to 36.1 percent in 2017. Decreased employment of locals was more drastic in governorates where conflict took place or that hosted refugees and IDPs. In Duhok, the employment ratio decreased by about 10 percentage points to reach 27 percent in 2017, the lowest in Iraq. Similarly, Babylon and Kirkuk both experienced decreases of more than 10 percentage points. The most severe decrease in female employment took place in Kirkuk, where almost all female employment was wiped out (a decrease from 26 percent employment to 5 percent).

Overall, a strong correlation exists between an increasing share of the forcibly displaced and deteriorating labor market conditions for the local population in Iraq. Panels c and d in figure 3.5 show simple correlations between the population share of IDPs and refugees (measured in 2017) and changing labor market indicators between 2012 and 2017 across governorates. The effect on LFPR is rather limited: a 10.0-percentage-point increase in the share of displaced people in the population correlates to about a 1.2-percentage-point increase in LFPR. In comparison, the unemployment effect is large: the same increase in displaced people's share leads to a 3.7-percentage-point increase in the unemployment rate. These results do not imply causality because other confounding factors may influence the correlation; nevertheless, these observations are in line with other circumstantial evidence.

JORDAN

From 2010 to 2016, the LFPR decreased and the unemployment rate increased among Jordanians: males dropped out of the labor force, and females became unemployed. The LFPR of all Jordanians decreased from 54 percent to 49 percent between 2010 and 2016, the two years for which we have comparable data (table 3.3). This drop was largely driven by a decrease in the male LFPR (from 86 percent to 78 percent); the female LFPR was rather stable over this period. At the same time, the Jordanian unemployment rate increased from 11 percent in 2010 to 16 percent in 2016. Unlike the LFPR dynamics, these increases were driven largely by female unemployment (increasing from 18 percent to 30 percent) and to a lesser extent by male unemployment (increasing from 9 percent to 12 percent).

To what extent are these deteriorations in the labor market outcomes related to the influx of the Syrian refugees? One potential avenue for exploring the relation between labor market outcomes and refugee arrival is to examine over time changes in the distribution of unemployment rate and LFPR across different population groups. Specifically, one would expect that Syrian refugees would compete with Jordanians with similar socioeconomic characteristics, mainly low-educated males and low-educated females. The idea here is that the influx of Syrian refugees might crowd out this section of Jordanian workers and thus impose a negative effect on the Jordanian labor market. Conversely, the deterioration of the labor market is less likely to be related to the refugee shock if it accrues to all cohorts, including those—like educated males and females—who are possibly less affected by the shock.

Differences in LFPR and unemployment dynamics between educated and uneducated groups are not significant nationwide. As documented in table 3.3, the LFPR changes between 2010 and 2016 were largely shared by both educated males (6-percentage-point decrease) and low-educated males (9-percentage-point decrease). The decrease in the LFPR of low-educated females was slightly bigger than that of educated females, but together they correspond to a small effect. Moreover, as for males, the unemployment effect was larger for educated females than for low-educated females, which further weakens the former effect. Overall, Jordanians with similar education profiles to Syrian refugees did not seem to face worse labor market outcomes than others.

Another way to analyze refugee effects in Jordan's labor market is to map labor market outcomes onto the distribution of refugees across different governorates. If the presence of Syrian refugees is a significant driver of deterioration in labor market outcomes, perhaps for those with a similar skill profile to that of refugees, then these effects must be greater in areas with a relatively higher concentration of refugees. To test the validity of this line of thought, we first present the distribution of employment numbers across Jordanian governorates by nationality (table 3.4). In relative terms, Syrians are most concentrated in Mafraq, Irbid, and Karak. Because the refugees' labor market effects could be higher for Jordanians whose skills are substitutes for, rather than complements to, those of refugees (that is, low-skilled Jordanians), we also amend the employment distribution by excluding Jordanians with tertiary education. This exclusion, however, does not significantly change the relative distribution.

Changes in the LFPR and the unemployment rate have not been homogenous across groups and governorates. For example, the unemployment rate for low-educated males rose by 3 percentage points in Amman, remained stable in Irbid and Zarqa, rose by 8 percentage points in Aqaba, and decreased by 1 percentage point in Balqa (table 3.5). This finding shows no signal of a unique negative shock in the main governorates. In comparison, the unemployment rate of low-educated females increased across the board (except in Madaba) and especially in Aqaba (by 39 percentage points) and Irbid (by 16 percentage points). A similar heterogeneity is also observed in the LFPR profiles, where the participation rates of low-educated males fell in all governorates, but those of females (educated or low educated) fell in many but increased in some.

TABLE 3.3. Labor force participation and unemployment rate trends in Jordan, 2010 versus 2016 (percent)

	LABOR FORCE PARTICIPATION RATE		UNEMPLOYMENT RATE		UNEMPLOYED/POPULATION	
	2010	2016	2010	2016	2010	2016
ALL	54	49	11	16	6	7
MALE	86	78	9	12	7	8
FEMALE	22	21	18	30	4	5
EDUCATED MALE	90	84	8	11	7	9
EDUCATED FEMALE	50	49	21	33	11	14
LOW-EDUCATED MALE	85	76	10	12	9	9
LOW-EDUCATED FEMALE	11	9	14	22	1	2

Source: Jordan Labor Market Panel Survey.

TABLE 3.4. Employment concentration in Jordan, by nationality, 2016 (percent)

	ALL				EXCLUDING TERTIARY-EDUCATED JORDANIANS			
	JORDANIAN	SYRIAN	EGYPTIAN	OTHERS	JORDANIAN	SYRIAN	EGYPTIAN	OTHERS
AMMAN	70	5	17	8	60	7	23	10
BALQA	70	4	16	9	60	5	22	12
ZARQA	76	2	8	13	69	3	11	17
MADABA	85	2	9	4	76	3	15	7
IRBID	81	6	10	3	74	8	14	3
MAFRAQ	75	9	13	3	69	11	16	4
JARASH	82	0	0	18	76	0	0	24
AJLOUN	100	0	0	0	100	0	0	0
KARAK	89	6	4	1	85	8	6	1
TAFILEH	100	0	0	0	100	0	0	0
MA'AN	95	0	4	0	94	0	6	0
AQABA	66	0	27	7	58	0	33	8

Source: Jordan Labor Market Panel Survey.

TABLE 3.5. Changes in Jordanian labor force participation and unemployment rates, 2010–16 (percentage points)

	CHANGE IN LABOR FORCE PARTICIPATION RATE					CHANGE IN UNEMPLOYMENT RATE				
	ALL	EDUCATED MALES	EDUCATED FEMALES	LOW-EDUCATED MALES	LOW-EDUCATED FEMALES	ALL	EDUCATED MALES	EDUCATED FEMALES	LOW-EDUCATED MALES	LOW-EDUCATED FEMALES
AMMAN	-3	-5	0	-7	-1	3	2	5	3	7
BALQA	-7	-5	-4	-11	-6	2	5	10	-1	7
ZARQA	-7	-7	-8	-11	-3	2	7	6	0	7
MADABA	-8	-18	-8	-11	-3	1	0	-4	4	-2
IRBID	-1	-2	0	-3	0	3	0	10	0	16
MAFRAQ	-2	-3	-5	-4	0	2	-1	8	2	2
JARASH	-2	1	3	-3	-1	1	4	-1	-1	10
AJLOUN	-1	0	4	-4	3	7	4	18	4	0
KARAK	-7	-5	-1	-11	-5	2	1	4	-1	4
TAFILEH	-6	-8	-6	-8	-4	6	9	20	0	8
MA'AN	-3	-6	-1	-9	2	3	5	9	1	0
AQABA	-2	-4	2	-8	2	14	0	21	8	39

Source: Jordan Labor Market Panel Survey.

The changes in the Jordanian LFPR and unemployment rate after 2010 show no clear relation with the population share of Syrian refugees. To relate the deterioration of the labor market indicators to the influx of Syrian refugees, the shock must disproportionately affect governorates that accommodate higher shares of refugees. Figure 3.6 shows the correlations between changes in the LFPR and unemployment rate between 2010 and 2016 and the share of Syrian refugees in the population of Jordanian governorates. Overall, nearly no correlation exists between Syrian refugee shares and LFPR changes across governorates. The changes in unemployment rates and refugee population are correlated negatively—that is, governorates with a lower refugee concentration experienced a higher increase in unemployment rate. Overall, these findings suggest that the injection of additional population may have had a partial and localized offsetting effect against a broader economic downturn faced by the country. Although a shifting of unemployment from high-refugee-intensity areas to low ones would also explain this pattern, such a shift would require major internal migration patterns of Jordanians. We do not have evidence that suggests such a movement.

The muted response of the Jordanian labor market dynamics to Syrian refugee arrivals could be related to the segregated nature of the labor market in Jordan. The overwhelming majority of working Syrian refugees (90 percent) are employed in the private sector,

FIGURE 3.6. **Labor market dynamics and Syrian refugees' presence in Jordanian governorates, 2010-16**

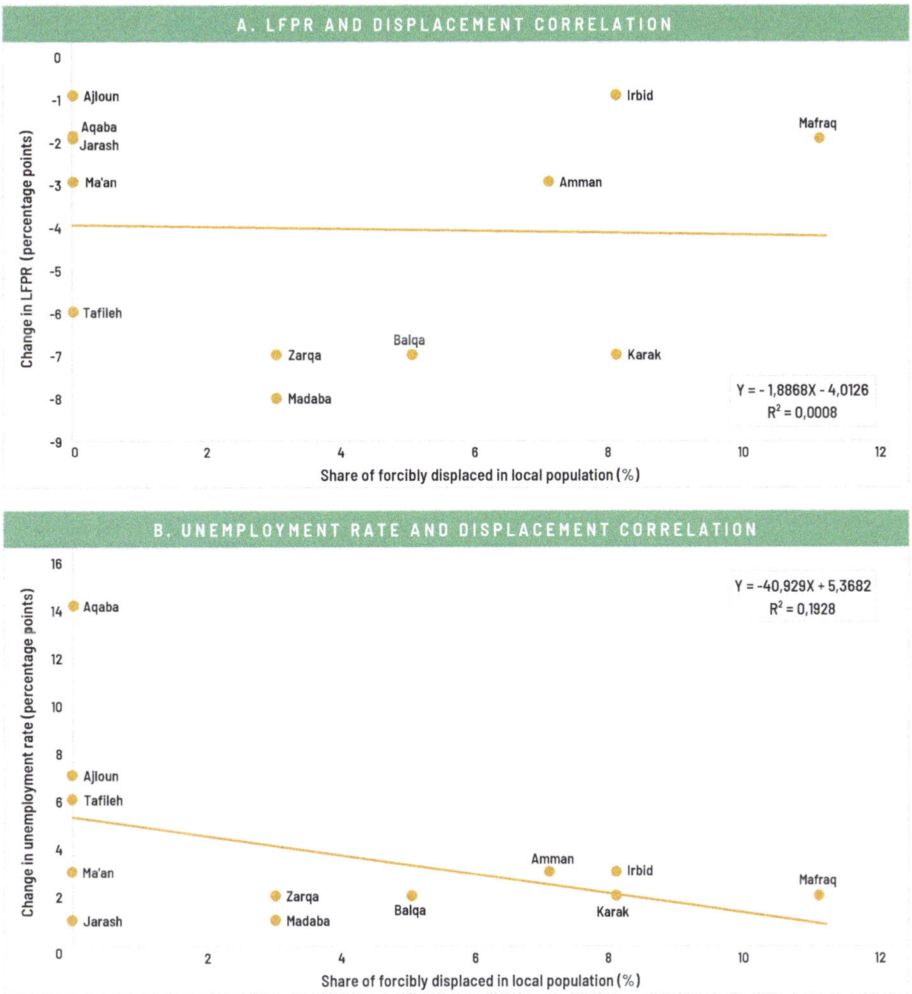

Source: World Bank staff calculations.

Note: Share of forcibly displaced population includes Syrian refugees in 2017. Changes in labor force participation rate (LFPR) and unemployment rate are defined between 2012 and 2017.

especially in the manufacturing sector, followed by construction, and wholesale and retail trade, which together represent 70 percent of working Syrian refugees. As for migrants from the Arab Republic of Egypt, most are employed in domestic household activities, agriculture, and construction, whereas workers from other nationalities are employed in wholesale and retail trade, construction, and agriculture. In comparison, the public sector is a main employer of Jordanians, employing about 40 percent of all Jordanian workers. On the private sector side, about 15 percent of all Jordanian workers are employed in wholesale and retail trade and about 11 percent in manufacturing. Thus, the sectoral overlap between employment patterns of Syrian refugees and of economic migrant groups in Jordan is much smaller than that between Syrian refugees and Jordanians.

TABLE 3.6. Links between Syrian refugees and wages across cohorts, Jordan, 2010-16

VARIABLES	ALL	EDUCATED MALES	LOW-EDUCATED MALES	EDUCATED FEMALES	LOW-EDUCATED FEMALES
BALQA#2016.YEAR	0.0414*** (3.818)	-0.0998 (-1.687)	0.0864*** (4.977)	0.0831*** (3.380)	0.103 (0.998)
ZARQA#2016.YEAR	-0.0432*** (-6.947)	-0.218*** (-16.50)	0.00744 (0.374)	-0.0104 (-0.261)	0.0778 (0.848)
MADABA#2016.YEAR	-0.0616** (-2.690)	0.00733 (0.120)	-0.0157 (-0.448)	-0.0389 (-0.575)	-0.624*** (-5.628)
IRBID#2016.YEAR	0.0359** (2.687)	-0.162*** (-18.26)	0.0612*** (3.264)	0.0269 (0.940)	-0.00883 (-0.0870)
MAFRAQ#2016.YEAR	-0.0582*** (-4.863)	-0.0746 (-0.749)	-0.0302** (-2.374)	0.00731 (0.156)	-0.275 (-1.567)
JARASH#2016.YEAR	-0.145*** (-19.27)	-0.225*** (-17.25)	-0.0865*** (-11.45)	-0.570*** (-8.063)	0.242*** (4.897)
AJLOUN#2016.YEAR	-0.260*** (-13.81)	-0.181*** (-4.081)	-0.250*** (-4.567)	-0.0589 (-1.251)	n.a.
KARAK#2016.YEAR	-0.139*** (-10.45)	-0.367*** (-10.25)	-0.0293 (-1.067)	-0.0875*** (-4.161)	-0.296*** (-3.944)
TAFILEH#2016.YEAR	-0.0978*** (-3.720)	-0.0886 (-1.443)	-0.105*** (-5.502)	0.0470 (1.186)	-0.390 (-1.502)
MA'AN#2016.YEAR	-0.115*** (-6.422)	-1.239*** (-9.739)	0.000479 (0.0153)	-0.0889 (-0.574)	-0.128* (-2.157)
AQABA#2016.YEAR	-0.129*** (-10.38)	-0.447*** (-3.943)	-0.0292 (-0.885)	0.150 (1.314)	-0.335** (-2.512)
CONSTANT	-0.332 (-1.292)	0.261 (0.933)	-0.384 (-1.164)	2.698*** (4.931)	3.733*** (9.017)
OBSERVATIONS	7,465	1,392	4,696	844	533
R-SQUARED	0.207	0.263	0.132	0.408	0.545
DEPVAR	LOGHRWG	LOGHRWG	LOGHRWG	LOGHRWG	LOGHRWG

Source: World Bank staff calculations.

Note: Robust t-statistics in parentheses.
*p < 0.1 **p < 0.05 ***p < 0.01; DEPVAR = Dependent variable; LOGHRWG = Hourly wages (in logs) ; n.a. = not applicable.

Another way the arrival of Syrian refugees could affect Jordanian labor market outcomes is through its effect on wages. An increase in labor supply could decrease the wages of those whose skills are the same as those of the newcomers. To test this hypothesis, analysis was carried out on changes in nominal hourly wages per worker before and after the shock, controlling for the effect of socioeconomic and demographic factors, occupation, industry, and type of job contract (permanent contract, temporary contract, or no contract), and whether a worker benefits from social security. The model also includes a set of dummy variables that control for governorate of residence and a year dummy in which 2010 is the reference year. The latter accounts for the change in the overall prices that might affect wages at the national level. The governorate dummies also control for factors that affect wages differently across governorates and change little over time. To examine the effect on wage change (after and before the shock) across governorates, an interaction variable (governorate by year of 2016) was introduced in which the reference governorate in 2016 is Amman. The estimates of the interaction terms measure the wage growth rate across governorates. The model was estimated across various Jordanian cohorts: all workers, educated males, educated females, low-educated males, and low-educated females. The sample used to estimate the wage model is limited to the private sector because Syrian refugees are not expected to compete with public workers.[4]

The wage analysis also provides mixed results. Table 3.6 shows the results of the wage regressions, with estimated coefficients showing the effects of country-year dummies. The wage growth in Mafraq is about 5.8 percent less than that in Amman, a significant result controlling for other factors. This difference is largely driven by a lower wage growth for low-educated males. In contrast, the wage growth in another high-refugee-intensity governorate, Irbid, is about 4 percent greater than that of Amman, again driven by low-educated males. In Zarqa, where refugees constitute about 8 percent of the population, a very large and significant gap emerged in educated male wages, relative to Amman. In Madaba, another relatively high-refugee-intensity area, males did not have major differences with Amman, but wage growth for low-educated females was much lower than that in Amman. In comparison, many governorates that did not receive a significant share of refugees performed much worse in wage growth relative to Amman. Ajloun, Aqaba, Jarash, Karak, and Ma'an all exhibited more than a 10 percent gap in wage growth relative to Amman, with Ajloun's gap standing at 26 percent. Overall, wage growth differentials do not provide a systematic result on the effect of refugee presence on wages.[5]

POVERTY TRENDS

Before the eruption of the Syrian civil war and the consequent political, economic, and social spillovers to its neighboring countries, poverty had been falling in both Iraq and Jordan. In Iraq, poverty fell from 22.4 percent in 2007 to 18.9 percent in 2012 (figure 3.7). At the height of the crisis, however, poverty is estimated to have risen to 22.5 percent in 2014 (Krishnan and Olivieri 2016) before falling back to 20.0 percent in 2017 (Sharma and Wai-Poi 2019), a decline but still higher than immediately before the crisis. In Jordan, poverty fell significantly by about 7 percentage points between 1997 and 2002, and by about 6 percentage points between 2006 and 2010 (figure 3.8). The 2004 and 2012 precrisis estimates in Lebanon are not comparable, and no postcrisis estimate exists.

Isolating the distributional impact of the Syrian crisis entails a more technical analysis. With the onset of the Syrian conflict, Jordan and Lebanon experienced a significant influx of refugees; Iraq was also hit by the related Islamic State militant crisis, displacing many Iraqis internally. The security crisis in Iraq was compounded by an economic shock triggered by the plunge of oil prices in the international market in 2014. This report evaluates the welfare and distributional impacts of the conflict in Syria on households in its neighboring countries of Iraq, Jordan, and Lebanon using a microsimulation-modeled analysis. The consequences of the crisis for the overall GDP, labor market, and population are likely to be among various channels through which the shock is transmitted to households and individuals in these countries. Moreover, there is likely to be significant heterogeneity across space (by country or within country) and between groups. We focus on the impact on host communities in Jordan and Lebanon rather than the impact on refugees; for an in-depth examination of the impact on refugees, see World Bank (2019). Because this assessment requires a simulation approach, we present the results in the next chapter.

FIGURE 3.7. **National poverty, Iraq, 2007–17**

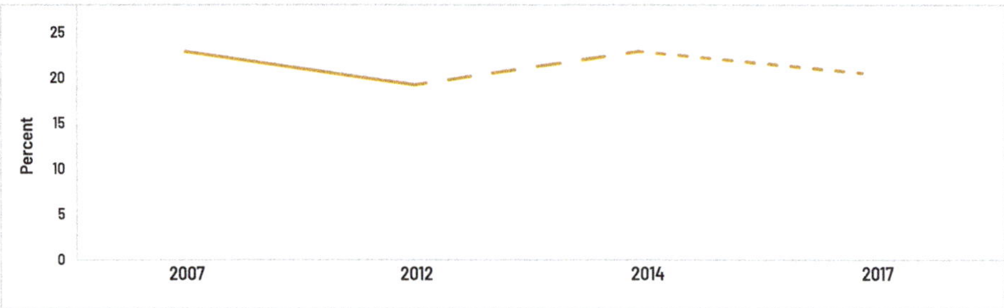

Sources: Iraq Household Socioeconomic Survey for 2007 and 2012; Krishnan and Olivieri 2016 microsimulations for 2014; Iraq SWIFT survey for 2017.

Note: The years 2007 and 2012 use the same consumption aggregate and are strictly comparable, but 2014 is based on microsimulations and 2017 uses a different consumption aggregate.

FIGURE 3.8. **National poverty, Jordan, 1997–2018**

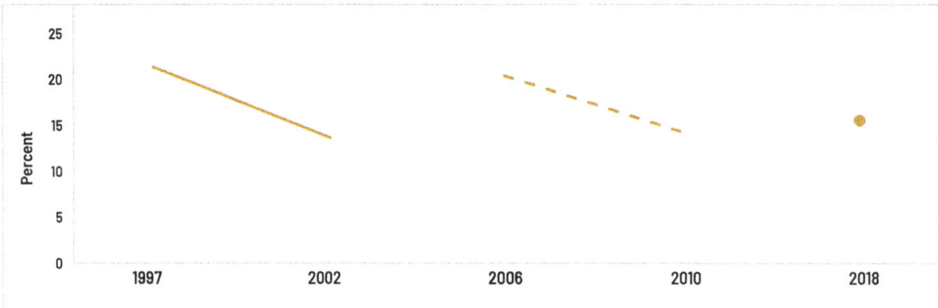

Source: Jordan Household Income and Expenditure Survey for all years.

Notes: The years 1997 and 2002 use the same consumption aggregate and are strictly comparable to each other. The years 2006 and 2010 use a different consumption aggregate and poverty line and are strictly comparable only to each other. The 2006 point has been reestimated using the 2010 methodology and is consistent with the 2010 point but is not the official 2006 rate. The year 2018 uses a different consumption aggregate and poverty line to all other points and is not comparable to earlier series.

ACCESS TO PUBLIC SERVICES AND INFRASTRUCTURE

A sudden hike in demand for publicly provided services could strain public service provision systems anywhere in the world. Public service provision systems in transportation, education, and health sectors are not built with a slack capacity to absorb a 20 percent increase in demand in a short time frame. Thus, when such a demand shock hit the governments of Iraq, Jordan, and Lebanon, it resulted in monumental challenges. On theoretical grounds, this demand can be met either by an equal adjustment of service provision (increase in supply) or by sharing of existing provision levels (decrease in host community access to services). In the former case, the impact is primarily fiscal. In the latter, it is a direct welfare (consumption) impact. In practice, what happens is often somewhere in between these boundary cases. Some adjustments in supply (possibly with the help of international aid) and some losses in the host community's access to services take place simultaneously; however, the exact magnitude of these adjustments may differ by sector, country, and time. In this section, we analyze such adjustments in the transportation, education, health, water and sanitation, and energy sectors.

TRANSPORTATION

At the outset of the Syrian conflict, the region's dominant transportation infrastructure, its road network, was well established but poorly maintained. According to available open source data, such as OpenStreetMap,[6] Iraq has about 50,500 kilometers (km) of roads, Jordan has about 10,300 km, and Lebanon has about 8,200 km (map 3.1). Road densities are high, especially in Lebanon, where road density is 79.9 km per 100 km^2 of land (figure 3.9). In Iraq, road density is about 11.6 km of roads per 100 km^2 of land area, and it rises to 56.5 km in the Kurdistan Region of Iraq (KRI). These networks support systems of domestic transportation dominated by trucking. The region has also suffered from a legacy of underinvestment and the absence of periodic maintenance, which reduce public spending efficiency.

The conflict in Syria has influenced the demand for transportation in Iraq, Jordan, and Lebanon, with consequences for depreciation and congestion. The transport sector provides ways for refugees to commute within the country or across borders, and it is directly affected by border closures and movement restrictions. To assess how these factors have influenced the quality of infrastructure and congestion effects, we have observed road density and demographic patterns between 2010 and 2019. These patterns have been reflected as a reduction in travel speed along major corridors, which was then used to produce indexes of host community accessibility to education and health care facilities.

Infrastructure depreciation

In Iraq, conflict-driven damage to infrastructure has compounded the displacement-driven depreciation. Syrian refugees and Iraqi IDPs are mostly situated in KRI, with no access to railway (railway infrastructure completely bypasses KRI, and operational railways are currently in the part of the country south of Kirkuk) or ability to afford air transport. This situation leaves road vehicles as the only means of transportation and—along with humanitarian relief efforts including heavy supply trucks carrying food, medicine, and construction material—puts pressure on the stagnant road network, accelerating its deterioration. It is estimated that the influx of refugees has increased the rehabilitation and upgrade needs of the road network by about $80 million to $100 million per year. Moreover, the Islamic State–driven conflict further accelerated deterioration and destruction of road infrastructure such as bridges and other major structures. The World Bank (2018b) estimated $3.3 billion worth of physical damages in transportation infrastructure. Ironically, the depreciation of the major road network could be higher if the trade volume between Iraq and Turkey continued at precrisis levels.

Despite the infrastructure needs, public expenditures in Iraq's transport sector have stagnated. The legacy of underinvestment and poor maintenance has continued since the onset of the crisis. An ambitious transport plan was developed in 2014 comprising road, rail, air, and water transport, covering the period 2014–33. The plan included completion of (at that time) ongoing projects, new expressways, rehabilitation of the existing rail network, development of the Euphrates High-Speed line, construction of several new airports (Duhok, Karbala/Najaf), and major expansions of existing seaports. The plan, however, did not consider maintenance of the existing infrastructure, but only the development component. It also did not account for the major impact of the Syrian crisis and the Islamic State. With such flaws, the master plan implementation failed in a relatively short time even before commencement.

MAP 3.1. Road network in the Mashreq region

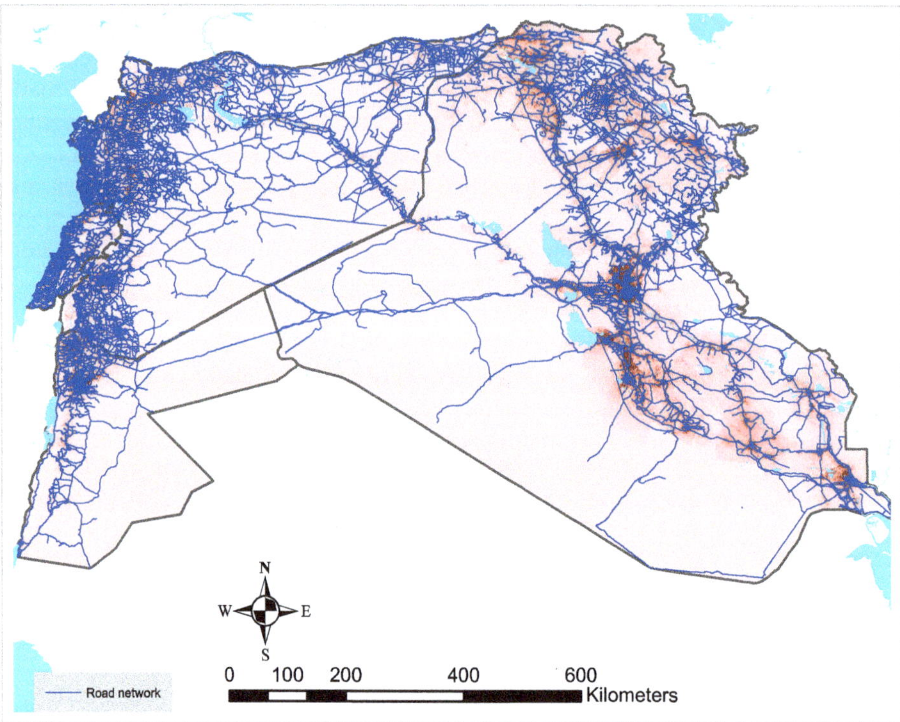

Sources: WorldPop and OpenStreetMap.

FIGURE 3.9. Population and road density, selected Mashreq countries

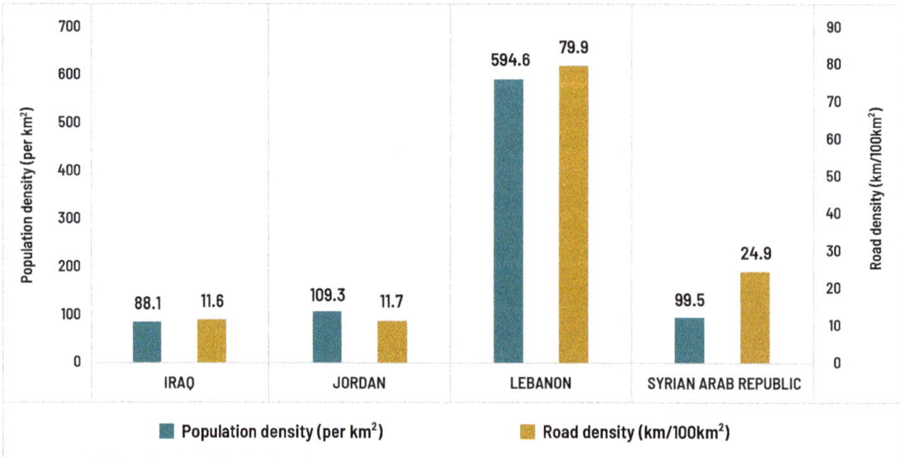

Source: World Bank staff estimates based on World Development Indicators (2010) and OpenStreetMap.
Note: km = kilometer.

Reconstruction of the Iraqi road network to its precrisis conditions would cost $4 billion, with another $1 billion required for the restoration of other transportation services. Most of the damage, as well as the wear and tear due to increased traffic load, has occurred in governorates with high intensity of conflict and high influx of refugees and IDPs. It is assumed that approximately 15 percent of the road network (about 6,500 km of main and secondary roads, and about 1,800 km of tertiary and municipal roads) would need to undergo reconstruction treatment.[7] The estimated amount may be increased by another 25 percent to take into account restoration of transportation services on roads (public buses and other facilities) as well as improvements to airport infrastructure.

Since the start of the Syrian crisis, the number of registered vehicles in Jordan has increased by half. According to the Jordanian Ministry of Transport, the number of registered vehicles has increased from 1,075,453 vehicles in 2010 to 1,583,458 vehicles in 2018. Although it is not possible to attribute this change to a single factor, the boom has nevertheless created significant strain on the road infrastructure—especially in urban areas, where most refugees are located—through significant and almost all-day congestion. This increased congestion has increased travel time, decreased accessibility for the host communities, and increased greenhouse gas emissions.

The collapse of Jordan's cross-border trade with Iraq and Syria has affected both the scale and the composition of vehicular traffic in Jordan. With increasing security concerns, regulatory obstacles, and the closure of the Jaber-Nasib border crossing point between Jordan and Syria in 2015, the number of buses entering Jordan from Syria dropped from 6,866 in 2010 to only 225 in 2018. Similarly, the number of private and public Syrian vehicles entering Jordan dropped from 331,636 vehicles in 2010 to only 8,172 vehicles in 2018. Somewhat counteracting the decrease in these inbound traffic numbers has been the diversion to Jordan's domestic market of many Jordanian trucks that transported internationally before the conflict. In 2016, the number of trucks crossing Jordan's international borders was only 20 percent of what it had been in 2011. Nearly all the trucks that previously served these markets diverted to the domestic market, exacerbating an already existing oversupply in Jordan.

In Lebanon, a high motorization density, insufficient maintenance of roads, and the influx of refugees have made a bad traffic problem worse. Road transport is by far the dominant form of transport in Lebanon for passengers, freight, and commerce, with about 400 vehicles per 1,000 inhabitants. Reliable public transport is nearly absent, and about 70–80 percent of the vehicular traffic in the Greater Beirut Area is estimated to be passenger cars (World Bank 2018a). The influx of Syrian refugees also put extra pressure on the road networks, which already suffered from the absence of rehabilitation and routine maintenance. The result has been a worsening of conditions over the years, which led to Lebanon's ranking at 121st in the world in terms of road quality (WEF 2018), dropping 20 places from 2010. Currently, the Ministry of Public Works and Transport (MPWT) estimates that about 15 percent of the main network is in good condition, 50 percent in fair condition, and 35 percent in poor condition. The condition of roads in rural and lagging regions is significantly worse compared to roads at the national level.

Lebanon aims to address some of its transport sector problems through a Capital Investment Plan (CIP). During the CEDRE (Conférence économique pour le développement, par les réformes et avec les entreprises) conference in Paris (April 2018), Lebanon presented an ambitious three-cycle CIP for the period 2018–30 (Harake and Kostopoulos 2018). The plan for about $11 billion in infrastructure investments (mainly transport, energy, and water) for the next five years coupled with an ambitious reform program received strong support from the international committee, with the World Bank Group pledging $4 billion in support of the CIP. About 27 percent of this budget is to be allocated for transport projects, including finalization of highways, expansion of the Tripoli Port, construction of the first modern railway linking the Tripoli Port to Syria, the introduction of a reliable public transport network and bus rapid transit lines, and the expansion of Beirut airport. The World Bank is currently financing two transport sector projects to address the decaying infrastructure and increasing traffic congestion in Lebanon. The Roads and Employment Project (REP), a $200 million project, aims to rehabilitate 500 km of roads all around Lebanon; and the Greater Beirut Public Transport Project (GBPTP), a $345 million project, aims to establish the first mass transit system on Beirut's northern highway.

These projects' design follows a win-win rationale. The two World Bank projects help Lebanon meet its important needs in the infrastructure sectors, reduce the large economic externalities of traffic congestion, improve transport services and reduce costs for the middle- and low-income Lebanese and Syrians, and create jobs for Lebanese and Syrians, thereby easing the economic and social pressures from the Syrian refugee crisis. The projects also highlight Lebanon's continuous efforts to weather the Syrian refugee crisis and the country's increasing needs for assistance from the international community to support it in providing a global public good. In addition, these two projects will also address Syrian unemployment by providing refugees with short- and long-term jobs in the construction sector. Initial estimates showed that REP will create 1.5 million labor days and GBPTP will generate 2 million labor days. Because of their impact in alleviating Syrian refugees' negative consequences, these two projects received Global Concessional Financing Facility (GCFF) financing.[8]

Congestion and service access

To what extent has the conflict-driven congestion reduced access to basic services in Iraq, Jordan, and Lebanon? To answer this question, we consider a comparison between 2010 and 2019 accessibility levels. Between the two periods, the capacity of the road network is assumed to be broadly unchanged and all roads passable and all-weather. Average speeds are 100 km/h for motorways, 80 km/h for trunk roads, 65 km/h for primary roads, 55 km/h for secondary roads, and 40 km/h for tertiary roads, respectively. Demographic distribution data are from WorldPop,[9] with spatial resolutions varying from approximately 100 meters to 1 km. In this approach, high population density increases traffic, particularly during peak hours, and therefore reduces traffic speed and accessibility (Nair et. al. 2019). With global city data, the elasticity is estimated at 0.089. For instance, with a population density of 1,000 persons per km^2, the average travel time during peak hours increases by 20 percent compared with the off-peak hours. If population density exceeds 10,000 persons per km^2, the average travel time would likely increase by 50 percent. Using this estimation, the above-average speeds are adjusted according to population density along each road segment. Finally, health care access is measured by the share of population with 30-minute access to the nearest health care facility, and school accessibility is defined by 10-minute access.

In Jordan and Lebanon—but not Iraq—accessibility improved slightly from 2010 to 2019. Estimates show that with population growth, which includes both refugees and the country's normal population increase, and congestion, the level of accessibility change is relatively small and positive in Jordan and Lebanon. In comparison, changes in Iraq are large and negative (figure 3.10). These changes are probably driven by the displacement of Iraqis from conflict-affected urban areas to other locations. People fled the civil war, and the road connectivity was damaged.

The positive results in Jordan and Lebanon are driven by the fact that the proximity effect dominates the congestion effect in these cases. Traffic congestion is projected to have increased, thus reducing travel speed and accessibility because of the arrival in Jordan and Lebanon of large numbers of refugees, who reside largely in urban areas. At the same

FIGURE 3.10. **Population with access to a health care facility or school, selected Mashreq countries, 2010 versus 2019**

Source: World Bank staff calculations.

time, the national populations have also increased naturally and are also estimated to live more in urban areas where the network of social facilities is well established. As a result, the proportion of the people who live within a 30- or 10-minute driving distance from a health care facility or school, respectively, is estimated to increase (map 3.2). This proximity effect appears to dominate the congestion effect, which slows the speed of access and potentially leaves out populations at the margins of the specified distance radius.

It should be noted, however, that the accessibility analysis described here does not consider service provision issues in the respective facilities. The accessibility analysis assumes a constant service provision per capita, both quantity and quality wise, in prevailing facilities. This assumption keeps the focus purely on transportation-driven problems. If these facilities did indeed have fixed capacities despite the increase of potential beneficiaries, then service access of everyone in a given area could decrease with increasing population even if their accessibility improved. We next turn to broader issues regarding the provision of such services and host community access to them.

MAP 3.2. **Population with access to a health care facility or school, selected Mashreq countries, 2010 versus 2019**

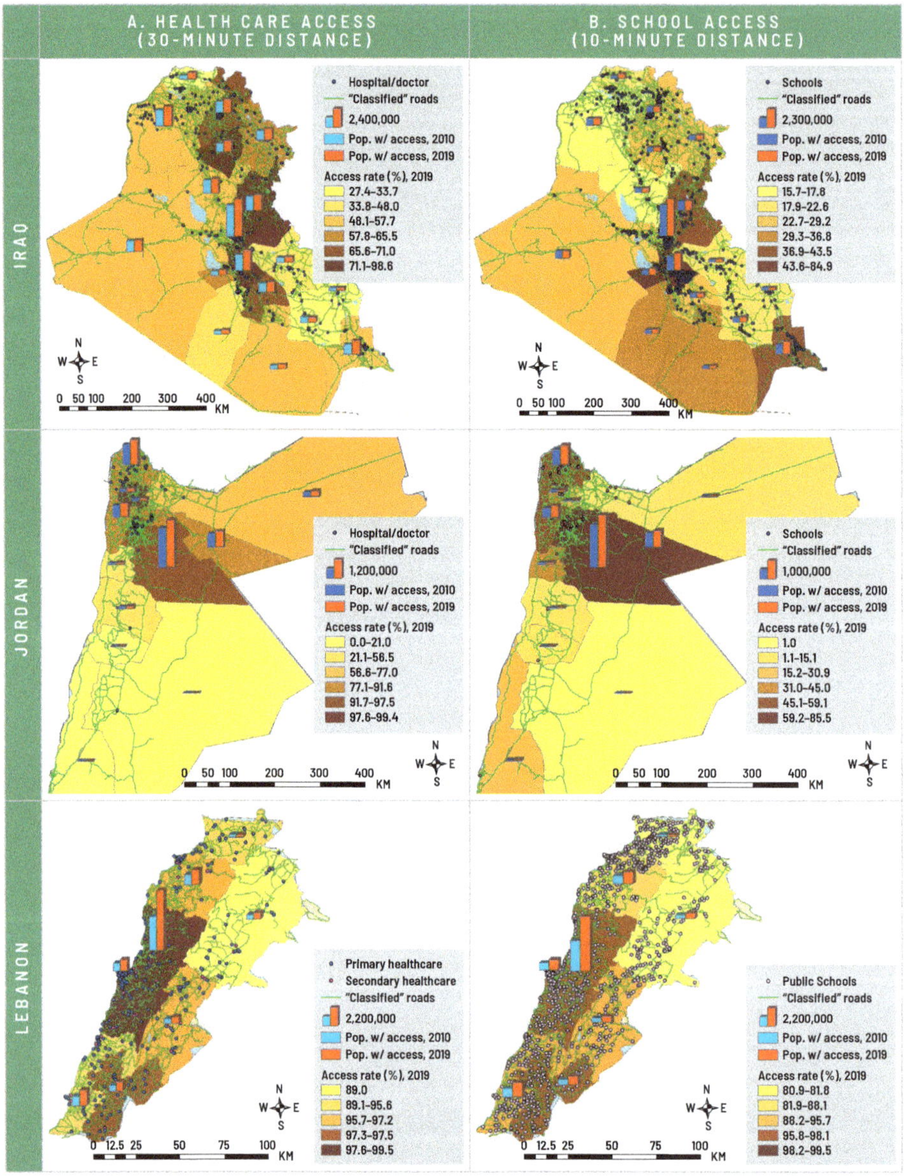

Source: World Bank staff calculations.

EDUCATION

The Syrian conflict has affected education service delivery drastically in host communities, primarily through refugee arrivals. Of the 1.9 million registered refugees in Iraq, Jordan, and Lebanon, nearly half are under the age of 18. Thus, the population of school-age registered Syrian refugees alone is close to about a quarter of the population of their peers in host communities. Equipping refugee children with the necessary skills and knowledge is a significant challenge for host governments, some of which already struggle to provide quality education to their own populations. In this section, we analyze the changes in education service delivery in Iraq, Jordan, and Lebanon between 2010 and 2018, outlining some of the explanatory factors and the fiscal implications for the host governments.

In Iraq, Syrian children attend either public schools for Iraqis or refugee-specific schools. Iraq has almost 70,000 Syrian refugee children registered, mostly concentrated in KRI: 30,000 are enrolled in schools, 16,000 are enrolled in some form of nonformal education, and the rest are not enrolled in any type of education program.[10] As of 2018, 71 percent of school-age Syrian refugee children living in camps and 46 percent living outside of camps attended school. Among Syrian children aged 6–11 years, 81 percent (88 percent of girls and 75 percent of boys) attend formal education, compared to 66 percent of children aged 12–14 (70 percent of girls and 62 percent of boys). Among Syrian children aged 15–17, 32 percent of boys and 35 percent of girls attend formal education. Generally, Syrian children's school attendance is lower than that of Iranian and Turkish groups. Only 1 percent of Syrian refugees is enrolled in tertiary education (UNHCR and IMPACT Initiatives 2019).

Despite improvements in attendance rates for Iraqi children in the last decade, student–teacher ratios have deteriorated. Data for middle-income countries show that in 2009–10, 90 percent of children at the primary school level were attending (93 percent for boys and 87 percent for girls) as were 49 percent of children at the secondary education level. According to the latest statistics (2018), Iraqi children have almost reached universal enrollment (92 percent) and gender parity in primary schools; however, enrollment in secondary education is significantly lower (58 percent) and varies by gender and urbanicity. Compared to 75 percent of males, only 55 percent of females aged 12–17 in rural areas are enrolled in school. Student–teacher ratios are a significant problem, especially as enrollment increases and not enough new teachers enter the education system. Although the number of teachers gradually increased between 2007 and 2017 (by 1.2 percent for the preprimary and primary levels and 3 percent for the secondary level), student–teacher ratios increased from an average of 16 to 23. The student–teacher ratio decreases in higher levels of education, likely because of student dropouts.

In Jordan, 56 percent of school-age Syrian refugees are enrolled in formal education, 13 percent follow some form of nonformal education, and 31 percent remain out of school. Enrollment decreases considerably with age for both genders (figure 3.11). Syrian refugees attend school in one of three ways: refugee camp schools, second-shifting, and mixed with Jordanian students.[11] Of Syrian children enrolled in school, 75 percent are either in refugee camp schools or in second shifts dedicated for Syrian children, whereas 25 percent are enrolled in the first shift alongside Jordanian children. The double-shift system is not available for secondary schools. Jordan has allowed Syrian refugee children to access tuition-free public schools in host communities since the start of the conflict. According to the Ministry of Education's Educational Management Information System (EMIS), Syrian children made up 9 percent of the student body in public schools in 2017–18. Accredited public schools were opened in the Zaatari refugee camp in 2012 and Azraq refugee camp in 2014.[12]

To what extent do Syrian children affect the education service delivery for the host community? A growing body of recent research suggests that the arrival of Syrian refugees in Jordan did not have a significant effect on the educational attainment and learning outcomes of Jordanian students (see, for example, Assaad, Ginn, and Saleh 2019; Rozo and Sviatschi 2018). Combining detailed household surveys with school-level records on the density of Syrians and using a differences-in-differences design across refugee prevalence and birth cohort, Assaad, Ginn, and Saleh (2019) find no evidence to support the idea

FIGURE 3.11. **School enrollment of Syrian refugee children in Jordan, by age, 2016-17 school year**

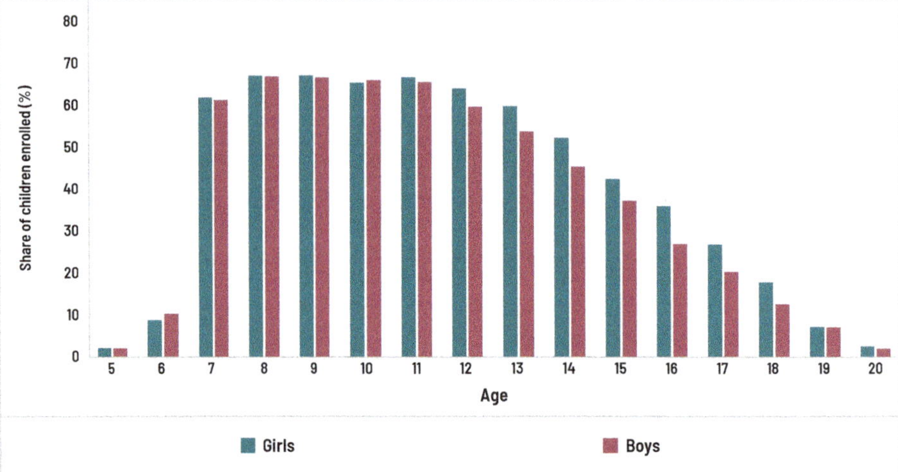

Source: United Nations Children's Fund based on 2016-17 school year data. Data refer only to those registered with the United Nations High Commissioner for Refugees.

that a greater exposure to Syrian refugees affected the attainment quantity or quality of Jordanian students. The intensive efforts of the Jordanian government, in collaboration with the international community, seem to have mitigated potential overcrowding and any resulting adverse effects on education outcomes. Relatively stable student–teacher ratio and classroom size statistics also support this view in Jordan.

In Lebanon, refugees make up almost one-third of the total enrollment in education (Government of Lebanon and UNHCR 2019). Currently, about 373,000 school-age Syrian refugee children (5–17 years) live in Lebanon (Government of Lebanon and UNHCR 2019).[13] The Syrian refugee population in Lebanon remains the largest concentration of refugees per capita and the fourth-largest refugee population in the world. The public system enrolls Syrian refugee children in three ways: in the first (morning) shift, together with Lebanese students, or in the second (afternoon) shift dedicated for Syrian refugee education (MEHE 2019a). Most Syrian refugee students are enrolled in the afternoon shift. Syrian refugee children from both shifts make up almost half the total number of students enrolled in public schools (MEHE 2019b).

To what extent did the arrival of Syrian refugee children affect the enrollment of Lebanese children? In 2010–11, Lebanon had almost achieved universal primary education enrollment for boys, whereas enrollment rates for girls lagged. Enrollment rates were significantly lower at the lower-secondary and secondary education levels, with only minor gender gaps (see figure 3.12). Rates did not reduce for Lebanese students by 2017–18; on the contrary, enrollment rates increased for lower- and upper-secondary education, in line with the overall trend of increases in schooling. Gaps between Lebanese and non-Lebanese students, however, remained stark in 2017–18. Despite major efforts, about half of refugee children do not attend school, with a strong bias in the age distribution. Refugees' enrollment rates significantly drop after primary education age and decrease even further at upper-secondary education age.

FIGURE 3.12. **School enrollment rates, by education level, 2010-11 and 2017-18**

Sources: United Nations Educational, Scientific, and Cultural Organization's Institute of Statistics database; Labor Force and Household Living Conditions Survey 2018-19.

Note: Figures are not repetition-adjusted.

In all three cases, the availability of enough funds has been crucial in extending service coverage to refugees and shielding the host communities from adverse impact. Estimates show that the provision of education services to all refugee children (not considering demand-side problems) could cost about $392 million in Lebanon, annually ($50 million in Iraq and $198 million in Jordan). Since the onset of the crisis, the international community has contributed substantially to the cost of service provision, including to some extent for Lebanese children, and the Lebanese government has provided the school infrastructure among other resources. As shown in figure 3.13, the cost for the 31 percent of non-Lebanese students enrolled in the second shift (afternoon) is shared by the European Union (40 percent), Germany (30 percent), the Netherlands (8 percent), and a number of other countries. Despite this contribution, a funding gap of 17 percent still exists at that level. Expanding the coverage, however, would require additional finances, especially considering the fact that bringing in those not yet enrolled may be costlier than providing services to those currently enrolled.

HEALTH CARE

The Syrian conflict could affect the health sector outcomes in neighboring countries mainly because of the expanding service demand led by refugee arrivals. Although possible short-term supply disruption (trade channel) and broader economic slowdown could theoretically affect the provision of health care services to Iraqi, Jordanian, and Lebanese constituents, these effects are likely to be dwarfed by that of refugee arrivals, which leads to a sudden increase in demand for health care services. If such demand is met by an equal increase in supply, the impact will fall on the fiscal cost of the additional supply of services (which may or may not be a burden for the country depending on the scale and composition of international support). If the supply does not adapt, then the burden will fall on the host community members in the form of reduced per capita accessibility of health care provision. The actual situation is often somewhere in between these two boundary cases: some fiscal cost (some burden on international community) and some service access reduction. In this section, we try to assess the size of these magnitudes.

In Iraq, two patterns seem to have driven health care sector results: displacement dynamics at the regional level and broader security and political challenges at the national level. Regionally, KRI observed a sudden and significant increase in demand for health care services as a result of refugee and IDP inflows, and the insurgence of the Islamic State has led to degradation of the health infrastructure in conflict-affected areas. Nationally, the subsequent instability and uncertainty have reduced strategic investments in service provision.

Over the course of the Syrian conflict and Islamic State insurgency in Iraq, the country's health sector has experienced considerable fallbacks. Access to health infrastructure, specifically to secondary and tertiary care, has been severely impacted. From 2010 to 2013, the total number of primary health care centers (PHCCs) had increased by 13.3 percent. After the onset the of Islamic State insurgency, however, this increase decelerated to only 2 percent (figure 3.14). Correspondingly, the PHCC density per 1,000 population on the national level peaked at 0.08 in 2013 and decreased to 0.071 in 2017. KRI has experienced the same trend. A combination of conflict damages, a massive influx of IDPs, and a protracted budget crisis in 2014 has tested the ability of the KRI government to respond to the growing health needs of the population. The total number and density of PHCCs in KRI dropped between 2013 and 2017, reaching 812 PHCCs and 0.12 PHCC per 1,000 persons.

Iraq's health sector also suffered major losses of human resources because of the death or emigration of its workforce. In just two years, between 2013 and 2015, Iraq lost 3,938 physicians and 6,787 nurses and midwives. Consequently, the density of physicians per 1,000 persons dropped by 0.17 points during the same period.

In 2017, it still had not recovered to precrisis values, and it remains below Organisation for Economic Co-operation and Development (OECD) levels of 2.9 and World Health Organization (WHO) standards of 1. As for nurses and midwives, the loss of human resources resulted in a decrease in density from its highest level of 1.97 in 2013 to its lowest level of 1.65 in 2015. This density has always been far from OECD (8 per 1,000) and WHO (4 per 1,000) standards. KRI has also suffered from a budgetary crisis since 2014, which has added to the ongoing Syrian refugee crisis and the Iraqi IDP situation. Although the nominal number of physicians increased from 6,693 to 7,755 between 2014 and 2017, the density remained relatively stable as a result of the huge influx of refugees and IDPs.

Refugees receive health care service through an extensive collaboration between the KRI government and the international community. Syrian refugees settled in camps benefit

FIGURE 3.13. **Donor commitments and funding gap for 2018–19 formal enrollment**

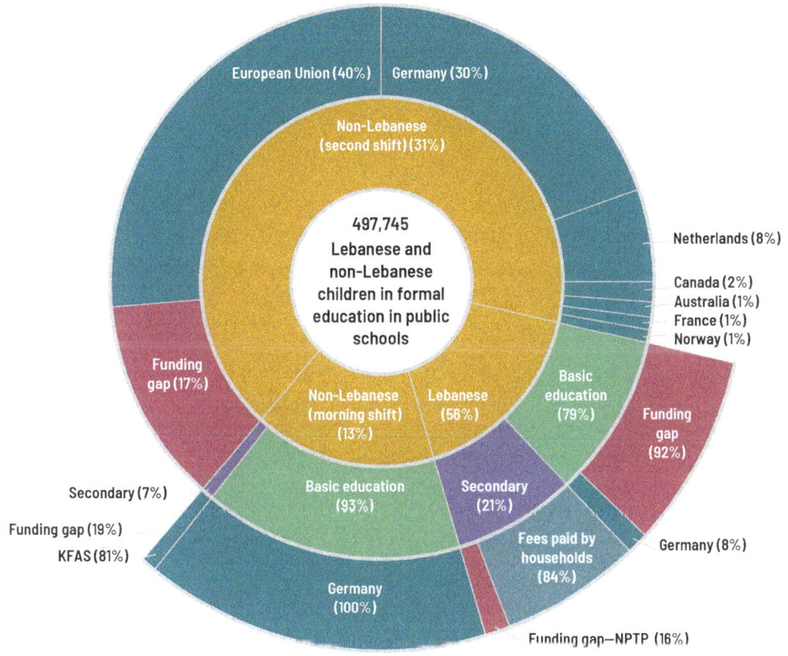

Source: MEHE 2018.

Note: KFAS = Kuwait Foundation for the Advancement of Sciences ; NPTP = National Poverty Targeting Program.

from PHCCs in the camps (a total of nine camps with one PHCC in each). Services are provided by the KRI directorate of health with the financial support of different agencies such as the United Nations High Commissoner for Refugees (UNHCR), WHO, and United Nations Population Fund. Like all nationals of KRI, refugees outside of camps can access all PHCCs, with a payment of 500 dinar per consultation. UNHCR supports these facilities through rehabilitation and procurement of medical equipment. For secondary and tertiary care, all refugees can be referred and have access to the public health facilities free of charge, with no distinction between refugees and others. Economic constraints as well as the high number of IDPs since 2014 have affected the capacity of the local health facilities in KRI to provide quality health services, particularly at secondary and tertiary health facilities. Problems have included irregular payment of salaries to medical staff and shortages of medical supplies and medicines, especially medicines for chronic diseases.

Iraq's health financing indicators have deteriorated. Between 2010 and 2016, government health spending as a share of general government expenditures decreased from 4.81 percent to 1.7 percent. The decrease in government funds for health drove private expenditure for health to increase from 26.1 percent in 2010 to 78.5 in 2016 (all of which is financed through out-of-pocket expenditures), which leaves Iraqis vulnerable to falling into poverty as a result of health expenditures.

In Jordan, health care supply has increased significantly over the last decade, in a trend mainly driven by private sector adaptation. On the supply side, both the infrastructure and the human capital portions of the sector exhibited significant increases since 2010 (figure 3.15).

The number of PHCCs has increased from a total of 1,453, accompanied by capacity increases in existing infrastructure and by the building of new hospitals (Tiltnes, Zhang, and Pedersen 2019), especially in refugee-intensive areas. These capacity increases were driven mostly by private sector response in governorates with the highest numbers of refugees (Amman, Irbid, and Mafraq) where the number of private hospital beds has grown at an average annual rate of 3.9 percent as opposed to the number of public beds, which has grown at an average annual rate of 1.9 percent. Similarly, the number of physicians increased drastically from 4,620 to 6,591 between 2010 and 2018 (figure 3.15).

Despite the increases in health care supply in Jordan, the demand for health care services has increased faster. From 2012 to 2014, the government of Jordan allowed registered Syrian refugees to pay the same rate as insured Jordanians at Ministry of Health facilities, which rendered health services almost free and boosted demand for health services by Syrian refugees. Although access to free health services helped meet the needs of refugees, it was fiscally unsustainable; in November 2014, the Ministry of Health began requiring Syrian refugees to pay the same copayment rate as poor uninsured Jordanians (20 percent of the prices listed for Ministry of Health services). In parallel, the number of PHCCs per 1,000 persons decreased from 0.2 to 0.16 between 2010 and 2018. Physicians per 1,000 persons fell gradually from 0.64 to 0.58 until 2017, but then picked up to 0.66 in 2018.

Jordan's public spending on health care decreased significantly in the last decade. Before the Syrian crisis, Jordan had reduced regressive health care out-of-pocket payments by half—from 42 percent to 22 percent of total health spending (2003–13). With the onset of the Syrian crisis, however, out-of-pocket expenses for Jordanians increased to approximately 28 percent of total health expenditures (2016). This increase is likely due to increased fiscal pressure beyond health service that limited the government's ability to provide financial protection for all. In fact, Jordanian government expenditures on health as a percentage of total government expenditures decreased from 18.39 percent in 2010 to 11.96 percent in 2016.[14] Fiscal pressure and the subsequent reduction in government expenditures on health may have driven Jordanians to seek private health services paid primarily out of pocket (Amnesty International 2016).

In Lebanon, supply-side adaptation to increasing demand has been sluggish in the health care sector. Although the total number of PHCCs in Lebanon increased from 870 to 965 between 2010 and 2018, in per capita terms, PHCC density fell from 0.18 PHCCs per 1,000 persons to 0.14 during that same period (figure 3.16). This decline is more prominent in Beqaa and the northern part of the country that have a higher concentration of refugees. Access to hospital care, measured as the number of hospital beds per 1,000 persons, also decreased from 2.76 in 2010 to 1.54 in 2017 because of both an increase in population and a decrease in the nominal number of beds. Interestingly, the movement of private and public sector beds is very similar over the years. Likewise, although the nominal number of physicians between 2010 and 2018 increased (from 12,163 to 13,837), the ratio of physicians per 1,000 persons saw a drop with the start of the refugee crisis from 2.46 to 2.01.

The lack of a more dynamic private sector response to a sudden increase in demand lies in distortions in the country's health care system. Even before the crisis, Lebanon's health care system struggled to ensure financial coverage to vulnerable Lebanese. The provision of health care services involved the Ministry of Public Health (MoPH) contracting hospitals and allocating a budget ceiling under which it can operate with financing from public funds. In practice, however, this ceiling was seldom enough to cover the health care demand of uninsured Lebanese, causing hospitals to accumulate arrears that the government is expected to pay back.

FIGURE 3.14. **Total number and density of PHCCs, physicians, and hospital beds, Iraq, 2010–17**

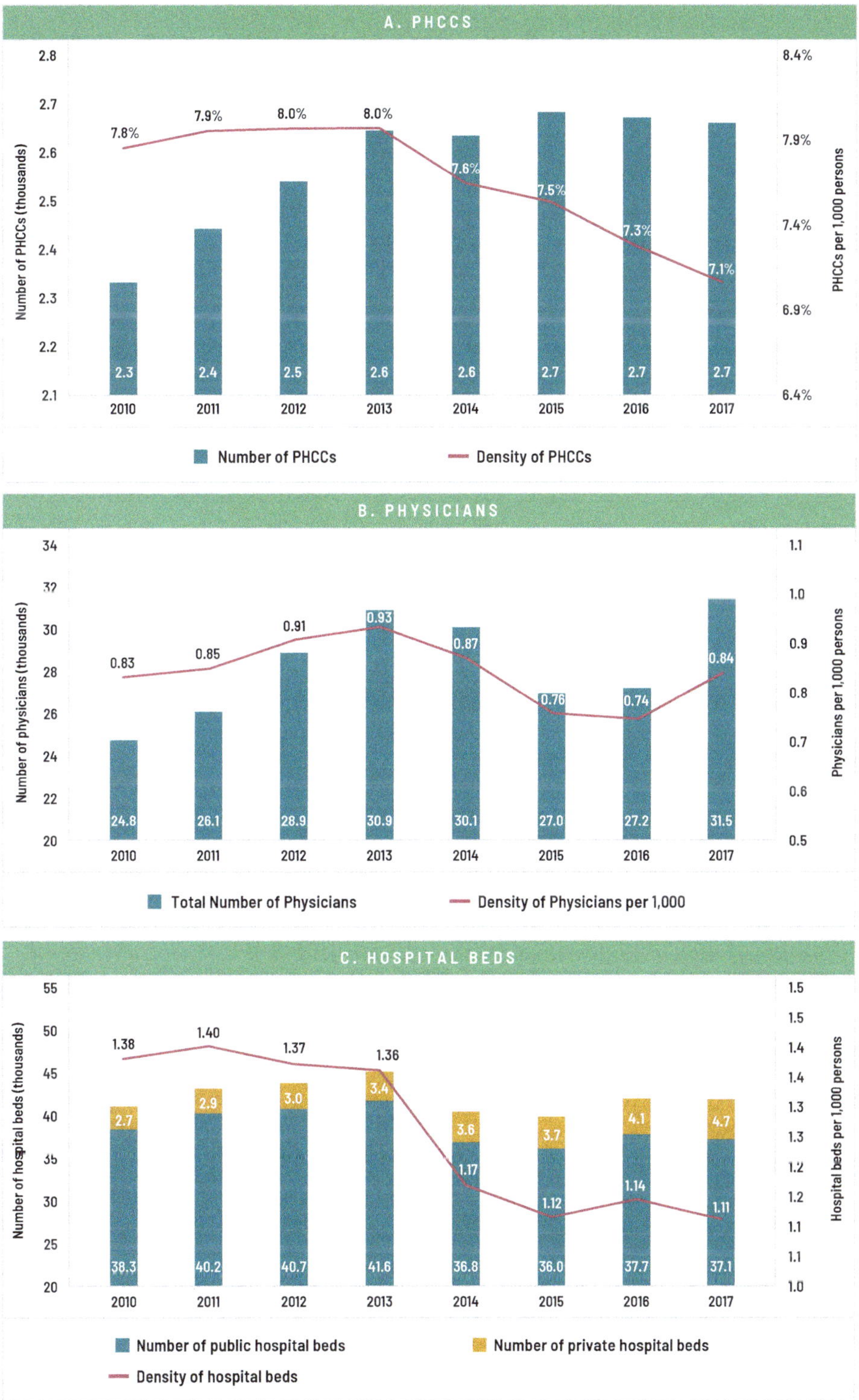

Source: Annual Statistical Reports, Iraq Ministry of Health.

Note: PHCCs = primary health care centers.

FIGURE 3.15. Total number and density of PHCCs, physicians, and hospital beds, Jordan, 2010–18

Source: Ministry of Health services.

Note: PHCCs = primary health care centers.

FIGURE 3.16. **Number and density of PHCCs, physicians, and hospital beds, Lebanon, 2010–18**

Source: Ministry of Public Health.

Note: PHCCs = primary health care centers.

A SURVEY OF THE OUTCOMES

According to the syndicate of private hospitals, arrears to private hospitals (only) for the period 2012–17 amount to $1.4 billion and an average of 94,000 Lebanese citizens annually are on hospital waiting lists because of insufficient financing and the limited budget ceilings for each hospital set by the MoPH. In fact, in certain cases, payments for services provided to Syrian refugees (which are financed by international aid) have been deemed more stable, making refugee treatment a desired business activity in private hospitals.

Financial coverage of health care service in Lebanon was further exacerbated by the onset of the Syrian crisis. The share of government health care expenditures in GDP increased from 3 percent in 2010 to 4.2 percent in 2016. With increasing fiscal pressures on the MoPH, extending coverage for citizens has proven difficult. In certain cases, although hospitals might have sufficient physical capacity to deal with the growing demand, insufficient financing due to increased fiscal pressures has constrained their ability to provide care to uninsured Lebanese.

WATER AND SANITATION

Before 2011, Iraq's water and sanitation systems suffered from low investment in wastewater treatment, low cost recovery, and an emerging gap between water-rich and water-poor areas. In KRI, which hosts the majority of refugees and IDPs, household water consumption was very high at over 350 liters per capita per day (the average for high-income countries is 120 liters per capita per day). This very high level of consumption was also highly subsidized, with only 12 percent of operation and maintenance costs recovered (United Nations 2013). This subsidy created a fiscal burden exceeding $100 million annually (without sewage costs). Nationwide, household access to improved drinking water services was relatively high at the aggregate level (87 percent); however, service interruptions (partially driven by energy supply interruptions) were common, especially in southern and central Iraq. Water quality, particularly salinity of water, in southern Iraq was already acknowledged as a growing problem. As a result, households in southern and central Iraq incurred coping costs in the form of investments in roof tanks, booster pumps, and treatment of drinking water including but not limited to the purchase of bottled water and desalinated water (figure 3.17).

Despite the emerging challenges, water access indicators since 2011 have improved in KRI thanks to supply-side adjustments, but the improvements are not without trade-offs. The KRI government and its development partners adapted quickly to match the hike in demand and improve water supply. The proportion of households with access to piped water increased from 88 percent to 91 percent after 2011. Authorities also made an effort to improve cost recovery, which improved from 12 percent before the crisis to 27 percent in 2017. With costs increasing by about a third and with an expanding demand, total water subsidies were estimated to grow by about 10 percent in the same period.

The supply-side adaptation, however, had other indirect consequences. With lower flows along the Euphrates and Tigris rivers, both biological pollution and salinity (due to tidal surges) have become major problems in southern Iraq. Although authorities increased investment in water treatment facilities in northern Iraq to match the hike in demand, the opportunity cost of this adaptation came in the form of forgone investments in upstream wastewater treatment, which magnified the impact of the upstream riparian developments (and so did not result from the influx of Syrian refugees). In 2018, about 88 percent of the Multiple Indicator Cluster Surveys (MICS) 2018 samples had no trace of E. coli in northern Iraq, and just 50 percent in central and southern Iraq.

FIGURE 3.17. Sources of drinking water in Kurdistan and central and southern Iraq, 2000–18

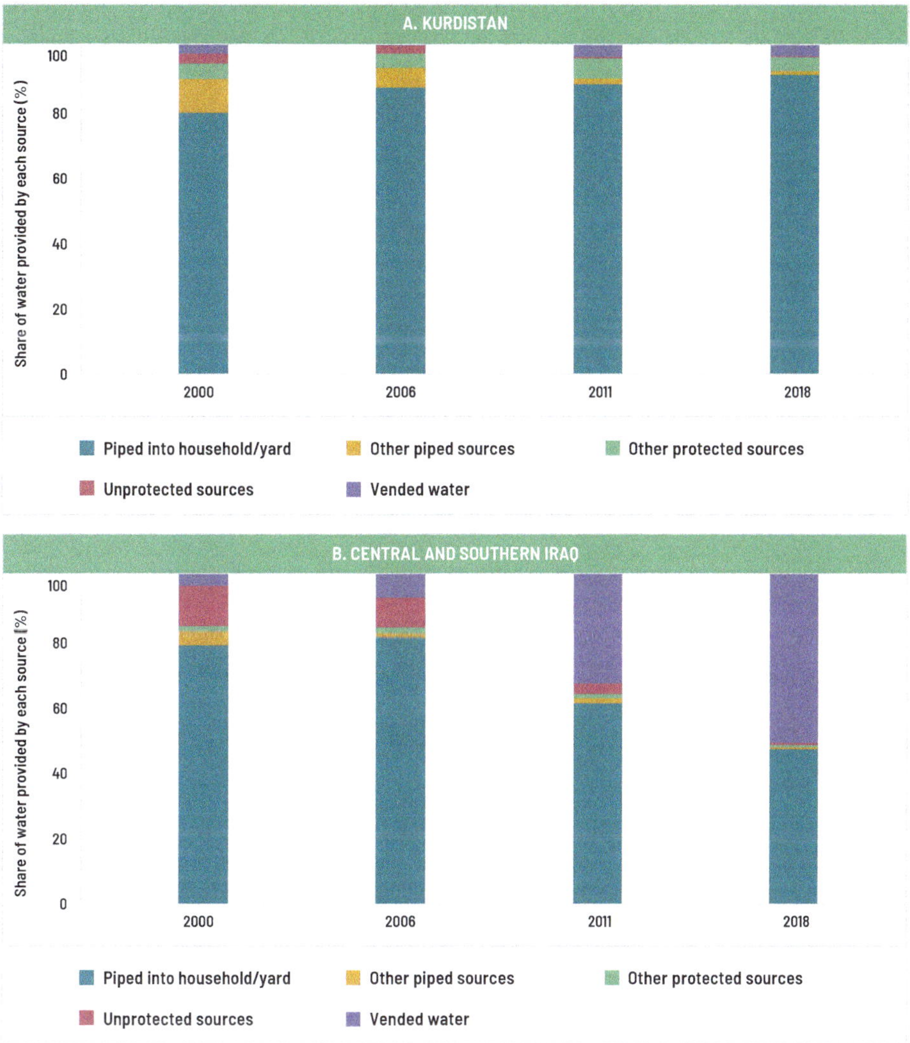

Source: Multiple Indicator Cluster Surveys (MICS) 2018.

Before the onset of the Syrian crisis, Jordan was one of the most water-stressed countries in the world, but service provision was relatively effective. Jordan's total renewable water resources are estimated to be 150 cubic meters (m^3) per capita per year, far below the threshold of severe water scarcity of 500 m^3 per capita per year (Swain and Jäkerskog 2016). Despite this estimate, Jordanians had near universal coverage to piped water at full cost recovery at the aggregate level (figure 3.18)—with the exception of Yarmouk utility company (one of Jordan's three utilities that handle the provision of water and sanitation services), which recovered only 59 percent of costs and provided intermittent services at high costs (pumping water from the Jordan River from more than 500 m below the service area). Household access to improved sanitation was near universal throughout the country; more than half of households were connected to a sewer network, and 24 wastewater treatment plants processed 111 million m^3 of sewage. The network had nearly 640,000 direct connections and provided the other half of households with septic tanks as a way of safely disposing of septage. Wastewater treatment plants were already used as a means of reclaiming 103 million m^3 of water for reuse in agriculture irrigation.

Jordan's water and sanitation sector suffered a double shock after 2011: a demand shock driven by the arrival of refugees and a supply shock driven by a hike in energy costs. The Arab Gas Pipeline, which fueled more than 90 percent of Jordan's power generation through natural gas imports from Egypt, was sabotaged in 2011 (Shenker 2011). With subsequent natural gas shortages, Jordan was forced to switch to more expensive and less efficient diesel and heavy fuel oil during a time of rising global oil prices. This switch had direct consequences for water services. Water utilities consumed 15 percent of all the electricity produced in the country, and electricity represented about half of these water utilities' operational costs. Along with the increased demand for services, additional costs and stagnant tariffs translated into an annual structural deficit of about $375 million and a $3.9 billion cumulative debt, a large share of which was short maturity and costlier than other sovereign borrowing, in Jordan's water and sanitation services. The authorities responded by developing an ambitious reform agenda, the Structural Benchmark Program, which aimed to increase the cost recovery from about 74 percent just before 2014 to 100 percent by 2021 by means of tariff adjustments and cost savings (figure 3.18). By 2017, the program hit the projected benchmark of 89 percent; however, with a further 40 percent increase in electricity tariffs in 2018, it regressed back to 68 percent.

Resolving the sustainability of water services in Jordan will require concerted efforts. At its core, the water and energy sector problems are intertwined: actions toward resolving energy insecurity will also help the water sector, but certain water-specific actions can be pursued as well. These actions include improving the energy efficiency of the water distribution systems (for example, directly connecting heavy loads such as water pumping stations to the grid and increasing water storage to reduce the need for 24/7 pumping) and a gradual tariff adjustment. In both cases, however, technical feasibility and distributional effects (affordability of the service by lower income segments) need to be studied carefully, and compensating mechanisms should be considered as needed. To this effect, synergies in service provision to Jordanians and Syrian refugees should be pursued. In fact, the Yarmouk water utility, which serves areas with high refugee intensity (Mafraq and Irbid), has been the most affected by the higher electricity costs (driven by subsidy removals). Thus, providing refugees water services sustainably can provide an opportunity to improve the overall utility system as well.

Before 2011, Lebanon's water and sanitation services suffered from low storage capacity, low cost recovery, and poorly designed reforms. With low water storage capacity, weak water supply networks, and rapidly rising demand from municipal and industrial sectors, water supply services were below the middle-income country averages and fluctuated seasonally. In the Mount Lebanon service area, for example, residents received only three hours of water a day during the summer season. Countrywide, only 25–35 percent of households relied on piped water as their main source of drinking water. Nearly half of households instead purchased bottled water or resorted to water trucks for their needs, whereas the remainder relied on their own wells and springs (map 3.3). In parallel, 92 percent of Lebanon's sewage was left untreated because of a poorly sequenced investment program and the absence of a viable business model for wastewater: wastewater treatment plants were built, but authorities did not have the financial or technical capacity to manage the plants. As a result, about half of the plants were managed through private sector contracts. The environmental degradation for untreated wastewater was estimated to be $144 million a year (World Bank 2010).

FIGURE 3.18. **Evolution and planned trajectory of operating cost coverage ratio, Jordan**

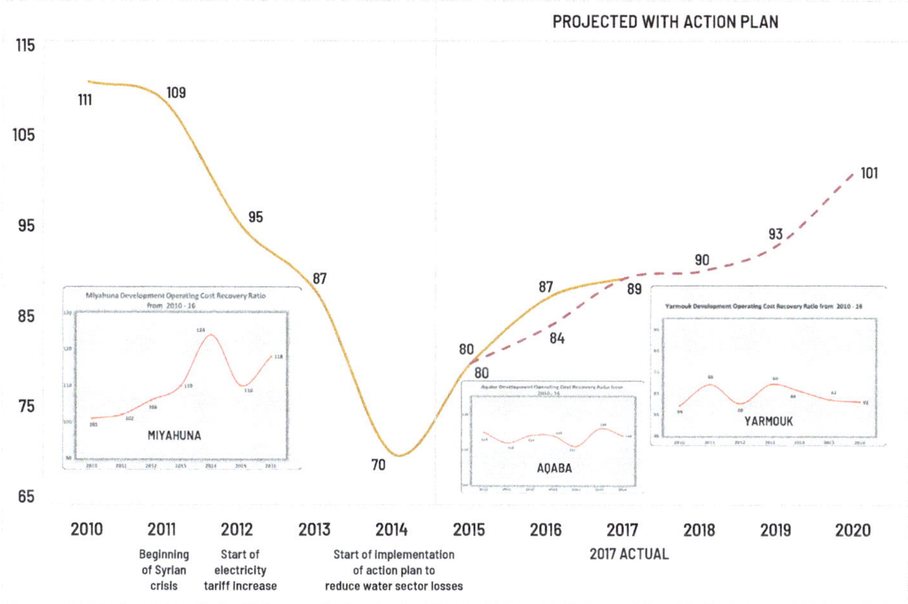

Source: World Bank staff calculations.

The arrival of Syrian refugees magnified Lebanon's prevailing water and sanitation problems in different ways, depending on the settlement type. Where Syrian refugees settled in urban areas (residential buildings), they largely have access to existing water and sanitation utilities. The main issue in urban areas is to prevent informal or unauthorized use of water, fully integrate refugees into commercial processes, and move toward cost-reflective tariffs. Supplying refugees in informal settlements was a bigger challenge. With lower infrastructure and higher proportions of refugees to local population, absorbing the hike in demand in informal settlements was more difficult than in urban centers. Since 2011, an estimated 1 million people are being served 32 million m^3 of water a year (88,000 m^3 a day) from boreholes and surface sources, largely financed by different programs of the United Nations and nongovernmental organizations. This service also comes at a higher average cost than for urban centers because much of this water has to be trucked from boreholes and springs to informal settlements. In certain cases, irregular activities near informal settlements (such as unauthorized access to water sources), which potentially could lead to disruptions in regular service provision, were also reported. Similarly, sanitation facilities in many informal settlements are not connected to existing sewer networks; in some cases, therefore, they are directing sewage into natural water courses. The Litani River Basin Authority actively worked with humanitarian agencies to move settlements away from these natural water courses and enforce improved sanitation solutions.

ENERGY

The Syrian crisis, especially the refugee arrival shock, has inevitably increased pressures on already strained energy utilities in neighboring countries. A recent World Bank assessment has pointed to considerable stress to the energy systems of the host countries, particularly Lebanon and Jordan, caused by the Syrian refugee crisis (World Bank 2019).

MAP 3.3. Water services, by type and location of Syrian refugees, Lebanon, 2019

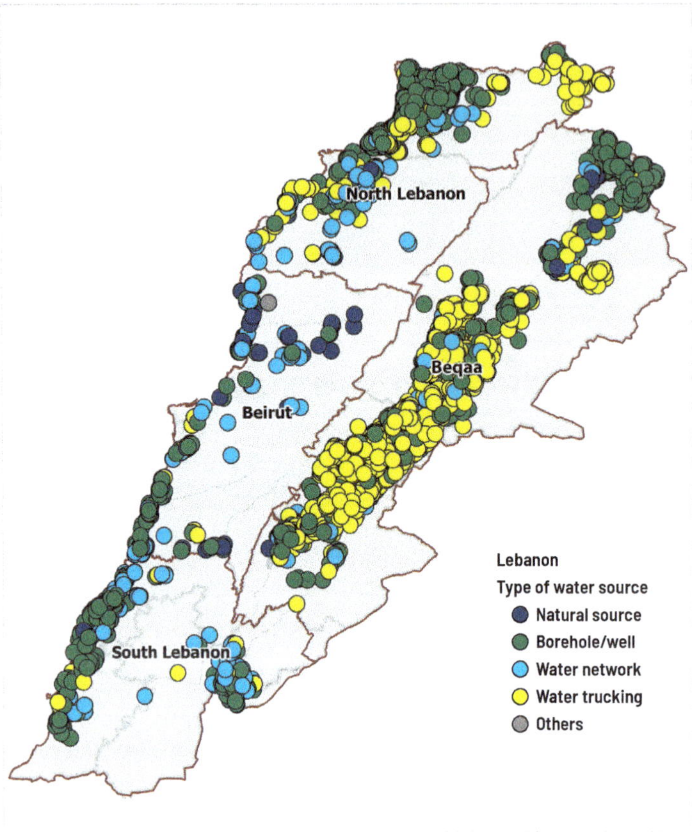

Source: Inter-Agency Mapping Platform, June 2019.

According to this analysis, fuel and electric power use have risen sharply since 2011, as have subsidy bills for the host country governments.

In Iraq, the small number of refugees and limited provision of electricity to them have limited the service access and fiscal impact of the Syrian crisis. Although all Syrian refugees are connected to the electricity grid, they received only about 9 hours of electricity per day on average, despite living in urban areas. In comparison, residents of Kurdistan received 18 hours of electricity per day. In Iraq, the cost of electricity supply is about $0.12 per kilowatt-hour (kWh) on average. With half of this cost recovered through the tariff, the fiscal cost of the refugee-induced demand to be covered by the treasury in 2018 was about $15 million. Since about 2012, the fiscal burden for the treasury would have been about $85 million to $90 million.

Jordan was already an energy-insecure country, importing 96 percent of its fuel demand; the influx of Syrian refugees has put a substantial strain on service provision. Total annual electricity consumption rose markedly from 4,296 Gigawatt-hours (GWh) in 2009 to 6,560 GWh in 2014 (an increase of 34.5 percent), and liquefied petroleum gas consumption increased from 300,000 tonnes per year to 366,000 tonnes per year during the same time period. The government of Jordan forecasted an additional 225 megawatts (MW) of energy required between 2016 and 2018. In November 2017, Jordan established the world's first refugee camp powered by renewable energy. The Azraq solar energy plant at the Zaatari refugee camp is a 12.9 MW solar photovoltaic plant and allowed UNHCR to increase power provision to refugees' homes from 8 hours to the current 14 hours.

The subsidized provision of electricity transmits the demand shock to fiscal balances. The cost of generation is estimated at $0.20/kWh on average, and the cost for the utility to supply the refugee-induced demand in 2018 would be $134 million. The tariff charged to households is about $0.05–$0.10/kWh, depending on the level of consumption per month (World Bank 2017a). The fiscal cost of the refugee-induced demand in 2018 is then about $60 million to $100 million. Since about 2012, the fiscal burden for the treasury could be close to six times as much, or $390 million to $595 million.

In Lebanon, a persistent excess demand prevails despite improvements in capacity. Lebanon was subject to significant load-shedding even before the arrival of Syrian refugees, resulting in supply cuts of roughly 3 hours (12.5 percent) daily in Beirut and up to 12 hours (50 percent) outside the capital and forcing locals to rely on diesel generators on a regular basis. Although 715 MW of total capacity has been added since 2010, the arrival of Syrian refugees necessitates the addition of 486 MW of additional power supply (inclusive of 15 percent technical losses during generation) to cover increased net demand. In total, 3,309,487 people need improved access to electricity. Lebanon currently has a peak demand of 3,400 MW, but only 2,720 MW installed capacity available at peak supply. Information on energy access and consumption is not available for refugees, but their access is almost certainly better than those currently within Syria. On average, between 2012 and 2016, Lebanese residents had roughly 14.0 hours daily (58.3 percent) of power available to them, compared to the 9.1 hours a day in Syria.

With less than complete cost recovery in service provision, Lebanon also faces fiscal consequences. In Lebanon, the cost of generation ranges from $0.17 to $0.23/kWh. At an average of $0.20/kWh, the cost for the utility to supply the extra demand induced by the refugee population from Syria in 2018 would be $252 million. Because the electricity tariff in Lebanon is subsidized, a large part of this cost is typically incurred by the treasury. Specifically, the reported average tariff of the state-owned electric utility—Electricité du Liban (EDL)—is $0.95/kWh (Obeid 2018). The cost recovered by the utility through the tariff (assuming that refugees do pay for the electricity they consume) would then be $120 million, with the remaining $132 million left for the treasury to cover in just one year, 2018. Since about 2013, the fiscal burden for the treasury must have been at least five times as much—that is, close to $750 million. Overall, regardless of the refugees, EDL incurs significant financial losses, $1.5 billion to $2 billion annually.

In all three countries considered in this analysis, a viable system of energy provision will require further efforts going forward. For electric power systems to function properly and deliver adequate services, a sufficient supply capacity to meet demand, including a reserve margin for contingencies, is needed. Because the influx of refugees increases the demand, host countries have several options to consider as coping strategies for their power systems, each involving its own costs. The options include building more generation capacity, introducing energy efficiency measures to curb the demand, and introducing coordinated regional expansion planning for generation and transmission capacity. A comparison between these alternatives, contingent on different population assumptions going forward, is considered in the last chapter of this study.

ENVIRONMENTAL TRENDS

The conflict in Syria could have direct and indirect effects on environmental trends in neighboring countries. First, changing air and water pollution levels inside Syria can affect other countries through transboundary movements of water and air bodies. Second, other things being equal, including per capita economic activity, the arrival of forcibly displaced Syrians could increase the environmental footprint in countries of asylum. Third, the conflict could have a composite effect (through trade, total factor productivity, and demographic shocks) on per capita economic activity in countries of asylum. Unfortunately, we cannot identify these channels independently by using available data sources. In this section, however, we describe the environmental trends in three categories and try to correlate them with refugee intensity subnationally to gain some inference about the correlation between the demographic shock and environmental outcomes. These three categories are the following:

1. *Water pollution*. We use a water clarity index to investigate whether water bodies (mainly lakes and ponds greater than 90 m^2 in surface area and with permanent presence) became more polluted because of the Syrian crisis, and whether a correlation exists between decreasing clarity and the level of refugee footprint. The index remotely detects the pollutants most likely to affect water translucence, algae, and sediment, but cannot identify the specific pollutant source reducing water clarity. May was selected as the month of observation because reservoirs peak around that time after peak precipitation and snow-melt.

2. *Land pollution*. We draw on solid waste management records and remote-sensing imagery to infer changes in land pollution between 2010 and 2019. The assessment focuses on solid waste district-level data and dumpsites, landfills, and burn pits where possible; and change is detected by measuring the size of each dumpsite over time. The analysis uses other sources such as the 2011 and 2016 dumpsite data from the United Nations Development Programme, spatial details of population trends from WorldPop, and 2014 government of Jordan survey data on municipal solid waste.

3. *Air pollution*. We examine whether there are high or increasing levels of fine particulate matter ($PM_{2.5}$) in areas of high refugee presence by using the Emerging Hot Spot Analysis developed by Esri. A hot spot is an area where statistically significant clustering of grid cells with high concentrations of particulate matter takes place, using the Getis-Ord local statistic, not because of a random process but because of a distinct spatial change pattern. This statistical test examines each grid cell within the context of neighboring cells, using a threshold distance of 15 km. The threshold that defines high $PM_{2.5}$ is relative to each country's distribution of values. The underlying data are retrieved from the Atmospheric Composition Analysis Group (van Donkelaar et al. 2016), which combines information from satellite, simulation, and monitor-based sources through a geographically weighted regression.

The water pollution effect of the refugee footprint has been mixed. The results of the water clarity and refugee intensity correlation analysis are presented in the first column of figure 3.19. The dots present the time trend estimates for each water site, and the vertical lines represent the confidence intervals. The water sites are sorted from low refugee presence (left) to high refugee footprint (right). Positive slope coefficients (dots) where the standard error range does not overlap with zero indicate a significant and increasing pollution trend. At the country level, no significant correlation exists between high refugee footprint and increasing levels of water pollution in the three countries. This lack of correlation is inferred by the absence of clustering of significant positives on the right-hand side. Nevertheless, the locations with higher refugee concentration are more likely to experience an increase in pollution, especially in Iraq and Lebanon.

Overall, the Syrian refugee influx has observed negative impacts on water clarity and quality in some local settings. Observed negative impacts in the context of this assessment include water pollution caused by unmanaged sewage and solid waste. Syrian refugees appear to compound existing water pollution challenges and increase the assessed water bodies' vulnerability to climatic, systemic, and regional dynamics. Jordan measures the most significant degradation overall in water clarity over time. Iraq measures the most stability, though minor water clarity degradation over time is apparent. Lebanon registered the most year-to-year variation, trending toward minor water clarity improvements during the period under examination, despite apparent periods of significant water clarity degradation.

Refugees have direct effect on solid waste generation in all three countries. The results for the correlation between changes in solid waste generation over time and refugee intensity are provided in figure 3.19. At the aggregate country level, the districts with the highest number of Syrian refugees registered the highest increases in solid waste. In Iraq, many official landfills analyzed annually between 2010 and 2019 using LANDSAT and Google Earth imagery did not exhibit significant area (m^2) expansion, because it is likely they are all managed to some degree. It is, however, possible that the m^3 measurements over time would register additional change, which can be missed in vertical observations from space. Such an expansion has been noted previously by other studies. For instance, the World Bank reported that refugees and IDPs generated over 1,690 tons of extra solid waste per day.

In Jordan, there have been significant increases in solid waste generation. Amman Governorate's Al-Jizah and Al-Quwasimah Districts and Irbid Governorate's Al-Kurah District registered the greatest change in municipal solid waste (MSW) generation (at least 256.7 percent, 172.1 percent, and 240.9 percent, respectively). The refugee share in Al-Quwasimah is among the ten highest in Jordan, estimated at more than 10 percent of the population in 2017. These observations are in line with other estimates. According to the government of Jordan, in the last 10 years, the total number of official landfills and dumpsites has increased from 20 to 24 (Aljaradin 2014; MMA and CVDB 2014). Similarly, a 2017 OXFAM report notes that the amount of waste transferred to landfill sites in Mafraq tripled since 2011 (Moodley 2017). Recent estimates show that the main cities hosting Syrian refugees, particularly Mafraq, Amman, Irbid, and Zarqa, could face increases of up to 60 percent in solid waste management costs given the strain of the rising population and insufficient infrastructure. Reportedly, most of Jordan's official landfills do not use advanced or ecologically tenable methods of waste disposal: the most common method of landfilling is the trenches method, which can leak waste into the soil and nearby water sources (Aljaradin and Persson 2012).

In Lebanon, refugee numbers correlate with increases in solid waste volumes. Based on United Nations Development Programme district-level data for MSW sites that were operational in both 2011 and 2016, the districts in Lebanon with the greatest increase in MSW between the 2011 and 2016 surveys are El Hermel District (12-fold increase), Aley (6-fold), El Batroun (3-fold), Bent Jbeil (2-fold), and Akkar (about 2-fold)

(UNDP and MoE 2017). It is likely that these significant increases have resulted in part because of pressure from Syrian refugees, at least in part from house-registered refugees and informal settlements (UNHCR 2016, 2020). Reportedly, only 48 percent of the MSW generated by refugees in 2014 was managed within the existing waste management infrastructure, and the rest is disposed primarily through burning and open dumping (MoE, EU, and UNDP 2014). Lebanon Inter-Agency Mapping Platform data from 2016 and 2018 comparing waste management strategies of 3,758 and 5,339 informal tented settlements, respectively, indicate this trend has largely persisted since 2014, with only an 8 percent increase in informal settlements using municipal collection since 2016 (UNHCR 2020).

It is difficult to attribute increases in ambient air pollution to specific sources, but some correlation between emerging hot spots and refugee settlements are observed. The literature typically identifies four channels through which the Syrian crisis is affecting air quality in Lebanese cities: on-road transport, residential heating, open burning of solid waste, and electricity production (MoE, EU, and UNDP 2014). Although it is not possible to decompose these channels, we can observe dynamic patterns around areas of interest and compare them with other areas to gain inferences regarding underlying mechanisms. Map 3.4 shows the results of such an attempt: the maps on the left show air pollution levels, as measured by $PM_{2.5}$ levels in a given volume, in 2016; and the maps on the right show the hot spot analysis for changes between 2005 and 2016.

Iraq shows the highest levels of $PM_{2.5}$ though the national average has decreased substantially since 2010 and has decreased, on average, from 65 micrograms per m^3 in 2006 to 41 in 2016. The reduction was particularly strong in northern, northeastern, and southwestern regions. Currently, the highest concentrations are in the western and southeastern regions, with both clusters recording temporally persistent hot spots. Significant emissions come from the use of low-quality fuel in transport, power generation, and the industrial sectors but also from gas flaring and dust storms (World Bank 2017b).[15]

In Jordan, two parallel but distinct trends in increasing air pollution are visible: urban and regional. Urban air pollution in Jordan is primarily driven by the country's heavy reliance on fuel oil and diesel, which emit high levels of sulfur dioxide, carbon monoxide, and nitrogen oxides. Some sporadic hot spots that are found in the urban core, and near refugee clusters (Irbid and Mafraq), are in this group. The influx of Syrian refugees has increased the number of vehicles on the road, causing an increase in the emission of air pollutants near refugee clusters (MPIC 2016). In addition, worsening air pollution hot spots are found in the eastern region in relatively less densely populated areas. These trends may be related to climate-driven changes in the amounts of sand and dust in air bodies over arid land.

In Lebanon, the concentration of pollution parallels the concentration of demography. In 2016, relatively high levels of $PM_{2.5}$ were observed along the western urban centers (Beirut and Tripoli). These centers are also the persistent hot spots; they exhibited increase in $PM_{2.5}$ intensity since 2005, reflecting the role played by increasing population. Intermittent hot spots are also identified in the northeast (Baalbek), where refugees have settled in large numbers, and the southwestern districts. Overall, these findings show that air pollution trends in Lebanon have largely been driven by demographic dynamics rather than climatic conditions.

FIGURE 3.19. **Water quality and land pollution trends, selected Mashreq countries**

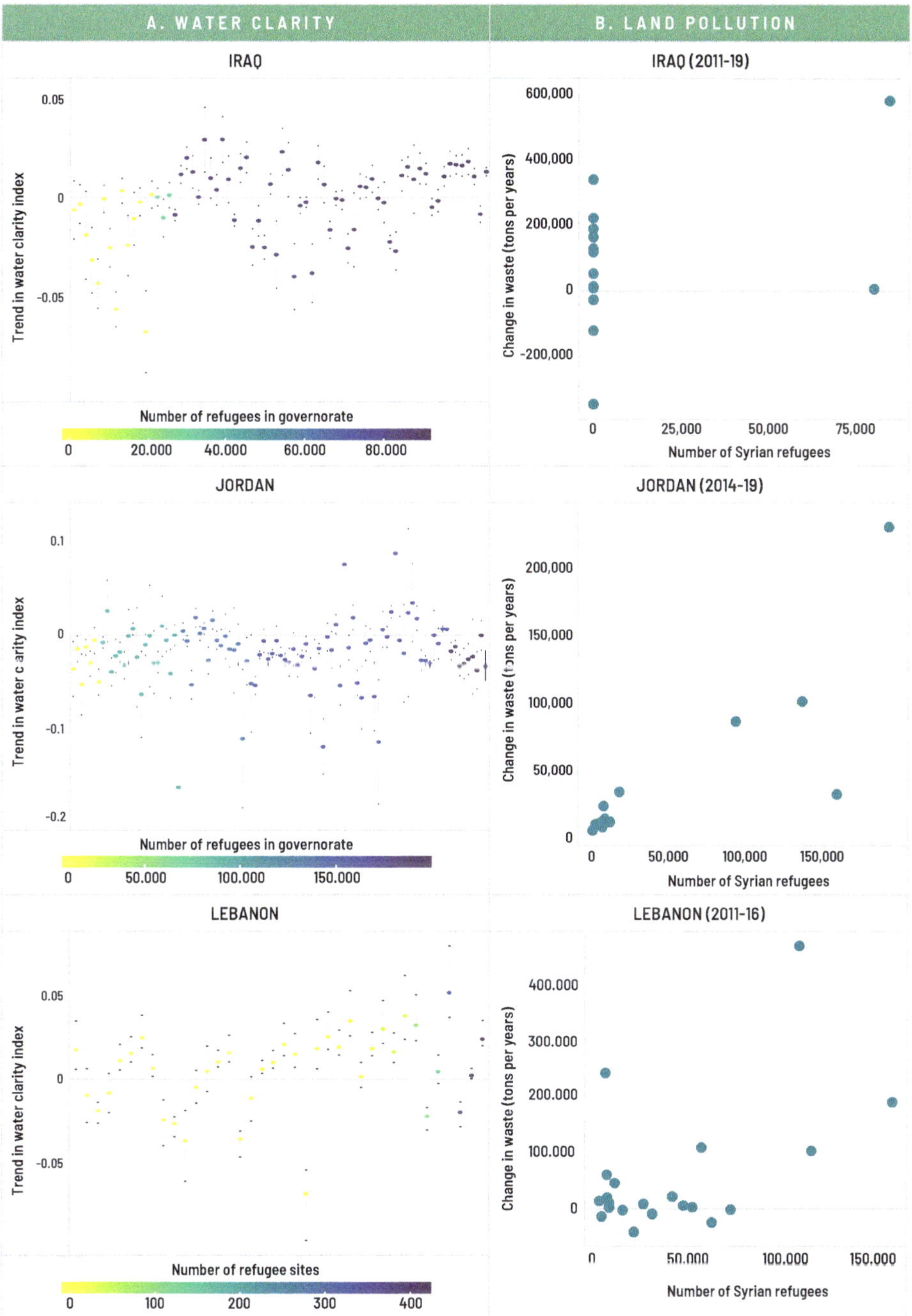

Source: World Bank staff analysis using LANDSAT data.

Note: Dots present time trend estimates for each water site; vertical lines represent confidence intervals. The water sites are sorted from low refugee presence (left) to high refugee footprint (right). Positive slope coefficients (dots) where the standard error range does not overlap with zero indicate a significant and increasing pollution trend.

MAP 3.4. **Fine particulate matter and emerging hot spot analysis, selected Mashreq countries**

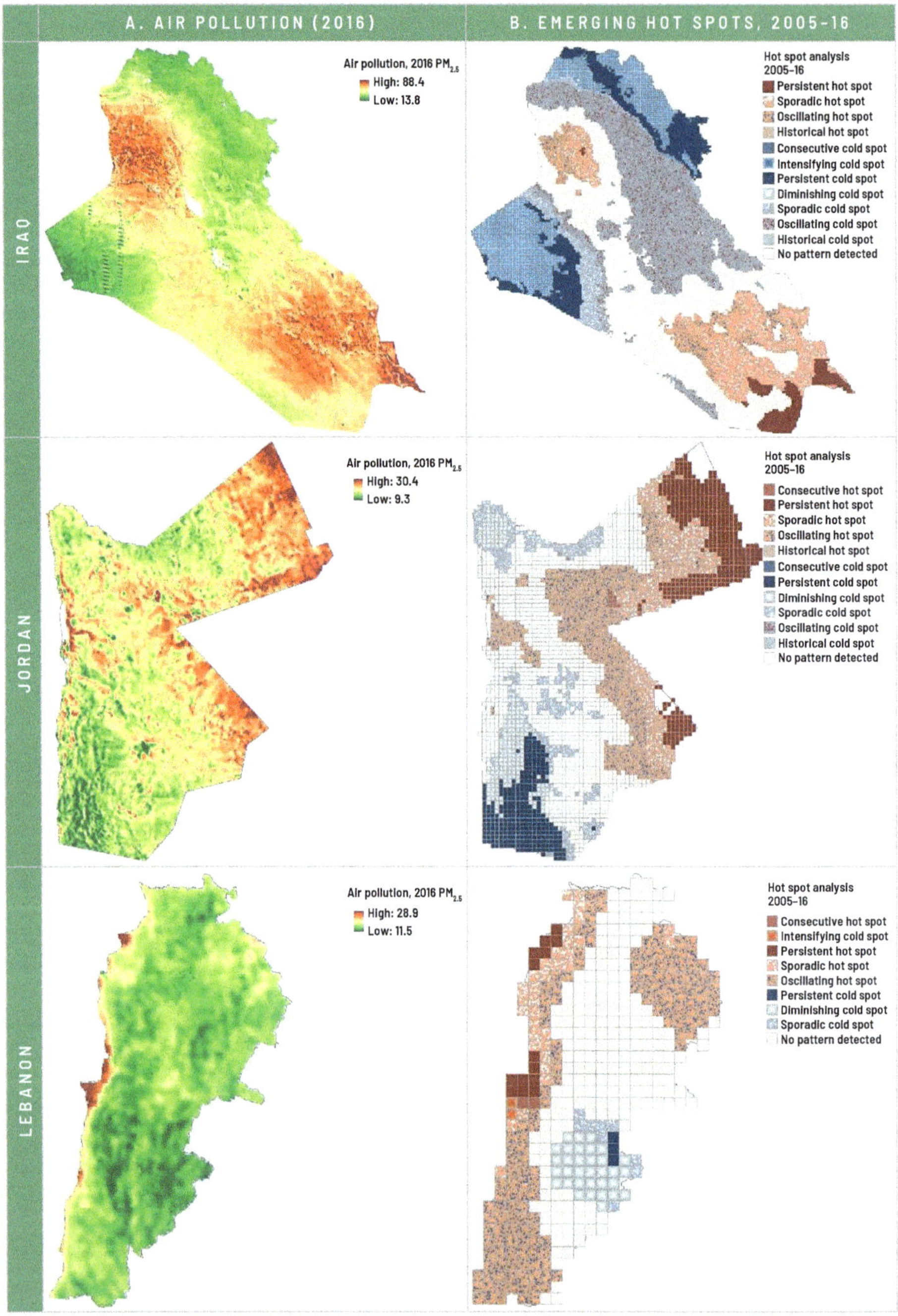

Source: World Bank staff analysis using LANDSAT data.

Note: $PM_{2.5}$ = fine particulate matter.

NOTES

1. On March 16, 1988, an Iraqi military operation code-named Anfal, which employed chemical weapons, led to the killing of an estimated 5,000 civilians in the Kurdish town of Halabja in just five hours.
2. Data from the US Energy Information Administration Database, https://www.eia.gov/.
3. Data from the Jordan Department of Statistics Database, http://dosweb.dos.gov.jo/.
4. One drawback of this methodology is that it does not separate the refugee shock from other factors that might change wage growth rates across governorates. Controlling for the national trend in wages, governorate fixed effects could partially account for this concern.
5. We have also limited the analysis to informal workers only, covering all, educated, and low-educated males. Informal workers are identified as those working without a formal contract or lacking social security coverage. The findings, mainly for the low-educated males (the main group of interest) were consistent with overall wage results.
6. OpenStreetMap is available at https://www.openstreetmap.org/#map=5/38.007/-95.844.
7. Assumed average cost of reconstruction of $500,000 per km of main and secondary roads and $300,000 per km of tertiary and municipal roads.
8. GCFF financing shares: REP = $45.4 million; GBPTP = $69.8 million.
9. For more on WorldPop, see https://www.worldpop.org.
10. In November 2018, there was a new influx of Syrian refugees from northern Syria; the number of children affected had not yet been estimated.
11. Jordan's preuniversity education system is composed of a preschool stage, which is almost entirely private; a basic compulsory schooling stage, which spans first grade to tenth grade; and a secondary stage, which includes the eleventh and twelfth grades, as well as academic and vocational tracks. As of the 2016–17 school year, Jordan had 3,925 basic schools, of which 2,621 (67 percent) were public schools. Similarly, it had 1,477 secondary schools, of which 1,215 (82 percent) were public.
12. Prior to 2014, the settlement process of refugees was somewhat arbitrary, and many were able to directly locate in host communities. Since 2014, the process was tightened and required refugees to start in one of three official refugee camps: Zaatari, Azraq, and the Emirati-Jordanian camp.
13. This number corresponds to the total number of children known to UNHCR (that is, both registered and others that have approached UNHCR for registration), but the number of the Syrian refugee children population varies depending on the source. The Vulnerability Assessment of Syrian Refugees in Lebanon (VASyR) 2018, a household survey on Syrian refugees in Lebanon, reports 488,000 registered Syrian children ages 3–17 whereas the Brussels Report 2018 reports close to 660,000 children.
14. 2020 World Development Indicators.
15. The continual flaring of associated and natural gas in oil fields leads to high levels of emissions. Iraq is flaring up to 70 percent of all the natural gas that it produces, costing billions and releasing about 20 million tons of carbon dioxide per year to the atmosphere. The increase in the frequency and severity of dust and sandstorms is the result of a host of factors including soil degradation and erosion, the deterioration of vegetation, desertification, and the deterioration of green spaces (World Bank 2017b).

REFERENCES

Alix-Garcia, Jennifer, Erhan Artuc, and Harun Onder. 2017. "The Economics of Hosting Refugees: A Host Community Perspective from Turkana." Report No. 113183, World Bank, Washington, DC.

Aljaradin, Mohammad. 2014. "Solid Waste Management in Jordan." *International Journal of Academic Research in Business and Social Sciences* 4 (11): 138–50.

Aljaradin, Mohammad, and Kenneth M. Persson. 2012. "Environmental Impact of Municipal Solid Waste Landfills in Semi-Arid Climates - Case Study – Jordan." *The Open Waste Management Journal* 5 (1): 28–39.

Amnesty International. 2016. "Living on the Margins: Syrian Refugees Struggle to Access Health Care in Jordan." Amnesty International, Amman. https://www.amnestyusa.org/reports/living-on-the-margins-syrian-refugees-struggle-to-access-health-care-in-jordan/.

Assaad, Ragui A., Thomas Ginn, and Mohamed Saleh. 2019. "Impact of Syrian Refugees on Education Outcomes in Jordan." CEPR Discussion Paper No. DP14056, Center for Economic and Policy Research, Washington, DC.

EIA (U.S. Energy Information Administration). 2014. "Jordan Country Analysis." EIA, Washington, DC. https://www.eia.gov/international/analysis/country/JOR.

Government of Lebanon and UNHCR (United Nations High Commissioner for Refugees). 2019. "Lebanon Crisis Response Plan 2017–2020 (2019 Update)." https://reliefweb.int/report/lebanon/lebanon-crisis-response-plan-2017-2020-2019-update.

Harake, Wissam, and Christos Kostopoulos. 2018. "Strategic Assessment: A Capital Investment Plan for Lebanon—Investment Opportunities and Reforms." Working Paper, World Bank, Washington, DC. http://documents.worldbank.org/curated/en/935141522688031167/Strategic-assessment-a-capital-investment-plan-for-Lebanon-investment-opportunities-and-reforms.

Hochberg, Michael. 2015. "Jordan's Energy Future: A Path Forward." Middle East Institute, Washington, DC, August 19. https://www.mei.edu/publications/jordans-energy-future-path-forward.

IMF (International Monetary Fund). 2019. "Second Review under the Extended Arrangement under the Extended Fund Facility." Country Report No. 19/127, IMF, Washington, DC.

Krishnan, Nandini, and Sergio Daniel Olivieri. 2016. "Losing the Gains of the Past: The Welfare and Distributional Impacts of the Twin Crises in Iraq 2014." Policy Research Working Paper 7567, World Bank, Washington, DC.

MEHE (Ministry of Education and Higher Education). 2018. "RACE II Fact Sheet: Issue November 2018." Fact Sheet, Ministry of Education and Higher Education, Beirut. http://racepmulebanon.com/images/fact-sheet-november-2018.pdf.

MEHE (Ministry of Education and Higher Education). 2019a. "RACE II Fact Sheet: Issue March 2019." Ministry of Education and Higher Education, Beirut. http://racepmulebanon.com/images/fact-sheet-march-2019.pdf.

MEHE (Ministry of Education and Higher Education). 2019b. "RACE II Fact Sheet: Issue September 2019." Ministry of Education and Higher Education, Beirut. http://racepmulebanon.com/images/RACE-PMU-Fact-Sheet-September-2019.pdf.

MoE (Ministry of Environment), EU (European Union), and UNDP (United Nations Development Programme). 2014. "Lebanon Environmental Assessment of the Syrian Conflict & Priority Interventons." UNDP in Lebanon. https://www.lb.undp.org/content/lebanon/en/home/library/environment_energy/lebanon-environmental-assessment-of-the-syrian-conflict.html.

Ministry of Transport (Jordan). 2014. "Annual Report." Transport Planning and Development Directorate, Amman.

Ministry of Transport (Jordan). 2018. "Annual Report." Transport Planning and Development Directorate, Amman.

MMA (Ministry of Municipal Affairs) and CVDB (Cities and Villages Development). 2014. "Development of a National Strategy to Improve the Municipal Solid Waste Management Sector in the Hashemite Kingdom of Jordan: Baseline Study on the Existing MSWM System in the Hashemite Kingdom of Jordan." http://www.mma.gov.jo/Files/Docs/11102018_043930BaselineReport.pdf.

Moodley, Soman. 2017. "Trash Talk: Turning Waste into Work in Jordan's Za'atari Refugee Camp." Oxfam Discussion Paper, Oxfam International, August. https://www.oxfam.org/en/research/trash-talk-turning-waste-work-jordans-zaatari-refugee-camp.

MPIC (The Ministry of Planning and International Cooperation). 2016. "Comprehensive Vulnerability Assessment." Jordan Response Platform for the Syria Crisis, MPIC, Amman. https://www.alnap.org/system/files/content/resource/files/main/cva-jordan.pdf.

Nair, Divya Jayakumar, Flavien Gilles, Sai Chand, Neeraj Saxena, and Vinayak Dixit. 2019. "Characterizing Multicity Urban Traffic Conditions Using Crowdsourced Data." *PLOS ONE* 14 (4): e0215728.

Obeid, Jessica. 2018. "Lebanon's Electricity Crisis: Getting to the Heart of It." *Executive*, December 17, 2018. https://www.executive-magazine.com/economics-policy/lebanons-electricity-crisis.

Rozo, Sandra, and Maria Micaela Sviatschi. 2018. "Are Refugees a Burden? Impacts of Refugee Inflows on Host's Consumption Expenditures." SSRN Scholarly Paper ID 3276870, Social Science Research Network. https://doi.org/10.2139/ssrn.3276870.

Sharma, Dhiraj, and Matthew Grant Wai-Poi. 2019. "Arrested Development: Conflict Displacement and Welfare in Iraq." Report, World Bank, Washington, DC. http://documents.worldbank.org/curated/en/914571554209012533/Arrested-Development-Conflict-Displacement-and-Welfare-in-Iraq.

Shenker, Jack. 2011. "Egyptian Pipeline Hit by Fourth Explosive Attack since January." *The Guardian*, July 12, 2011. https://www.theguardian.com/world/2011/jul/12/egypt-pipeline-explosion-fourth-attack.

Swain, Ashok, and Anders Jägerskog. 2016. *Emerging Security Threats in the Middle East: The Impact of Climate Change and Globalization*. Lanham, MD: Rowman & Littlefield.

Tiltnes, Åge A., Huafeng Zhang, and Jon Pedersen. 2019. *The Living Conditions of Syrian Refugees in Jordan: Results from the 2017–18 Survey of Syrian Refugees Inside and Outside Camps*. Fafo Report 2019:04. Oslo: Fafo Research Foundation.

United Nations. 2013. "Water in Iraq Factsheet." Fact Sheet, United Nations, New York, March. https://reliefweb.int/sites/reliefweb.int/files/resources/Water-Factsheet.pdf.

UNDP (United Nations Development Program) and MoE (Ministry of Environment.) 2017. "Updated Master Plan for the Closure and Rehabilitation of Uncontrolled Dumpsites throughout the Country of Lebanon." UNDP and Ministry of Environment. https://www.undp.org/content/dam/lebanon/docs/Energy%20and%20Environment/Publications/Updated-Master-Plan-Volume-A_Final-ilovepdf-compressed.pdf.

UNHCR (United Nations High Commissioner for Refugees). 2016. "Syria Refugee Response: Lebanon Syrian Refugees Registered." UNHCR Lebanon Country Office, Beirut. https://data2.unhcr.org/en/documents/download/53961.

UNHCR (United Nations High Commissioner for Refugees). 2020. "Lebanon Information Hub Data Portal." CARTO. 2020. http://ialebanon.unhcr.org/.

UNHCR and IMPACT Initiatives. 2019. "Multi-Sector Needs Assessment (MSNA) IV of Refugees Living out of Formal Camps in the KR-I." https://reliefweb.int/report/iraq/multi-sector-needs-assessment-msna-iv-refugees-living-out-formal-camps-kr-i-may-2019.

Van Donkelaar, A., R. V. Martin, M. Brauer, N. C. Hsu, R. A. Kahn, R. C. Levy, A. Lyapustin, A. M. Sayer, and D. M. Winkler. 2016. "Global Estimates of Fine Particulate Matter Using a Combined Geophysical-Statistical Method with Information from Satellites, Models, and Monitors." *Environmental Science and Technology 50 (7)*: 3762–72.

World Bank. 2010. "Republic of Lebanon—Water Sector: Public Expenditure Review." Report No. 52024, World Bank, Washington, DC. http://documents.worldbank.org/curated/en/965931468265767738/Republic-of-Lebanon-Water-sector-public-expenditure-review.

World Bank. 2017a. "Jordan Economic Monitor Fall 2017: Towards Stronger External Trade Performance." Working Paper No. 122139, World Bank, Washington, DC. http://documents.banquemondiale.org/curated/fr/444331513705915370/Jordan-economic-monitor-Fall-2017-towards-stronger-external-trade-performance.

World Bank. 2017b. "Iraq—Systematic Country Diagnostic." Report No. 112333-IQ, World Bank, Washington, DC. http://documents.worldbank.org/curated/en/542811487277729890/Iraq-Systematic-Country-Diagnostic.

World Bank. 2018a. "Greater Beirut Public Transport Project, Project Appraisal Document." Report No.PAD2574,WorldBank,Washington,DC.http://documents.worldbank.org/curated/en/471241521338566907/pdf/PAD-final-02262018.pdf

World Bank. 2018b. "Iraq Construction and Investment: Part 2 Damage and Needs Assessment of Affected Governorates." World Bank, Washington, DC. http://documents.worldbank.org/curated/en/600181520000498420/pdf/123631-REVISED-Iraq-Reconstruction-and-Investment-Part-2-Damage-and-Needs-Assessment-of-Affected-Governorates.pdf.

World Bank. 2019. *The Mobility of Displaced Syrians: An Economic and Social Analysis*. Washington, DC: World Bank.

World Bank. 2020. *World Development Indicators*. Washington, DC: World Bank. https://databank.worldbank.org/home.aspx.

WEF (World Economic Forum). 2018. *The Global Competitiveness Report 2017–2018*. Geneva: WEF.

4. UNRAVELING THE NATURE OF THE IMPACT

What is the impact on Iraq, Jordan, and Lebanon of the conflict in the Syrian Arab Republic? In chapter 1, we discussed the challenges of identifying the impact of a conflict on neighbor economies. With global, regional, and national factors that took place around the same time period, a perfect counterfactual case, which would show the economic and social outcomes in the absence of the Syrian conflict, is not available. Moreover, because the conflict has had multidimensional influences in the region, selecting the right indicators for an impact assessment becomes a serious problem. No single indicator would summarize this impact completely. Alternatively, we can use multiple indicators, but this approach has its own problems. On the one hand, in the absence of an attempt to aggregate the impact, this effort would provide a list of effects, but it is not always clear how far the list can be extended and if there is any overlap between the entries on the list. On the other hand, aggregation is not always possible across different dimensions of impact. In light of these difficulties, we need to accept a trade-off.

To isolate the impact of the Syrian conflict, we restrict our attention to the impact on gross domestic product (GDP). In the previous chapter, we analyzed the changes in economic and social conditions (real economy; fiscal balances; labor markets; publicly provided goods and services including transportation, energy, water, education, and health; and environmental pollution) in Iraq, Jordan, and Lebanon during the Syrian conflict. This analysis helped us take stock of changes that can potentially be associated with the conflict. We did not attempt, however, to identify the impact of the conflict in a strict sense because it was not always possible (data issues) or feasible for such a wide range of issues. In this chapter, we focus our attention on the impact of the conflict on GDPs in neighboring countries and try to identify such impact more crisply, by estimating counterfactual GDP levels. We then consider secondary channels of impact, that is, how the GDP impact translates into effects on poverty rates and fiscal outcomes. This approach is not ideal, but it is feasible. It helps us build a better sense of the extent to which the Syrian conflict has been responsible in explaining the trends in these dimensions.

THE IMPACT ON GDP

For many countries around the world, the current millennium commenced with a golden decade, albeit a short one. From 2002 onward, economic growth rates soared significantly above those in the previous decade in many countries. Global GDP growth increased from 2.8 percent in the 1990s to 3.2 percent in 2000–08, annually. Middle-income countries (MICs) performed even better, with growth rates doubling from 3.1 percent per annum to 6.2 percent over the same period. Countries in the Middle East and North Africa (MENA) also observed an acceleration in growth rates from 3.6 percent in the 1990s to 4.6 percent during 2000–08. This trend ended abruptly with the global financial crisis.

The global financial crisis triggered a period of anemic economic performance that has lasted to date. Between 2008 and 2010, global GDP growth retreated to 1.3 percent per annum and has since remained sluggish at 2.8 percent. Similarly, the average annual growth rate in MICs has remained at 4.6 percent between 2010 and 2018, and in MENA countries at 3 percent. In fact, average growth rates in all income groups in the current decade have yet to catch up with that of the short golden decade (figure 4.1).

In Iraq, the volatility driven by conflict and oil dwarfed other factors that may have influenced economic trends. In the past three decades, Iraq has experienced three wars, major sanctions, and numerous political bottlenecks. Its invasion of Kuwait in 1990, imposition of nearly total sanctions four days after (which largely prevailed until 2003), the First Gulf

War in 1990–91, the Oil for Food Program (initially in 1991 in a limited manner, and more effectively after 1997), the Second Gulf War in 2003, major escalation in insurgency from 2011 onward, and the rise of the Islamic State in 2013–14 have all contributed to an exceedingly volatile economic and political context in the country. During this period, the economy rebounded rapidly, but briefly, after the cessation of wars (31.5 percent annual growth for two years after the First Gulf War and 54.2 percent for only one year after the Second Gulf War) and during the Oil for Food Program (24.3 percent annual growth between 1997 and 1999). Despite continuing uncertainty, the country did not experience a major economic crisis after 2010, rendering the average growth rate 2.2 points higher than that between 2000 and 2010, annually.

Jordan, in contrast, has exhibited a more balanced economic trajectory, one that traced global trends relatively more closely. From the 1990s to the 2000s, Jordan's economic performance became stronger and more stable. The average annual growth rate increased from 5.1 percent in the 1990s to 6.9 percent between 2000 and 2008, and the standard deviation of growth decreased threefold (from 4.6 to 1.5) at the same time. Starting from 2010, however, growth has stalled. The average annual growth rate has been a modest 2.5 percent, marking a 3.9 percent drop from the previous decades.

Lebanon's growth record is marked with episodic spurts with long pauses in between. Lebanon experienced two strong growth episodes after the early 1990s, both preceded by wars. The first episode came after 16 years of brutal Lebanese civil war and boosted GDP 2.5-fold (about 16.3 percent growth per year) between 1990 and 1996. From 1997 onward, growth stalled, leaving GDP only 30 percent larger a decade later in 2006 (about 2.7 percent growth per year). Following the brief war with Israel, the economy took off once more and grew by about 9.2 percent per year until 2010 despite the global financial crisis. Since then, Lebanese GDP has grown by only 1.4 percent per year, which makes the difference between growth rates in two consecutive decades the largest (4.4 percentage points) among comparators (figure 4.1).

Can global or regional factors explain the post-2010 slowdown in Jordan and Lebanon? The parallelism between the global trends and the GDP trajectories in Jordan and Lebanon suggests that at least some of the post-2010 slowdown in these two countries could be driven by global trends. The differences in economic performance between the two consecutive decades (2000s and 2010s) are much larger in Lebanon and Jordan (4.4 and 3.9 percentage points per year, respectively) than in comparable countries (1.3 percentage points in MICs) and even in countries affected by fragility, conflict, and violence (1.6 percent), as shown in figure 4.1. Similarly, several region-specific factors, including Arab Spring events, regional tensions, and the 2014 oil price collapse, could also contribute to the slowdown in Jordan and Lebanon; but the slowdown in these two countries is also much more significant than the average decrease in MENA (1.2 percentage points). Overall, these differences suggest that other factors may have influenced the post-2010 economic performances.

To separate the impact of the Syrian conflict from that of global and regional factors, we run an analysis using the synthetic control method (SCM). In the absence of a direct measure of the impact of the conflict, this approach helps generate counterfactual series for analyzing the impact of a treatment, for example, an exogenous shock or policy. It involves assigning weights to the members of a control group not subjected to the treatment. This weighted control group becomes a synthetic benchmark. Once the weights are optimized to make sure the synthetic series mimics the pretreatment trajectory of the main subject, then the post-treatment (after-shock) performances are compared between the main subject of the analysis (actual data) and the synthetic series (counterfactual) to assess the impact of the treatment.

FIGURE 4.1. GDP growth comparison across decades, selected Mashreq countries versus comparators, 2008–18

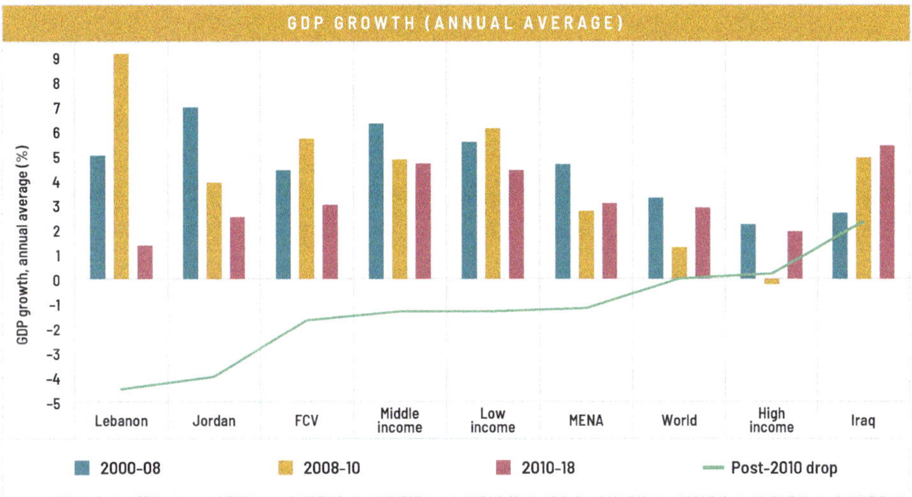

Source: World Bank staff calculations.

Note: Figure shows average annual changes in constant 2010 US$. FCV = (countries affected by) fragility, conflict, and violence; MENA = Middle East and North Africa.

For the purposes of this study, three different specifications of the SCM are used. The first specification puts greater emphasis on maximizing the model's fit in preconflict years with no consideration of dimensionality of data. The second specification allows a trade-off by incorporating several covariates at the expense of the model's fit. Finally, the third specification amends the second one by imposing a MENA-specific shock, which is estimated in a growth regression with MENA-year fixed effects for post-2010 years. Box 4.1 provides a more detailed description of these approaches, and figure 4.2 shows the estimation results. Overall, all three methods have desirable characteristics and drawbacks. Thus, we use an unweighted average of the three specifications as our preferred method.

The estimated impact of the Syrian conflict on GDPs in Iraq, Jordan, and Lebanon has unambiguously been negative and sizeable. Figure 4.3 compares the actual average annual GDP growth rates (yellow bars) with the counterfactual estimates (red bars) between 2010 and 2018. In Jordan, the average GDP growth rate in the counterfactual scenario (no Syrian conflict) is estimated at 4.1 percent annually since 2010, which is 1.6 percentage points higher than the actual growth rate. The counterfactual growth rate in Lebanon, at 3.1 percent, is estimated to be 1.7 percentage points greater than the actual in the same time frame, and in Iraq, at 6.7 percent, 1.2 percentage points higher.

Overall, the Syrian conflict seems to have reinforced the adverse effects of the global and regional factors on GDPs in Jordan and Lebanon since 2010. Our estimates show that not all economic slowdown in Jordan and Lebanon between the 2000s and 2010s can be attributed to the Syrian conflict. Even in the absence of a conflict in Syria, global factors (such as stalling economic recovery in the aftermath of the global financial crisis and oil price collapse in 2014) and MENA-specific factors (such as Arab Spring events other than the Syrian conflict and tensions in the Persian Gulf) alone would lead to a decrease in average annual GDP growth by 2.0 percentage points in Jordan and 2.3 percentage points in Lebanon between the 2000s and 2010s, as shown in figure 4.3 (the difference between the blue and green bars). In comparison, the extreme fluctuations in the Iraqi economy in the 2000s hinder a meaningful comparison over decades along these lines.

BOX 4.1. Estimations based on the synthetic control method

In the absence of a truly valid way to measure counterfactual gross domestic product (GDP) growth rates in neighbors of the Syrian Arab Republic, as a second-best attempt to assess how GDP series would behave in the absence of a conflict in Syria we employ a synthetic control method (SCM) developed by Abadie and Gardeazabal (2003) and extended in Abadie, Diamond, and Hainmueller (2010, 2015).

This method searches for a weighted combination of other countries (donors) that resemble as closely as possible the characteristics of the target country in the pretreatment period in terms of an outcome variable (GDP level in this case) and a set of other specific covariates. This is achieved by minimizing for the pretreatment period the root mean squared prediction error (RMSPE).

The predictors we considered to conduct the analysis are GDP level (our outcome variable, in constant 2010 US$), population growth (annual percentage), inflation (annual percentage), trade openness (trade as percentage of GDP), industry share (agriculture and industry as percentage of GDP), a measure of human capital (secondary and tertiary gross school enrollment), and some indicator of investment share (gross fixed capital formation as percentage of GDP).

The donor pool includes all countries except those directly or indirectly affected by conflicts in the period of our analysis. To account for regional shocks that could have affected the Middle East and North Africa (MENA) region independently from the Syrian conflict, we also implement a simple economic growth regression model, and use MENA region effects to amend results.

We consider the following alternative SCM specifications:

First specification (Sp #1). All preintervention outcome years are used as predictors, which helps to create a remarkably well-fitting model to the observed pretreatment model (minimizing RMSPE). Other covariates are assigned very small weights, however, which can introduce bias.

Second specification (Sp #2). The number of preintervention outcome years is restricted to three, which reduces the fit of the model but assigns greater weights to other covariates.

Third specification (Sp #3). The predictions in Sp #2 are amended by introducing a MENA growth differential in the posttreatment period, by using MENA fixed-effects from a cross-country growth regression.

Accounting for Iraq's oil GDP in synthetic control-based estimations has proven to be a daunting challenge. Oil production is the single most important driver of Iraq's GDP, and it increased drastically in recent years regardless of the Syrian conflict, the Islamic State insurgency , and internal displacement. To address this special situation, the actual growth rate in oil GDP in the posttreatment period is imposed on the synthetic series.

Overall, whereas the first two specifications would incorporate only global factors that may affect the post-2011 growth dynamics in Iraq, Jordan, and Lebanon (for example, oil price shocks and global economic slowdown), the third specification would also incorporate MENA-wide factors (for example, average Arab Spring effects, including the Syrian conflict, and region-wide tensions). In the absence of a dominating approach, the analysis employs an average synthetic series, in which equal weights are assigned to each specification. Technical explanations of these estimates are provided in appendix C.

FIGURE 4.2. **Synthetic GDP estimates, Iraq, Jordan, and Lebanon, 2000–18**

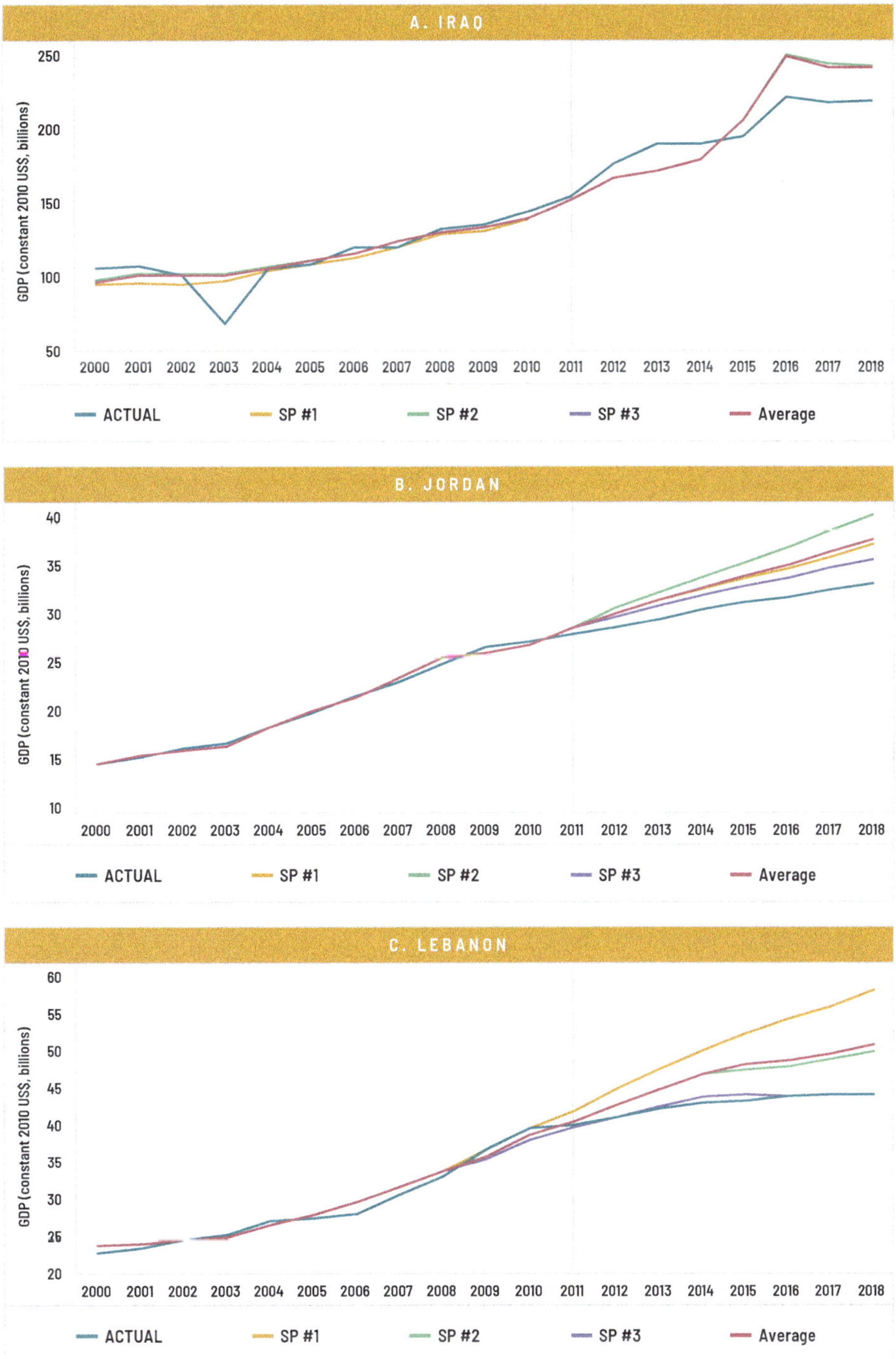

Source: World Bank staff calculations.

Note: Sp #1 denotes the first specification with all pretreatment outcome values used as predictors, Sp #2 uses three pretreatment outcome values as controls (beginning, middle and end of period years), Sp #3 amends the Sp #2 by incorporating MENA-specific growth shocks in the post-2010 period, and finally the Average series presents the average of these three series with equal weights. MENA = Middle East and North Africa.

To mitigate the adverse impact of the conflict effectively, we need to better understand the mechanisms through which such impact is manifested. A conflict can affect the economic and social outcomes in neighboring countries through multiple channels, including via cross-border flows of goods, people, and money. The relative significance of these channels often varies across cases, and their effects are not necessarily in the same direction (that is, whereas one flow could depress economic growth, the other one might stimulate it). Thus, an accurate mapping of these channels, and their role in explaining the economic impact, is a natural first step in designing effective policies to mitigate the undesired effects of the conflict. This mapping is what we turn to next.

DRIVERS OF THE GDP IMPACT

The conflict in Syria has likely affected other economies in many ways, but we cannot measure or identify all these factors. Conflicts have multidimensional effects on economic, social, and political spheres within their zone of influence. Unfortunately, some of these effects (for example, cultural and political) are not quantifiable in detail given our current tools and techniques. In this study, we estimate the impact of the Syrian conflict on the growth dynamics in Iraq, Jordan, and Lebanon between 2011 and 2018, and isolate the marginal effects of refugee arrival shocks and trade shocks, while also considering a residual effect (total factor productivity [TFP] shock) that combines other factors. Doing so does not mean that other factors are not important; it is just that we cannot separate those effects given data limitations. The three shocks considered are defined as follows:

- *Refugee arrival shock* reflects the increase in population with both supply and demand shocks in labor and goods markets being affected, along with the injection of associated international aid.
- *Trade shock* reflects the closure of trade routes through Syria and Iraq, with an adverse effect on exports, the decrease in import demand in Syria, and the decline in demand for tourism services in the region.[1]
- *TFP shock* reflects unobserved characteristics that affect growth but are not explicitly captured in the modeling framework (for example, overall investor or consumer confidence, innovation, and so on) and is treated as residual.

These shocks are calibrated to match the observed outcomes. For the period under consideration (2011–18), the following series are observed and used in the simulations: GDP growth, private and government consumption, exports and imports growth, population, and skilled and unskilled labor force. For analysis of counterfactual series, we use the SCM estimates of counterfactual GDP growth as the basis. Next, we employ a structural gravity model (explained in the appendix) to generate counterfactual exports and imports series for all three countries. Population trends reflecting the natural evolution in the absence of the Syrian conflict were gathered by using United Nations Population Division's population growth rates as specified in the 2010 vintage.

Computations are performed by means of a computable general equilibrium (CGE) model tailored for the countries in consideration. The model underlying the simulations is the Global Trade Analysis Project (GTAP) model—a multiregion, multisector, and multifactor CGE model solved in a dynamic recursive setting (Hertel 1997).

FIGURE 4.3. **GDP growth rate comparison, 2000-10 versus actual 2010-18 versus counterfactual 2010-18**

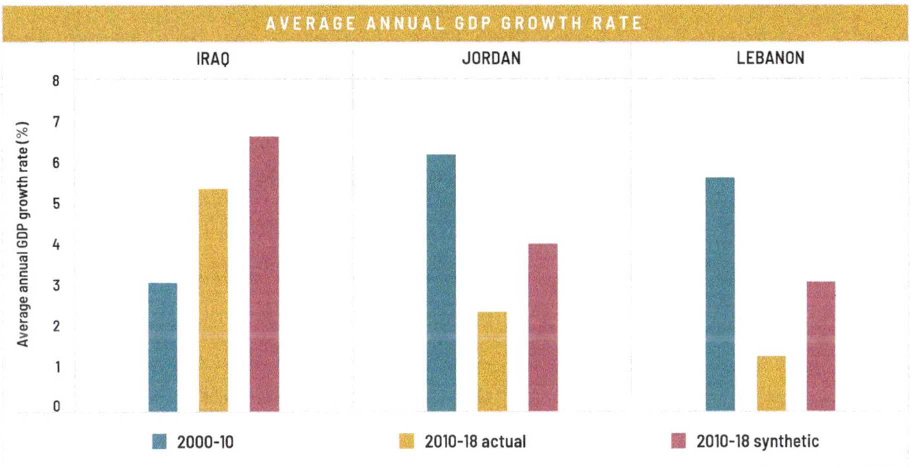

Source: World Bank staff calculations.

The GTAP model is calibrated using the GTAP 9 database representing the global economy in 2011 extended to include Iraq, Syria, and Lebanon, which are missing in the standard version of the database (Aguiar, Narayanan, and McDougall 2016; Aguiar et al. 2019). For the purpose of the simulations, the GTAP database was aggregated into 34 sectors and 8 countries and regions (Iraq, the Islamic Republic of Iran, Jordan, Lebanon, Syria, the rest of MENA, Turkey, and the rest of the world). The model is ideal for measuring the impact of policies that have wide-ranging effects because it takes into consideration general equilibrium links. These links include interactions between consumers, producers, and governments; inter- and intraindustry links; interactions between domestic and foreign markets; investment decisions; and resource constraints.[2]

The model is used to estimate the marginal impact of each shock. As a first step, the GTAP model is estimated using actual outcomes to generate a dynamic path for the evolution of these economies for 2011–18. In the next step, actual outcomes (shocks) are replaced with counterfactual assumptions representing their evolution in the absence of the Syrian conflict. One step at a time, counterfactual shocks for population, trade, and TFP growth are used in order to isolate the marginal impact of these factors on GDP growth in Iraq, Jordan, and Lebanon between 2011 and 2018. Thus, starting from real outcomes, for which all shocks are calibrated to generate a transition from actual 2010 data to actual 2018 data, we exclude each shock one by one to measure the marginal impact. For instance, the interpretation of the trade shock is an answer to the question "What would happen to GDP if all other shocks—except the trade shock—were to hit the country?"

Marginal effects are not decompositions. In our framework, results of the three simulations discussed above cannot be interpreted as additive, but rather they capture the marginal effects of population, TFP, and trade shocks. With general equilibrium and feedback effects, the combined impact of these shocks differs from the sum of the different components. In other words, the sum of marginal shocks on GDP is not equal to the overall GDP shock of the conflict because of the interaction effects.

THE MARGINAL EFFECTS OF THE REFUGEE SHOCK

In this scenario, the actual population and labor force growth observed in the data are replaced with counterfactual population and labor force estimates. All other shocks replicating the actual growth path of these economies are kept at their observed levels. The left-hand graph in panel a of figure 4.4 highlights the differences between actual and counterfactual population growth for the 2011–18 period. Notably, in the absence of refugees, population growth in Lebanon would have been only 0.7 percent per annum, compared to the actual 4 percent including refugees. In the case of Jordan, the difference between actual and counterfactual is slightly less but still significant at 3.8 percent and 1.8 percent, respectively. For Iraq, refugee arrivals were modest relative to the total population, and they added only 0.1 percentage point to annual population growth for the period 2011–18.

Results show that the marginal effect of the refugees on GDP was positive in all three host countries but more pronounced in Lebanon and Jordan. The right-hand graph in panel a of figure 4.4 shows the GDP effect of removing the refugee shock from observed outcomes in each country. In the absence of refugees, Lebanon's GDP would have grown on average 0.9 percentage points more slowly between 2011 and 2018, by 0.5 percent per year instead of the actual 1.4 percent we have observed, other things being equal. Similarly, in the absence of refugees, Jordan's GDP would have grown 0.9 percentage points more slowly, at 1.5 percent per year instead of the observed 2.4 percent. As expected, the impact of the refugees on growth in Iraq was beneficial but modest. Note that GDP is an indicator of aggregate economic activity, and it does not capture distributional consequences. Thus, although the overall economic activity increases with a hike in population, per capita income of certain individuals or groups can still be reduced by the shock.[3]

The positive GDP effects are driven by supply- and demand-side factors reinforcing each other at the aggregate level. In this simulation, refugees become part of the unskilled labor force at the rate of participation described in World Bank (2019). As a result, the decline in the labor force in the counterfactual scenario has different supply- and demand-side implications. On the supply side, slower labor force growth has adverse implications for economic activity in the host countries, resulting in a binding resource constraint. Sectors intensive in unskilled labor contract and decreasing demand for inputs have a dampening effect on the rest of the domestic economy. The slowdown in activity negatively affects wages and rates of return as well as exports and investment. On the demand side, a decline in wages leads to a fall in income for consumers.

THE MARGINAL EFFECTS OF THE TRADE SHOCK

The Syrian conflict had a significant adverse effect on the trade flows of both Jordan and Lebanon (figure 4.4, panel b). In this scenario, observed export and import growth are replaced with the counterfactual estimates.[4] These suggest that, in the absence of conflict, export growth in Jordan would have been much stronger, at an average of 6.9 percent per annum for 2011–18, compared to the observed 0.6 percent. Similarly, without the Syrian conflict, imports are estimated to have grown at 5.0 percent per annum, compared to the actual 0.3 percent. In the case of Lebanon, the dampening impact of the Syrian conflict on imports is shown to be insignificant compared to the actual for the 2011–18 period.

Results show that the trade shocks associated with the Syrian conflict had a significant dampening effect on growth in Jordan and Lebanon. The right-hand graph in panel b of figure 4.4 shows the marginal GDP effects of the trade shocks in Jordan and Lebanon; due to data limitations, Iraq was not included. Everything else equal, with the higher counterfactual trade growth, Lebanon's GDP would have grown on average 2.9 percentage points faster between 2011 and 2018 (by 4.3 percent instead of the actual 1.4 percent). Similarly, in the absence of refugees, GDP in Jordan would have grown 3.1 percentage points faster (at 5.5 percent instead of the observed 2.4 percent). The analysis could not be repeated for Iraq in a reliable manner given the extreme volatility of the country's oil exports.

Trade shock has widespread effects in the economy. Higher export growth in the "no conflict" counterfactual boosts the output of export-oriented industries and benefits other domestic sectors indirectly, through higher input demand. Economic expansion benefits factors of production through higher rates of return, and workers benefit from higher wages. Import demand also expands as a result of increasing income, but this effect is dominated by the income effect of export expansion driven by better access to markets and lower transportation costs (in simulations, import level is set at its actual and counterfactual levels, respectively).

THE MARGINAL EFFECTS OF THE TFP SHOCK

In all three countries, especially in Lebanon, counterfactual TFP growth rates are significantly higher than the actuals. TFP captures a series of unobserved and not explicitly modeled factors such as consumer, producer, and investor confidence; innovation; and technological change. There are two sets of TFP estimates generated: the first associated with actual outcomes and the second with counterfactual outcomes. In order to estimate the marginal effect of the TFP shock associated with the Syrian conflict, actual TFP growth is replaced with counterfactual TFP growth. Model estimates reflecting actual outcomes suggest a negative average annual TFP growth of −0.6 percent in Lebanon and close to zero in Jordan (figure 4.4, panel c). In comparison, TFP growth in the counterfactual scenario is positive, at 0.5 percent for both countries from 2011 to 2018. In the case of Iraq, TFP growth is estimated to be positive in both scenarios, but 0.5 percentage points lower in the counterfactual.

Results suggest that the negative TFP shock associated with the Syrian conflict had a dampening effect on growth in all three countries. Everything else equal, assuming the TFP growth of the counterfactual scenario, Lebanon's GDP would have grown on average 2.8 percentage points faster between 2011 and 2018, by 4.2 percent instead of the actual 1.4 percent per year. Similarly, results show that GDP in Jordan would have grown 2.6 percentage points faster, at 5.0 percent instead of the observed 2.4 percent per year (figure 4.4, panel c). Finally, although Iraq did not experience a large trade and refugee arrival shock, lower TFP growth associated with actual outcomes had a dampening effect on growth of 1.9 percentage points for 2011–18.

Overall, the marginal effects analysis shows that the collapse of trade and the intangible consequences of the Syrian conflict have been detrimental for neighbors of Syria. In both Jordan and Lebanon, a substantial decrease in exports and imports, culminating in trade balance compression, has been the most significant driver of the slowdown in GDP growth. This effect is followed by the intangible factors that have depressed the growth through stalling TFP growth. Finally, the arrival of refugees has been found to boost the GDPs in these countries; however, this effect has not been large enough to mitigate the adverse effects from the trade and TFP shocks.

FIGURE 4.4. **The sizes and marginal effects of different shocks on GDP in Iraq, Jordan, and Lebanon, 2011–18**

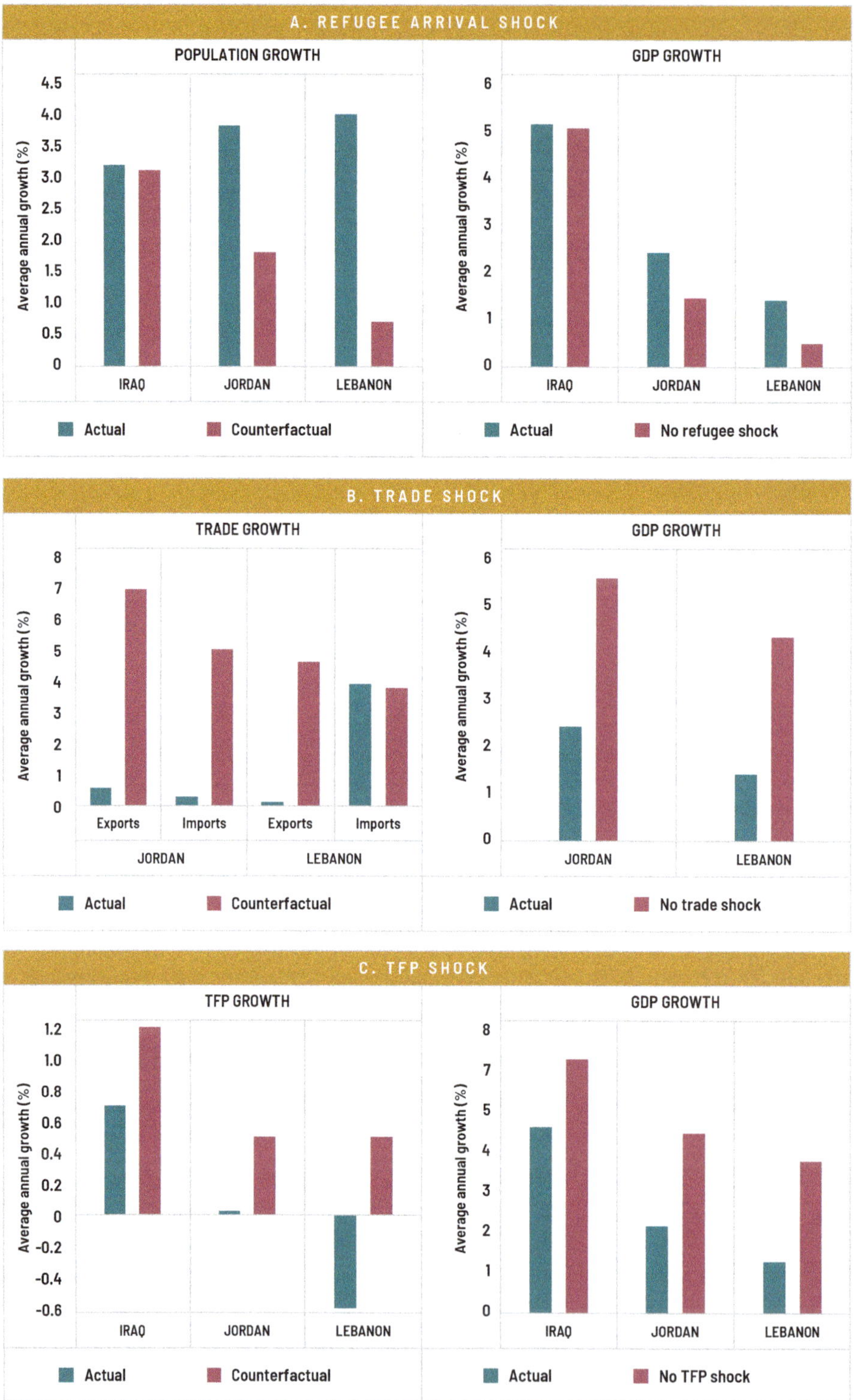

Source: World Bank staff calculations.

Note: TFP = total factor productivity.

The marginal impacts on GDPs should be interpreted in a limited manner. It is important to note that even in ordinary cases GDP trends and individual welfare are not always closely correlated. In the case of the three countries covered in this study, the changes in aggregate economic activity are accompanied by a population hike, and the shocks are likely to have nonuniform effects across the local populations. Unfortunately, it is not possible to take stock of all these heterogeneities; however, in the next section we attempt to infer certain distributional consequences of the GDP impacts.

DISTRIBUTIONAL IMPLICATIONS OF THE GDP IMPACT

How did the GDP impact of the Syrian conflict affect the well-being of Iraqis, Jordanians, and Lebanese? Variations in a country's GDP are rarely accompanied by equivalent changes in everybody's income, yet the distributional characteristics of such aggregate dynamics represent an important aspect of the welfare impact. In this section, we evaluate the welfare and distributional effects of the conflict in Syria on households in Iraq, Jordan, and Lebanon using a microsimulation-based analysis. The simulations focus on how the macro-shock in the form of GDP growth reduction driven by the Syrian conflict (as captured by the counterfactual simulations earlier), as well as demographic and labor market adjustments (as captured in the actual data), are transmitted to households and individuals living in these countries. Special attention is paid to heterogeneity across space (by country or within country) and between groups.

The microsimulation approach integrates the GDP impact analysis with a complete household distribution analysis based on national surveys. Unlike aggregate approaches (for example, using historical GDP elasticity of poverty rates), the microsimulation technique employed here uses a household micro-dataset with national survey data comprising households across spatial and income distributions, and incorporates the multiple channels through which a shock affects households. This technique links the sectoral and aggregate macrodata of the three countries to their household surveys to extrapolate microeconomic snapshots under different scenarios. The model accounts for multiple channels through which macro-changes are transmitted into microlevel household impacts. Specifically, it accounts for changes in a country's employment shares and sectoral GDP, overall population growth, and social assistance programs. Additionally, the microsimulation model is designed to explicitly account for a large-scale displacement in Iraq due to the Islamic State crisis. A more technical description of the microsimulation methodology is provided in appendix C.

The poverty rate in Iraq would have been 6 percentage points lower without the Syrian crisis, including the Islamic State and internal displacement. The first panel in table 4.1 shows the poverty statistics in Iraq using national poverty rates in 2012. Switching from the actual growth to counterfactual growth, as estimated earlier in this section, leads to a 6.0-percentage-point drop in overall poverty headcount. Households in rural locations and with male heads were most affected by the crisis—poverty was 6.8 and 6.2 percentage points higher, respectively, than in the counterfactual scenario. By comparison, the impact of the crisis on poverty was 5.7 and 4.6 percentage points among households in urban areas and with female heads, respectively.

The crisis also has worsened the welfare of those who were already poor. The poverty gap—a measure of how far below the poverty line the average poor household's consumption is—has increased by almost 2.0 percentage points because of the crisis, while the severity in poverty (weighting more to those most below the line) has increased by 0.7 points.

TABLE 4.1. Poverty Implications

IRAQ		2012	IMPACT
POVERTY HEADCOUNT	OVERALL	18.89	6.01
	URBAN	13.46	5.67
	RURAL	30.65	6.75
	FEMALE HH HEAD	14.81	4.60
	MALE HH HEAD	19.32	6.16
POVERTY	GAP	4.13	1.84
	SEVERITY	1.36	0.74
VULNERABILITY	HEADCOUNT	29.20	0.96
INEQUALITY	GINI	0.30	0.01
	THEIL	0.15	0.01
	90/10 PERCENTILE	3.71	0.32
	90/50 PERCENTILE	1.98	0.05
	75/25 PERCENTILE	1.98	0.08

JORDAN		2010	IMPACT
POVERTY HEADCOUNT	OVERALL	14.40	3.85
	URBAN	13.88	3.33
	RURAL	16.83	6.31
	FEMALE HH HEAD	11.11	3.55
	MALE HH HEAD	14.73	3.88
POVERTY	GAP	2.81	0.73
	SEVERITY	0.87	0.21
VULNERABILITY	HEADCOUNT	26.63	5.99
INEQUALITY	GINI	0.33	-0.01
	THEIL	0.19	-0.01
	90/10 PERCENTILE	4.07	-0.40
	90/50 PERCENTILE	2.19	-0.03
	75/25 PERCENTILE	2.07	-0.09

LEBANON		2012	IMPACT
POVERTY HEADCOUNT	OVERALL	27.38	7.10
	FEMALE HH HEAD	21.80	7.58
	MALE HH HEAD	28.29	7.02
POVERTY	GAP	7.47	2.11
	SEVERITY	3.06	0.98
VULNERABILITY	HEADCOUNT	27.64	0.83
INEQUALITY	GINI	0.32	0.00
	THEIL	0.17	0.00
	90/10 PERCENTILE	4.23	0.07
	90/50 PERCENTILE	2.05	0.03
	75/25 PERCENTILE	2.06	0.02

Source: World Bank staff calculations.

Note: HH = household.

Moreover, the vulnerability rate (those only slightly above the poverty line) also increased by about a percentage point. Aggregate inequality between the scenarios, however, remained stable across all measures with impact ranging from 0.3 points for the 90/10 ratio to 1 point for the Gini and Theil indexes, reflecting the broad distribution of internally displaced persons across the precrisis population.

Compared to Iraq, Jordan has experienced a more modest, although nevertheless significant, impact on poverty as a result of the Syrian crisis. The second panel in table 4.1 shows the impact of the crisis on poverty and inequality in Jordan, using the 2010 Household Expenditure and Income Survey (HEIS) survey as the baseline. Results show that with lower GDP growth the overall poverty headcount in Jordan has increased by 4.0 percentage points. As in Iraq, households in rural locations suffered the most, with poverty increasing by 6.3 percentage points. Poverty impacts among both male- and female-headed households and in urban locations, in contrast, are similar to the overall impact, between 3.3 and 3.9 percentage points. The impacts on the gap and severity indexes are also lower compared to the impacts in Iraq; however, the number of vulnerable individuals under the actual with-shock scenario increased much more significantly (6 percentage points) in Jordan, suggesting that, although not as many households were affected to the point of falling below the poverty line, many more were affected to the point of bringing them near to it.

Among the three countries analyzed in this study, Lebanon is estimated to have been hit hardest in terms of the incidence of poverty. In Lebanon, poverty is 7.1 percentage points higher between the counterfactual and actual scenarios—the highest estimated among the three countries. The crisis had similar impacts on male- and female-headed households (7.0 and 7.6 percentage points, respectively). Similarly, the gap and severity indexes are affected more significantly than in the other two countries. Impacts on vulnerability and inequality are negligible.

Overall, the simulation results suggest that the poverty impact of the crisis has been substantial in all three countries. In Lebanon and Iraq, the impacts are greater than 6 percentage points, roughly 30 percent and 25 percent increases, respectively, in poverty incidence from their 2012 values. In Jordan, the impact on the poverty rate is relatively small. Vulnerability impacts, however, are much higher in Jordan, indicating that the overall impact across all three countries was similarly broad. Inequality measures remained relatively stable compared to the precrisis period in all three countries.

FISCAL IMPLICATIONS OF THE GDP IMPACT

To what extent can the increasing debt burden in the region be attributed to the GDP shock imposed by the Syrian conflict? If the Syrian conflict has reduced GDP growth in Iraq, Jordan, and Lebanon, it must also have implications for fiscal outcomes in these countries. Ratios of public debt to GDP could be especially responsive to changes in GDP trajectories; however, although the sign of this effect is somewhat predictable (higher growth often reduces debt-to-GDP ratios), its magnitude is not. Unfortunately, estimating the overall fiscal impact of the Syrian conflict in Iraq, Jordan, and Lebanon with precision is a daunting task. In order to map the debt dynamics in these countries onto the conflict in Syria, counterfactual estimations for revenues, expenditures, and interest rates would be needed. In the absence of such estimates, we conduct a thought experiment to assess the responsiveness of debt dynamics to the changes in GDP, fiscal revenue and expenditure trends, and interest rate patterns. Specifically, we consider three scenarios:

1. *Counterfactual GDP scenario.* This first scenario simulates the debt-to-GDP ratio by using the counterfactual (no Syrian conflict) GDP series and the actual revenue-to-GDP and primary expenditure–to-GDP ratios.

2. *Counterfactual GDP and preconflict primary balance scenario.* In addition to the first scenario, this scenario also assumes that the revenue-to-GDP and primary expenditure–to-GDP ratios are maintained during the 2011–19 period at the historical, five-year average ratios observed prior to the conflict (2006–10). Intuitively, this scenario indicates a debt path unaffected by the changes in fiscal policy manifested during the conflict, which may have been influenced by the conflict itself.

3. *Counterfactual GDP, preconflict primary balance, and lower real interest rate scenario.* In addition to the second scenario, this scenario also assumes that the real interest rate facing the government during the conflict is 200 basis points lower than the actual rate. This scenario estimates a debt path while excluding broader uncertainty driven by the conflict onset for the sole purpose of assessing the impact of less expensive government borrowing.

In Iraq, the counterfactual growth rates by themselves would not drive the debt-to-GDP ratio down significantly. In contrast, should the country manage to maintain the preconflict fiscal trends (in which, on average, the primary balance was near zero), the debt-to-GDP ratio in 2019 would have been nearly 20 percentage points lower than the actual ratio (figure 4.5, panel a). The latter was pushed up by an average primary deficit of 2 percent of GDP—largely explained by the collapse of oil prices since mid-2014. Finally, a lower real interest rate may not have had a significant impact. With all factors (counterfactual GDP, preconflict primary balance, and an improved interest rate) taken into consideration, the debt-to-GDP ratio would decrease from an actual ratio of 49.3 percent to 25.9 percent.

FIGURE 4.5. Debt-to-GDP ratios under alternative growth and fiscal trend scenarios, Iraq, Jordan, and Lebanon

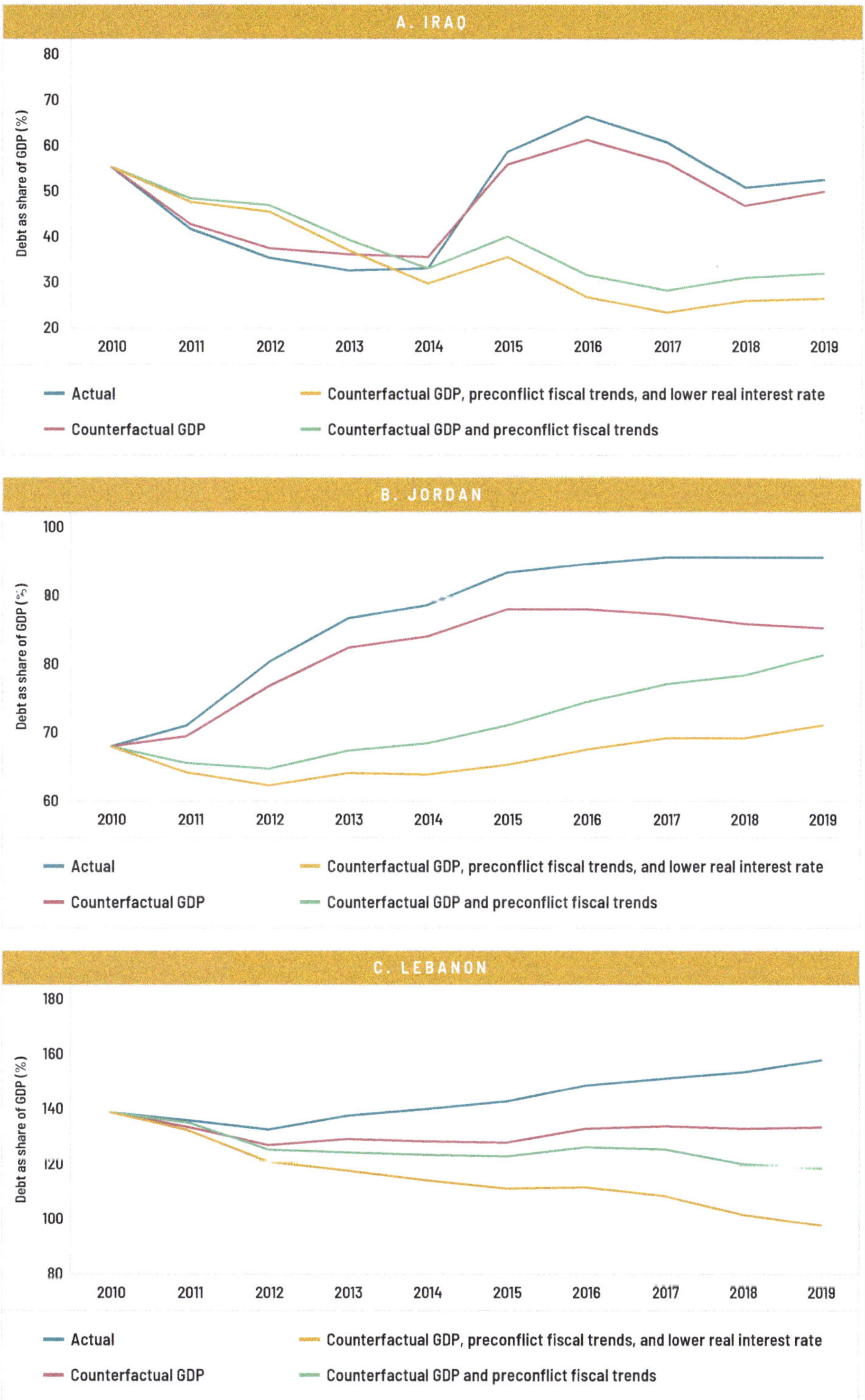

Source: World Bank staff calculations.

In Jordan, even all three factors together would just maintain the debt-to-GDP ratio and not reduce it. Without a 1.6-percentage-point annual reduction in GDP growth imposed by the Syrian conflict, Jordan's debt-to-GDP ratio in 2019 would have been 10 percentage points lower than the actual one (decrease from 94.6 percent to 84.4 percent). If the country were to maintain the preconflict primary balance (an average of 3.8 percent of GDP) rather than the actual primary balance (an average of 4.5 percent of GDP) after the onset of the conflict, the debt ratio in 2019 would not have been affected much (only 3.6 percentage points lower than that in only the counterfactual GDP scenario). The marginal effect of such primary balance switching, however, would be stronger in the earlier years of the conflict (between 2012 and 2015), where the primary balance reached double-digit deficits at its height. A lower real interest rate, instead, would have a more uniform depressing effect on the debt-to-GDP-ratio and, by 2019, would further reduce the debt ratio by 10 percentage points. Even with all three factors combined, the debt-to-GDP ratio (at 70.7 percent in 2019) does not decrease below its preconflict level (67.1 percent in 2010).

Lebanon's debt-to-GDP ratio could decrease with either one of the three factors and would do so much more with all of them together. Without the conflict's GDP impact (a 1.7-percentage-point decrease in growth annually), Lebanon's debt-to-GDP ratio in 2019 would have been 23 percentage points lower than the actual one. In addition, had the country managed to maintain the preconflict primary surplus (2.3 percent of GDP) rather than the actual primary surplus (0.7 percent of GDP), the debt-to-GDP ratio in 2019 would have been reduced by another 15 percentage points. Finally, a 200-basis-point decrease in the real interest rate would also have reduced the ratio further, by 20 percentage points. With all factors combined, the debt-to GDP ratio would decrease from about 137 percent in 2010 to about 97 percent in 2019 (instead of climbing up to 155 percent in reality).

DISCUSSION

How significant is the impact of the Syrian conflict on the GDPs of neighboring countries? The analysis in this chapter shows that the Syrian conflict is accountable for about 1.2 percent, 1.7 percent, and 1.6 percent reduction in average annual growth rates in Iraq, Jordan, and Lebanon, respectively. To put these numbers into perspective, a background paper to this report estimated the average GDP effects of conflicts on neighboring countries by using simple cross-country growth regressions (Onder, Onder, and Rojas 2020). The analysis first pools all civil conflicts (intrastate) and then focuses on high-intensity civil conflicts only.

The Syrian conflict's impact on neighboring countries' GDPs has been larger than the average effects elsewhere. Figure 4.6 shows the estimated GDP effects, globally, where time 0 denotes the onset year of the conflict and each number to the right shows the number of years after the onset, and each number to the left shows the number of years before the onset. In both cases (all conflicts and high-intensity conflicts), the 95 percent confidence intervals contain the horizontal axis, 0 line. In other words, globally speaking, on average, conflicts do not have a statistically significant effect on the neighbor's GDPs. Even when we ignore the significance problem, the estimated magnitude of effects on especially Jordan and Lebanon (1.7 percent and 1.6 percent, respectively) are larger than the global estimates in any given year after the onset of the conflict.

FIGURE 4.6. Average GDP growth effects of conflict in a neighboring country

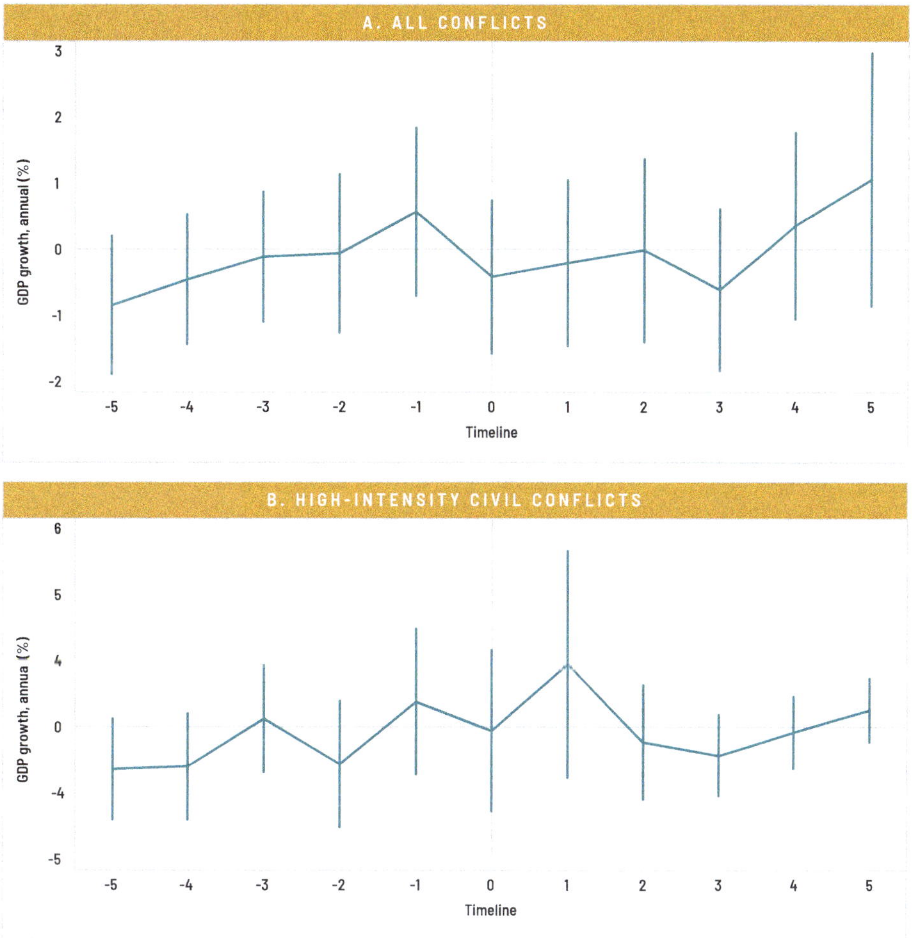

Source: Onder, Onder, and Rojas 2020.

Note: Vertical lines denote confidence intervals (5 percent).

What makes the Mashreq different for such large effects to take place? It is difficult to find precise answers to this question without comparing all conflict cases in detail. We know from the analyses in previous sections, however, that a number of contributing factors can be potential culprits. These factors are as follows:

- *The sheer scale, composition, and duration of the Syrian conflict*. With more than 400,000 directly conflict-driven casualties, displacement of more than half of the preconflict population, and no end in sight in its ninth year, the Syrian conflict has been brutal by any measure. According to *The Toll of War*, Syria's GDP had shrunk by more than 60 percent by the end of the sixth conflict year (World Bank 2017). Therefore, the scale of the economic collapse in the original conflict country is much larger than average. As a result, the negative fallout can also be expected to be higher.

- *The high exposure of Mashreq economies to the Syrian crisis.* As discussed in previous chapters, although bilateral trade between Syria and its neighbors was not particularly high in proportional terms, the country still played important roles. For Lebanon, Syria provided the only viable land connection, and for Jordan it served as a major transit trade route. Moreover, the displacement crisis ensuing the conflict has reached unprecedented levels, about a quarter of the population in Lebanon and a fifth of that in Jordan. Although a positive demographic shock by itself does not necessarily lower GDP, this effect nevertheless shows the magnitude of the spillovers, which can be captured by other channels, like TFP shocks.

- *The low institutional resilience of the Mashreq economies.* The analysis in the previous chapters has shown that, when the Syrian crisis hit, Iraq, Jordan, and Lebanon did not have high state capacity or policy space. Despite significant heterogeneity across the countries in details, overall, the countries were already struggling with a downward trend in economic and fiscal performance, and complex political economy dynamics complicated the policy responses. As a result, with less than ideal mitigation efforts, the already sizeable shocks were propagated in the economy, magnifying the impact of the conflict.

Overall, the Syrian conflict has taken a heavy toll in neighboring countries, and this process has not finalized yet. The impact of the Syrian conflict is likely to continue as long as the conflict lasts, and beyond. Although analyzing the factors that may help to stop the war is beyond the scope of this report, considering alternative ways in which Syria's neighbors can mitigate the negative fallout of the conflict in the future is squarely within our scope. In the next chapter, we will consider these options while also recognizing the uncertainty surrounding the evolution of the conflict inside Syria.

NOTES

1. The counterfactual trade shock is implemented through an exogenous, nonrevenue-generating technological change that affects the efficiency of trade transactions at the border. This change could be best conceptualized as, for instance, improvements in trade facilitation indicators, opening of previously blocked trade routes, or removal of red tape. As such, the efficiency improvements come at no cost and, although they generate no revenues, result in welfare gains for the economy as a whole. Welfare gains translate into income gains for consumers, which in turn boost demand and production. Because of these indirect effects, the effect of the trade shock on GDP is bigger than the net counterfactual trade growth effect.
2. The core specification of the GTAP model broadly replicates a standard global dynamic CGE model. Production is specified as a series of nested constant elasticity of substitution (CES) functions using various inputs—unskilled and skilled labor, capital, land, natural resources (sector-specific), energy, and other intermediate inputs. Demand by each domestic agent is specified at the so-called Armington level—that is, demand for a bundle of domestically produced and imported goods. Armington demand is aggregated across all agents and allocated at the national level between domestic production and imports by region of origin. The dynamics of the model are of recursive dynamic type and are characterized by capital accumulation.
3. Similarly, the unmeasured consequences of refugee arrivals (for example, political, cultural, and sentimental aspects) cannot be fully captured by the GDP analysis, despite being important. To the extent these factors affect economic activity, some of these factors are captured by the TFP analysis; but even there it is not possible to separate them from other intangible effects in the absence of data.
4. Estimating the model for Iraq was not feasible because of large swings in yearly trade growth.

REFERENCES

Abadie, A., and J. Gardeazabal. 2003. "The Economic Costs of Conflict: A Case Study of the Basque Country." *American Economic Review* 93 (1): 113–32.

Abadie, A., A. Diamond, and J. Hainmueller. 2010. "Synthetic Control Methods for Comparative Case Studies: Estimating the Effect of California's Tobacco Control Program." *Journal of the American Statistical Association* 105 (490): 493–505.

Abadie, A., A. Diamond, and J. Hainmueller. 2015. "Comparative Politics and the Synthetic Control Method." *American Journal of Political Science* 59 (2): 495–510.

Aguiar, Angel, Maksym Chepeliev, Erwin L. Corong, Robert McDougall, and Dominique van der Mensbrugghe. 2019. "The GTAP Data Base: Version 10." *Journal of Global Economic Analysis* 4 (1): 1–27.

Aguiar, Angel, Badri Narayanan, and Robert McDougall. 2016. "An Overview of the GTAP 9 Data Base." *Journal of Global Economic Analysis* 1 (1): 181–208.

Hertel, Thomas, ed. 1997. Global Trade Analysis: Modeling and Applications. Cambridge: Cambridge University Press.

Onder, Harun, Stefanie Onder, and Claudio Rojas. 2020. "Good Fences for Bad Neighborhoods? Cross-Border Growth Effects of Civil Wars." Background paper, *The Fallout of War*, World Bank, Washington, DC.

World Bank. 2017. *The Toll of War: The Economic and Social Consequences of the Conflict in Syria.* Washington, DC: World Bank.

World Bank. 2019. *The Mobility of Displaced Syrians: An Economic and Social Analysis.* Washington, DC: World Bank.

5. THE AFTERMATH: A TALE OF TWO FUTURES

Although the crisis in the Syrian Arab Republic is not the only cause of problems in the Mashreq, the analysis in this report shows that it continues to fuel them. Since its beginning, the Syrian conflict has had important consequences for Mashreq countries. The analysis thus far has shown the nature of this impact in detail. The economic interconnectivity between Syria and its neighbors has been shrinking as a result of the economic collapse in the former and the erection of new barriers (such as border closures) in the latter. This reduced interconnectivity limits the nature of Syria's impact on its neighbors as compared to the earlier years of the conflict. Nevertheless, Syria's influence continues to extend outward, even if in the form of a security black hole that threatens the stability of the region as a whole.

Going forward, the economic and political trajectories of the Mashreq countries will remain intertwined. Future developments in Syria are likely to influence the economic and social outcomes in other Mashreq economies. An economic recovery fueled by a credible political resolution and subsequent improvements in security and service access conditions in the country would have significant positive repercussions in the region. Conversely, deteriorating conditions, including the rekindling of the conflict or a deepening economic bottleneck in Syria, would add to the adverse impact of the conflict so far. In the end, the scale and the composition of such future impact will depend on the policy measures adopted going forward in the Mashreq economies.

For the purposes of this study, and based on policy options, we consider two paths ahead: a unilateral approach and a regional approach. A unilateral approach defines a state in which each country implements its desired policies by taking the conditions and policies in other Mashreq countries as given at their current specifications. In addition, international support in a given country is not linked with other cases either. In comparison, a regional approach characterizes a state in which the Mashreq countries coordinate their efforts in addressing cross-boundary issues including migration, trade, and infrastructure. Likewise, support from the international community is determined within a regional strategical framework. Thus, whereas the unilateral approach presents an adaptive policy path where countries try to implement their best responses to changes in the regional context with the support of an international community (which shares the same country-specific focus), the regional approach enables a cooperation in which jointly beneficial policies can be implemented with the support of the international community that shares the same regional perspective.

In this chapter, we characterize the elements of such future paths, albeit in an incomplete manner. As this report is drafted, the active conflict situation in Syria and looming regional uncertainties do not lend themselves to a fully fledged policy road map. Nevertheless, we take a pragmatic view and use the technical analysis on the backward-looking impact analysis to shed some light on the policy options going forward. In the following sections, we characterize the two policy approaches (unilateral and regional) and analyze their implications under different conditions. In order to account for the uncertainty regarding the conditions in Syria, we adopt with modifications the three scenarios developed in *The Mobility of Displaced Syrians: An Economic and Social Analysis* (World Bank 2019). In the first scenario (which we adopt as our baseline), the insecurity index[1] decreases from 1.70 to 0.54 and only 5 percent of the damaged infrastructure is rebuilt by 2025. In comparison, the second scenario envisages that the insecurity index decreases further to 0.15 and the reconstruction ratio reaches 16 percent, over the same period. Finally, the third scenario considers a decrease to 0.07 in the insecurity index and a reconstruction ratio of 30 percent. These scenarios do not mean to project the likely outcomes in Syria; they are merely assumptions that help us incorporate uncertainty into our forward-oriented thinking.

At the outset, we should emphasize that the regional approach we consider is not about economic or political integration, but is about cooperation. As we discuss in the following sections, much ink has been spilled on the economic and political integration in the Arab world in the past several decades. In this report, we do not discuss those issues. Our focus is on internalizing cross-border externalities, whether those be about taking advantage of common market prospects, infrastructure cooperation, and mobility of labor or about promoting security and stability in the region as a whole.

THE FALLOUT PROSPECTS

Economic recovery in Syria is expected to be slow going forward. The scenario analysis of economic recovery in Syria foresees somewhat modest improvement in security conditions and limited service restoration activity across all scenarios. As a result, in the first scenario (baseline), gross domestic product (GDP) growth increases by 0.8 percentage points annually in the next five-year period. In comparison, the second and third scenarios yield GDP growth of 1.7 percentage points and 2.5 percentage points, respectively. It is important to remember that these are incremental growth rates brought about by security improvements and service restoration only and should not be interpreted as GDP growth projections. These estimates are based on the simulation analysis in *The Mobility of Displaced Syrians* report (World Bank 2019), and they take into consideration the productivity-enhancing aspects of better security and greater infrastructure stock, as well as the endogenous response of refugees outside the country in the form of spontaneous returns.

A positive fallout from Syrian recovery is possible; however, it will largely be driven by better regional security and confidence rather than by immediate economic opportunities. The muted economic recovery in Syria will translate into a slow reversing of the adverse economic and social impact of the conflict on Iraq, Jordan, and Lebanon so far. In the baseline case (scenario 1), the additional GDP growth in Iraq, Jordan, and Lebanon is estimated to be limited to 0.2–0.3 percentage points (figure 5.1). In the other two scenarios, in which security improvements and service restoration are both more significant, the growth increments are between 0.3 and 0.6 percentage points (scenario 2) and 0.6 and 0.9 percentage points (scenario 3). A large share of these additional growth rates (more than 90 percent) is driven by the security- and confidence-driven total factor productivity (TFP) improvements.

The complementarity between potential material requirements for service restoration and the current trade profile of Syria's neighbors is low. In order to see why the trade channel may be relatively small, we compare the current trade patterns in the Mashreq region with the likely import demand associated with service restoration in Syria. To do so, we first calculate the material demand for reconstructing damaged structures, by using a back of the envelope calculation based on previous examples. Accordingly, the following materials constitute the top five (by value) across all three scenarios: concrete structure (cement, sand, aggregate), rebar steel, wood, concrete block, and waterproofing. These five are followed by electrical copper, roof tiles, wood doors, paint putty, and ceramic tiles; but their demand is on average much smaller compared to the top-five list. Table 5.1 shows the estimated value of each material in different scenarios in US$ billions. We next turn to the trade patterns of Iraq, Jordan, and Lebanon. According to the latest statistics from UN Comtrade, both Jordan and Lebanon ran significant trade deficits in all top-five materials we calculated for Syria (table 5.2).[2] Thus, in current economic conditions, we do not observe a revealed advantage in either country (besides proximity) that would grant these countries a competitive edge or first mover advantage in supplying these materials to Syria in the future.

FIGURE 5.1. GDP growth gains in neighboring countries from security and service restoration in Syria

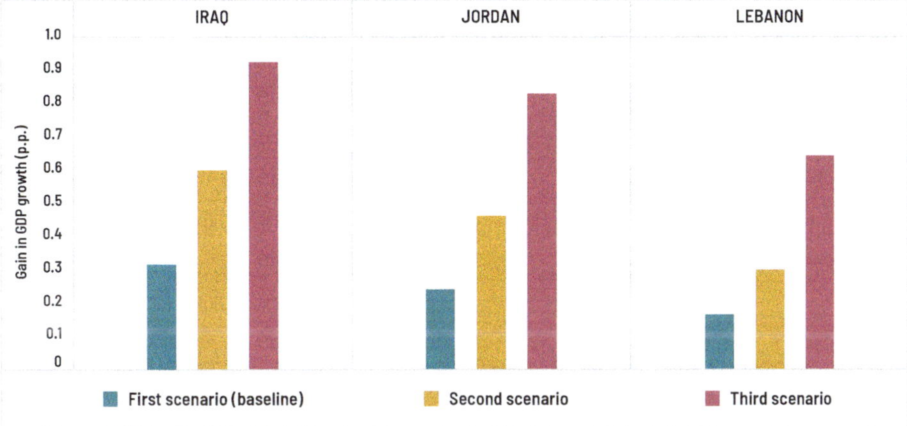

Source: World Bank staff calculations using *Mobility of Displaced Syrians* (World Bank 2019) scenarios.

Note: In the first scenario (baseline), the insecurity index decreases from 1.70 to 0.54 and only 5 percent of the damaged infrastructure is rebuilt by 2025. In the second scenario, the insecurity index decreases further to 0.15 and the reconstruction ratio reaches 16 percent. The third scenario considers a decrease in the insecurity index of 0.07 points and a reconstruction ratio of 30 percent. p.p. = percentage point.

TABLE 5.1. The top-five estimated demands for materials in Syria, 2020–25 (US$, billions)

	FIRST SCENARIO (BASELINE)	SECOND SCENARIO	THIRD SCENARIO
CONCRETE STRUCTURE	0.54	1.66	3.07
REBAR STEEL	0.48	1.48	2.76
WOOD	0.20	0.61	1.13
CONCRETE BLOCK	0.20	0.61	1.12
WATERPROOFING	0.17	0.54	1.01

Sources: World Bank staff calculations; World Bank 2019.

Note: The material requirements for construction were estimated by using previous construction experience in similar regional markets (for example, Jordan and Lebanon) and the infrastructure damage assessments from World Bank (2019), which reflect conditions as of mid-2018. The quantity/size needed for each material was calculated based on the estimated damage area and factors/coefficients determined at the sector level based on the minimum requirements for proper construction of similar structures in terms of type and size. The total cost for each type of construction material was obtained by multiplying the amount needed with the unit cost for each sector for each governorate, with unit costs based on market reference points in the region.

TABLE 5.2. Current trade patterns of Lebanon and Jordan corresponding to the top-five estimated demands for materials in Syria, 2018 (US$, millions)

	LEBANON			JORDAN		
	EXPORT	IMPORT	BALANCE	EXPORT	IMPORT	BALANCE
CONCRETE STRUCTURE	0.1	2.0	-1.9	0.7	3.4	-2.7
STEEL BAR	0.2	46.3	-46.1	0.2	1.9	-1.7
WOOD	8.1	221.6	-213.5	8.2	179.6	-171.4
CONCRETE BLOCK	1.5	6.7	-4.7	0.9	2.9	-2.0
WATERPROOFING	3.1	135.6	-132.6	5.0	96.6	-91.6

Source: World Bank staff calculations.

A UNILATERAL APPROACH

Regardless of the other factors, the governments in the Mashreq can and should address structural weaknesses and eliminate inefficiencies to better mitigate shocks. The analysis in the previous chapters has shown that the Syrian conflict has significantly affected the neighboring countries. This impact occurred partially because the initial exposure was high: the region had significant economic interconnectivity, and the demographic shock emanating from the conflict loomed at an unforeseen scale. The other side of the problem, however, was about the imperfections in the mitigation efforts. Despite the heroic effort to accommodate the proportionally largest refugee population in the world in recent decades, a complex set of factors has so far limited the efficiency of the response in the countries considered in this report. We elaborate on these factors in the following paragraphs.

A persistent short-termism has been an obstacle against developing an effective mitigation strategy in the region. The lack of medium-term planning is a common problem for both the governments in the region and the international community (donors). On the government side, this problem manifests itself as formulating mitigation policies as a series of ad hoc measures in sequence. This approach is costly and open to political exploitation. On the donors' side, a 12-month funding cycle remains the norm, which does not encourage or facilitate multiyear, cross-agency, and cross-sector planning. In fact, the number of projects running 24 months or more has decreased substantially in the past three years in the region.

The lack of an adequate medium-term perspective in coping with the repercussions of the Syrian conflict is costly for all. Inefficiencies emanating from the lack of a medium-term perspective abound in the three countries covered in this study. More specifically, these inefficiencies include the following:

- *Costly and ineffective service provision*. In many instances, ad hoc solutions to protracted issues are both less effective and more costly. For instance, in Jordan and Lebanon, a relatively high share of water supply to refugees, especially to those who live in nonpermanent shelters or camps, is provided by tanking or trucking, and is more prone to quality (E. coli) problems than piped water. Among Syrian nationals living in camps in Zarqa and Mafraq, about 32 percent rely on tanker trucks for drinking water. Of the Syrians in camps relying on bottled water for drinking, as many as 62 percent rely on tanker trucks and bottled water for nondrinking purposes also. These ad hoc solutions lead to both higher operating costs and higher health care costs. A United Nations Children's Fund (UNICEF) study for 20 villages in Lebanon (UNICEF 2018) estimated that a piped water alternative to trucking could reduce service provision costs by about 70 percent over two years (UNICEF 2018). Estimates for this study show that the 2018 national disease burden from inadequate household drinking water, sanitation, and hygiene in Jordan and Lebanon stood at 0.55 percent and 0.74 percent of GDP, respectively.

- *Lost economic opportunities.* Despite all efforts, school attendance of Syrian refugees is limited relative to their host country peers, leading to significant losses in human capital. These losses can be analyzed by using the Expected Years of Education (EYE) component of the Human Capital Index (HCI) methodology.[3] In Jordan, Syrian children are expected to have 8.3 years of education on average, about 3.7 years fewer than Jordanian children (table 5.3). The gap is wider in Lebanon, at 5.4 years (6.3 years for Syrians and 11.7 years for Lebanese). Next, we can calculate the economic gains from closing this gap by using a simple methodology.[4] Results show that the convergence of Syrian refugees' school attainment with that of locals would increase the GDP growth rate by 0.4 percentage points in Jordan and 1.1 percentage points in Lebanon. In other words, the low school attainment of Syrian refugees not only reduces their human capital but also costs the host countries in terms of forgone growth opportunities.

- *Underfunded programs.* Although aid to the region has exhibited an upward trend, the volume of funding has not kept up with growing needs. The governments in the region routinely fall short of their financing targets, and United Nations response plans for the region and for each country remain substantially underfunded. Interestingly, the lack of a medium-term strategy is a likely driver of this outcome. As the host country governments refrain from committing to a medium-term path, the international community could limit aid for different reasons. For instance, as discussed previously, with costly and inefficient service provision driven by short-termism, the marginal impact of an additional dollar spent would be lower. Thus, donors may choose to spend money elsewhere, to get a higher return on their investment in the form of a greater impact on the ground. Another mechanism is the donors' desire to avoid a moral hazard problem (for example, aid reduces the governments' incentives to perform pertinent actions). Without regional government commitment to medium-term programs, the risk of moral hazard increases, rendering donors less willing to contribute.

Shifting from a short-term focus to a medium-term strategy also provides a golden opportunity to build institutional resilience. The analyses in this report have shown that both state capacity and policy space were limited in the Mashreq region at the outset of the Syrian conflict, especially in Iraq and Lebanon. Over the course of the conflict, they have deteriorated further. With the right approach, progress in these areas is within reach—even in the absence of a major external change. A comprehensive approach that carefully combines the deployment of a medium-term strategy for addressing the protracted challenges of the Syrian crisis and reinforcing public service delivery to own constituents can achieve great results because potential synergies exist between the two objectives. Some examples are as follows.

Bring "Robin" into the "hood." Refugee arrivals and other spillover effects from conflicts have heterogenous effects on well-being in neighboring economies. For instance, a higher demand for accommodation can increase rents in certain areas; whereas tenants suffer

TABLE 5.3. School attainment differences between Syrians and locals (percent unless otherwise noted)

	LEBANON		JORDAN	
	LEBANESE	SYRIAN	JORDANIAN	SYRIAN
PREPRIMARY ENROLLMENT (2 YEARS)	90.7	23	35.1	25
PRIMARY ENROLLMENT (6 YEARS)	92.4	75.4	98.3	75.4
LOWER-SECONDARY ENROLLMENT (3 YEARS)	78.5	28.7	98.3	67
UPPER-SECONDARY ENROLLMENT (3 YEARS)	64.9	15	81.3	41
AVERAGE YEARS OF SCHOOLING	11.7	6.3	12	8.3
GAIN FROM CONVERGENCE (% OF GDP)	1.1		0.4	

Source: World Bank staff calculations.

losses as a result of such increases, landlords can make gains. The overall impact of the conflict on a given individual's material well-being is a sum of all changes that affect his or her real purchasing power. This is a multidimensional problem. Nevertheless, some people are set to be affected more negatively than others, and the main channels through which this happens can be identified. An important role that can be played by governments in the three countries we cover is to smooth out the gains and losses by means of appropriate public policies. Progressive social insurance and assistance mechanisms are examples in this regard. The former comprises functions like unemployment insurance, which could help mitigate the short-term effects of the shock and facilitate a less costly transition for locals.

In all three countries in this study, these automatic stabilizers were weak, especially in nonpublic sector employment. In comparison, social assistance programs were more prevalent yet much less targeted, which reduced their progressivity, especially in Iraq and Lebanon. In Iraq, the main social protection program is the Public Distribution System (PDS), which provides households with four food items every month: wheat flour, rice, sugar, and vegetable oil. In 2012, food receipts from the PDS provided about 70 percent of total calories of the poorest 40 percent of the population (World Bank 2014b). Even the richest quintile drew 45 percent of its calories from PDS receipts. In Lebanon, significant public spending on energy subsidies has been the main source of assistance for households. To put this into perspective, Lebanon's nonsubsidy social safety net program spending did not exceed 1 percent of GDP in 2013; however, if electricity subsidies are included, particularly transfers to EDL (Electricité du Liban, the state-owned utility), this spending increases dramatically to above 5.6 percent of GDP. As in any other place, these subsidies are highly regressive, benefiting mainly richer households. Although the National Poverty Targeting Program (NPTP) provides a more effective and targeted approach, in 2019 it covered only 230,000 beneficiaries (43,000 households) with education and health assistance, and only 50,000 beneficiaries (10,000 households) received the e-card food voucher (4 percent of the poor). In all countries, better protection of the poor and vulnerable, and redistribution from the winners of the impact to the losers, is needed. To this effect, synergies between refugee assistance mechanisms and national social assistance systems should be explored.

Improve service access for all. The analyses in the earlier chapters in this report have shown several areas where the governments' provision of public goods and services can be improved upon. For instance, in the transportation sector, insufficient attention to periodic maintenance seemed to be a common problem in all three countries before the onset of the conflict. This problem continues. Similarly, in the energy sector, Lebanese citizens resorted to costly alternatives like diesel generators because supply shortages render grid access unreliable (with up to 12 hours a day of load-shedding). Since the onset of the conflict, the situation has improved modestly (about 14 hours of grid electricity) but still has much room for further improvement. Examples abound in other sectors as well. Although constituents' service access levels are less than perfect, the efficiency of service provision is not better. In all countries, utility tariffs are well below cost-recovery levels. EDL's deficits in Lebanon, for example, which run more than US$1 billion each year, with or without refugees, are covered by general fiscal revenues. In practice, the presence of refugees makes these prevailing inefficiencies more visible. Thus, while trying to improve the efficiency and effectiveness of service provision to own constituents and refugees, countries can exploit synergies between the two provision systems. Another important case in this regard is the education sector. As described previously, the low school attainment of refugees translates into a major economic loss for the host countries. Thus, developing a plan to overcome this loss should include consideration of opportunities to improve the provision of services for own constituents. Developing a joint medium-term strategy would also be useful in this regard.

Invest in state capacity and build policy space. The successful implementation of the preceding two areas requires building further public sector capacity and policy space. Currently, major discrepancies exist between public sector shares of employment (too much) and service delivery capacities (too little) of public sectors in the region. They are partially driven by a common perception of public sector employment as a redistribution mechanism and a prize to be allocated across various groups. It is important to establish a civil service that is relatively immune to political rivalries and rent-seeking. Again, developing a medium-term strategy for better service delivery for locals and refugees alike can provide an opportunity in this regard. The heavy presence of international organizations and civil society organizations in service delivery for refugees could provide an opportunity to align the two systems in a transparent manner. It should be noted that it is not enough for a current government to practice meritocracy and transparency. That government should also install mechanisms that prevent future governments from doing otherwise, which requires a careful design of institutional constraints over discretion.

While aspiring to deliver on these fronts, reformers should be cognizant of a complex political economy that surrounds the policies in these countries. The short-termism and low institutional resilience of countries should not be regarded simply as poor policy choices. In fact, these results themselves are outcomes of a complex political economy in these countries. For instance, in Lebanon, confessional patronage is embedded in the Lebanese political system: power-sharing arrangements and the electoral system encourage sectarian groups to compete for the key levers of the state and for access to lucrative patronage opportunities (USIP 2013). Large numbers of businesspeople have entered politics, and large numbers of politicians have extensive economic interests, blurring the lines between political and business elites and entrenching and normalizing the exploitation of public funds for personal gain (El Kak and Zoughaib 2020). The result is a suboptimal equilibrium, in which successive governments do not find it incentive compatible to invest in state capacity or to develop a longer-term vision.[5]

In the next section, we consider the elements of a vision that could also possibly change the dynamics of such political economy constraints. A determined policy maker can go a long way in improving conditions for constituents despite the political economy constraints. This rationale—that policy makers can unilaterally make changes to improve their constituents' quality of life—guides the discussion in the current section. Nevertheless, major shifts that relax some of the political economy constraints faced by policy makers could open more space for such improvements. In the next section, we discuss the possibility of one such major shift—that is, taking a more regional approach to peace and stability.

A REGIONAL APPROACH FOR A BETTER EQUILIBRIUM

Although unilateral approaches do help, a regional approach can deal more effectively with problems that have significant transboundary aspects. Public policy studies have long established a principle of "perfect correspondence" formulated by Oates (1972). This principle can be summarized as a complete match between each governance unit that provides a public service and a group of constituents who consume it. For instance, if consumers of a municipal service like solid waste collection reside solely in a limited geographic area, then the service should be provided by the corresponding municipality (not higher or lower in the governance chain). This match ensures allocative efficiency because it minimizes information problems and strategic interactions across units.

In the case of the Syrian crisis, the conflict clearly has major transboundary effects as shown in the previous chapters. From broader regional insecurity to sudden demographic changes, the conflict in Syria has imposed numerous changes on the neighboring countries, and it will continue to impose new ones going forward. Overall, in net terms, the "public bad" emanating from the conflict is consumed by everybody in the region, if not beyond. Theoretically, therefore, we would expect a regional mitigation strategy to be more effective in coping with the fallout of the conflict. This argument, however, will need to be substantiated further. What are the mechanisms though which regional cooperation can contribute to peace, stability, and prosperity in each country? Does a regional approach offer clear gains for everyone? If yes, why have these potential gains failed to mobilize the policy makers for such an approach so far?

To analyze the advantages and limitations of a regional perspective, we employ a model-based framework. A background paper to this report, Karayalcin and Onder (2020), builds a game theoretic model to analyze regionalism, provision of public goods and service, and conflict dynamics in the same framework. More specifically, the analysis compares how public services are provided in unilateral and regional schemes, and how these affect the likelihood of conflict. On the basis of this comparison, the analysis then studies the incentive structure behind the two schemes. A more detailed description of the methodology is described in box 5.1.

The main idea here is that, if governments could internalize the cross-border effects of their actions, it could translate into better service provision and lower tendency toward conflict. The core argument is built on the observation that, in Mashreq, public goods have cross-border implications. For instance, better roads in Syria make transportation costs lower not only for Syrians but also for Iraqis, Jordanians, and Lebanese.[6] This effect is also true for public bads, which became evident during the conflict when road closures inside Syria affected the trade patterns of neighboring countries.

BOX 5.1. Regionalism, conflict, and public services

A background paper for this report, Karayalcin and Onder (2020), develops a game theoretic model of regional integration, which analyzes the incentives for rent-seeking and conflict in the presence of publicly provided services and cross-border externalities of such services. This model allows us to study the interaction of domestic conflict and regional integration that takes the form of coordination of the provision of public services.

The model comprises two economies, each of which is inhabited by two groups in contest. Each of these economies produces a composite good employing both private and public capital. The groups engaged in domestic contest undertake private investments not only in productive activities but also in unproductive (rent-seeking or conflictual) activities. An important characteristic of the model is that public capital in one economy leads to productivity-enhancing spillovers in the other member of the union. In practice, this reflects a case in which investments in, say, transportation infrastructure in one region reduce production costs in a neighboring jurisdiction by improving its connectivity as well. These spillovers play an important role for the results.

In the case of a unilateral scheme, governments use their tax proceeds (supplemented potentially by foreign aid) in provisioning public capital. The decision-making problem faced by the national government is that of maximizing the welfare of its constituent groups by choosing both the optimal level of investment in public capital and the distribution of public services across rival groups. While solving this optimization problem, however, national governments do not internalize the productivity spillovers across jurisdictions.

In comparison, in the case of a regional integration scheme, spillover-generating investments in each economy are chosen at the regional level in a coordinated manner. The difference between the two schemes (unilateral and regional) mainly lies in the fact that the cross-border externalities are internalized in the case of a regional scheme, which national governments would not do unilaterally. Therefore, perceived returns on a given investment are greater in the case of a regional scheme than under a unilateral scheme. As a result, the optimal levels of investment in both economies are greater under a regional scheme.

The first result of the analysis builds on this observation: given two identical economies, all groups prefer a regional scheme over the unilateral one. If the economies differ with respect to initial income, however, then at least one group in the richer economy could lose from transitioning into a regional scheme because coordinated public investments in that scheme would de facto amount to a redistribution from rich to poor economies.

Next, the model investigates interactions among domestic conflict, migration, and the incentives for regional integration. Within this framework, if migration does not affect the relative sizes of the two contesting groups, then it also does not alter the incentives for regional integration. Migration that does affect this balance, however, could lead to changes in domestic conflict outcomes and thus interact with fiscal policy outcomes. Overall, such an outcome can also reduce the incentives for regional schemes for at least some of the groups.

Finally, the analysis also shows that foreign aid could influence the incentives for regional schemes by changing income differentials across regions.

In a unilateral framework, governments do not take these spillovers into consideration when deciding the level of public services. In contrast, a regional scheme considers all spillovers. Thus, because the perceived benefits are greater (for the whole region) in the regional scheme, the optimal levels of public good and services are also greater. A direct conjecture from this result is that, with greater provisioning of public goods and services, investments in state capacity would increase and the conflictual activities of various groups within a country would decrease at the margin.[7]

Although a necessary condition for regionalism to take place, by itself an efficiency gain is not enough for governments to choose such a path. When regional schemes are not mutually beneficial, they cannot take place. Moreover, a cross-border externality can be internalized differently by participants. The analysis by Karayalcin and Onder (2020) shows that, when countries are significantly dissimilar in terms of their initial income levels, productivity, and relative sizes of groups that contest for resources, then regional schemes can amount to a de facto redistribution from the relatively well-off country to the relatively less well-off. Thus, even if a regional approach to investments can eliminate a systemic inefficiency, it would not be preferred by the former country because the redistribution effect may dominate the efficiency gain.

Overall, the validity of a regional perspective is an empirical question. Whether the prospects in the Mashreq region can support a regional paradigm or not depends on the specific circumstances each country faces. In the following sections, we provide brief assessments of potential gains from cross-border cooperation, potential obstacles, and lessons from historical experiences.

CROSS-BORDER SYNERGIES IN THE MASHREQ REGION

The Syrian conflict motivated the erection of new barriers in the Mashreq. The conflict has dramatically broken the system of cross-border flow of people and goods across Mashreq countries. With violence in the country's interior and changing hands of border crossings, economic connectivity disintegrated quickly.

- Trade between Mashreq countries had built steadily in the 2000s, but then dropped sharply after 2011. The intraregion trade between the Mashreq countries increased substantially over the 2000–10 period thanks to a series of initiatives to liberalize trade (table 5.4 and table 5.5), including the Pan-Arab Free Trade Area (PAFTA), which removed tariffs (but not nontariff barriers) on intraregional merchandise trade among its 17 members starting from 2005. Since the onset of the Syrian war, however, the intraregional share of total merchandise trade in the Mashreq countries declined from 7.0 percent to 1.5 percent (not shown). The most dramatic declines have occurred in trade between Jordan and Syria and between Jordan and Iraq. The rise and fall of intraregional trade were accompanied by a similar pattern in the complementarity of trade across the Mashreq countries.[8] The trade complementarity index measures the extent to which the export pattern of one country matches the import pattern of another. The index ranges from 0 to 100; the higher the index, the higher the potential for that country's trade with the other countries. Table 5.6 shows that the trade complementarity of Mashreq countries increased over the 2000–10 decade and then fell drastically across all bilateral relationships.

- The exodus of more than 5 million Syrian refugees increased domestic pressure on Mashreq states to institute new restrictions on the movement of people. The first restrictions targeted Palestinian Syrians. Jordan began denying entry to Palestinians

TABLE 5.4. Intraregional export value, share in merchandise exports, and CAGR, selected Mashreq countries, 2010–18

		US$, MILLIONS			SHARE OF MERCHANDISE EXPORTS (%)			PERCENT CHANGE		
	EXPORTS TO	2000	2010	2018	2000	2010	2018	CAGR 2000–07	CAGR 2008–10	CAGR 2011–18
IRAQ	JORDAN	684	187	2	4.2	0.4	0	–44	156	–46
	LEBANON	1	3	5	0	0.0	0	4	–53	2
	SYRIAN ARAB REPUBLIC	—	96	—	—	0.2	—	–7	–52	–49
JORDAN	IRAQ	141	911	661	11.0	14.8	8.7	21	6	–6
	LEBANON	41	228	129	3.2	3.7	1.7	11	46	–14
	SYRIAN ARAB REPUBLIC	23	238	47	1.8	3.9	0.6	37	10	–22
LEBANON	IRAQ	29	267	147	3.7	8.4	4.1	26	0	–4
	JORDAN	39	108	74	4.9	3.4	2.1	15	–5	–6
	SYRIAN ARAB REPUBLIC	26	221	205	3.3	7.0	5.8	35	–1	–1
SYRIAN ARAB REPUBLIC	IRAQ	—	2,295	—	—	20.6	—	17	–5	—
	JORDAN	45	376	70	0.9	3.4	9.7	35	4	–21
	LEBANON	283	339	92	5.8	3.1	12.7	–4	12	–16

Source: UN Comtrade database.

Note: CAGR = compound annual growth rate; — = not available.

living in Syria in April 2012, and in January 2013 officially implemented a policy of not admitting them (HRW 2014). Jordan then closed its last border crossing to Syrian refugees after a car bomb killed six Jordanians near the Rukban border crossing in June 2016 (Sweis 2016). Prior to 2015, travel between Lebanon and Syria was largely unrestricted. The International Labour Organization estimates that 300,000 Syrian workers were in Lebanon before 2011, many of them working in construction (Ajluni and Kawar 2015). Like Jordan, Lebanon began barring Palestinians from entry in 2013, but non-Palestinian Syrians were automatically entitled to a six-month stay in Lebanon. In January 2015, as domestic opposition to Syrian refugees rose, the Lebanese government instituted a visa requirement for Syrians (BBC News 2015). In May of that year, the Lebanese government instructed the United Nations to stop registering Syrian refugees.

Nevertheless, prospects for cross-border cooperation remain significant. The previous analysis shows that, in the medium term, a rapid economic recovery in Syria and possible fallout in the form of trade opportunities are not likely. Many other factors, however, could make a better regional cooperation desirable. Refugee return is more likely when borders are more permeable, that is, the refugees would know they can have a second chance should their return attempt fail.

TABLE 5.5. Intraregional import value, share in merchandise imports, and CAGR, selected Mashreq countries, 2000–18

		US$, MILLIONS			SHARE OF MERCHANDISE EXPORTS (%)			PERCENT CHANGE		
	IMPORTS FROM	2000	2010	2018	2000	2010	2018	CAGR 2000–07	CAGR 2008–10	CAGR 2011–18
IRAQ	JORDAN	141	911	661	5.2	3.1	1.9	21	6	−6
	LEBANON	29	267	147	1.1	0.9	0.4	26	0	−4
	SYRIAN ARAB REPUBLIC	—	2,295	—	—	7.8	—	17	−5	−39
JORDAN	IRAQ	684	187	2	17.2	1.3	0	−44	156	−46
	LEBANON	31	104	86	0.8	0.7	0.5	18	−7	−5
	SYRIAN ARAB REPUBLIC	45	376	70	1.1	2.5	0.4	35	4	−21
LEBANON	IRAQ	1	3	5	0	0	0	4	−53	2
	JORDAN	34	195	107	0.7	1.2	0.6	16	24	−13
	SYRIAN ARAB REPUBLIC	283	339	92	5.9	2.1	0.5	−4	12	−16
SYRIAN ARAB REPUBLIC	IRAQ	0	96	0	0	0.5	0	−7	−52	−100
	JORDAN	23	238	47	0.6	1.3	0.8	37	10	−22
	LEBANON	26	221	205	0.7	1.2	3.6	35	−1	−1

Source: UN Comtrade database.

Note: CAGR = compound annual growth rate; — = not available.

TABLE 5.6. Intraregional Trade Complementarity Index, 2000, 2010, 2018

		IMPORTERS											
		JORDAN			LEBANON			IRAQ			SYRIAN ARAB REPUBLIC		
		2000	2010	2018	2000	2010	2018	2000	2010	2018	2000	2010	2018
EXPORTERS	JORDAN				33	37	33	25	33	32	23	30	30
	LEBANON	33	49	44				25	54	43	29	44	41
	IRAQ	5	9	9	15	20	20				7	12	3
	SYRIAN ARAB REPUBLIC	12	28	25	25	39	23	12	28	24			

Source: UN Comtrade database.

Note: The index is computed using mirror data. Index varies from 0 to 100. Exporters in row and importers in columns. For instance, in 2000, Jordan's trade potential to Lebanon is 33 whereas Syria's trade potential to Iraq in 2000 is 7.

Simulations in *The Mobility of Displaced Syrians* showed that, with such re-exit options, the spontaneous returns of Syrian refugees could be up to 1.6 percent, 2.4 percent, and 7.4 percent higher in the next decade in the first, second, and third scenarios, respectively (World Bank 2019). Formalizing such mobilization capacity across borders would not only facilitate more returns but also empower market mechanisms that help match jobs with workers and, thus, improve allocative efficiency in job markets.

Perhaps the most important gains from a regional approach are in service market integration and infrastructure cooperation. Although the intraregional complementarity of trade has been relatively low in strictly tradable sectors (for example, merchandise), the potential gains from removing barriers to service market integration and infrastructure cooperation are large. Opportunities to exploit cross-border synergies in energy, transport, and digital technologies (that is, information and communications technologies) are particularly promising. In what follows, we summarize these prospects.

- *Energy*. There is much room for deeper mutual integration of countries' electricity sectors at the regional level. Coordinated expansion planning for generation and transmission capacity, joint projects to build transmission interconnections, and joint efforts to build and strengthen the institutions for a common electricity market can all contribute to cost savings and better security of supply, thus mitigating the impact of the Syrian refugee crisis. To illustrate this point, table 5.7 presents the case of cross-border Interconnectors of Jordan with West Bank and Gaza, Saudi Arabia with Iraq, Jordan with Iraq, and Saudi Arabia with Jordan. Total economic benefits from these projects amount to $9.2 billion, derived mainly from avoided capital expenditures, as well as reliability benefits and fuel cost savings. Although the 2018–35 time horizon for this estimate is relatively long, the nature and magnitude of the benefits are instructive. Least-cost planning models show huge potential benefits from integrating infrastructure and markets at a regional level. Ideally, the scope of cooperation for promoting these benefits would not be limited to the four countries considered in this study but would include at least the whole eight-country group that has established the Mashreq interconnection. Furthermore, cooperation is already underway to integrate the electric power systems of the entire Pan-Arab region, including the Mashreq, Gulf Cooperation Council, and Maghreb subregions. In the Pan-Arab context, the creation of regional institutions for a common electricity market would bring the four countries of this study into the orbit of a much wider market integration effort. The proposed institutions include three Sub-Regional Transmission System Operators responsible for technical aspects of electricity trade, Market Facilitators responsible for the commercial aspects of trade, and a Pan-Arab Advisory and Regulatory Committee responsible for regulatory aspects.

- *Transport*. The lack of integrated transport systems and infrastructure poses a bottleneck that prevents the region from establishing regional value chains and participating in the global system of production and distribution. The three main action areas are as follows. First, accelerate railway systems. All countries in Mashreq suffer from weak railway interconnectivity, with Lebanon entirely lacking railway lines. According to the Agreement on International Railways in the Arab Mashreq,[9] 60 percent of the total railway network remains to be built (PGLOBAL 2011). Railway infrastructure and related transport of heavy and bulk loads are also prerequisites for preservation of road infrastructure. Improvement of the existing infrastructure and services,

TABLE 5.7. Benefits of cross-border interconnectors between Iraq, Jordan, Saudi Arabia, and West Bank and Gaza

	TOTAL SYSTEM COST (US$, MILLIONS)	FUEL COST[a] (US$, MILLIONS)	CAPITAL COST[b] (US$, MILLIONS)	RELIABILITY[c] (US$, MILLIONS)	O&M COST[d] (US$, MILLIONS)
IRAQ, JORDAN, SAUDI ARABIA, AND WEST BANK AND GAZA WITHOUT INTERCONNECTORS	625,177	316,552	94,550	147,179	66,896
IRAQ, JORDAN, SAUDI ARABIA, AND WEST BANK AND GAZA WITH PROPOSED INTERCONNECTORS	615,997	309,882	94,720	144,007	67,389
BENEFITS[e]	9,180	6,670	-169	3,172	-493

Source: World Bank staff calculations.

Note: Total discounted cost of operating the regional power system in the period of 2018–35, assuming discount rate of 6 percent.

a. Total cost of fuel consumed in the 2018–35 period.
b. Total annualized cost of building new generation capacity in the period 2018–30, assuming a weighted average cost of capital of 6 percent.
c. Includes the cost of unserved energy plus the cost of unserved reserves.
d. Includes fixed and variable operation and maintenance (O&M) cost.
e. Economic benefits are estimated as the difference between the discounted cost of the power system without using cross-border interconnectors minus the discounted cost of the system using selected, planned cross-border interconnectors.

as well as development of missing links would provide better connectivity for their ports with internal and export markets. Second, improve cross-border facilities and procedures. Customs authorities and the related system are chaotic in the region. An underdeveloped transit system causes delays and increases freight rates. No unified procedures exist at customs, so streamlining them—with upgraded information and communications technologies systems and reduced red tape and delays—should be a priority. Third, expand the TIR (Transports Internationaux Routiers) system. The TIR system of transit guarantees reduces the need for complicated procedures and specific arrangements for movement of goods (for example, convoys), as well as the associated fees and delays. The TIR system is complex institutionally, but it is effective and helps reform the transport sector because firms must meet professional standards set by the International Road Transport Union (IRU). Jordan has recently revived its membership to the TIR Convention. By the beginning of 2019, Iraq had finalized all the formalities in order to join the TIR Convention. The Iraqi Parliament has yet to approve ratification of the TIR Convention. Although it has not yet acceded to the harmonization, Lebanon has been a contracting party to the TIR since 1997.

- *Digital market*. The digital transformation of the Mashreq region would greatly benefit from a regional integration of infrastructure and data markets. The region has two major advantages: (i) a very young population promising a stronger participation in the global digital market and a rapid increase in local content and data bandwidth consumption and (ii) a strategic geographic position that allows it to be at the center of advanced services, trade, and connectivity. The Single Digital Market in East Africa is estimated to benefit every country (with the greater incidence of gains accruing to lower-income countries) by an additional 0.6 to 1.6 percentage points of GDP growth and an additional 2.0 to 6.2 percentage points of job creation. For deeper markets like the European Union, the GDP growth effect increases to about 2.4 percentage points. The effect in the Mashreq region is likely to remain between these two points. This approach comprises the following three-point strategy:

1. *Increase connectivity through infrastructure deployment.* This step includes improving connectivity between the countries, reducing the costs of access to regional networks, and positioning the region as a hub for international connectivity carrying Europe–Asia traffic (see box 5.2 for details). To this effect, when security and political conditions permit,

   - Undertake investments in regional fiber backbones and last-mile connectivity within countries to promote universal broadband access (especially in Iraq and Syria) in the medium term;

   - Reduce taxes, fees, and procedures for infrastructure deployment, including import duties for network equipment and fees for licensing and spectrum allocation for rural distribution, and provide easier access to rights-of-way to lay cables and mount equipment along other public infrastructure in the short term (can be done elsewhere regardless of the conditions in Syria); and

   - Explore the feasibility of issuing a single regional 4G or 5G license that specifies coverage obligations for each country, to improve scalability of business operations for the licensee. This would require a positive outlook in Syria and stability in the region as a whole.

2. *Lower regional transit costs.* Create a standardized open-access regime for regional backbone interconnection. Adopt a regional open access policy, including rights for any licensed operator in the region to purchase wholesale transit capacity. ISP licenses and IXP policies in the region must also be incentivized to promote regional connectivity and traffic exchange. This incentive would be mutually beneficial for Lebanon, which has two IXPs that it can monetize, and for Iraq, Jordan, and Syria, which do not house any IXPs at present. This initiative can be implemented in the short to medium term and is of a moderate priority. It may be possible to implement even with a negative outlook on the conflict in Syria.

3. *Improve affordability and quality of connectivity services.* Undertake a detailed stocktaking exercise of telecom policies in each region and collect data points for factors such as interconnection fees, number portability, infrastructure sharing challenges, price regulation of dominant market players, and so on; and implement or update policies where deficient. This exercise is urgently required in Iraq and Syria, which lack easily available data on many policies regarding telecom and connectivity (for example, the gaps in International Telecommunication Union and World Economic Forum data for the two countries). It is of high priority and can be undertaken even with a negative outlook on the conflict in Syria. In addition, coordinate a regional reduction or elimination of import and services taxes for consumer devices and connectivity services. Doing so would provide Iraq and Syria with advantageous technology transfers to fill existing gaps in the digital value chain and provide Jordan and Lebanon with improved access to talent pipelines and consumer markets. Conditions in Syria could influence the feasibility of this initiative.

BOX 5.2. Digital infrastructure outlook

The Mashreq internal bandwidth market—most of which is linked to Europe—is increasing at a brisk rate. International bandwidth in the Middle East and North Africa grew at a 41 percent compound annual growth rate (CAGR) between 2014 and 2018. Most of this traffic, however is linked to Europe, and only 8 percent is deployed within the region. With the growth in local demand and the increase in content generation, this regional traffic is expected to increase with an estimated CAGR of 30 percent between 2018 and 2025. Content providers' use of international bandwidth is expected to grow at an even higher CAGR of 54 percent between 2018 and 2025. This growth would inevitably require a stronger integration of networks within the region and between the region and other global markets.

The Mashreq is at the crossroads of the highest growth segment of global data connectivity. The Europe–Asia route is among the most dynamic of global routes, with a CAGR for bandwidth a whopping 59 percent over the past five years. Most broadband networks linking Europe and Asia are delivered through submarine cables, and transit through the Arab Republic of Egypt (map B5.2.1). Egypt has long been a choke point for vital traffic links between Europe and Asia, and disruption in the Red Sea landing points has had an impact on hundreds of millions of customers. This problem has provided incentive for alternative terrestrial routes to crop up, and routes traversing Iraq have gained some traction. A notable advantage of terrestrial Europe–Asia routes is that they typically follow more direct paths between Europe and Asia than do submarine cables, resulting in lower latency. Hence, the Mashreq region is an important region to increase the overall redundancy of the global internet infrastructure by offering alternative routes to global internet connectivity.

MAP B5.2.1. Terrestrial and submarine cables in Mashreq

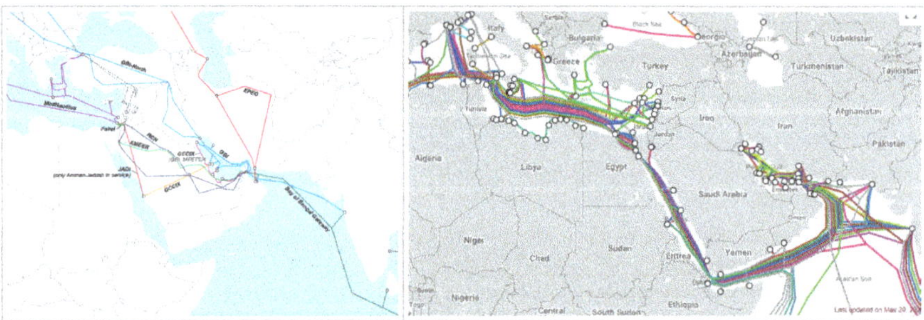

Source: TeleGeography 2018. https://www2.telegeography.com.

Interconnecting the data traffic infrastructure between the four countries has stalled because of conflict. Gulf Bridge International (GBI) currently passes through Iraq, linking Red Sea traffic to Turkey and Europe; however, two other regional networks—RCN (Regional Cable Network) and JADI (Jeddah, Amman, Damascus, and Istanbul)—have stopped operation in Mashreq because of the conflict in the Syrian Arab Republic. RCN, for instance, intended to reach Europe from the United Arab Emirates via Saudi Arabia, Jordan, Syria, and Turkey; however, the Syrian conflict has stalled this endeavor, and the system carries traffic only between Jordan and the Gulf. Looking forward to a time of stability, integrating infrastructure and positioning the region as a hub for international connectivity have a strong business case and can be carried out by the private sector. Governments, however, control much of the physical infrastructure in the region, which is the case for Iraq,

BOX 5.2 (continued)

Lebanon, and Syria. Stepping up the game in this regard would require stronger cooperation between the various governments, or the liberalization of the domestic and international fiber infrastructure in these countries.

THE LIMITS OF REGIONALISM: LESSONS FROM HISTORY

In the Mashreq, the idea of cross-border integration is as old as the borders themselves. From the 1920s onward, Arab nationalism was the dominant ideology of the Mashreq, and Pan-Arab aspirations have risen and fallen throughout the 20th century. Although not as old as the idea of political integration, the idea of economic integration has also surfaced frequently, especially in the last few decades. In the 2000s, various initiatives sought to capitalize on the economic opportunities of increasing cross-border integration in the Mashreq. The PAFTA between 17 MENA countries was signed in 1997 and entered into force in 2005. It removed tariffs on intraregional merchandise trade, but nontariff barriers and barriers to services endured (Secretary General of the League of Arab States 1997). Mashreq countries also pursued bilateral free trade agreements with Turkey in the 2000s (Ianchovichina and Ivanic 2014). Some Mashreq countries also signed Euromed Association Agreements (EAAs), which aimed to create a deep Euro-Mediterranean free trade area.[10] An EAA with Jordan went into effect in 2002 and with Lebanon in 2006, and talks were initiated with Syria in 2008. Turkey also spearheaded the Shamgen agreement, an ambitious customs union initiative between Jordan, Lebanon, Syria, and Turkey. The agreement was based on the European Union model and was due to come into effect in 2011.

Progress toward a unified Mashreq economy has been limited. Despite numerous attempts to enhance economic integration in the Mashreq in the 2000s, various obstacles to the movement of goods endured and intraregional trade remained very low.[11] Of all Mashreq states, Syria imported the highest share of its imports from within the region in 2010, but two-thirds of its imports still came from outside the region. Jordan had the second-highest proportion of regional imports, at 16.2 percent; Lebanon had less than 7 percent, and less than 3 percent of Iraq's imports came from the region. Average tariffs across the region have come down but remain high compared to East Asia, the Americas, and Europe. High nontariff measures pose even more significant barriers. MENA remains one of the most restrictive regions in services trade, globally the fastest-growing segment. High transport costs and technical barriers also impede progress, and, despite advances in the Gulf and elsewhere, logistics lag, especially when it comes to decreasing the cost of cross-border trading. Further challenges include lack of common standards and red tape. Overlaying these barriers and challenges are often protectionist, inward-looking economies, with public and private sector incumbents safeguarding "their" markets—precluding greater market contestability, which is key to opening to the outside.

Aspiring to integrate but failing to do so stems from incentive structures within countries, between countries in the region, and between the region and the rest of the world. Within individual economies, the political elites in Mashreq countries operate within a fractured socioeconomic context. Despite a growing dissatisfaction with governance that cuts laterally across society, majority-minority group dynamics (largely ethnic and sectarian, but not limited to those) continue to reinforce the elites' preferences to maintain the status quo. The confessional system in Lebanon is one, but not the only, example in this regard. As for incentive structures between the region's economies, major economic and political asymmetries across countries have played an important regressive role. On the one hand, as shown by Karayalcin and Onder (2020), asymmetries in economic sizes and productivities can reduce willingness of the relatively richer countries to integrate economically if doing so leads to a significant redistribution. On the other hand, the elites in smaller countries can also refrain from integrating if doing so can lead to a loss of monopoly over state apparatus control and public resources. Finally, this picture becomes even more complex when considering external factors. Through bilateral relationships with the rest of the world, the elites in each state can bargain for support to maintain the status quo, which is somewhat stable until inherent fragilities render it otherwise. With conflicting interests, these alliances can block prospects for economic integration. Major shocks like conflicts, however, can provide a break point in this equilibrium as has happened before in the region's history.

Historically, integration has been a multilayered process, with each layer playing an important role, and the sequence of the layers being determined by the nature of the leading shock. To motivate a long-term vision for the Mashreq, we have investigated the long history of the region. Accordingly, three periods stood out for their success in improving economic connectivity in the region: the Umayyad and Abbasid caliphates (661–1258) and the Golden Age of Islam, the Pax Ottomanica during the early modern period, and the Euro-Ottoman modus vivendi of the long 19th century (1800–1945). In each of these periods, both the driver of economic integration and the corresponding sequencing of integration layers (infrastructure integration, labor mobility, and trade integration) were different (box 5.3). In the first period (Golden Age of Islam), a mass migration shock driven by noneconomic (religious) motives triggered trade links and eventually infrastructure integration. In comparison, in the second period (Pax Ottomanica), the provision of security and links to the imperial trade networks, both of which were enforced externally, were the main drivers. Finally, in the third period, a strong trade shock (supplying raw materials to Europe, where the Industrial Revolution was unfolding) was the main culprit. Three main lessons from this analysis for the contemporary problems covered in this report are as follows:

1. Large-scale demographic shocks can provide an opportunity to increase cross-border connectivity by supporting trade, as happened in the Umayyad and Abbasid caliphates period. The immediate corollary from this lesson applies to the large-scale Syrian displacement. As discussed above, with a slow economic recovery in Syria going forward, the trade benefits for neighboring countries are likely to remain modest. With the support of a common regional vision, and eventual infrastructure cooperation (including physical and institutional dimensions), the gains can be transformative.

2. External factors can play a major role in facilitating economic integration. In the Pax Ottomanica period, this external factor was the stability and trade gains facilitated by the Empire, which was imposed from above. In comparison, in the 19th century the trade expansion with Europe promoted a bottom-up economic integration, in which the market dynamics shaped the labor mobility and infrastructure provision across the Mashreq geography. This is especially true when none of the regional actors can be the locomotive of such process, as is currently the case.

3. The right balance between competition and cooperation is essential in promoting a dynamic regional economy. The Pax Ottomanica period suffered from stagnant economic dynamics because urban guilds, empowered by an imperial institutional setup

BOX 5.3. Regionalism across three historical periods in the Mashreq

The Mashreq region has a rich history of successes and failures in terms of expanding economic connectivity (see figure B5.3.1). A background paper for this report, Ozveren (2020), has analyzed three types of connectivity, trade, labor mobility, and infrastructure cooperation, in the region's long history.

Golden Age of Islamic Conquests in Mashreq

The Muslim conquerors who advanced from the Arabian Peninsula into Iraq and Syria were adventurers with noneconomic motives, that is, religious zeal. Large numbers of incomers settled land, introduced new crops, and expanded commercial agriculture. They were thus integrated into the workforce as farmers and peasants, pushing others up to employment in urban manufacturing and trade sectors. Others specialized in setting up and running the caravan trade. Empire building was flexible, with the center occasionally shifting while borders remained porous and flexible. The central power sought agricultural innovation and undertook major irrigation projects in Iraq. Bagdad became not only an international trade and finance center but also a center of learning comparable to Renaissance Florence. Such an empire was convenient to maintain at a low cost during normal times but suffered from a defense deficit when faced with sudden massive attacks from the lands beyond. Mongol conquest and then the Crusades demonstrated this vulnerability and the edifice disintegrated into numerous rival principalities.

- This period shows that large-scale population movements driven by noneconomic reasons can still carry a strong impetus through labor mobility to trade across borders, which then triggers further positive developments in infrastructure cooperation (both institutional and physical).

Sixteenth-Century Pax Ottomanica in the Fertile Crescent

Ottomans imposed political unity under their defensive umbrella in the Fertile Crescent. This unity brought stability, low-cost international protection, and infrastructural integration. At this time, oceanic trade routes were shifting at the expense of the Mediterranean. By creating a large imperial network, Ottoman policy boosted economic development by shifting the center of gravity from the East toward the Mediterranean. Aleppo, Basra, and Damascus were revived as trade nodes in a vast network. Mediterranean ports served Aleppo and Damascus and linked to overland trade in the imperial system. This large-scale trade integration compensated for losses due to shifts in favor of oceanic routes. The Ottoman production system was conservative, relying on urban guilds that preserved traditional technology, enforced quality, and served as depositories of skills and know-how. This system, however, reduced growth potential or adaptation capability. When it gave in under external pressure, the empire left behind a legacy of country-size units coinciding with Ottoman administrative units.

- This period shows that infrastructure integration can be an effective policy instrument for triggering change, but it needs to be accompanied by flexible, market-sensitive trade integration and labor mobility to be able to sustain dynamic economic growth and structural change.

Euro-Ottoman Modus Vivendi of the 19th Century

This period's momentum came from a very strong external shock stimulating trade integration with Europe. The region was inscribed into the international division of labor as an

BOX 5.3 (continued)

exporter of first primary and later semiprocessed agricultural products. Overseas trade expanded just as the economic center of gravity shifted to the Syrian coastline bordering the Mediterranean. Port cities like Beirut became poles of economic growth, until the growth of grain trade reintegrated the littoral with the hinterland much later. With such a trade integration shock, infrastructural integration was bound to take big steps. The Egypt and the Ottoman Empire competed for administrative reform and good governance. The greatest physical project was the Suez Canal, which boosted trade integration through Basra with the Indian Ocean route. Railways, roads, and river transport means were built rapidly yet often lacked compatibility across subregions. Labor integration comprised limited European settlement in ports. In the later stages, both agriculture and domestic manufacturing gained significant market responsiveness, creating their own labor markets.

- If the previous phase was too change-resistant, this period was far too dynamic. Every segment of the integration in this era was activated often with contrasting orientations. Inherent in chaotic short-sighted transport projects was a tendency to foster lock-ins and suboptimal line choices in the next period. The littoral–hinterland (Syrian Civil War of the 1860s) and Iraq–Syria fault lines just waited to play themselves out when circumstances permitted.

FIGURE B5.3.1. Dynamics of regional integration in three distinct episodes

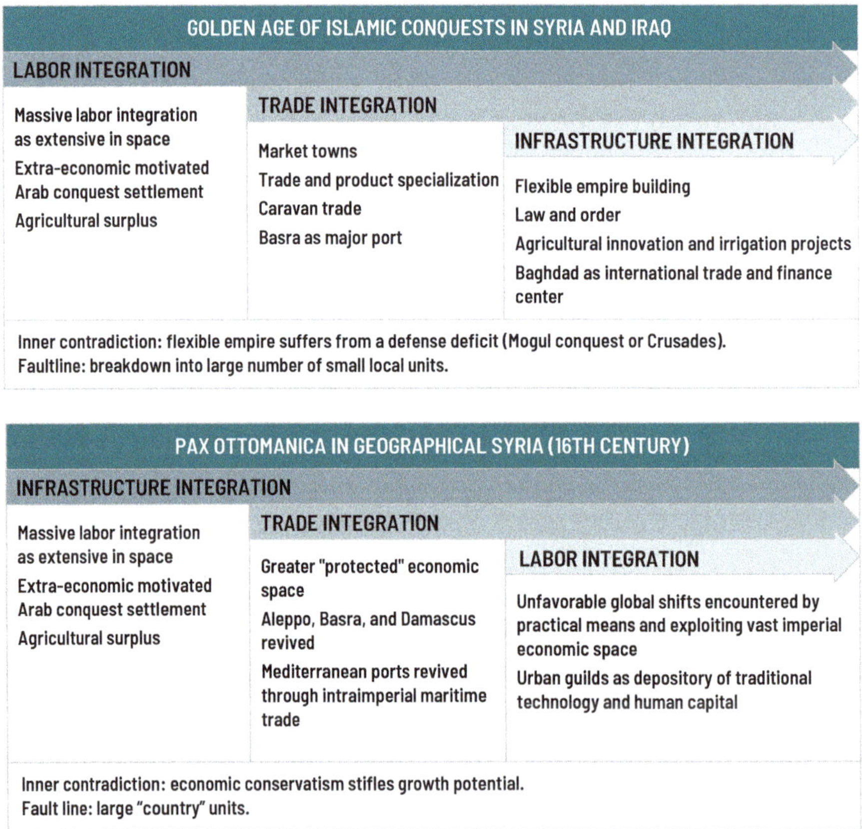

BOX 5.3 (continued)

EURO-OTTOMAN MODUS VIVENDI (19TH CENTURY)

TRADE INTEGRATION

With European trade as exporter of raw and semiprocessed (spun silk, etc.) materials
Expansion of overseas trade and rise of ports
Domestic grain trade

INFRASTRUCTURE INTEGRATION

Reform
Rise of Beirut as a port city
Suez Canal project
Railways, roads, river transport

LABOR INTEGRATION

Limited European entrepreneur settlement
Market-oriented agriculture
Manufacturing restructured by local demand

Inner contradiction: security deficit causes concentration of private interests on the coastline. Railway projects with incompatible gauges imply suboptimal lock-ins for the next period.
Faultline: coastline versus inner heartland (1860s civil war in greater Syria); and Iraq and Syria look in different directions after Suez Canal.

and effectively operating as trade unions, somewhat reduced incentives for innovation and competition. In comparison, the Euro-Ottoman modus vivendi of the long 19th century witnessed a chaotic race to establish natural monopolies by means of infrastructure investments, which led to incompatibility across regions. Contemporarily, this shows that a regional integration should encourage market principles and contestability, yet it should nurture markets with strategic and supportive infrastructural and institutional systems.

Overall, our analysis shows both challenges and opportunities in the Mashreq. Cross-border externalities, either public goods or public bads, are significant in the Mashreq. In the absence of a regional focus, governments can still undertake actions to enhance their ability to mitigate the negative fallout of conflicts in neighboring countries and improve the well-being of their constituencies. Considering major cross-border spillovers, and the political economy constraints governments operate in, a regional approach to stabilization and prosperity is likely to be more effective. Potential gains from a regional cooperation are sizeable, and they can help stabilize the region by improving the well-being of all constituents in the region. There are several impediments, however, to a regional perspective: major asymmetries within each country and between the countries of the region have so far prevented a regional perspective. Nevertheless, history shows us a better outcome is possible. Should an international consensus on stabilizing the region as a whole materialize, a switch from a bad equilibrium to a good equilibrium can take place, which has happened several times in the region's history. Under the right conditions, service restoration and economic recovery in Syria can provide an opportunity for such a consensus for a regional perspective. In the next, and final, section, we provide a number of recommendations on such external help.

A DEUS EX MACHINA FOR THE MASHREQ THEATER?

Shifting to a regional focus for stability and prosperity necessitates a concerted international effort. The overview of gains from regional cooperation, and the factors that may render efforts for such cooperation futile, shows that transitioning from a unilateral approach to a regional one cannot be induced by cheap talk. In game theoretic language, a renewed round of communication among parties that does not affect their payoffs is unlikely to shift the regional equilibrium to a better one.[12] Instead, what is needed is a supra-national commitment to stability at the regional level. Such commitment, which can be achieved only by a concerted effort of the international community, can make the actors of the region feel safe enough to perform deeper social and economic change, which would help to relieve the exclusion of certain segments of the local populations and alleviate the inherent interdependent fragility. The right combination of local, regional, and international inputs can thus help surpass the inherent limitations observed in the past. Achieving that combination is no easy task. Yet no alternative at hand is equally desirable or feasible, at least not for the foreseeable future.

Fully characterizing a concerted international effort is beyond the scope of this study; however, experiences elsewhere can help to define the elements of such an approach. The lessons from regional stabilization and economic cooperation experiences in Africa and Europe can potentially be useful for envisaging a regional perspective for the Mashreq despite several differences. The following selected experiences are likely to be relevant for the Mashreq.

- *External support.* Under a common perceived threat from the Soviet Union, Western Europe's uniform alignment with the United States facilitated deep economic and political integration along rule of law, democracy, and open markets. Although such integration is not feasible (and not necessarily desired by all parties) for the Mashreq, the current nonalignment of external actors hampers even developing a more regional perspective for stabilization and prosperity. On an ironically positive note, however, the "global public bads" from an unstable Mashreq region, including the sudden demographic shocks and security threats, provide incentives for all parties to wish for better stability and prosperity for all in the region.

- *Popular support and ownership.* After two devastating world wars left a profound mark on Europe's peoples, the desire for no more war in Europe was deep and very widely shared. Nevertheless, the lack of popular support derailed further integration efforts despite elite interests, as illustrated by the French and Dutch rejection of the European Union Constitution. In the Mashreq, conditions are quite different. Historically, it has been the elites who, despite using a popular discourse in favor of a regional perspective, hindered such regionalism for fear of losing control. In contrast, cross-border ties of constituents remained resilient despite borders. Thus, the popular support condition may not be a strongly binding constraint in the Mashreq, especially if occurring in tandem with the following condition.

- *Inclusiveness.* A regional perspective can be stabilizing and beneficial only if it is inclusive. The phenomena of inward-looking protectionism, insufficient provision of public services, and economic and political exclusion of segments of societies are often manifestations of the same underlying political economy conditions. Thus, if international commitment can facilitate the participation in regionalism of otherwise suspicious elites, the inclusiveness of this approach, which can promote convergence between the lagging groups or regions and others, can facilitate the necessary political support and, thus, better stability. Otherwise, a noninclusive regionalism can further fuel instability by increasing the opportunity cost of exclusion, and peace, for the excluded.

- *Settlement of major conflicts.* Promoting regional stability requires the settlement of previous armed conflicts. The conflict in Syria will make such regional perspective impossible unless the conflict is settled. The region teems with unresolved grievances, including interstate conflicts (for example, Arab–Israeli), large-scale displacements (for example, Palestinian refugees), and domestic tensions (for example, sectarian divides in Iraq, Lebanon, and Syria). Some of these grievances do not necessarily present a stumbling block for a regional perspective and may even find relief in such processes, but the Syrian conflict is not one of them. With the large cross-border effects, reaching a regional stability without ending the Syrian crisis is unlikely to happen.

- *Honest broker*. The international community has the right agents to steer a medium-term regional agenda for stability and prosperity. Under the auspices of the United Nations system, and when the political conditions allow, the World Bank Group is well positioned to take a steering role on policy dialogue and reform with individual countries, coordinate and influence partner country strategies, and help to create a more effective platform for coherent donor–government dialogue on key issues. The process would involve developing structured finance solutions, innovative approaches, and instruments to leverage additional funding for a regional agenda, including, but not limited to, outcome-based models like public-private partnerships, challenge funds, and impact bonds pooled under umbrella funds.

In sum, although the conditions are less than ideal for a regional drive, such a motive can provide a feasible exit from a fragile regional equilibrium. Studies on regional cooperation often highlight the importance of stability before attempting cooperation. In the Mashreq, however, we do not have this option. Drivers of instability in the Mashreq are numerous and powerful, and overcoming them will be a formidable task. Thus, in this report, we took a different approach and asked if a regional perspective that is owned locally but supported internationally can help stabilize the region as a whole. Our answer is affirmative, albeit cautiously so. If and when an international consensus is established, the international community has the means to facilitate such a vision. The most uncertain, and perhaps the most difficult, part is building such consensus. We are optimistic because the alternative is in no one's interest.

NOTES

1. The insecurity index represents the broader safety of Syrians and is calculated by normalizing security incidents over years (assigning 0 to no incidents and 1 to the highest incidents, which took place in 2017). For more information, please see World Bank (2019).
2. The UN Comtrade database (the United Nations International Trade Statistics Database) is available at https://comtrade.un.org.
3. The HCI measures the human capital of the next generation, defined as the amount of human capital that a child born today can expect to attain by his or her 18th birthday given the risks of poor health and poor education in the country where he or she lives (Kraay 2018). One component of the HCI is EYE, which measures the number of years of schooling a child can expect to obtain by age 18 given the pattern of enrollment rates. It is calculated as the sum of age-specific enrollment rates between ages 4 and 17.
4. This calculation involves converting an additional year of completed education into a metric of productivity. To do so, we use estimates from Hanushek and Woessmann (2007), associating an additional year of schooling with a 0.58-percentage-point increase in GDP per capita. Please note that this approach necessarily assumes closing the gap between Syrian refugees and locals not only in years of expected education but also in job opportunities. Otherwise, the Hanushek and Woessmann (2007) estimate would be an overshooting for our purposes.
5. The mechanisms through which low state capacity (formulated as ineffectiveness in enforcing contracts, protecting property, and providing public goods and raising revenues) and political violence either in the form of repression or civil conflict can emerge are explored in detail by Besley and Persson (2011).
6. Such mechanisms also underlie the arguments for scale economies, in which removing barriers across markets not only leads to the removal of a direct inefficiency (for example, trade costs) but also helps produce goods more cheaply.
7. In Besley and Persson (2011), greater investments in fiscal and legal capacities and lower investments for conflictual investments can be explained by a greater willingness to provide own constituents with public goods and services. In our framework, the willingness to do so is endogenous: internalizing the cross-border externalities of public goods induces an increase in this willingness.
8. For a detailed analysis of services and goods trade in MENA (and between countries inside and outside MENA), see Rouis and Tabor (2012) and World Bank (2014a).
9. Adopted on March 14, 2003, and entered into force on May 23, 2005. The Agreement has been ratified by 16 countries in the region.
10. For more on the Euro-Mediterranean free trade area, see https://ec.europa.eu/trade/policy/countries-and-regions/regions/euro-mediterranean-partnership/.
11. See Karasapan (2020) for a detailed overview of the history of integration attempts in the Arab World.
12. In certain situations communication by itself can change the equilibrium by focal point effect; however, in the Mashreq, the payoff profile and the nature of the strategic interactions do not provide such an example.

REFERENCES

Ajluni, Salem, and Mary Kawar. 2015. *Towards Decent Work in Lebanon: Issues and Challenges in Light of the Syrian Refugee Crisis*. Beirut: International Labour Organization.

BBC News. 2015. "Syrians Entering Lebanon Face New Restrictions." BBC News, January 5, 2015, sec. Middle East. https://www.bbc.com/news/world-middle-east-30657003.

Besley, Timothy, and Torsten Persson. 2011. "Fragile States and Development Policy." *Journal of the European Economic Association* 9 (3): 371–98.

El Kak, Nadim, and Sami Zoughaib. 2020. "Grappling between Past and Future: Will Lebanon's Political Economy Reproduce Itself?" OpenDemocracy (blog), January 10, 2020. https://www.opendemocracy.net/en/north-africa-west-asia/grappling-between-past-and-future-will-lebanons-political-economy-reproduce-itself/.

Hanushek, Eric A., and Ludger Woessmann. 2007. "The Role of Education Quality for Economic Growth." Policy Research Working Paper 4122, World Bank, Washington, DC.

HRW (Human Rights Watch). 2014. "Not Welcome | Jordan's Treatment of Palestinians Escaping Syria." Human Rights Watch, August 7, 2014. https://www.hrw.org/report/2014/08/07/not-welcome/jordans-treatment-palestinians-escaping-syria.

Ianchovichina, Elena, and Maros Ivanic. 2014. "Missed Opportunities: Economic Effects of Potential Deep Trade Integration in the Levant." Conference Paper Presented at the 17th Annual Conference on Global Economic Analysis, Dakar, Senegal. http://www.gtap.agecon.purdue.edu/resources/res_display.asp?RecordID=4383.

Karasapan, Omer. 2020. "The Mashreq and a Search for Integration and Stability." Background paper, *The Fallout of War*, World Bank, Washington, DC.

Karayalcin, Cem, and Harun Onder. 2020. "Domestic Conflict, Public Services, and Regional Integration." Background paper, *The Fallout of War*, World Bank, Washington, DC.

Kraay, Aart C. 2018. "Methodology for a World Bank Human Capital Index." Policy Research Working Paper 8593, World Bank, Washington, DC.

Oates, Wallace E. 1972. *Fiscal Federalism*. New York: Harcourt Brace Jovanovich.

Ozveren, Eyup. 2020. "The Past Experience in Patterns of Integration of Syria, Iraq, Lebanon, and Jordan: Delineating a Historical Trajectory with Implications for the Foreseeable Future." Background paper, *The Fallout of War*, World Bank, Washington, DC.

PGLOBAL (PGlobal Global Advisory and Training Services). 2011. "A Study of International Transport Corridors in OIC Member Countries." Report prepared for the Islamic Development Bank, PGlobal Global Advisory and Training Services. http://www.comcec.org/wp-content/uploads/2015/02/IDB-TransportCorridors-Study.pdf.

Rouis, M., and S. R. Tabor. 2012. *Regional Economic Integration in the Middle East and North Africa: Beyond Trade Reform*. Directions in Development. Washington, DC: World Bank Group.

Secretary General of the League of Arab States. 1997. "Declaration Pan-Arab Free Trade Area Economic and Social Council's Resolution No. 1317-O.S. 59." https://wits.worldbank.org/GPTAD/PDF/archive/PAFTA.pdf

Sweis, Rana. 2016. "Jordan Closes Border to Syrian Refugees After Suicide Car Bomb Kills 6." *New York Times*, June 21, 2016. https://www.nytimes.com/2016/06/22/world/middleeast/jordan-syria-attack.html.

UNICEF (United Nations Children's Fund). 2018. "20 Villages Assessment Report." World Engineering and Technology, UNICEF, New York.

USIP (United States Institute of Peace). 2013. "The Syrian Conflict's Impact on Lebanese Politics." Peace Brief 158, USIP, Washington, DC. https://www.usip.org/sites/default/files/PB158.pdf.

World Bank. 2014a. "Over the Horizon: A New Levant." Report no. 86946-IQ, World Bank, Washington, DC.

World Bank. 2014b. "The Unfulfilled Promise of Oil and Growth: Poverty, Inclusion and Welfare in Iraq 2007–2012." World Bank, Washington, DC. http://documents.worldbank.org/curated/en/752991468261314600/The-unfulfilled-promise-of-oil-and-growth-poverty-inclusion-and-welfare-in-Iraq-2007-2012.

World Bank. 2019. *The Mobility of Displaced Syrians: An Economic and Social Analysis*. Washington, DC: World Bank.

Appendixes

A. DATA SOURCES FOR CHAPTER 2

IRAQ HOUSEHOLD SOCIO-ECONOMIC SURVEY 2012

The survey was an improved version of the Iraq Household Socio-Economic Survey (HSES) conducted in 2006–07. HSES-2012 intends to provide estimators of comparable quality for each of Iraq's 118 gadahs (districts), implying that the sample should be explicitly stratified by *gadah*, with a similar sample size allocated to each gadah, regardless of its size. A sample size of 216 households per gadah is proposed, equivalent to a total sample of 25,488 households for the country. The response rate of HSES-2012 was 98.7 percent; HSES-2012 surveyed 25,146 households. The dataset includes comprehensive social, demographic, and economic information of 176,041 individuals. One-quarter of the surveyed households lived in the Kurdistan Region of Iraq (KRI), and 9 percent lived in Baghdad. Of the families surveyed, 7.5 percent lived in Ninawa, the governorate hugely affected by the violence that took place two years after.

IRAQ RAPID WELFARE MONITORING SURVEY 2017

The Rapid Welfare Monitoring Survey (SWIFT), conducted in 2017, replaced the HSES, which stopped in 2014. SWIFT-2017 intended to provide interim estimates of welfare and well-being until another survey comparable in scope and coverage to HSES could be fielded. Although this survey includes Iraqi residents and internally displaced persons (IDPs) in addition to some refugees from the Syrian Arab Republic, one should use it cautiously because it includes a smaller number of households and excludes 14 districts, including 9 in Ninawa and 3 in Anbar, for security reasons. It also excludes Syrian refugees and IDPs living in camps then.[1] SWIFT-2017 includes 52,966 individuals living in 8,615 households—equal to 34 percent of the 2012 sample size. Of these households, 202 are Syrian, whereas 1,053 (12.3 percent of the sample) host at least one IDP. Of these Syrian families, 99 percent came from Syria. A few of them (3.5 percent) were living in Iraq before 2003, but the majority (72 percent) arrived between 2003 and 2014; the remaining 24.5 percent arrived after 2014. Of the households surveyed in 2017, 31 percent live in KRI; that share is 6 percentage points higher than the HSES-2012 results, consistent with the fact that KRI received about 40–50 percent of all IDPs. Compared to the population share of KRI, KRI is overrepresented in the sample. In contrast, Ninawa governorate is underrepresented because of security reasons and because the SWIFT-2017 includes just 1 district out of 10 in that governorate.

NOTES

1. Whereas 8 percent of the Syrian refugees in the Middle East and North Africa region live in camps (Krishnan and Olivieri 2016), 37 percent of Syrian refugees in Iraq live in camps according to the United Nations High Commissioner for Refugees (see https://data2.unhcr.org/en/situations/syria).

REFERENCES

Krishnan, N., and S. D. Olivieri. 2016. "Losing the Gains of the Past: The Welfare and Distributional Impacts of the Twin Crises in Iraq." Policy Research Working Paper 7567, World Bank, Washington, DC.

B. ESTIMATING THE IMPACT OF THE SYRIAN CONFLICT ON CAPITAL FLOWS

Many factors—global, regional, and domestic—may have affected capital inflows into Iraq, Jordan, and Lebanon following the onset of the crisis in the Syrian Arab Republic. We analyze the role that the Syrian conflict may have played using regression analysis on a panel data of 236 emerging markets and developing economies (EMDEs) from 1976 to 2018 within a push-pull framework that is frequently used in the capital flows literature. This framework divides the determinants of capital flows into external push factors and domestic pull factors. The underlying concept is a portfolio approach in which expected returns, risk, and risk preferences determine capital flows across countries.

Push factors are external conditions (or supply-side factors) that underpin the supply of global liquidity and encourage investors to increase their exposure to EMDEs. Typically, the push factors include variables like global risk aversion, US (or a group of advanced economies) economic growth, and US (or a group of advanced economies) interest rates. Pull factors are the domestic country characteristics (or demand-side factors) that influence risks and returns to investors, and they depend on local macroeconomic fundamentals, government policies, and the overall investment climate. To this framework we add several conflict-related variables.

Our specification of the model is

$$F_{it} = \alpha_0 + \sum_{j=1}^{5} \lambda_j X_{jit} + \sum_{k=0}^{3} \rho_k dconf_{i(t-k)} + \sum_{l=0}^{3} \theta_l dconfneighbor_{i(t-l)} + \gamma dMENA + \alpha_i + \beta_t + u_{it}$$

where F_{it} is the inward capital flow for country i at time t; the flows include direct investment (di_l), portfolio (pi_l), and total inflows ($sumi\_l$). X_{jit} are the push and pull factors used as controls: US real gross domestic product (GDP) growth ($l.usgdpg$), the US Federal Reserve Bank's shadow interest rate ($l.usshadir\_nzcb$) and country real GDP growth ($l.gdpg$) all as one time period lags, as well as the Standard & Poor's VIX volatility index (vix), the heritage index ($heritage$)—used as an indication of the general investment climate—and a 2008 year dummy to capture the 2008 global financial crisis ($d2008$). We also include two variables to be able to address the broader question of how conflict affects capital flows: the country conflict variable ($dconf$), which is a dummy variable controlling for presence of conflict[1] in a given year, and a variable ($dconfneighbor$), which controls for the presence of conflict in the country's immediate neighbors. To separate the impact of the Syrian conflict specifically, we add two further Syria-related variables: (i) a 2011 year dummy interacted with distance to Syria ($d2011\_ldistcapSYR$) and (ii) a Syria neighbor dummy interacted with a post-2011 year dummy ($d3C\_2011,\ d3C\_2012, \dots, d3C\_2016$). This last variable is intended to capture any changes in investor behavior that may occur over time after the start of the conflict (in this case after 2011). The t and i are the time and country identifiers. Variables and data sources are defined in table B.2.

The model is estimated using ordinary least squares (OLS) with a panel fixed country effects specification, and statistical inference is made using robust standard errors. The results are given in table B.1.

Focusing on the non-Syrian-conflict-related variables, we observe the following:

- The results for foreign direct investment (FDI) inflows (columns 1 and 2) show the significance of the *L.usshaqdir_nzcb* variable in the direction that is normally expected (negative). The *L.usgdpg* and *d2008* variables, both significant, are with signs that would not necessarily be a priori determined. Faster growth in mature economies could support larger capital inflows to emerging markets (positive relationship), or it could divert investor interest away from emerging markets (negative relationship). With regard to the 2008 dummy, although global FDI flows were affected, as were FDI flows within mature economies, FDI flows to emerging markets initially showed comparatively greater resilience. Most other variables, although insignificant, show the expected signs.

- In the case of portfolio inflows, (columns 3 and 4), the VIX volatility variable is significant with the expected negative sign. The *d2008* dummy variable is also found to be significant and with the expected negative sign generally found in the literature with respect to portfolio flows because of a sharp retrenchment of portfolio flows to EMDEs immediately with the onset of the global financial crisis in 2008.

- The results for total capital inflows (columns 5 and 6) show that all the variables that were significant for each of the components of capital inflows remain significant for total inflows as well.

Turning to the Syrian conflict–related dummies we find the following:

- For FDI inflows, the dummy for the distance to Syria in 2011 (*d2011_ldistcapSYR*) (column 1) shows an expected positive significant effect (that is, the greater the distance between the capital-receiving country and Syria, the greater the FDI inflows to the country; or conversely the smaller the distance between the capital-receiving country and Syria, the lower the FDI inflows into the country). FDI inflows for Syria's immediate neighbors in 2011–15 (column 2) also experienced a statistically significant negative trend after controlling for other factors.

- For portfolio flows there is a negative effect for Syria's neighbors in the two years after 2011; however, this trend reverses to a positive trend in 2015 and 2016 (column 4).

- For total inflows we find both the distance variable (*d2011_ldistcapSYR*) and the neighbor variable for 2012 and 2015 (both negative) to be significant (columns 5 and 6, respectively).

To the extent that the Syrian conflict affected domestic GDP growth in the three neighboring countries, this result would be picked up in the coefficient on domestic GDP. The significance of the Syrian conflict–related dummies suggests that, even controlling for the effect through domestic growth, the Syrian conflict had an adverse effect, perhaps reflecting generalized uncertainty. FDI flows were the most consistently affected by the generalized uncertainty—in that both measures of conflict are found to be of the expected sign and significant throughout the 2011–15 period. Although portfolio flows also reacted negatively—both as measured by the distance variable and the Syria neighbor conflict variable—the latter variable is negative only at the beginning and reverses from 2015 onward. The difference between the behavior of FDI inflows and portfolio flows is perhaps not surprising because FDI flows tend to reflect a longer-term commitment in a country and are arguably more sensitive to the host country climate and outlook. The results show that total capital inflows were also negatively affected by uncertainty.

TABLE B.1. Determinants of capital inflows—all emerging markets and developing economies

VARIABLE	FDI INFLOWS (*di_l*)		PORTFOLIO INFLOWS (*pi_l*)		TOTAL INFLOWS (*sumi_l*)	
	(1)	(2)	(3)	(4)	(5)	(6)
L.usgdpg	−0.419** (0.016)	−0.249** (0.027)	−0.343** (0.011)	−0.335** (0.010)	−1.537** (0.013)	−1.099*** (0.008)
L.usshadir_nzcb	−0.532* (0.057)	−0.668** (0.047)	−0.138 (0.132)	−0.144* (0.090)	−0.676* (0.056)	−1.023** (0.040)
L.gdpg	0.0372 (0.346)	0.0507 (0.176)	0.0284 (0.325)	0.0295 (0.317)	0.281*** (0.010)	0.326*** (0.005)
vix	−0.0903** (0.021)	−0.0196 (0.335)	−0.0743*** (0.001)	−0.0710*** (0.005)	−0.423*** (0.004)	−0.240*** (0.004)
heritage	−0.0103 (0.905)	−0.0119 (0.891)	−0.0184 (0.653)	−0.0187 (0.647)	0.0148 (0.930)	0.00505 (0.976)
d2008	5.668*** (0.006)	5.099*** (0.005)	−1.099* (0.093)	−1.123 (0.102)	8.777*** (0.002)	7.289*** (0.001)
dconfneighbor	−0.296 (0.560)	−0.185 (0.703)	−0.109 (0.516)	−0.111 (0.514)	0.330 (0.821)	0.577 (0.686)
dconf	0.255 (0.622)	0.329 (0.541)	−1.508 (0.109)	−1.539 (0.106)	−1.987 (0.261)	−1.820 (0.299)
dconf_1	−0.687 (0.419)	−0.792 (0.374)	0.395 (0.391)	0.384 (0.406)	−0.630 (0.621)	−0.834 (0.541)
dconfneighbor_1	0.345 (0.200)	0.176 (0.505)	0.261 (0.435)	0.260 (0.431)	0.306 (0.574)	−0.0930 (0.870)
dconf_2	1.335 (0.225)	1.370 (0.218)	0.250 (0.446)	0.220 (0.500)	4.131 (0.177)	4.121 (0.179)
dconfneighbor_2	0.351 (0.275)	0.490 (0.158)	−0.0553 (0.863)	−0.0525 (0.869)	1.414* (0.097)	1.787* (0.060)
dconf_3	1.795 (0.221)	1.831 (0.225)	0.0980 (0.739)	0.117 (0.691)	4.404 (0.153)	4.472 (0.161)
dconfneighbor_3	1.120 (0.178)	1.002 (0.205)	−0.163 (0.603)	−0.165 (0.605)	1.384 (0.367)	1.041 (0.456)
d2011_ldistcapSYR	0.391** (0.021)		0.00520 (0.909)		1.031** (0.043)	
d3C_2011		−2.326* (0.064)		−1.040** (0.034)		−1.936 (0.285)
d3C_2012		−3.265* (0.063)		−1.293** (0.011)		−4.603* (0.088)
d3C_2013		−4.225* (0.050)		−0.667 (0.414)		−4.522 (0.157)
d3C_2014		−4.183* (0.065)		0.707 (0.542)		−3.854 (0.284)
d3C_2015		−2.574** (0.023)		−0.459 (0.594)		−3.239** (0.038)
d3C_2016		−2.014 (0.100)		3.102*** (0.003)		1.354 (0.495)
_cons	6.712 (0.220)	5.277 (0.289)	5.211* (0.052)	5.139* (0.056)	15.79 (0.160)	12.39 (0.216)
R2	0.687	0.686	0.375	0.376	0.540	0.538
AR2	0.665	0.662	0.327	0.324	0.504	0.500

P	4.52E-13	2.84E-15	1.57E-10	1.52E-12	5.13E-14	2.73E-20
BIC	13988.2	14136.8	10100.7	10207.9	15077.5	15236.2
N	1835	1851	1653	1667	1652	1666

Source: World Bank staff calculations.

Note: FDI = foreign direct investment.

Significance levels: * = 10 percent, ** = 5 percent, *** = 1 percent.

TABLE B.2. List of variables used in regressions

	VARIABLE	VARIABLE NAME	SOURCE	UNIT
CAPITAL FLOWS	DIRECT INVESTMENTS	*di_l*	IMF BOP	US$, BILLIONS
	PORTFOLIO INVESTMENTS	*pi_l*	IMF BOP	US$, BILLIONS
	TOTAL INWARD INVESTMENTS	*sumi_l*	IMF BOP	US$, BILLIONS
PUSH FACTORS	US REAL GDP GROWTH	*usgdpg*	IMF WEO	PERCENT
	US FED. SHADOW INTEREST RATE	*usshadir_nzcb*	HAVER	PERCENT
	S&P VOLATILITY INDEX	*vix*	HAVER	INDEX
PULL FACTORS	REAL GDP GROWTH	*gdpg*	IMF WEO	PERCENT
	INDEX OF ECONOMIC FREEDOM	*heritage*	HERITAGE FOUNDATION	–
CONFLICT VARIABLE	CONFLICT PRESENCE	*dconf*	UCDP	–
	CONFLICT IN NEIGHBOR	*dconfneighbor*	–	–
MENA VARIABLES	DISTANCE TO SYRIA AND YEAR 2011	*d2011_ldistcapSYR*	CEPII	LOG (KILOMETERS)
	POST-2011 YEAR AND SYRIA NEIGHBOR DUMMY (IRAQ, JORDAN, AND LEBANON) INTERACTION VARIABLE	*d3C_[2011-2016]*	–	–

Source: World Bank staff.

Note: CEPII = Centre d'Etudes Prospectives et d'Information Internationales; IMF BOP = International Monetary Fund Balance of Payments; IMF WEO = International Monetary Fund World Economic Outlook; MENA = Middle East and North Africa; S&P = Standard & Poor's; UCDP = Uppsala Conflict Data Program; US Fed. = US Federal Reserve Bank; – = not available.

NOTES

1. The Uppsala Conflict Data Program (UCDP) dataset defines a conflict as "a contested incompatibility that concerns government and/or territory where the use of armed force between two parties, of which at least one is the government of a state, results in at least 25 battle-related deaths in a calendar year." See https://ucdp.uu.se.

C. TECHNICAL NOTES FOR CHAPTER 4

COUNTERFACTUAL GROSS DOMESTIC PRODUCT ESTIMATIONS

Using the approach pioneered by Abadie and Gardeazabal (2003), popularly known as the synthetic control method (SCM), this report attempts to estimate a counterfactual gross domestic product (GDP) for Iraq, Jordan, and Lebanon for the period following the 2011 onset of the civil war in the Syrian Arab Republic.

Data

The pretreatment characteristics considered in this report for the calculation of the counterfactuals are based on a standard set of economic predictors commonly used in similar literature (for example, Abadie and Gardeazabal 2003; Abadie, Diamond, and Hainmueller 2015; Billmeier and Nannicini 2013; Campos, Coricelli, and Moreth 2019; Coffman and Noy 2012). Because our goal is to study an event with major social and economic repercussions at an international level, we have taken a series of specific considerations to consolidate both the dataset and the pool of donor countries. First, in terms of the outcome variable, given the nature of the conflicts affecting Iraq, Jordan, and Lebanon, we discarded the use of per capita indicators, frequently used in this type of study. The high degree of uncertainty related to the number of refugees emerging across the Middle East and North Africa (MENA) region since the early 2000s brings into question the reliability of the indicators and the results that could come from them.

Second, because our goal is to obtain a synthetic control free from conflict, we dropped from the donor pool all countries directly or indirectly affected by an exogenous shock during the period of analysis. Excluded countries range from MENA countries affected by the Arab Spring to other countries dealing with national upheavals, like Japan and the Fukushima disaster of 2011.

Third, this report relies on the use of the *synth* command for STATA. The algorithm behind it requires having countries with complete data for all years in the outcome variable and, in case of the covariates, at least one year of data for the preintervention period. Countries without both specifications have also been dropped from the sample.

Fourth, traditional datasets, like the World Bank's World Development Indicators (WDI), are likely to include refugees in their population measures. Because refugees are an essential part of the treatment effect we are trying to measure, we used a counterfactual population dataset to generate the annual population growth for Iraq, Jordan, and Lebanon between 2010 and 2018. These counterfactuals consist of vintage population projections made in 2010 by the United Nations Population Division (UN Population). The data for the rest of the countries and periods come from the 2019 UN Population Prospects.

Finally, for the post-2010 period, Iraq's GDP presents a volatile behavior that implies a challenge for the creation of its synthetic counterfactual. As can be seen in table C.1, between 2010 and 2013, the country's nonoil GDP enjoyed particularly high growth rates. With an annual average of 11.43 percent, nonoil GDP not only contrasts with the more modest 6.13 percent growth of oil GDP for the same period but also implies an unexpected positive development in times when the Syrian conflict was unfolding.

TABLE C.1. Oil and nonoil annual GDP growth rates for Iraq, 2010–18 (percent)

	2010	2011	2012	2013	2014	2015	2016	2017	2018
OIL GDP	0.96	8.46	12.97	2.14	5.40	18.42	24.62	-3.54	-1.55
NONOIL GDP	12.88	6.58	14.99	11.29	-3.89	-14.63	1.55	-0.59	1.18

Source: World Bank staff calculations based on World Bank's World Development Indicators (2019a).

During the Islamic State crisis between 2013 and 2014, however, nonoil GDP plunged, reaching its lowest point in 2015 (–14.63 percent) and setting an annual average of –3.28 percent for the remaining period of analysis. Oil GDP, in contrast, bounced during the same years, gaining strong dynamism and reaching a peak of 24.62 percent of growth in 2016 and an average annual rate of growth between 2014 and 2018 of almost 9 percent. This behavior is very difficult to replicate by a synthetic counterfactual. The conditions imposed on the donor pool of countries described in the previous section make it difficult to find countries that, without being affected by internal or external shocks, can show similar fluctuations during the same period of time. Additionally, SCM has certain limitations. A traditional synthetic counterfactual is, for instance, incapable of predicting discretionary increases in oil production, an element that could explain Iraq's post-2010 economic volatility. In order to generate an estimate that is better able to account for these unexpected changes, we calculate for Iraq an additional oil-adjusted synthetic series estimated in the following way. We calculate the post-2011 growth rate from our original synthetic series, then we applied the rate of growth obtained to the oil GDP series. We then take the oil GDP growth in excess of that counterfactual number, incorporate a fiscal multiplier effect of 1.8, and add this result on top of our original synthetic series. In favor of consistency, all synthetic counterfactuals calculated for Iraq included in this report have been adjusted with this method.

The predictors considered to conduct the analysis are GDP level (our outcome variable, in constant 2010 US dollars), population growth (annual percentage), inflation (annual percentage), trade openness (trade as percentage of GDP), industry share (agriculture and industry as percentage of GDP), a measure of human capital (secondary and tertiary gross school enrollment), and some indicator of investment share (gross fixed capital formation as percentage of GDP). Aside from the data on population growth, all the variables supporting the calculation of the synthetic counterfactuals and the econometric model come from the World Bank's WDI database (2019a). For a full description of the variables used in this analysis, please refer to table C.2.

The final country-level panel data cover a period of analysis that goes from 2000 to 2018 and provide for the calculation of each country's synthetic control from a donor pool of 121 countries.

Finally, to adjust the results of the synthetic control models to regional shocks that could have affected the MENA region regardless of the Syrian conflict, we implement a simple economic growth regression model whose dependent variable is GDP growth (annual percent). To avoid incorporating in the model the immediate impacts of the Syrian conflict, we dropped from the sample the countries more closely affected by the event: Iraq, Jordan, Lebanon, Libya, Syria, and the Republic of Yemen.

TABLE C.2. Variable definitions

INDICATOR NAME	DEFINITION
GDP (CONSTANT 2010 US$)	GDP at purchaser's prices is the sum of gross value added by all resident producers in the economy plus any product taxes and minus any subsidies not included in the value of the products. It is calculated without making deductions for depreciation of fabricated assets or for depletion and degradation of natural resources. Data are in constant 2010 US$. Dollar figures for GDP are converted from domestic currencies using 2010 official exchange rates. For a few countries where the official exchange rate does not reflect the rate effectively applied to actual foreign exchange transactions, an alternative conversion factor is used.
POPULATION GROWTH (ANNUAL %)	Based on total population by sex, reported by the United Nations Population Division's 2019 World Population Prospects. Link: https://population.un.org/wpp/Download/Standard/CSV/.
INFLATION, CONSUMER PRICES (ANNUAL %)	Inflation as measured by the consumer price index reflects the annual percentage change in the cost to the average consumer of acquiring a basket of goods and services that may be fixed or changed at specified intervals, such as yearly. The Laspeyres formula is generally used.
TRADE (% OF GDP)	Trade is the sum of exports and imports of goods and services measured as a share of gross domestic product.
SCHOOL ENROLLMENT, SECONDARY (% GROSS)	Gross enrollment ratio is the ratio of total enrollment, regardless of age, to the population of the age group that officially corresponds to the level of education shown. Secondary education completes the provision of basic education that began at the primary level, and aims at laying the foundations for lifelong learning and human development, by offering more subject- or skill-oriented instruction using more specialized teachers.
SCHOOL ENROLLMENT, TERTIARY (% GROSS)	Gross enrollment ratio is the ratio of total enrollment, regardless of age, to the population of the age group that officially corresponds to the level of education shown. Tertiary education, whether or not to an advanced research qualification, normally requires, as a minimum condition of admission, the successful completion of education at the secondary level.
AGRICULTURE, VALUE ADDED (% OF GDP)	Agriculture corresponds to ISIC divisions 1-5 and includes forestry, hunting, and fishing, as well as cultivation of crops and livestock production. Value added is the net output of a sector after adding up all outputs and subtracting intermediate inputs. It is calculated without making deductions for depreciation of fabricated assets or depletion and degradation of natural resources. The origin of value added is determined by the International Standard Industrial Classification (ISIC), revision 3 or 4.
INDUSTRY, VALUE ADDED (% OF GDP)	Industry corresponds to ISIC divisions 10-45 and includes manufacturing (ISIC divisions 15-37). It comprises value added in mining, manufacturing (also reported as a separate subgroup), construction, electricity, water, and gas. Value added is the net output of a sector after adding up all outputs and subtracting intermediate inputs. It is calculated without making deductions for depreciation of fabricated assets or depletion and degradation of natural resources. The origin of value added is determined by ISIC, revision 3 or 4.
GDP GROWTH (ANNUAL %)	Annual percentage growth rate of GDP at market prices based on constant local currency. Aggregates are based on constant 2010 US$. GDP is the sum of gross value added by all resident producers in the economy plus any product taxes and minus any subsidies not included in the value of the products. It is calculated without making deductions for depreciation of fabricated assets or for depletion and degradation of natural resources.
GROSS FIXED CAPITAL FORMATION (% OF GDP)	Gross fixed capital formation (formerly gross domestic fixed investment) includes land improvements (fences, ditches, drains, and so on); plant, machinery, and equipment purchases; and the construction of roads, railways, and the like, including schools, offices, hospitals, private residential dwellings, and commercial and industrial buildings. According to the 1993 SNA, net acquisitions of valuables are also considered capital formation.
GDP GROWTH (ANNUAL %)	Annual percentage growth rate of GDP at market prices based on constant local currency. Aggregates are based on constant 2010 US$. GDP is the sum of gross value added by all resident producers in the economy plus any product taxes and minus any subsidies not included in the value of the products. It is calculated without making deductions for depreciation of fabricated assets or for depletion and degradation of natural resources.

Source: World Bank staff calculations.
Note: SNA = The System of National Accounts.

Specifications and overview of the synthetic control method

To investigate what would have been the GDP levels in Iraq, Jordan, and Lebanon if the Syrian civil war had not been present, we use the method developed by Abadie and Gardeazabal (2003) and extended in Abadie, Diamond, and Hainmueller (2010, 2015). This method searches for a weighted combination of other countries (donors) that resemble as closely as possible the characteristics of the target country in the pretreatment period in terms of an outcome variable (GDP level in this case) and a set of other specific covariates. It does so by minimizing for the pretreatment period the root mean squared prediction error (RMSPE).

To describe it more formally, let's use the notation described by Abadie, Diamond, and Hainmueller (2010). Let's assume that Y_{it} is the outcome variable of interest (GDP level) of a country i at a time t. The country affected by the event is represented by $i = 1$, and $i = 2, \dots, N + 1$ represent those not impacted and $t = 1, \dots, T_0, \dots, T$, with T_0 being the year the event of interest occurred.

Let's assume also that Y_{it}^I is the outcome variable of interest of the country affected by the event and Y_{it}^N the outcome variable of interest of the country had the event never occurred.[1] The average treatment effect estimator can be represented as

$$\tau_{it} = Y_{it}^I - Y_{it}^N \tag{C.1}$$

Because we cannot observe the outcome variable of the treated country had the treatment never occurred (when $\tau_{iT_{0+1}}, \cdots, \tau_{iT}$), to estimate the treated country's hypothetical outcome (τ_{it}) we rely on the general model proposed by Abadie, Diamond, and Hainmueller (2010):

$$Y_{it}^I = \delta_t + \tau_{it} + v_{it} \tag{C.2}$$

$$\tau_{it} = \alpha_{it} D_{it} \tag{C.3}$$

$$Y_{it}^N = \delta_t + v_{it} \tag{C.4}$$

$$v_{it} = \theta_t Z_i + \lambda_t \omega_i + \varepsilon_{it} \tag{C.5}$$

where D_{it} is a binary indicator adopting the value of 1 when $i = 1$ and $t > T_0$ and zero otherwise; α_{it} is the effect of the event on the variable of interest; Z_i is a vector of country-level covariates; θ_t is a vector of time-specific parameters; λ_t a vector of unobserved common factors; ω_i the country-specific observable term; and ε_{it} the unobserved transitory shocks with zero mean.

The counterfactual will be given by an estimate of Y_{it} (when $i > 1$) as close as possible to Y_{1t} for every $t < T_0$, based on the previously defined country-level covariates (Z_i). A series of weights ($W = w_2, \dots, w_{N+1}$) will be assigned to construct the counterfactuals, where $\sum_{i=2}^{N+1} w_i = 1$ and $w_i \geq 0$. Therefore,

$$\sum_{i=2}^{N+1} w_i Y_{it} = Y_{it} \tag{C.6}$$

and

$$\sum_{i=2}^{N+1} w_i Z_i = Z_i \tag{C.7}$$

lead to the unbiased estimator of τ_{it}:

$$\hat{\tau}_{it} = Y_{it} - \sum_{i=2}^{N+1} w_i Y_{it} \tag{C.8}$$

The optimal set of weights is chosen to minimize the RMSPE, which is given by

$$RMSPE = \sqrt{\frac{1}{T_0}\sum_{t=1}^{T_0}(Y_{it} - \sum_{i=2}^{N+1} w_i Y_{it})^2} \tag{C.9}$$

In addition to the counterfactuals, this report also attempts to evaluate regional effects not necessarily linked to the Syrian conflict that could have affected the GDP levels of the three treated countries. The econometric strategy to identify these potential effects is given by

$$y_{i,t} = c_0 + u_i + u_t + \beta_{i,t} D_{i,t} + \varepsilon_{i,t} \tag{C.10}$$

where i and t denote countries and event years respectively; $y_{i,t}$ represents the dependent macroeconomic variable (GDP growth, annual percentage); u_i and u_t country and time fixed effects, respectively; $\beta_{i,t}$ the coefficient of interest; $D_{i,t}$ a dummy variable that identifies MENA countries in the post-2010 period; and $\varepsilon_{i,t}$ the error term.

Precisely because we want to isolate regional effects other than the one generated from the Syrian conflict, we have excluded the following countries from the panel regression: Iraq, Jordan, Lebanon, Libya, Syria, and the Republic of Yemen.

COUNTERFACTUAL TRADE CALCULATIONS

In order to calculate counterfactual export and import trends, we employ a structural gravity approach in which changes in aggregate and bilateral trade (both exports and imports) are functions of GDP growth rates. More specifically, the exports from origin i to destination j can be expressed as

$$X_t^{ij} = \frac{Y_t^i E_t^j}{Y_t}\left(\frac{t^{ij}}{\Pi_t^i P_t^j}\right)^{1-\sigma} \tag{C.11}$$

where Y_t^i is the total output of country i, E_t^j is the total expenditure, Π_t^i is the price index, Y_t is the global output, and

$$P_t^j = \left(\sum_k \left(\frac{t^{ij}}{\pi_t^k}\right)^{1-\sigma} \frac{Y_t^k}{Y_t}\right)^{\frac{1}{1-\sigma}} \tag{C.12}$$

$$\Pi_t^j = \left(\sum_k \left(\frac{t^{ij}}{P_t^k}\right)^{1-\sigma} \frac{E_t^k}{Y_t}\right)^{\frac{1}{1-\sigma}} \tag{C.13}$$

Note that, without savings, GDP is equal to the expenditure $Y_t^i = E_t^i$. The term $\left(t^{ij} / \Pi_t^i P_t^j\right)$ captures trade cost and bilateral frictions. We assume that it is constant, given fixed prices.

We perform counterfactual exercises using cost structure of different years and the counterfactual GDP estimations described previously, which are denoted as Y_t^{i*}. We assume that global GDP, Y_t, is unaffected by the conflict.

We do not have a good measure of P_t^i; therefore, we will assume that it is constant. We do not use theory to predict price changes, because prices increase, and GDP decreases in Syria with conflict. In most cases GDP and prices move together in the same direction. Therefore, we cannot easily predict price changes using GDP.

Case 1: Counterfactual (no conflict) based on 2010 trade cost structure

We can estimate bilateral trade as follows:

$$\widetilde{X_t^{ij}} = X_{2010}^{ij} \frac{Y_t^{i*}}{Y_{2010}^i} \frac{Y_t^{j*}}{Y_{2010}^j}, \tag{C.14}$$

and total imports as

$$\widetilde{M_t^j} = M_{2010}^j \sum_i \left(w_{M,2010}^{ij} \frac{Y_t^{i*}}{Y_{2010}^i} \frac{Y_t^{j*}}{Y_{2010}^j} \right), \tag{C.15}$$

where $w_{M,2010}^{ij}$ is the share of origin i in destination j's imports. We will assume that Y_t^{i*} is equal to Y_{2010}^j for other countries (that is, countries other than Syria and its neighbors).

Estimating total exports:

$$\widetilde{X_t^i} = X_{2010}^i \sum_j \left(w_{X,2010}^{ij} \frac{Y_t^{i*}}{Y_{2010}^i} \frac{Y_t^{j*}}{Y_{2010}^j} \right) \tag{C.16}$$

where $w_{X,2010}^{ij}$ is the share of destination j in exports of i. We will assume that Y_t^{j*} is equal to Y_{2010}^j for other countries.

Case 2: Counterfactual (conflict, actual GDP) based on 2010 trade cost structure

Estimating bilateral trade:

$$\widehat{X_t^{ij}} = X_{2010}^{ij} \frac{Y_t^i}{Y_{2010}^i} \frac{Y_t^j}{Y_{2010}^j} \tag{C.17}$$

Estimating total imports:

$$\widehat{M_t^j} = M_{2010}^j \sum_i \left(w_{M,2010}^{ij} \frac{Y_t^i}{Y_{2010}^i} \frac{Y_t^j}{Y_{2010}^j} \right) \tag{C.18}$$

where $w_{M,2010}^{ij}$ is the share of origin i in destination j's imports. We will assume that Y_t^i is equal to Y_{2010}^j for other countries (that is, countries other than Syria and its neighbors).

Estimating total exports:

$$\widehat{X_t^i} = X_{2010}^i \sum_j \left(w_{X,t}^{ij} \frac{Y_t^i}{Y_{2010}^i} \frac{Y_t^j}{Y_{2010}^j} \right) \tag{C.19}$$

where $w_{X,t}^{ij}$ is the share of destination j in exports of i. We will assume that Y_t^j is equal to Y_{2010}^j for other countries.

Case 3: Counterfactual (no conflict) based on current trade cost structure

Estimating bilateral trade:

$$\overline{X_t^{ij}} = X_t^{ij} \frac{Y_t^{i*}}{Y_t^i} \frac{Y_t^{j*}}{Y_t^j} \tag{C.20}$$

Estimating total imports:

$$\overline{M_t^j} = M_t^j \sum_i \left(w_{M,t}^{ij} \frac{Y_t^{i*}}{Y_t^i} \frac{Y_t^{j*}}{Y_t^j} \right) \tag{C.21}$$

where $w_{M,t}^{ij}$ is the share of origin i in destination j's imports. We will assume that Y_t^{i*} is equal to Y_t^i for other countries (that is, countries other than Syria and its neighbors).

Estimating total exports:

$$\overline{X_t^i} = X_t^i \sum_j \left(w_{X,t}^{ij} \frac{Y_t^{i*}}{Y_t^i} \frac{Y_t^{j*}}{Y_t^j} \right) \tag{C.22}$$

where $w_{X,t}^{ij}$ is the share of destination j in exports of i. We will assume that Y_t^{j*} is equal to Y_t^j for other countries.

MICROSIMULATION STRATEGY

The microsimulation model employed in this report is a macro-micro approach where SCM, structural gravity, and computable general equilibrium (CGE) simulation results are applied to the full household distribution as given by the household micro-dataset. It links the sectoral and aggregate macrodata of the three countries to their household surveys to extrapolate microeconomic snapshots under different scenarios. The model accounts for multiple channels through which macro-changes are transmitted into microlevel household impacts. Specifically, it accounts for changes in a country's employment shares and sectoral GDP, overall population growth, and changes in social assistance programs. Additionally, the microsimulation model is designed to explicitly account for a large-scale displacement in Iraq due to the Islamic State crisis. Figure C.1 illustrates the basic microsimulation modeling process. The first step is to prepare model assumptions and macro-projections under different scenarios. The second step of the simulation involves imposing the macro-projections on the baseline household survey data.

FIGURE C.1. Microsimulation modeling process

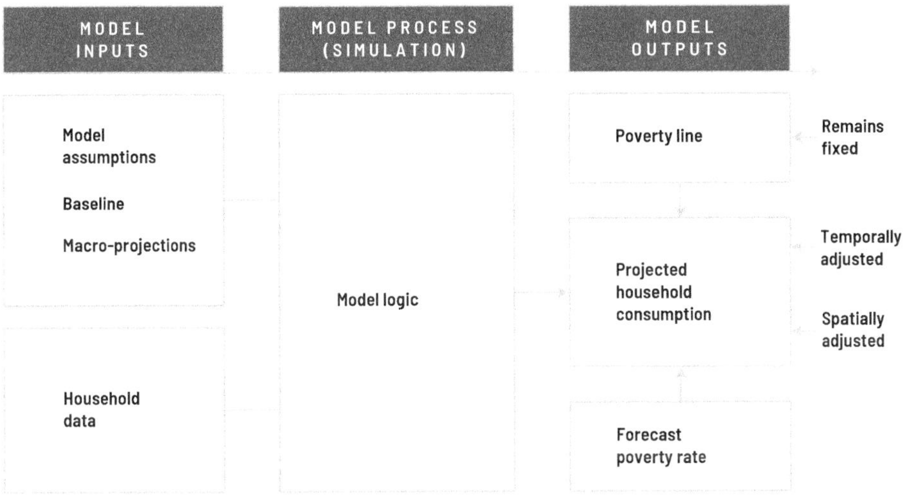

Source: World Bank.

In the simulation phase, we adjust the survey weights according to the growth in population. Similarly, using the Displacement Tracking Matrix (DTM) of the International Organization for Migration (IOM), we account for the displaced and returnee population in Iraq starting in 2014.

Using baseline survey data, the simulation extrapolates the consumption of each household for the subsequent years, which then are used to create poverty and inequality measures. Formally, our ex ante microsimulation uses the following equation to transform macromodeling results into results based on household survey data:

$$C_{i,t+1}^{s} = \left(C_{i,t}^{s} - \frac{C.transfer_{i,t}}{HHsize_{i}}\right) \times \left(1 + g_{i,t+1}^{cons,s}\right) + \frac{C.transfer_{i,t+1}}{HHsize_{i}} \quad (C.23)$$

where, subscripts and superscripts i, s, and t index household i employed in a sector s at time t. The per capita consumption, C, at time $t+1$, is a function of the previous period's per capita consumption net of any per capita cash transfer or other governmental assistance, $\frac{C.transfer}{HHsize}$, growth in per capita consumption of the sector in which the household is employed, $g^{cons,s}$, and cash assistance it received at time $t+1$. The sectoral consumption growth at time $t+1$ is a function of sectoral income growth, $g_{i,t+1}^{inc,s}$, and the overall population growth, p_{t+1}, adjusted by a ratio of the sectoral share of employment, E^{s}. This relationship can be defined by the following equation:

$$g_{i,t+1}^{cons,s} = g_{i,t+1}^{inc,s} - \left(\frac{E_{i,t+1}^{s}}{E_{i,t}^{s}} \times (1 + p_{t+1}) - 1\right) \quad (C.24)$$

where

$$g_{i,t+1}^{inc,s} = g_{i,t+1}^{s} \times pass_{t} \quad (C.25)$$

and

$$E_{t+1}^{s} = \frac{E_t^s \times (1 + e_{t+1}^s)}{\sum_{\forall s} E_t^s \times (1 + e_{t+1}^s)} \tag{C.26}$$

In equation (C.25), while g^s is a sectoral growth in GDP, $pass_t$ is a pass-through factor from GDP growth to income. Similarly, in equation (C.26) sectoral share of employment E^s depends on its value in the previous period and the growth in sectoral employment e^s.

As seen in equations (C.23) to (C.26), the microsimulation model takes sectoral GDP growths, changes in sectoral share of employment, and population growth as three macro-inputs (as produced by the SCM, structural gravity model, and the CGE models in this report and UN Population Division's population growth projection in 2010 vintage as the counterfactual population growth). These are included in order to capture multiple transmission avenues for poverty and inequality impacts.

We use the latest available household surveys from the precrisis period and calibrate poverty and inequality till 2017: the 2012 Household Socio-Economic Survey (HSES) in Iraq, the 2012 Household Budget Survey (HBS) in Lebanon, and the 2010 Household Expenditure and Income Survey (HEIS) in Jordan. All three are nationally representative surveys of the people living in those countries at the time of the survey enumeration. We use the observed macroeconomic inputs for the actual scenario and exploit the counterfactual GDP and population results described above. The scope of the analysis is to isolate and quantify the impacts due to the crisis in Syria; therefore, both states of the world—actual and counterfactual—incorporate the macroeconomic impacts due to the collapse of oil prices in 2014. The resulting gap between the two states, thus, is likely the net of the impacts due the oil crisis. Next, we discuss in detail the assumptions we make regarding the macroeconomic states of the three countries under the two scenarios.

GDP. Our microsimulation model uses the sectoral GDP growth rather than the overall GDP growth and their pass-throughs to household income. We classify the economies into three sectors; namely agriculture, industry, and services, and assume a pass-through of 75 percent for all three sectors. The CGE model provides counterfactual sectoral growth rates for Jordan and Lebanon; however, it reports only the aggregate counterfactual GDP for Iraq. We assume growth of a particular sector's GDP share in Iraq would have followed its historical trend starting in 2004 till the year of the survey, 2012, and project the sectoral shares till 2017. We then apply these projected shares to the aggregate counterfactual GDP and calculate yearly sectoral GDP growth in Iraq. For the group that is not working, we assign the weighted average growth rate of the three sectors in all three countries.[2]

Given the nature of the population represented by the baseline surveys, we need to exclude the contribution of refugees to the actual observed GDPs in order to find the actual outcome on the precrisis host country population. The CGE model produces actual aggregate GDPs without the refugees' contribution. We then apply the sectoral shares reported by the WDI (World Bank 2019a) to create sectoral GDP growth.

Employment. The microsimulation model uses sectoral shares of employment, E^s, from the WDI (World Bank 2019a) for the actual scenario. In order to calculate employment shares under the counterfactual scenario, we assume sectoral employment to sectoral GDP elasticities would have followed the historical trend (between 2004 and 2010 for Jordan and between 2004 and 2012 for Iraq and Lebanon). We combine this information with the counterfactual sectoral GDP growth calculated previously and estimate counterfactual sectoral growth in employment, e^s. We then employ equation (C.26) to estimate counterfactual shares of sectoral employment. Growth in share of employment for the nonworking group is assumed to be zero. When applying to the microdata, the model makes two important assumptions regarding employment in both the frameworks. First, a household's sector of employment is assumed to be same as that of its head.[3] Second, the model makes a stronger assumption that employment status of a household remains constant over time and, thus, does not account for switches in occupation nor entry or exit from the labor force. These are strong assumptions, and a careful consideration is required while interpreting results. Large-scale disruptions to labor markets are not modeled. The evidence suggests that Syrian refugees have not affected Jordanian employment outcomes, and the number of refugees in Iraq is very small relative to the total population—the main impact of the crisis is through internal displacement, which is modeled explicitly (see Fallah, Krafft, and Wahba 2019; Wahba 2018). No evidence exists for the impact of refugees on labor markets in Lebanon, but restrictions on employment and differences in skill level between refugees and residents likely mean they have been limited (see Conway et al., forthcoming; World Bank 2019c).

Cash transfers. Cash transfers are treated differently from consumption due to other household income because they are not necessarily tied to economic growth but instead depend upon government social policy. Iraq has a universal Public Distribution System (PDS), which was instituted in 1990 with 10 subsidized food items. The program is entrenched and significant to Iraqis to such an extent that the national surveys, including the 2012 HSES, collect detailed information regarding its accessibility and each household's consumption of ration food items. We use the value of the ration food items consumed by the households observed in the HSES 2012 as the cash transfer input in the microsimulation model for both the with- and without-shock scenarios. Additionally, we assume no change in the PDS program during the analytical period; hence, the value of the transfer remains the same in real terms beyond 2012. Because the transfer is in-kind, no inflationary impacts are modeled. During the Islamic State crisis, however, a significant portion of the displaced population lost access to the PDS (World Bank 2019b). Below, we discuss the adjustment we make regarding the cash transfer for the internally displaced (and returnee) population in Iraq.

Lebanon and Jordan, in contrast, have much smaller social assistance programs in terms of coverage.[4] Beneficiaries of the Lebanese governmental aid program (National Poverty Targeting Program) receive $27 monthly per capita, capped at six members per household, whereas the main Jordan cash assistance program (National Aid Fund) transfers on average 100 Jordanian dinars per household per month. The microsimulation assumes no changes in these two programs over time. Hence, the nominal transfer values to each remain constant (and are thus decreasing in real terms, unlike the in-kind transfer in Iraq). Additionally, both Jordan's HEIS 2010 and Lebanon's HBS 2012 lack information regarding whether the sampled households receive cash assistance and the amount they receive. We use the information on program coverage by income distribution—decile in Jordan and quintile in Lebanon[5]—and randomly assign beneficiary status and match the coverage rate within decile or quintile. The cash transfer beneficiary status and amount remain the same in both actual and counterfactual analyses.[6]

Internally displaced persons (IDPs) in Iraq. Microsimulation models of shocks usually model the impact on household economic welfare through macroeconomic channels. Although this is done for Jordan and Lebanon in the current analysis, an additional channel is used for the Iraq simulation. Using economic growth scenarios to simulate household outcomes would fail to capture the full impact of the Syrian crisis on Iraqi households because they do not capture other key dimensions of the crisis. In particular, they fail to capture the effect of internal displacement on households through the loss of productive assets, access to employment and livelihoods, and access to the PDS. To address this limitation, we include an additional modeling element in the Iraq microsimulation.

Starting in early 2014, the Islamic State crisis compelled many Iraqis to abandon their homes and flee to safer areas. At its height, in March 2016, 3.4 million people (net of returnees) were internally displaced in Iraq (IOM 2019). The count of IDPs was 2.1 million people in 2014, 3.2 million in 2015, 3.0 million in 2016, and 2.6 million people in 2017 (IOM 2019).[7] In order to identify the likely forced displaced and impact on their consumption among the HSES 2012 households, we exploit the 2017/18 Rapid Welfare Monitoring Survey (SWIFT) that included a separate sampling stratum for the IDP population, representative at the national level.

To replicate the impact of the Syrian and Islamic State crises on households in Iraq, we adopt the following steps. For non-IDP households, consumption and the impact of the crisis on welfare are modeled in the same way as previously described for Jordan and Lebanon. For IDP households, the impact of displacement is modeled in three stages, described in the rest of this section: (i) which households are displaced; (ii) which displaced households lose access to PDS; and (iii) which households return from displacement to their original locations and how much consumption rebounds.

First, we implement a logistic model of the following form in the SWIFT data:

$$\Pr(Displaced_i = 1) = F(\beta_0 + \beta_1 X_i) \tag{C.27}$$

where $Displaced_i$ is a household $i's$ displacement status (= 1 if displaced, 0 otherwise), and X is a vector of place of origin (governorates) and other household characteristics that are likely to be correlated with the displacement status and $F(z) = e^z/(1 - e^z)$. Using $\hat{\beta}_0$ and $\hat{\beta}_1$ estimates from the SWIFT data, we calculate each household's probability of displacement in the HSES 2012 data. Starting in 2014, we begin displacing households with the highest probability to match each year's net displacement numbers from the DTM matrix. Note that the net displacement declines after 2015, indicating increasing numbers of returnees. Therefore, to match the IOM numbers, from 2016 onward we start returning displaced households with the lowest probability of displacement.[8]

Second, the PDS program in Iraq plays an important role in Iraqi households' budgets and expenditures.[9] A significant portion of IDPs, however, lost their access to the PDS.[10] We analyze IDPs only in the SWIFT data and implement a regression analogous to equation (C.27) but with PDS access as the dependent variable and a vector X that reflects covariates likely affecting access to the PDS. Again, using the estimated parameters, we predict the probability of losing PDS access among those already predicted as becoming IDPs in the HSES 2012 data. We then assign a zero PDS transfer to those with the greatest probability and match the portion of IDPs with zero PDS to the percentage of IDPs without PDS in the SWIFT data.[11]

Third, as discussed, displacement is likely to significantly alter household economic welfare through nonmacroeconomic channels. Using the SWIFT data among IDPs, we fit a simple ordinary least squares regression to explain postdisplacement consumption levels. The estimated parameters of the explanatory covariates then are used in the 2012 data to predict the consumption level of an IDP household for the year when it gets displaced (as described earlier). After this one-time adjustment, the consumption level changes normally as per the standard microsimulation approach used for non-IDPs in Iraq and host communities in Jordan and Lebanon. As pointed out earlier, in the model we start returning some of the IDPs after 2015. For a returnee household, we make a one-time adjustment during its year of return—we assume that the returnee household will recover about 80 percent of its consumption level from the year before its displacement as well as recovering access to PDS.

NOTES

1. In order to implement a synthetic control model, we need to assume that the event does not have any impacts on the outcome variable of the treated country before $t=T-_0$.
2. The assumption is that those neither working nor looking for work have alternative sources of income (such as pensions, remittances, or interest and rent), which grow in line with the broader economy.
3. Usually welfare analysis is done at the household level, especially for consumption and income, applying individual level survey weights to produce population estimates. Individual survey weights are calculated by multiplying survey weights of households with their sizes. Head of household characteristics are usually incorporated with other variables to characterize a household.
4. The governmental cash transfer aid in Jordan (NAF) reached 7.5 percent of its population in 2010 and the coverage of the Lebanese cash assistance program (NPTP) was 2.0 percent in 2012.
5. Coverage in Lebanon was 4, 3, 2, 2, and 2 percent proceeding from the poorest quintile to the richest quintile, respectively (calculated from the 2012 HBS). Similarly, in Jordan it was 31, 11, 6, 5, 6, 5, 4, 4, 2, and 1 percent from the poorest decile to the richest decile, respectively (calculated from the 2010 HEIS).
6. In reality, Jordan has expanded the NAF significantly in 2019 and 2020 with further expansion planned in 2021. This expansion occurs, however, after the 2017 actual end point modeled here, and it is unclear whether such an expansion would have occurred in the counterfactual scenario without the Syrian crisis.
7. These are net displacement counts from the last round of the year of the IOM DTM matrix.
8. The SWIFT survey was conducted before large-scale return of IDPs in Iraq, so a returnee probit could not be conducted; in all likelihood, probability of displacement is not the same as the inverse of the probability of return.
9. In 2007, rations provided 1,998 calories per person per day on average, accounting for 85 percent of required calories and 68 percent of actual calories consumed, with the proportion as high as 78 percent for the poor (World Bank 2010). In 2012, food receipts from the PDS provided about 70 percent of total calories of the poorest 40 percent of the population (World Bank 2014).
10. Only 63 percent of the displaced Iraqis reported consumption of ration food compared to 96 percent of the nondisplaced Iraqis.
11. We assume returnee households to recover 79 percent of their consumption enjoyed in the year before they became displaced. This is the average consumption of IDPs compared to the non-IDPs in the SWIFT data.

REFERENCES

Abadie, A., and J. Gardeazabal. 2003. "The Economic Costs of Conflict: A Case Study of the Basque Country." *American Economic Review* 93 (1): 113–32.

Abadie, A., A. Diamond, and J. Hainmueller. 2010. "Synthetic Control Methods for Comparative Case Studies: Estimating the Effect of California's Tobacco Control Program." *Journal of the American Statistical Association* 104 (490): 493–505.

Abadie, A., A. Diamond, and J. Hainmueller. 2015. "Comparative Politics and the Synthetic Control Method." *American Journal of Political Science* 59 (2): 495–510.

Billmeier, A., and T. Nannicini. 2013. "Assessing Economic Liberalization Episodes: A Synthetic Control Approach." *Review of Economics and Statistics* 95 (3): 983–1001.

Campos, N. F., F. Coricelli, and L. Moretti. 2019. "Institutional Integration and Economic Growth in Europe." *Journal of Monetary Economics* 103: 88–104.

Conway, M., A. Khandros, A. Della Guardia, M. Wai-Poi, and G. Seshan. Forthcoming. *Forced Displacement in the Mashreq: Impact on Household Welfare*. Washington, DC: World Bank.

Coffman, M., and I. Noy. 2012. "Hurricane Iniki: Measuring the Long-Term Economic Impact of a Natural Disaster Using Synthetic Control." *Environment and Development Economics* 17 (2): 187–205.

Fallah, B., C. Krafft, and J. Wahba. 2019. "The Impact of Refugees on Employment and Wages in Jordan." *Journal of Development Economics* 139: 203–16.

IOM (International Organization for Migration). 2019. "The Displacement Tracking Matrix (DTM). IOM, Grand-Saconnex, Switzerland. http://iraqdtm.iom.int/.

Wahba, J. 2018. "The Impact of the Syrian Refugee Influx on the Jordanian Labour Market." Policy Brief No. 32, Economic Research Forum, Cairo.

World Bank. 2010. *Confronting Poverty in Iraq*. Washington, DC: World Bank.

World Bank. 2014. "The Unfulfilled Promise of Oil and Growth: Poverty, Inclusion, and Welfare in Iraq, 2007–2012." World Bank, Washington, DC. http://documents.worldbank.org/curated/en/752991468261314600/The-unfulfilled-promise-of-oil-and-growth-poverty-inclusion-and-welfare-in-Iraq-2007-2012.

World Bank. 2019a. "World Development Indicators." World Bank, Washington, DC. https://datacatalog.worldbank.org/dataset/world-development-indicators.

World Bank. 2019b. "Arrested Development—Conflict Displacement and Welfare in Iraq." Note, World Bank, Washington, DC.

World Bank. 2019c. *The Mobility of Displaced Syrians: An Economic and Social Analysis*. Washington, DC: World Bank.